Film Noir Reader 4

Other Limelight Editions by the same Authors

The Vampire Film
More Things Than Are Dreamt Of
What Ever Happened to Robert Aldrich?
Film Noir Reader
Film Noir Reader 2
Horror Film Reader
Film Noir Reader 3 (with Robert Porfirio)

Also by Alain Silver

David Lean and His Films
The Samurai Film
Film Noir: An Encyclopedic Reference to the
American Style, Editor
The Film Director's Team
Raymond Chandler's Los Angeles
The Noir Style
Film Noir (Taschen Film Series)

Also by James Ursini

David Lean and His Films
The Life and Times of Preston Sturges, An American Dreamer
Film Noir: An Encyclopedic Reference to the
American Style, Co-editor
The Noir Style
Film Noir (Taschen Film Series)

Film Noir

R E A D E R 4

EDITED BY

ALAIN SILVER AND JAMES URSINI

LIMELIGHT EDITIONS • NEW JERSEY

First Limelight Edition October 2004

LIBRARY OF CONGRESS CATALOGING-IN-PUBLICATION DATA

Film noir reader 4 : the crucial films and themes / [edited by] Alain Silver and James Ursini.—1st limelight ed.
    p.   cm.
  ISBN 0-87910-305-1 (pbk.)
   1. Film noir—United States—History and criticism. I. Silver, Alain, 1947- II. Ursini, James.

PN1995.9.F54F64 2004
791.43'6556—dc22
                                        2004002792

Contents

Part Two: Noir Themes

Acknowledgments

As with the first three volumes, the idea for an anthology on film noir still goes back to fall of 1974, so we again acknowledge our prospective collaborators from that project as well as the co-editors of *Film Noir: An Encyclopedic Reference to the American Style,* Elizabeth Ward, Robert Porfirio, and Carl Macek. Thanks also to Fred Lombardi for soliciting the *Variety* list in 1993 and providing a record of opinions from a decade ago. Deep appreciation to Dominique Mainon for invaluable research and consultation.

Most of the illustrations not from the editors' personal collections were kindly provided by David Chierichetti. Other illustrations came from Glenn Erickson and Cassandra Langer of Private Eye: Noir Arts Ltd. Scene stills are reproduced courtesy of Allied Artists, Columbia, MGM, Paramount, RKO, Selznick International, 20th Century-Fox, United Artists, Universal, and Warner Bros. Filmographic research was done at the AMPAS Library and on-line at the Internet Movie Database (imdb.com). As they have many times before, James Paris and Glenn Erickson kindly proof read the entire manuscript. The book was designed by David Balk. Of course, Mel Zerman at Limelight Editions again made the entire endeavor possible.

"Gun Grazy," originally appeared as part of "In Focus: Ten Shades of Noir" in *Image: A Journal of Film and Popular Culture,* no. 2 (1996), copyright © 1996 by Gary Johnson and is reprinted by permission of the author.

"Violently Happy: Gun Crazy," originally appeared in *Metro,* no. 109 (March, 1997), copyright © 1997 by Adrian Martin and is reprinted by permission of the author.

"The Unsuspected and the Noir Sequence: Realism—Expressionism—Style" and "The Noir Title Sequence" are adapted from *The Dark Age of American Film: A Study of American Film Noir* (1940–1960) [doctoral dissertation, Yale University], copyright © 1979 by Robert Porfirio and are reprinted by permission of the author.

"*Rancho Notorious*: A Noir Western in Colour" originally appeared in *Cineaction* No. 13/14, Summer 1988, copyright © 1988 by Robin Wood and is reprinted by permission.

All previously unpublished materials are, as applicable, Copyright © 2004 by the individual authors and are printed here by permission.

Film Noir Reader 4

Above, Humphrey Bogart as Philip Marlowe dines with Vivian Sternwood (Lauren Bacall) in Howard Hawks' adaptation of Raymond Chandler's novel, *The Big Sleep*. Below, Lucky Gagin (Robert Montgomery, standing at left) is unimpressed by government agent Bill Retz (Art Smith) in *Ride the Pink Horse*.

Introduction

Alain Silver

Why *Film Noir Reader 4*? It is certainly not because James Ursini and I have not fully expressed ourselves on the subject. Still, while the seminal essays collected in the first two Readers, as well as the interviews in the third, continue to be pertinent, the 21st century brings a new perspective. More than forty years after the close of the classic period, the term film noir is now firmly embedded in the English language (and its dictionaries, so it is no longer being italicized by us) and is acquiring a third new generation of viewers. This volume consists almost entirely of new material, and what the various essayists offer is a fresh look at the key pictures and the key themes of film noir.

As may be obvious, the case studies in Part One focus on the films which are most often screened in retrospectives and in classrooms. But the movies included should not be mistaken for a "ten best" list. For the record my film noir top "ten" was compiled for *Variety* back in 1993. Free to indulge in glib value judgments, the titles I selected and comments I made back then were:

1. *Kiss Me Deadly*	6. *Ride the Pink Horse*
2. *Gun Crazy*	7. *Out of the Past*
3. *Double Indemnity*	8. *Night and the City*
4. *Criss Cross*	9. *Caught*
5. *Woman in the Window*	10. *White Heat* and *The Big Sleep*

I cheated with number ten; but this list is neither chronological nor alphabetical. I admire Sam Fuller's *Underworld U.S.A.* and Kubrick's *The Killing* and think they are better movies than *White Heat*; but they're not better film noir. I love *Cry of the City*, *Phantom Lady*, and *The Killers*, too, but I did have one rule: a single movie per director, otherwise Siodmak, Lang, Ophuls and Wilder might have overwhelmed the field and made it an all-émigré list. No Anthony Mann? Another great filmmaker with a lot of noir titles, but no. No John Huston, either; *Maltese Falcon* helped start it all but got left in the dust and *Asphalt Jungle*, just not quite. A nearer miss for the lesser-known Henry Hathaway and John Farrow, whose *The Dark Corner* or *Kiss of Death* and *His Kind of Woman* or *The Big Clock* are nothing to sneeze at. I'm out of words, so you figure out why. Hint: this list has it all: tortured, obsessed, war-scarred, psychotic, truck-driving, insurance-selling escapees and ex-cons and their exotic, blonde and brunette femme fatales.

3

A quick flip of the page back to the Contents of this volume will confirm that only five of the eleven pictures in my decade-old list are discussed herein. More recently (in 2000), I compiled another list of "the ten best titles which video has to offer" for the UK-based *Good Book Guide*. Those titles in no particular order were: *Kiss Me Deadly; White Heat; Gun Crazy; Force of Evil; In a Lonely Place; The Killers; Woman in the Window; Caught; The Big Sleep;* and *His Kind of Woman*. Only three of these films made our current contents page. Finally James Ursini and I have just completed another book on film noir for Taschen, which approaches the noir cycle through ten thematic prototypes: *Criss Cross; Detour; Double Indemnity; Gun Crazy; In a Lonely Place; Kiss Me Deadly; Out of the Past, The Reckless Moment; T-Men;* and *Touch of Evil*. Six of these ten are discussed in this volume.

Opinions certainly vary about what the best prototypes of film noir may be. French critic Nicolas Saada has five of them in his essay on the noir style in Part Two; but only one, *Kiss Me Deadly*, is on any of my lists. In *Film Noir Reader 2*, Philip Gaines outlined a 12-week college course on noir. His classic period selections broken down by screening weeks were:

1. Opening with a Bang: *Double Indemnity* (alternate title, *Out of the Past*)

3. The Classic Period: *The Maltese Falcon*

4. Post-war angst: *Nobody Lives Forever*

5. Docu-noir: *The Naked City*

6. Fugitive Couples: *Gun Crazy*

7. Psychological Melodrama: Auld Lang Noir: *Woman in the Window* or *Scarlet Street*

8. The A's, B's, and Z's of Noir: *Detour* and *DOA*

9. Apocalypse Noir: *Kiss Me Deadly*

10. The Classic Period Ends: *The Killing* and *Touch of Evil*

The sardonic Mr. Gaines is nothing if not idiosyncratic; and yet, when one compares his course outline to the contents in Part One, there are the most matches of all: seven. Those who teach film and noir in particular have learned this distinction through practice; or, as Gaines said about *Double Indemnity* in FNR2:

> It also exemplifies more aspects of noir than just about any other film. It was based on a hard-boiled novel (by James M. Cain), co-written by a major hardboiled guy as well (Raymond Chandler), directed by a refugee not from German Expressionism but German Fascism (Billy Wilder), and shot and scored by preeminent noir craftsmen, John Seitz and Miklós Rósza, at a major studio (Paramount). So in introductory comments on film noir, one can touch on the source literature, earlier film movements, the political context in the world (war in Europe) and in Hollywood (the first film noir nominated for an Academy Award®), or visual and aural

styles and have examples right at hand. In terms of the narrative, which is the aspect of film noir that is readily accessible to most students, *Double Indemnity* really packs a wallop: femme fatale (in spades); flashback; first person narration (heavily ironic to boot); ace investigator; more greed than von Stroheim could throw at you; hetero- and a soupçon of homo-eroticism; and, even without the cut scene of Keyes watching Neff entering the gas chamber, some pretty harsh shuffling off this mortal coil by assorted characters.

While one might be hard pressed to put it as colorfully as that, many of the same points hold true for all the films in Part One. In fact, what I opined in 1993—that what best exemplifies film noir is not necessarily the best film—figured heavily into our current editorial choices. That and the consideration that some of the possible choices, such as *The Killers* and *Night and the City,* had already been "case studies" in earlier volumes in this series. Ultimately, after reviewing and researching anew to create our list, only two films were de rigueur: *Double Indemnity* and *Kiss Me Deadly* (and these two are extensively discussed in Part Two as well). They were closely followed by *Gun Crazy, Out of the Past, The Big Sleep, DOA,* and *Touch of Evil.* Among Fritz Lang's noir films, the reputation of *The Big Heat* has risen while that of *Woman in the Window* (and *Scarlet Street*) has diminished. Despite Philip Gaines' disparagement, Detour and its doomed narrative, however mawkish, is number nine. Barton Palmer has written and edited his own books on film noir, and his reconsideration of "Lounge Time" (created by Vivian Sobchack in her 1998 essay on noir figures and their "world of bars, diners, and seedy hotels") is a search for reconciliation between her approach and a crucial film in the noir canon, *Out of the Past.* Similarly, Kevin Hagopian examines the factors that created the two versions of *The Big Sleep.* Rounding out the dozen are Tony Williams' reassessment of Losey's *The Big Night* as a coming-of-age saga produced in the face of an impending blacklist; Grant Tracey's dissection of *The Big Heat* and the sexual dynamics in Joe Lewis' *The Big Combo;* and Bob Porfirio's close reading of visual style in *The Unsuspected.*

Part Two ranges a bit more widely over the subject. While commentators may agree on the boundaries of the "classic period," such issues of source works, mixed genres, and socio-political context remain significant and without clear consensus. In that sense, the chapter titles speak for themselves, although it may not be clear from the titles what examples figure most prominently in the articles.

J. P. Telotte, who has also written his own volume on noir, examines the elements of depth and darkness, focusing in particular on *Sunset Boulevard* and *Kiss Me Deadly.* Sheri Chinen Biesen considers the female protagonist in noir, particularly its title characters in movies such as *Laura, Mildred Pierce,* and *Gilda.* Reynold Humphries analyzes the complex relationship after World War II between crime on screen in film noir and off screen in the minds of the House Un-American Activities Committee.

Nicolas Saada's essay is an overview from a decidedly non-American (and non-English) viewpoint. As a former *Cahiers du Cinéma* critic who is more than a generation removed from his countrymen who coined the term, his essay neatly summarizes the key aspects of noir style. Saada generally surveys the concept of noir's interaction with other arts, other movements, and other genres. Eric Somer and James Ursini specifically consider noir vis-à-vis the horror films produced by Val Lewton at RKO and the Western respectively. Robin Wood goes even deeper into the latter relationship in his article on Lang's saga of "hate, murder, and revenge," the noir Western shot in color, *Rancho Notorious*. Finally, Robert Porfirio examines how the title sequence sets up viewer expectation and a noir mood in a dozen key films including *The Maltese Falcon, Double Indemnity, Kiss Me Deadly, In a Lonely Place, The Killers* and *Touch of Evil*; Ginny Schwartz revisits *Double Indemnity* from the point of view of Generation X; and Constantine Verevis analyzes neo-noir's approach to remaking classic period films with special consideration for *The Postman Always Rings Twice*.

It should be clear that all these essays are intended to complement a viewing of the film. But those who have read any of our earlier introductory comments will already be aware of our editorial belief that all texts are secondary to the films themselves. These essays range widely over the subject to form a collection of pieces appropriate for the film noir novice and aficionado alike.

Having given our usual admonition not to confuse the comments with the artifacts, to refer the reader to the "things themselves" is not to suggest they did or do exist in a vacuum. If we have been rhetorical in past introductions, it is not because we are seeking something akin to Henri Bergson's élan vital, nor are we subscribing to Croce's anti-fascist polemic that "every true history is contemporary history." If anything we are echoing Samuel Butler's warning that "God cannot alter the past, though historians can." The continuing "relevance" of film noir is that of any art defined by a particular style and narrative content to any era which succeeds it. The key relationship in any work is transcendentally simple: between an author, whose intentionality is contained entirely within the work, and a viewer. Also relevant is the relationship between similar works from the same era. Many of the revisionist approaches to the brief history of motion pictures seem intent on bypassing these. Certainly placing a work "in its contexts" can broaden understanding and may reveal alternate aesthetic readings; but as Barton Palmer aptly warns any rigid system, traditional or alternative, is exclusionary.

At its core, an excessively contextual approach to excavating a "film site" is tantamount to plying a pick and shovel only at the perimeter. Perhaps a better analogy would be trying to explicate a painting by looking at the frame. It might be interesting to read transcripts of the comments of all the spectators who attended the Salon des Réfusés in 1863, just as audience response cards from sneak previews of the classic noir period might be fascinating. As evaluatory benchmarks, however, they rank with using a "laugh meter" to rate a comedy. Whether one believes the film noir phenomenon is a movement, a genre, or a hybrid, the extraneous (and sometimes gratuitous) comments applied by revisionists often obfuscate as much as clarify. For Marc Vernet to posit the "invention" of film noir post hoc is still like saying that the Impressionist movement in France did not exist before 1874. Finding a consensus appellation for a group of works is just that, and nothing more. Events contemporary to the production and release of any film noir may be relevatory; but the imaginary preview cards from which many commentators seem to be reading provide neither fact nor exegesis. The primary relationship remains the transient interaction created every time someone watches a film noir, then, now, or any time in the future.

Now that there are four readers and well over a thousand pages of writing, one might well ask if the task is accomplished. For the time being, certainly. But if the length of this volume is any indication, no matter what one's critical bias, the more time that passes since the end of the classic period the more pertinent that era becomes. We are pleased that this volume can address the Crucial Film and Themes while including essays with a very wide range opinions from essayists with a very wide range of experience, as the Notes on Contributors will readily confirm. The internet helped not only to focus our editorial choices but also to discover several of the essayists in this volume. This seems all the more appropriate in light of what an uncharacteristically restrained Gaines astutely observed at the conclusion of *FNR2*:

> For many students, particularly mine, the ultimate question is not what noir was, but what it might be. They see film noir as an open-ended experience. Of course, with the short-sightedness of the young, they also see their own times—where slow internet access can be a most grievous fate—as more angst-ridden than any previous. The encapsulation effect, a selective view of the 1940s and 1950s through a noir filter, is not an easy read for those whose parents were not yet born when *The Maltese Falcon* was released. Still the through-line of film noir is undeniable and, in what may be the greatest irony, can be exhilarating to perceive for the first time [after] the turn of millennium.

Phyllis Dietrichson (Barbara Stanwyck) hides as a nervous Walter Neff (Fred MacMurray) watches insurance inspector Keyes leave in *Double Indemnity*.

"Murder Can Sometimes Smell Like Honeysuckle": Billy Wilder's *Double Indemnity* (1944)

James A. Paris

It is difficult to imagine how radically new and different *Double Indemnity* appeared at the time of its release in 1944. Inasmuch as many of the genres that made the American cinema of the 1940s and 1950s so vital have run their course, we can sit back and examine both the film and the genre as cultural artifacts, which is ostensibly what we are doing here. In this article, I will attempt to approach the film on two fronts: first, from the point of view of its uniqueness not only in Billy Wilder's career but also among the films of its time; secondly, as a work whose excellence continues to be even more apparent today than when it was released.

We tend to forget that Billy Wilder, who gave us so many great Hollywood films, was not himself an American, although his films are quintessentially American. "To know me," said Wilder, "you must think of me in terms of what Austria was like in 1906, when I was born. Austria in those days was a huge monarchy of 56 million people—the Austro-Hungarian Empire. The monarchy seemed indestructible."[1] The First World War destroyed the empire so utterly that scores of talented writers, artists, musicians, and filmmakers fled in all directions, while the empire fragmented (and continues to fragment) into numerous nation-states of variable stability. Most of the Austrian filmmakers who came to the United States continued to make films that identified them in one way or another as émigrés. One of them, Billy Wilder, turned out to be somewhat different.

On his arrival in Hollywood in 1934, Wilder started out as a writer. This in itself forced him out of the European mold and to adapt to the new language and culture quickly: One cannot think and speak in German and still write films for an American audience. Fortunately, he was usually teamed up with American screenwriters the likes of Borden Chase and Charles Brackett. (In fact, the partnership with Brackett continued during a large part of Wilder's directorial career.)

As an émigré, Wilder frequently found himself working with other émigrés such as Ernst Lubitsch, Joe May, Erich Pommer, Joe Pasternak, and Victor Schertzinger, initially on projects that were a continuation of themes from the European cinema. Eventually, by the time he teamed up with Brackett on Howard Hawks's *Ball of Fire* (1941), Wilder had to know his English well, as the film was a comedy about American slang. Coincidentally, it starred Barbara Stanwyck, whom Wilder engaged on *Double Indemnity* three years later. Wilder's directorial debut, *The Major and the Minor* (1941) was to all intents and purposes a Hollywood film comedy. His second film, *Five Graves to Cairo* (1943)

9

was an obligatory but entertaining war film, which included in its cast Erich von Stroheim as General Rommel; and, again, it was not significantly different from other WWII
propaganda films signed by native-born Hollywood directors.

His third film was something else again.

A New Hardness

Film noir had its antecedents in gangster films such as Joseph Von Sternberg's *Underworld* (1927) and its many 1930s successors. But in 1941, two Warner Brothers films
burst onto the scene that were qualitatively different from the gangster and detective
films that had preceded them: I am speaking of Raoul Walsh's *High Sierra* and John Huston's *The Maltese Falcon*. Both films starred Humphrey Bogart, in the first case as a
gangster on the run putting together his last heist; in the second, as a detective out to
avenge his murdered partner. There was a new hardness in both films. Bogart's Roy
Earle is an old time hood with feelings. When the heist turns bad, he is hunted down
by the police and stages a hopeless gunfight to the death amid casual onlookers who
are gathered to rubberneck at the last minutes of the notorious gangster's life. This is
a far cry from *Roaring Twenties* (1939) by the same director, in which two unlikable violent gangsters come to a bad end.

While there is a good deal of comic byplay in *The Maltese Falcon*, it was a new
phenomenon to see the suddenly enraged Sam Spade have the feckless Brigid
O'Shaughnessy (Mary Astor) hauled away by the police on a murder rap while sardon-
ically professing his love for her.

I am reminded by Marcel Proust's description in *The Guermantes Way* of how Au-
guste Renoir's painting changed the way that people saw reality:

> People of taste tell us nowadays that Renoir is a great eighteenth-century painter.
> But in so saying they forget the element of Time, and that it took a great deal of
> time, even at the height of the nineteenth century, for Renoir to be hailed as a
> great artist. To succeed thus in gaining recognition, the original painter or the orig-
> inal writer proceeds on the lines of the oculist. The course of treatment they gave
> us by their painting or their prose is not always pleasant. When it is at an end, the
> practitioner says to us: "Now look!" And, lo and behold, the world around us
> (which was not created once and for all, but is created afresh as often as an orig-
> inal artist is born) appears to us entirely different from the old world, but per-
> fectly clear. Women pass in the street, different from those we formerly saw,
> because they are Renoirs, those Renoirs we persistently refused to see as women.
> The carriages, too, are Renoirs, and the water, and the sky....[2]

From where did this new pessimism come? The United States and Europe had endured a grim depression, and now a new world war was pulling in our country—a
land that had hitherto prided itself on its isolation. In our literature and our film, we
had endured the hard times cheerfully, but the hopelessness that had engulfed much

of Europe in the 1930s finally dragged us in as well as our boys started to die on the battlefields of Europe, Asia, and North Africa. New writers had been writing dark new stories in periodicals such as *Black Mask*. Dashiell Hammett, Raymond Chandler, Horace McCoy, Cornell Woolrich and James M. Cain saw a different America in which the race was not always to the strong and pure, but to the most ruthless and the most cynical. Somewhat later than the novelists and short story writers, the films eventually began to reflect this cynicism.

James M. Cain was definitely one of the most hard-boiled of the bunch. The success of his novels *The Postman Always Rings Twice* (1934) and *Double Indemnity* (1938) on one hand interested the studios and on the other alerted the Breen Office of the Motion Picture Production Association that here was a potential threat to the moral fiber of the nation. Cain's novels had this quality of looking at human concupiscence and greed from a high vantage point, as if we were staring at insects, with about as much emotional involvement.

There are many stories about how Paramount came to film *Double Indemnity*, but suffice it to say that it was made and that Wilder jumped at the chance. "I wanted Cain, who wrote the short story [sic]," says Wilder, "but he was busy. My producer, Joseph Sistrom, said, 'Look, there is a good writer who knows the climate of Southern California, and you will like him.' So we found Mr. Chandler. Raymond Chandler wasn't known then the way he is now."[3] By this time, the new scriptwriter had published a respectable number of short stories, *The Big Sleep* (1939), *Farewell My Lovely* (1940), and *The High Window* (1942).

Although Chandler and Wilder did not really hit it off personally, the screenplay they wrote was the only one honored by publication in the prestigious Library of America series. Chandler continued on in Hollywood for a while, but never got the hang of the place. In an essay entitled "Writers in Hollywood" (1946), he slammed the industry for not giving more power and prestige to writers such as himself.[4] I believe that, to the end of his days, Chandler did not understand that his travails with Wilder as a fledgling screenwriter resulted in one of the greatest of all scripts.

The Auteur Theory

Like many of my generation, I came to become interested in film during the heyday of the *politique des auteurs*, especially as exemplified on this side of the Atlantic by the work of Andrew Sarris. His book, *The American Cinema: Directors and Directions 1929–1968*, was nothing less than a manifesto. Sarris evaluated directors under such picturesque classifications as "Pantheon Directors," "The Far Side of Paradise," "Expressive Esoterica," and—the category where we find Billy Wilder—"Less Than Meets the Eye."

Having seen at least half a dozen major critical movements arise since the auteur theory, I see it at worst as a self-consuming artifact. Auteurism had the virtue of sending its adherents to actually see movies, including those that had previously been rejected as too insignificant to analyze. Once one went back to the originals, one can make up one's own mind and see that Sarris was right about many things and wrong about others. Sarris was merely attempting to translate a French critical tendency to our shores.

In France, Auteurism dates back to a *Cahiers du Cinéma* article by François Truffaut entitled "About a Certain Tendency of the French Cinema." This article was ostensibly an attack on the dominance of the French cinema of the Fifties by writers who brought too literary an approach to their work. Naturally, Sarris inherited the French prejudice against screenwriter-directors (though somehow granting absolution to Alfred Hitchcock).

Sarris aims a number of shots at Wilder, but the target is moving too fast for him. We are stuck with such observations as "Billy Wilder is too cynical to believe his own cynicism" and of his "penchant for gross caricature, especially with peripheral characters." Finally: "All of Wilder's films decline in retrospect because of visual and structural deficiencies,"[5] none of which are specified.

There actually are unifying themes that run through Wilder's work. The fact that Wilder emerged from the ruins of the Austro-Hungarian Empire did not mean that he had to confine himself to European themes. Having begun as a writer, Wilder was more or less impelled to become a chameleon, such that even his films set in Europe are seen through American eyes. Sarris was right about the director's cynicism: Especially in his more dramatic films, the lead characters tend to use one another for their own purposes. Altruism and sentimentality give way to opportunism and outright insensitivity.

Let us look at *Double Indemnity* in this light. Walter Neff is a high-powered insurance salesman out to "game" the system for his benefit, at the same time indulging his sexual fantasies about Phyllis Dietrichson and her stepdaughter Lola. Phyllis, on the other hand, sees in Neff a way to rid herself of her husband, who has refused to divorce her. She strings Neff along insofar as it suits her purpose. They both talk about going "straight down the line," but I am not convinced that they are talking about the same line. There is no real love here: Neff is driven by his hubris and lust; and Phyllis, by her venality. Even the teenaged Lola uses Neff as a way of meeting her unsavory boyfriend Nino Zaccetti and justifying her relationship with him, while Neff, pasha-like, dreams of bagging the mother and daughter. To quote Kurt Vonnegut Jr.'s calypso singer in *Cat's Cradle*:

> Nice, nice, very nice.
> So many people in the same device.

The Exception That Proves the Rule

The one exception to the rule is the insurance investigator, Barton Keyes. What Wilder and Chandler did with the character of Keyes is a good example of why the film is so superior to the novel. Here is how Cain introduces him in the novel:

> When I got back to the office, I found Keyes had been looking for me. Keyes is head of the Claims Department, and the most tiresome man in the whole

world.... He gets fatter every year, and more peevish, and he's always in some kind of a feud with other departments of the company, and does nothing but sit with his collar open, and sweat, and quarrel, and argue, until your head begins spinning around just to be in the same room with him. But he's a wolf on a phony claim.[6]

In both the film and the novel, we see him in this latter role: He savages a Mr. Gorlopis who had set fire to his truck to collect the insurance. Like a Javert, Keyes singlemindedly goes after Gorlopis until he signs a waiver releasing the insurance company from the claim. What makes the character of Keyes so interesting is that he feels compelled to be "a wolf on a phony claim." On a number of occasions, he refers to his "little man," who ties knots in his stomach whenever he feels that there is something wrong with a claim.

It does not take long after the murder for Keyes's little man to act up. He shows up suddenly at Neff's apartment and complains that he ate dinner two hours ago, and that it stuck half way down his craw. "The little man is acting up again."[7] When Neff says he has no bicarbonate of soda, he asks if he at least has a peppermint. As he leaves, he says, "I've got to get to a drugstore. It feels like a hunk of concrete inside me."[8] The notion of a shark like Keyes being driven to discern the truth in a case tends to hint at a certain softness in him.

His character undergoes a further softening as it becomes apparent that he is a father figure of sorts to Neff. He even tries to get his star salesman to take a pay cut to join him in the Claims department:

KEYES: Now, look, Walter. The job I'm talking about takes brains and integrity. It takes more guts than there is in fifty salesmen. It's the hottest job in the business.

NEFF: It's still a desk job. I don't want a desk job.

KEYES: A desk job. Is that all you can see in it? Just a hard chair to park your pants on from nine to five. Just a pile of papers to shuffle around, and five sharp pencils and a scratch pad to make figures on, with maybe a little doodling on the side. That's not the way I see it, Walter. To me a claims man is a surgeon, and that desk is an operating table, and those pencils are scalpels and bone chisels. And those papers are not just forms and statistics and claims for compensation. They're alive, they're packed with drama, with twisted hopes and crooked dreams. A claims man, Walter, is a doctor and a blood-hound and a cop and a judge and a jury and a father confessor, all in one.[9]

Although he does not accept Keyes' offer, Neff treats him with respect and even love. In his voice-over, he reminisces, "I really did [love you], too, you old crab, always sore at everyone. But behind the cigar ashes on your vest I kind of knew you had a heart as big as a house."[10]

At several points in the film, Neff lights Keyes' cigar after Keyes fails to; and Keyes submits like a pleased father.

At the end, as Neff is leaking blood from his bullet wound, Keyes comes upon him and hears him incriminate himself over the Dictaphone. Are we in the presence of Keyes the father or Keyes the ruthless bloodhound? The answer is both.

NEFF: And now I suppose I get the big speech with all the two-dollar words in it. Let's have it, Keyes.

KEYES: You're all washed up, Walter.

NEFF: Thanks, Keyes, that was short, anyway.[11]

Neff is in a delirium and tries to make his way out of the office. Keyes offers to call a doctor, while remaining obdurate about turning him in for murder and insurance fraud. Now comes the last scene in the film:

NEFF: (slowly and with great difficulty). You know why you didn't figure this one, Keyes? Let me tell you. The guy you were looking for was too close. He was right across the desk from you.

KEYES: Closer than that, Walter. (The eyes of the two men meet in a moment of silence)

NEFF: I love you, too.

Neff fumbles for the handkerchief in Keyes' pocket, pulls it out and clumsily wipes his face with it. The handkerchief drops from his hand. He gets a loose cigarette out of his pocket and puts it between his lips. Then with great difficulty, he gets out a match, tries to strike it, but is too weak. Keyes takes the match out of his hand, strikes it for him and lights his cigarette. The scene fades out.[12]

So while all the other characters are attempting to step over one another, Keyes stands alone as a strict, yet kind and highly principled force. His character is the exception that proves the rule. Curiously, if Edward G. Robinson's Keyes were more similar to Neff and Dietrichson, the film would more like Cain's original novel. The fact that he isn't adds a more satisfying texture to the finished film.

Other Wilder films that have similar cynical, self-interested leading characters are *Sunset Boulevard* (1950); *Ace in the Hole* AKA *The Big Carnival* (1951); *Stalag 17* (1953); *Witness for the Prosecution* (1957) with the Tyrone Power role a classic example; *The Apartment* (1960); and *The Fortune Cookie* (1966). In his later films, Wilder allowed some sentimentality to creep back into his work—see especially *Avanti!* (1972). Looking over his œuvre as a whole, however, the note that is struck in much of his best work is a scornful cynicism that does not admit of any concessions to sentimentality.

The wonder of it all is that Wilder's films do come across as being so likeable despite it all. It seems to be very much in keeping with the man, who was nothing if not realistic about the film industry. Woe to him who asked Wilder about film as an art form! Here is Wilder's response to one interviewer:

Now, you must understand that a man who makes movies and certainly some-body like myself that makes all kinds of movies, works in different styles. I don't make only one kind of movie, like say Hitchcock. Or like Minnelli, doing the great Metro musicals. As a picture-maker, and I think most of us are this way, I am not aware of patterns. We're not aware that "This picture will be in this genre." It comes naturally, just the way you do your handwriting. That's the way I look at it, that's the way I conceive it. Just like I do not imagine Monet painting his land-scapes and telling himself, "Now wait a minute, I'm an Impressionist. Therefore I must do it this way."13

As one unnamed filmmaker quipped, you don't interview Anaxagoras by asking him how it feels to be a Pre-Socratic.

Sex and Hubris

Double Indemnity is a film that will be viewed and admired for years to come. What makes the film unique is one thing; what makes it memorable is something else again. There are, after all, filmmakers who are far more consistent throughout their careers without one scintilla of what constitutes greatness, either in their individual works or their work as a whole.

As in Greek tragedy, we see the hubris of the insurance salesman, Walter Neff, as he overreaches himself to sell an accident policy to an unhappy young wife. A bache-lor in his thirties, Neff is excited by the blonde with the anklet on her left leg. Early in his voice-over, Neff says, "I killed him for money—and a woman—and I didn't get the money and I didn't get the woman."14 The whole story is told from Neff's point of view: We never see Phyllis's point of view except insofar as Neff is present.

The central action is the murder of Phyllis's husband, identified only as Dietrichson. It is Neff who suggests that Dietrichson's death be in a train accident:

NEFF: Look, baby. There's a clause in every accident policy, a little something called double indemnity. The insurance companies put it in as a sort of come-on for the customers. It means they pay double on certain accidents. The kind that al-most never happen. Like for instance if a guy got killed on a train, they'd pay a hundred thousand instead of fifty.

PHYLLIS: I see. (Her eyes widen with excitement.)

NEFF: We're hitting it for the limit, baby. That's why it's got to be a train.15

Here is where Neff overreaches. That extra fillip of murder on a train is what arouses Keyes' suspicion. When, earlier, Neff and Phyllis decide on collaborating on the mur-der, Neff's voice-over Dictaphone narration says, "That was it, Keyes. The machinery had started to move and nothing could stop it."16

After the murder, and after his impersonation of Dietrichson on the train, Neff

Phyllis Dietrichson (Barbara Stanwyck) displays her signature anklet to a lust-filled Walter Neff (Fred MacMurray) while the cuckolded husband (Tom Powers) absorbs himself in insurance papers in *Double Indemnity*.

feels uneasy despite the fact that everything seemingly went well. On the Dictaphone, he muses:

> That was all there was to it. Nothing had slipped, nothing had been overlooked, and there was nothing to give us away. And yet, Keyes, as I was walking down the street to the drug store, suddenly it came over me that everything would go wrong. It sounds crazy, Keyes, but it's true, so help me: I couldn't hear my own footsteps. It was the walk of a dead man.[17]

That most seemingly un-noir-like of all actors, Fred MacMurray, was cast for the part of Neff. It was a brilliant coup. Known primarily for his comedies, both before and after *Double Indemnity,* he gave a performance that validated Wilder's judgment and showed him to be a more wide-ranging actor than anyone could have guessed. MacMurray's fundamental amiability made him all the more effective as a tragic protagonist. (Later, in 1960, MacMurray played the even more unsympathetic role of J. D. Sheldrake in Wilder's *The Apartment*).

It is ironical that the one person in the film to whom Neff can turn as a friend is Keyes, the incorruptible insurance claim investigator from whom he has the most to fear for his transgression. After the meeting in the executive's office, Phyllis pays a surprise visit to Neff in his apartment:

PHYLLIS: How much does he know?

NEFF: It's not what he knows. It's those stinking hunches of his.

PHYLLIS: But he can't prove anything, can he?

NEFF: Not if we're careful. Not if we don't see each other for a while.

PHYLLIS: For how long a while? (She moves toward him but he does not respond.)

NEFF: Until all this dies down. You don't know Keyes the way I do. Once he gets his teeth into something he won't let go. He'll investigate you. He'll have you shadowed. He'll watch you every minute from now on. Are you afraid, baby?

NEFF: What are you talking about?

PHYLLIS: And you don't really care whether we see each other or not.

NEFF: Shut up, baby.

He pulls her close and kisses her as the scene fades out.[18]

The Second Mrs. Dietrichson

In Cain's novel, Phyllis Dietrichson was not new to murder. Before her marriage to Dietrichson, she had worked as a nurse. In this capacity, she had killed not only her husband's previous wife but other patients as well who were entrusted to her care. Chandler and Wilder bring up this angle as a strong suspicion of Lola's in one of her meetings with Neff. There isn't time in this fast-paced script to provide much of a backstory.

The blonde wig that Barbara Stanwyck wore in the role of Phyllis was one of Wilder's biggest regrets. "Mistake there," he said. "Big mistake!"[19] The director regarded her make-up as a form of cheap symbolism. As a way of underlining Phyllis's dime store eroticism (she uses a perfume she bought in Ensenada), it is also crudely effective.

When we first see her, she is wearing nothing but a bath towel as she stares down at Walter Neff, who had just gained admittance by putting his foot in the door, figuratively speaking, when the maid answered the door. That Wilder and Chandler managed to tightrope walk around the Breen Office during wartime with all this suggestiveness was a major surprise to the Paramount studio executives; and, even today, it is no small measure of the film's artistry.

The racy repartee at this first meeting between Walter and Phyllis underscores the tawdriness of their respective approaches with some of Chandler's best dialogue:

NEFF: Accident insurance? Sure, Mrs. Dietrichson. (His eyes fall on the anklet again.) I wish you'd tell me what's engraved on that anklet.

PHYLLIS: Just my name.

NEFF: As for instance?

PHYLLIS: Phyllis.

NEFF: Phyllis, I think I like that.

PHYLLIS: But you're not sure?

NEFF: I'd have to drive it around the block a couple of times.

PHYLLIS: (standing up again) Mr. Neff, why don't you drop by tomorrow evening around eight-thirty. He'll be in then.

NEFF: Who?

PHYLLIS: My husband. You were anxious to talk to him, weren't you?

NEFF: Sure, only I'm getting over it a little. If you know what I mean.

PHYLLIS: There's a speed limit in this state, Mr. Neff. Forty-five miles an hour.

NEFF: How fast was I going, officer?

PHYLLIS: I'd say about ninety.

NEFF: Suppose you get down off your motorcycle and give me a ticket.

PHYLLIS: Suppose I let you off with a warning this time.

NEFF: Suppose it doesn't take.

PHYLLIS: Suppose I have to whack you over the knuckles?

NEFF: Suppose I bust out crying and put my head on your shoulder.

PHYLLIS: Suppose you try putting it on my husband's shoulder.

NEFF: That tears it.[20]

Neff is properly hooked. He obsesses about Phyllis's anklet and is well on his way to helping her kill her husband. Blonde wig and all, Phyllis is a figure that radiates both sexuality and danger, like the younger Joan Crawford when her face assumes "the mask." Although after the murder, she and Neff continue to profess desire for each other, it is very evident that what unites them now is the shared fear of being caught. There is the now-famous scene in the neighborhood supermarket where they push

A distraught Keyes (Edward G. Robinson) turns his head as the condemned Neff (Fred Mac-Murray) is taken into the gas chamber. This scene was eventually cut from the release print of *Double Indemnity*.

separate shopping carts and talk like zombies without looking at each other to avoid the prying eyes of the insurance company's investigators.

The culmination occurs when they can no longer continue in this vein. Neff has been meeting with Lola, who reinforces his negative feelings about Phyllis; and it seems that Phyllis has been consoling herself with none other than Nino Zaccetti. All this comes out in their final meeting at her house. After airing mutual recriminations, Phyllis pulls out a handgun and shoots:

> NEFF: What's the matter? Why don't you shoot again? Maybe if I come a little closer? (Taking a few more steps toward her and stopping again) How's that. Do you think you can do it now?

Phyllis is silent. She doesn't shoot. Her expression is tortured. Neff goes on until he is close to her. Quietly he takes the gun out of her unresisting hand.

> NEFF: Why didn't you shoot, baby? (In reply Phyllis puts her arms around him in complete surrender.) Don't tell me it's because you've been in love with me all this time.

PHYLLIS: No. I never loved you, Walter. Not you, or anybody else. I'm rotten to the heart. I used you, just as you said. That's all you ever meant to me—until a minute ago. I didn't think anything like that could ever happen to me.

NEFF: I'm sorry, baby. I'm not buying.[21]

At this point, with her gun in his hand, he shoots her dead. At this point, he realizes that Phyllis's gunshot did not go astray, and that he was bleeding. It is from this wound, unnoticed at first, that he dies.

In the original release of the film, Neff was arrested, tried, and executed in the gas chamber for double murder. There exists a still reproduced in Richard Schickel's fine monograph on the film that shows Neff flanked by two police officers through the window of the chamber, while Keyes holds on to the rail outside and looks down.[22] Either preview audiences did not like to see the amiable MacMurray put to death, or else Wilder thought there was a neater way to wrap everything up. Although Cain's ending was different, it was highly unsatisfactory: Neff and Phyllis are on an oceanliner off the Mexican coast about to commit suicide. What Chandler and Wilder did was neater and more emotionally satisfying. The sound of sirens as Neff dies in Keyes' arms put the final touches on one relationship that never got off the ground and another that Neff took entirely for granted.

Hitchcock and the Tulips

In his now famous series of interviews by François Truffaut, Alfred Hitchcock reminisces about a scene he would have liked to put in *Foreign Correspondent* (1940):

Had the picture been done in color, I would have worked in a shot I've always dreamed of: a murder in a tulip field. Two characters: the killer, a Jack-the-Ripper type, behind him the girl, his victim. As his shadow creeps up on her, she turns and screams. Immediately, we pan down to the struggling feet in the tulip field. We would dolly the camera up to and right into one of the tulips, with the sounds of the struggle in the background. One petal fills the screen, and suddenly a drop of blood splashes all over it.[23]

That kind of incongruity is what pervades *Double Indemnity*. In the Thirties, a nice little house in the suburbs was such a dream object that the thought of a callous murder being plotted there was too jarring to the viewer's sensibilities. To this, add the concept of insurance (which was Cain's unique contribution), and you have a combination that had never been conceived of before. According to Schickel, Charles Brackett thought Cain's story line "disgusting" and begged off the project.[24] It was by penetrating the inconceivability barrier that Wilder, with the help of Chandler, created a noir masterpiece.

The opening of *Double Indemnity* is pure noir: an erratic, speeding car in the night crashes a stop light and pulls up to the curb. An overcoated figure lurches from the car and rings the bell at a high-rise building. It was the wounded Walter Neff, making his way to the Pacific All-Risk Insurance offices to dictate his message to Keyes. As he begins his narrative, we cut to a sunny day in a foothill suburban development full of Spanish-style houses. After passing an ice-cream truck, Neff pulls up to a two-story house that looks expensive. As he finagles his way inside, we see a living room with light streaming in through half-closed venetian blinds. There is more than a touch of dust motes drifting in the burdened air on a hot day. The smell of honeysuckle pervades the area. This is the point where Phyllis enters on the second floor landing draped only in a towel.

In his interview with Robert Porfirio, Wilder describes the mood of the Dietrichson house's interior:

> This, the *stimmung* [mood] in *Double Indemnity*, the idea there was that this was kind of a California house, and the furniture and everything was right there where I would like to sense that, as the sunshine comes through, that it has not been dusted. The dust is floating around, and she [Phyllis] is a bad housewife, and the daughter doesn't give a damn.[25]

Much of the credit for translating this vision into film goes to director of photography John Seitz. From the unlikely Spanish suburban house to the cavernous offices of the insurance company, to the dark railroad yard, there is a sense of rightness to the look of the scenes. The look is pure noir, even when we are seeing things that were never shown in a noir film before. In this film, murder does smell like honeysuckle, and something else besides, perhaps a touch of Phyllis's cheap perfume from Ensenada. We can absorb the contrasts because there is a natural rightness to the way the shots look in every case. Even when the sun is shining, the leaden feeling that something is not quite right is conveyed and helps build a feeling of suspense—suspense despite the fact that we already know that the whole murder plot unraveled in the first few minutes of the film.

The score by Miklos Rózsa is not heavy like a Max Steiner score, yet it builds on the growing feeling of dread by a subtle slow rhythm reminding one of a steam locomotive in the distance.

Perhaps it took a European who had lost an entire world to see life with such a bittersweet sense of irony. From the credits, where we see Walter Neff in on crutches as he impersonates the murdered Dietrichson and hear the foreboding notes of the music well up, *Double Indemnity* grabs our attention and keeps it engaged throughout. There are no adventitious scenes to cut: every scene is dead on. What in Cain's novel seems merely sordid is converted by Wilder's magic touch into something rich and strange.

It is ironic that *Double Indemnity* did not win an Oscar the year of its release. That honor went to Bing Crosby and Barry Fitzgerald in *Going My Way*. But Billy Wilder had the last word after all: He stuck out his foot and tripped Leo McCarey on his way to the podium to receive the award for Best Director.[26]

NOTES

1. Charlotte Chandler, *Nobody's Perfect: Billy Wilder, A Personal Biography,* New York: Simon & Schuster, 2002, p. 15.

2. Marcel Proust, *The Guermantes Way, In Search of Lost Time,* Volume III, translated by C. K. Scott-Moncrieff and Terence Kilmartin and revised by D. J. Enright, New York: The Modern Library, 1993, p. 445.

3. C. Chandler, p. 115.

4. Reproduced in Raymond Chandler, *Later Novels and Other Writings* (New York: Library of America, 1995), pp. 993–1003.

5. Andrew Sarris, *The American Cinema: Directors and Directions, 1929–1968,* New York: E.P. Dutton & Co., 1968, pp. 165–67.

6. James M. Cain, *Double Indemnity* (New York: Vintage Books, 1992), pp. 7–8.

7. Raymond Chandler [and Billy Wilder], "*Double Indemnity,*" in *Later Novels and Other Writings,* New York: Library of America, 1995, p. 944.

8. Chandler and Wilder, p. 945.

9. Chandler and Wilder, pp. 917–18.

10. Chandler and Wilder, p. 891.

11. Chandler and Wilder, p. 970.

12. Chandler and Wilder, p. 972.

13. Robert Porfirio, Alain Silver, and James Ursini, editors, *Film Noir Reader 3: Interviews with Filmmakers of the Classic Noir Period,* New York: Limelight Editions, 2001, p. 101.

14. Chandler and Wilder, p. 879.

15. Chandler and Wilder, pp. 909–910.

16. Chandler and Wilder, p. 904.

17. Chandler and Wilder, p. 934.

18. Chandler and Wilder, p. 947.

19. Porfirio et al, p. 116.

20. Chandler and Wilder, pp. 884–85.

21. Chandler and Wilder, p. 969.

22. Richard Schickel, *Double Indemnity,* London: British Film Institute, 1992, p. 62.

23. François Truffaut, *Hitchcock,* New York: Simon and Schuster, 1967, pp. 96–97.

24. Schickel, p. 32.

25. Porfirio et al, p. 114.

26. Apocryphal but very much in character.

The doomed and sadomasochistic couple (Ann Savage and Tom Neal) of *Detour*, posed against a typically minimalist background.

Fate Seeks the Loser:
Edgar G. Ulmer's *Detour* (1945)

Glenn Erickson

Did you ever want to forget anything? Did you ever want to cut away a piece of your memory or blot it out? You can't, you know. No matter how hard you try. You can change the scenery, but sooner or later you'll get a whiff of perfume or somebody will say a certain phrase or maybe hum something. Then you're licked again!

Film noir has a short list of core masterpieces, the films that most successfully exemplify the style, or initiated important trends. The majority of titles on this short list are studio films made by some of the best talent in Hollywood. But near the top of the list, one Poverty Row title persists. It's a lowly effort from Producer's Releasing Corporation, an outfit with an output that rarely saw the top half of a grind-house double bill, let alone an Oscar.

Detour is a 68-minute potboiler with an unpromising premise and a no-star cast. One of the earlier 'cult' pictures that surfaced in the 1970s rediscovery of film noir, it's a title of legendary proportions. Because of the lack of documentation down at its level of production, the film has accumulated its share of erroneous myth.

Detour's compressed storyline illustrates the despairing thoughts of pianist-vagrant Al Roberts (Tom Neal) as he sits at the counter of a roadside diner outside Reno, Nevada. As the lighting on his face undergoes a radical shift into inner darkness, Al's bitter voiceover recalls happier days in a Manhattan club. In flashback we see Roberts accompanying his singer girlfriend Sue (Claudia Drake). Sue leaves for Hollywood to try her luck, and soon thereafter Al hitchhikes across the country to be with her. But his fateful ride with Haskell (Edmund MacDonald), a talkative gambler with a heart problem, is the beginning of a nightmarish, absurd chain of coincidences and bad decisions that strand Al in a desert of crime, guilt, and blackmail. Abetting Al's bad luck is the consumptive, self-destructive Vera (Ann Savage), a fellow hitchhiker who ruthlessly exploits his mistakes. By the time the tale reaches its downbeat finale, Al has hit one of the lower rungs of degradation to be found in film noir. Miserable, convinced he is a wanted criminal and can never take his troubles to Sue, he roams the highways and back roads wondering when his inevitable arrest will come.

Almost all of the credit for *Detour* can be attributed to the limitless creativity and resourcefulness of director Edgar G. Ulmer, the patron saint of no-budget filmmaking.

Before the noir rediscovery, Ulmer was virtually unknown in America and acknowledged only by the French *Cahiers du Cinema* critics. He was abused as a cheap joke in
critic Andrew Sarris' auteurist *American Film*. Not until his filmography could be properly assessed did it become evident that Ulmer had a valid claim to *auteurship*. He not
only exercised complete artistic control over his often-tiny productions, but his flamboyant directing style left clear tracks for critics to trace—from minimalist musicals
to ethnic melodramas, to ambitious science fiction thrillers.

Back when it first became a hot topic of discussion, *Detour's* reputation was long
on rumor and short on good information. When many curious fans caught up with it
in the late 70s, they were surprised to find that it wasn't all shot, as was often repeated, on two tiny sets in front of a process screen. Some notions about the film
persist to this day. It took six days to shoot, not three as often reported. Compared
to a big-studio production it was a real cheapie, but by Poverty Row standards *Detour* was almost lavish. Budgeted at $89,000, it was completed for a stratospheric
$117,000. This was at a time when most of Ulmer's other PRC pix cost less than 30
grand, a figure that included the studio's overhead. Ulmer's personal salary on this
particular show was miniscule. He took home less than a third of what was paid to
the film's initial director, Lew Landers. Landers left before filming even commenced,
but collected most of what was budgeted for the director.

Detour doesn't have the typical grayish Poverty Row photographic look, especially
when seen in a print of reasonable quality.[1] A few carefully lit master scenes—the
wraparound bookend in the Reno diner, the roadside exterior in the rain—give the
picture its pervasive atmosphere. The average PRC would all take place in nowhere
sets like the motel room, and employ dull stock shots as filler. *Detour's* finishing details include a number of carefully crafted montage sequences, precision lab opticals
that are a far cry from the crude $50 bargain lap dissolves found in other PRC films.
To preserve the 'right to left' screen orientation for his cross-country montage,
Ulmer takes the time and effort to optically flop a hitchhiking shot—shifting cars to
the wrong side of the road in the process. The carefully mixed soundtrack blends
several carefully arranged themes, among them a hit pop song, "I Can't Believe That
You're In Love With Me," something unexpected in an ordinary Poverty Row production.

Ulmer's ability to squeeze good-looking pictures from his limited resources was
legendary. The picture never suffers for its cheapness. There are no sagging back-
drops, bare stage floors, etc. There is a lot of rear projection, but it's expertly done.
The production even ran out to the desert north of Los Angeles for a few roadside
pickup shots. In his interview excerpted in *Kings of the Bs*,[2] Peter Bogdanovich got
the crafty director to talk about his practice of filming 'PRC Hour' shots at the end
of each film shoot—rapid-fire coverage and bits needed to finish scenes that didn't
fit into the schedule. To give key scenes proper attention Ulmer shrewdly reduced
other parts of the film to easily shot fragments that could be knocked off wholesale
in just a few hours.

A big part of Ulmer's economy can be attributed to the long patches of narration built into his shooting script. The hardboiled pulp tradition was known for its first-person narratives, which here translate into a wall-to-wall flashback voice-over. Al Roberts tells his story almost as a radio drama, in the lightly cynical, arch manner associated with Raymond Chandler stories, and would soon decorate the hep performances of proto-beats like Robert Mitchum. Scenes of tense character interaction alternate with Roberts' woefully cynical interior monologues:

> Ever done any hitchhikin'? It's not much fun, believe me. Oh yeah, I know all about how it's an education and how you get to meet a lot of people and all that. But me, from now on I'll take my education in college, or in P.S. 62 or I'll send $1.98 in stamps for ten easy lessons.

> While the mechanic inspected the car, we haggled. At last, when we were all worn out, we hit a compromise—his price.

> If this were fiction, I would fall in love with Vera, marry her and make a respectable woman of her. Or else she'd make some supreme class-A sacrifice for me, and die.

Detour's originality enables it to hold its own against the top titles in the noir field. From within the confines of the PRC budget straightjacket it established an original genre thread, the Tale of the Loser Hero. Roberts isn't a cop, a private detective, a criminal or a crooked politician, but instead a passive schmoe, a professional victim. Critic Blake Lucas[3] correctly pegged Al's detour from the straight and narrow path as the road he really wants to take. Unlike other noir antagonists who struggle in dark corners, Al's destiny has a definite self-willed quality.

Al's self-constructed fate in *Detour* is clearly expressed in his narration. He perceives himself as existing in a friendless isolation, a claustrophobic exile visually enhanced by the fog on Riverside drive. At every opportunity, Roberts collapses into a pessimistic cynicism, an attitude he appears to enjoy. Nothing's good enough for Al; not even the ten-dollar tip he receives in appreciation for his musical talent:

> "What was it?" I asked myself. A piece of paper crawling with germs. It couldn't buy anything I wanted.

Al Roberts has his health, a measure of talent, and a woman who likes him but he prefers to wallow in morbid self-attention. After Sue departs, she seems to exist only as an unattainable concept in Al's negative thinking. When Al phones her, we only hear his end of the conversation. We see her only in a couple of silent cutaways (surely filmed during Ulmer's 'PRC Hour' at the end of production). Al's concern for Sue is sincere and his hitchhike Odyssey across America is well intentioned, but he doesn't have the resolve to see it through.

Al's cross-country trip is a journey of self-discovery. His perverse pleasure, playing victim, finds concrete expression as he is reduced to a beggar thumbing rides, meekly accepting handouts from strangers. On The Road is where things happen in America, and *Detour* expresses a post–Jack London, pre–Jack Kerouac consciousness of the Road as the lonely mirror of the soul.

Al makes two crippling decisions, choices proving that character determines his fate, not the 'mysterious force' he whines about at the film's end. He's convinced that his vagrant status will prejudice the law against him, but Haskell's accidental death isn't all *that* mysterious. The dead man's pills should prove that he had an existing heart condition. Al makes the accident appear to be a crime and takes Haskell's identity, thus guaranteeing a murder charge if he's caught. These are the acts of a masochist. So thoroughly does Roberts frame himself, the only explanation is that he secretly wants to be a criminal.

Later on Al laments the fact that he can't hook up with Sue *"with a thing like that hanging over my head."* In actuality, that happened as soon as he left his ID on Haskell's body. Roberts is really that kind of complicated man who professes to have strong goals yet all the while purposely engineers his own failure. In real life these maladjusted types want attention, or for someone else to step in and relieve them of their responsibilities. It's the urge that keeps a potential high-class musician like Al playing piano in a dive: he can curse his cruel fate while avoiding the feared struggle for success in the competitive world. This allows him to trumpet his superiority while cursing the system that he claims has victimized him. Ever see an artist create something promising, only to destroy it? They always make sure they have an audience, someone to disappoint.

A standard Cornell Woolrich short story would stop with this twist alone and follow Roberts' effort to extricate himself from the trap of assuming Haskell's identity. Mickey Rooney makes one mistake in the minor Loser Hero effort *Quicksand,* and spends an hour foolishly getting himself in deeper. But Ulmer and Goldsmith throw in another complication almost immediately when Roberts-disguised-as-Haskell tops his bad judgment by picking up the hitchhiking Vera. Why does he do such a risky thing, when he should be sneaking into San Bernardino and ditching Haskell's car as quietly as possible? Again, the only answer is his self-destructive itch. Roberts is the scorpion who stings not the frog, but himself. This unaccountability of human actions is much more interesting and believable than the 'mysterious fate' that Roberts claims is responsible for his troubles.

Vera is a woman who looks like she's been on the highway for several days. Her face is shiny and her hair is like a bird's nest. This particular kind of realism was unknown in American pictures, where women roughing it were never less glamorous than Veronica Lake in *Sullivan's Travels.* But Vera soon shows her true colors. With one sharp turn of her head she transforms from a cameo-like unknown female, into Al's worst nightmare. Immediately accusing and threatening, she takes control of both Al and the movie. With predators like Vera roaming the roads, perhaps Roberts was correct in believing that the authorities would railroad him into a murder charge. Piercingly suspicious, she sees beyond Al's foolish impersonation and is soon prepping him for the gas chamber.

In the mostly-civilized world of romantic drama there's nothing quite like the intensity of *Detour's* duel of wills between Al and Vera. The crackling banter lifts the picture onto a higher theatrical plane. Roberts' voice-over admiration of Vera grudgingly acknowledges his attraction for her. Does he want to be abused? Why else would he put up with her interrogations, an insinuating verbal onslaught that would drive any normal man into a blind rage?

> Say, I've been around. And I know a wrong guy when I see one. What'd you do, kiss him with a wrench? ... Why should I believe you? You've got all the earmarks of a cheap crook. Shut up! You're a cheap crook and you killed him. For two cents I'd change my mind and turn you in. I don't like you!

Again, it soon becomes clear that Vera is Al's destined mate, and not simply because he voluntarily gives her a lift at the worst possible time. Sinful lovers in films noir constantly use the line, 'We were made for each other—we're both bad', but whereas the couples in *Double Indemnity* or *Out of the Past* are making extreme judgments on themselves, "tawdry" and "sordid" form the sum total of Al and Vera's relationship. He's a chump in a frame of his own making, and she's a consumptive harpy out to throttle the world until it gives her what she wants. Radio's popular *The Battling Bickersons* are echoed in their incessant arguing. *Detour* becomes a perverse situation comedy, one where Lucy blackmails Ricky Ricardo to commit suicidal crimes. Vera's sexual desires are no more under control than her criminality and show a potential weakness that Al fails to exploit to effect an escape. One must assume that, like some married couples who fight yet stay together, something in Al senses the rightness of his pairing with Vera.

If a vestige of romance remains in *Detour*, it's in the fact that Roberts keeps Sue free of his problems. His willingness to suffer alone instead of dragging Sue in, as does Jeff Bailey with his innocent girlfriend in *Out of the Past*, makes Roberts praiseworthy on at least one level. His not contacting Sue comes off as his only selfless gesture.

One very important reason for *Detour* 's success is that its scale of production is perfectly tailored to its subject. Al's present in the Reno diner finds him surrounded by unwelcome strangers. He rejects a truck driver's attempt to be friendly. But reality in the flashback story is reduced to his claustrophobic interior world. New York is a tiny club set and a foggy nowhere with street signs. Middle America is a map and an endless desert existing mostly as an unreal rear-projected backdrop. Los Angeles is a hotel room and a few cramped exteriors. This is how Al Roberts perceives the world. In Technicolor and wide screen, opened up for more characters and more 'realism', *Detour* would be beyond pointless.

The crime, drinking and sexuality in the storyline attracted the attention of the censors and were not overlooked because of the film's modest means or for any other reason. Small outfits like PRC were subject to the same Breen office oversight that the majors were. Arriane Ulmer Cipes, the director's daughter,[4] reports

that multiple changes mandated by the censors resulted in Ulmer rewriting much
of the script, which initially gave more emphasis to the Vera character. Thus, a
"Poverty Row quickie" that shouldn't have had the time to become a one-man
artistic effort, did.

1945's Production Code mandated that murderers of any stripe be brought to justice. A gas chamber execution scene was shot for *Double Indemnity*, in case the censors didn't think Fred MacMurray's imminent arrest made his fate sufficiently clear to
audiences. Ulmer ingeniously satisfied the censor by illustrating, as a foregone conclusion Al's dark prediction of eventual arrest. The visual employed is a simple shot of Al
being picked up by a police car on a dark road, but Al's plaintive voiceover is haunt-
ingly wistful:

> I know. Someday, a car will stop to pick me up that I never thumbed. Yes, Fate,
> or some mysterious force, can put the finger on you or me for no good reason
> at all.

Like the eloquent epigram that plunges Jean Brooks into doom at the end of Val Lewton's *The Seventh Victim*, Roberts' words consign him to a unique cinematic limbo, forever wandering between the noir winds. Many noirs strike appropriately dark moods,
while imposing absurd external ironies on their protagonists, random jokes of fate
that have little to do with who they are. *Detour* asserts that the 'fate' in film noir, no
matter how absurd or ironic, can really be explained in terms of the quixotic human
character.

What *Detour* resembles is a perverse take on Theodore Dreiser's *An American
Tragedy,* a variation in which the unlucky male hero is doomed not by ambition or a
desire for a rosy *Place in the Sun,* but by a self-willed exile from paradise. Al Roberts
may be a tawdry underclass loser, but his rejection of society's optimistic mirage
makes him a forerunner of the nonconformists and counterculture antiheroes to
come.

NOTES

1. Good copies of *Detour* are hard to come by, in 35mm, 16mm, or video. Various archival efforts to create a new negative have reportedly been blocked by a collector-producer with
   a marginal claim to copyright ownership of the film. Not even he has an intact copy of the
   picture, although cooperation between collectors and archives could conceivably result in
   a title-saving restoration before the prints themselves deteriorate.

2. Todd McCarthy and Charles Flynn, editors, *Kings of the Bs,* E.P. Dutton and Co., New York,
   1975. p. 387.

3. *Film Noir: An Encyclopedic Reference to the American Style,* Alain Silver & Elizabeth Ward, editors, The Overlook Press, 1979. p. 90.

4. Arianne Ulmer Cipes, interview with the author, March 17, 2003, Los Angeles. The specific production information and details of Detour's original budget, originate from this interview. Ms. Ulmer has organized The Edgar G. Ulmer Preservation Corporation, an entity that has been very successful in preserving and further popularizing his films.

Vivian Sternwood (Lauren Bacall) literally and figuratively pulls the dour Philip Marlowe (Humphrey Bogart) out of another complexity.

"How You Fixed for Red Points?": Anecdote and the World War II Home Front in *The Big Sleep* (1946)

Kevin Hagopian

"Every clue told me a different story..."
> —Humphrey Bogart as Philip Marlowe, in voice-over,
> *The Big Sleep* trailer, 1946

"This began as a simple case of blackmail, and all at once, things started to happen for no reason at all. No reason at all..."
> —Marlowe, in dialogue from a scene filmed but
> deleted from *The Big Sleep*'s 1946 release

I.

Critics have marveled at the impenetrability of *The Big Sleep*'s labyrinthine plot since the film went into its long-delayed release in August, 1946, fully a year after it had first been previewed by thousands of American servicemen overseas. When it premiered in New York, the conscience of middlebrow movie tastes, *The New York Times*' Bosley Crowther, called *The Big Sleep* "one of those pictures in which so many cryptic things occur amid so much involved and devious plotting that the mind becomes utterly confused." Crowther's review makes it seem that he knew less about *The Big Sleep*'s narrative world after seeing the film than before.[1] In recent years, analysts have rightly come to regard this convolution as one of the chief satisfactions of the film. David Thomson refers to the pleasurable bafflement induced by *The Big Sleep* as the film's "nearly lyrical impossibility."[2] The source of this bafflement is a slippage between the entire narrative universe of the film—in narrative theory terms, the "story," including the film's immense backstory and off-screen characters, as well as everything that happens on screen—and those portions of the story which only appear on screen; again, using narrative theory, the "plot."[3] Just who killed Arthur Gwynn Geiger, the smut peddler with the chinoiserie bungalow on Laverne Terrace? Who killed (more famously) the Sternwoods' chauffeur, Owen Taylor? Why, exactly, did Geiger's shadow, Carol Lundgren, kill Joe Brody? And who killed Sean Regan?[4]

Much has been made of the elaborate plotlines of classic-era film noir in general. However, there is an important distinction to be made between the heavily articulated temporality and spatiality of films such as *The Killers* (Robert Siodmak, Universal, 1946),

The Enforcer (Bretaigne Windust/Raoul Walsh, Warner Brothers, 1949), or *Passage to Marseille* (Michael Curtiz, Warner Brothers, 1944), an overlooked war movie-noir, with their flashbacks within flashbacks, on the one hand, and *The Big Sleep*, with its massive accumulation of plot material, underexplained events, and insufficient motivations, on the other. The first group of films are complex, but decipherable using the normal amount of cognitive skill a trained movie viewer could be expected to bring to the theater. Such is *L.A. Confidential*. But *Lost Highway* is much more like *The Big Sleep*, whose narrative elaborations are only decipherable through far more advanced elliptical reasoning than the classical Hollywood cinema regularly demands of its viewers. These elaborations constantly threaten to distend the film into insensibility.[5]

By providing a forum for understanding story/plot slippage in a major Hollywood production as something other than "error," a violation of codes to which unreflective obedience is taken for correctness, and then making a virtue of this slippage, *The Big Sleep* may be said to have given distant advance permission for films such as David Lynch's *Mulholland Drive* and Quentin Tarantino's *Pulp Fiction*. In the process, *The Big Sleep*'s opaqueness created a well from which that part of neo-noir which does not consist simply of `Forties pastiches could draw, in an effort to explain modern life by not refusing to linearize the ambivalences of that life. Given the dedication of neo-noir screenwriters such as *Lost Highway*'s Barry Gifford and *L.A. Confidential*'s writer-director Curtis Hanson to classic noir viewing, acknowledged in many interviews, and the related attachment of their films to complex storylines, it is entirely possible that *The Big Sleep* has grown, if anything, more influential as the years go by.[6]

However, the refreshing anarchy of *The Big Sleep*'s plot has been neutralized by the way in which the history of the film's own production is used against these impulses toward an open text. The story of *The Big Sleep* is often told as an antic tale of improvisation and whimsy, a screwball comedy of the soundstages. This dismisses as slapdash filmmaking the film's dark comedy and denatures its smirking, bloody ironies, themselves harbingers of the disturbingly nihilistic gore of the late 1960's in films such as *Bonnie and Clyde* and *The Wild Bunch*. Like those films, *The Big Sleep* was the product of a period of social distress, and the unhingeing of old class, race, and gender verities, as much as it was (also) the work of a recognized auteur. *The Big Sleep* is as intricate a social text as it is a narrative one, its contorted plot an index of a garbled and anxious wartime society, its lyrical impossibilities alluding to social possibilities the conservative ethos of the classical Hollywood cinema could barely contain.

The "explanation" of the film as a funny story, with its own punchline, began with a series of interviews given by Howard Hawks in the 1960's and early 1970's. The way Hawks told the story of the production of *The Big Sleep* is thus: sometime during the shooting of the film, Humphrey Bogart asked Hawks who had killed Owen Taylor, who is discovered dead behind the wheel of the Sternwood family car. Hawks told Bogart that he didn't know, and claimed that he then asked the screenwriters, Leigh Brackett, Jules Furthman, and William Faulkner. They didn't know either, went Hawks' story, and neither did Raymond Chandler, author of the novel *The Big Sleep*, when Hawks wired him. The Owen Taylor story was a pretext, however, for Hawks' real point, which has to do with the anarchy of the film's narrative: "Actually, we didn't care. It was the first time I made a picture and just decided I wasn't going to explain things. I was just going to try and make good scenes."[7] The story was a staple in Hawks' years on the lecture and film festival circuit, and continues to keynote analysis of the film even by critics who should know better than to trust Hawks' compulsive talespinning, such as Andrew Sarris and Robin Wood.[8] Hawks, more loquacious and gregarious than his fellow classic era giants of the action cinema, John Ford, Raoul Walsh, and William Wellman, nonetheless shared with them a deep need to downplay notions of either artiness or social commentary in his work. If Ford famously referred to the creation of his films as "just a job of work," Hawks more often gave the impression of considering film directing a manifestation of the strenuous life, rather like fly-fishing, an act which required not only the demonstration of manly professionalism, but also the expression of native wisdom associated with the craft acquired through practice, wisdom which could not be associated with either dry intellectualism or ungovernable creative passion.[9] After the Owen Taylor story became gospel, everything of note in the film seemed to become a Hawks invention, casual yet incisive. This meant that *The Big Sleep* film was even harder to categorize as film noir. For film noir, at its most effective as a critical concept, is a mode of social analysis, and is therefore primarily a social, rather than a Romantic, kind of filmmaking.[10]

Howard Hawks was American auteurism's poster child. No self-styled anti-intellectual in American popular culture has ever benefited so much from intellectual attention. In his lifetime, he was the focus of one of the most influential thematic studies of a single director, Robin Wood's *Howard Hawks,* which compared him to Shakespeare, Bach, and Mozart. Peter Wollen's equally influential theoretical treatise, *Signs and Meaning in the Cinema,* uses Hawks to prove that artists working within the very maw of the popular culture machine (in Hawks' case, the film studios), can create an ouevre of thematic uniqueness and stylistic consistency.[11]

It is this cult of personality, expressed through the Owen Taylor story, which has made consideration of *The Big Sleep* as a film noir so difficult: put simply, how can a film diagnose the social and psychological ills of its day, and thus speak in some way for its society (perhaps the primary functions of film noir as a critical concept), if it is so completely the projection of a single ego? When even its mistakes turn out to be another name for the flourish of genius? The answer lies in something the talkative Hawks rarely discussed, a production circumstance which made *The Big Sleep* the most chaotic of all his films. *The Big Sleep* was really two films, the first of which finished shooting in January, 1945, and was completed in March, 1945. The film was then previewed to an overseas audience of servicemen. After these previews, an extensive process of retakes, deletions, and the shooting and inclusion of new scenes, took place beginning in January, 1946, to ready the film for its domestic release in late August, 1946. Between January 1945 and August 1946, the stars of the film, Bogart and Lauren Bacall, were married, World War II came to a close, Warner Brothers was the site of a violent labor lockout which virtually shut down the studio, the infamous Hollywood Red Scare began, and the long prosperity of the film industry during the sound era began to wane. The enormous energies generated by the experience of World War II, both within society, and at the movie studios, began to dissipate, or to find expression in new ways—the celebrated "post-war disillusionment" of Paul Schrader's four-part definition of film noir.[12] At the center of these developments, *The Big Sleep* was subject to many powerful external forces, direct and indirect, institutional and social forces, many of which have left distinctive marks on the finished film. The result is a film text whose narrational strategy is episodic to the point of disjointedness, whose backstory is so confusing as to be cognitively counterproductive, and many of whose plot points go unexplained or unmotivated. In this fragmentation, the film effectively responds to the psychological and social displacement of the war years as well as any studio film made between 1942 and 1946. It does so because its controlling anti-logic arises from the frantic conditions of wartime, both in society at large, and within the hothouse environment of the movie studios, and not from the agency of a single gifted individual. Perhaps Hawks invented the Owen Taylor story as a way of asserting, after the fact, control over a project whose most powerful authorial presence had been wartime society itself.

II.

With the rise of "greatest generation" romanticism about World War II, it is difficult to recreate the anxiety and division that existed on the home front, not only out of fears for loved ones abroad, but because the turmoil of war brought disputes over the equality of both sacrifice and rewards associated with wartime life.[13] America at war was a stew of changing gender norms, racial and ethnic conflicts, and economic discrimination.[14] Southern California in particular experienced these shifts as collisions. Emigration from the South and Southwest of poor whites, and of Blacks, to the burgeoning war industries, especially aerospace and shipbuilding, made the region a microcosm for the race and class frictions which also boiled over in bloody rioting in Detroit and Harlem.[15] Transportation and, even more seriously, housing shortages further exacerbated intergroup tensions in what was already one of the nation's fastest growing metropolitan regions.

Southern California, studded with defense installations, and relatively closer to Japanese forces than other regions of the US, was captivated by war hysteria. The region experienced the psychological terror of Japanese shelling of Santa Barbara by a Japanese submarine on February 23, 1942, as well as a massive phantom "air raid" prompted by jittery air defense gunners, the next night; 1,400 rounds of anti-aircraft shells and countless thousands of machine gun rounds were fired at reports of massed formations of Japanese aircraft. On May 16, 1942, newspapers headlined a poison gas scare; 350,000 gas masks were shipped to West Coast ports.[16] Air raid precautions were taken across the region, including at the film studios, where air raid drills were staged. But if the victory at Midway in June, 1942, abated the military threat, the social upheaval occasioned by war continued without letup across Southern California. In the infamous anti-Mexican-American zoot suit riots of June 3–10, 1943, marauding soldiers and sailors, abetted by civilians and even police officers, stripped and beat Chicano zoot suiters—who were then arrested for indecency and vagrancy. The violence spread to Pasadena, Long Beach, and San Diego, and targeted anyone of Hispanic appearance. A witness, Staff Sergeant William D. Eastlake wrote to *Time* on July 5, 1943: "I could find nothing to distinguish the behavior of our soldiers from the behavior of Nazi storm troop thugs beating up outnumbered non-Aryans." In addition to noting the racist causes of the rioting, he stated flatly, "This is a form of class war." In the "Sleepy Lagoon" affair of late 1942, 22 male Chicanos were railroaded into a trial, and 20 were jailed, for the unexplained murder of one Jose Diaz; 12 were sentenced to life imprisonment at San Quentin. Although the verdicts were eventually reversed for lack of evidence, the case was as significant in the history of race relations on the West Coast as the Scottsboro Case had been several years previous for the South.[17] Race also figured in perhaps the most carefully-organized single act of government-sanctioned oppression of a minority group in American history. By the end of 1942, over 120,000 Americans of Japanese descent living on the West Coast, most from California, had been relocated to internment camps scattered across the most desolate parts of the American interior. In many cases, their property and businesses were forfeit.

These were the celebrated instances. Just as significant was the climate of generalized fear and uncertainty in which they took place. This generation was the same one which had experienced the physical and psychological uprooting of the Depression; wartime offered yet another massive blow to social stability. Trepidation over the fate of loved ones overseas, frustration with fragmented family units (with attendant concerns over child care), a swiftly rising cost of living, apprehension over the end of the wartime boom and the much-discussed return of economic depression, as well as the impact of returning veterans on economic and family life, were all features of wartime life. Not surprisingly, wartime exaggerated the remarkable ethos of crime in Los Angeles. Though the city was relatively small, it was known as a center of police corruption, a mecca for illegal gambling, a center of gay club and drag culture, and a city with more than its share of violent and bizarre homicides.[18] Wartime in the region meant larger paychecks, the presence of large numbers of service personnel, a transient civilian population, increased teenage prostitution, juvenile crime, and the black market. These were all accelerants for a radical reconsideration of the notion of the illicit, in which existing socially delineated arbitrary standards of right and wrong (legality) no longer functioned as effectively to restrain inappropriate behavior, and new behaviors and activities grew up along the margins of legality which had not yet been assigned a place in this arbitrary world of legality.

Los Angeles, even more so than the nation at large, experienced the war not only as a time of patriotic fervor, but also as one of personal and social flux. More than anything else, wartime was a period of the suspension of social certainties, a time best characterized by a specifically narrative question: "what next?"[19] Given this atmosphere of personal uncertainty and group tension, the notion of post-war disillusionment as a determinant on film noir should be reconceived as not only a set of impulses growing out of post-1945 disappointments with unfulfilled wartime optimism, but also with angst raised by the wartime social experience itself.

The Big Sleep was conceived and executed in this atmosphere of turbulence on the home front, and the film would cause its own turbulence at Warner Bros. The work on the screenplay began on August 29, 1944, and the film began production on October 10, 1944, with principal photography completed, far behind schedule, on January 12, 1945. The film was scored, titled, and ready for release in March, 1945. Warners decided to hold the film up because the studio had several films awaiting release which touched on military or geopolitical aspects of the war, which was fast coming to a close.[20] For instance, *Escape in the Desert,* directed by Edward Blatt, a war-rewritten remake of *The Petrified Forest* starring Helmut Dantine as a German prisoner of war on the loose in the American desert, was released on May 19, 1945, just after Germany had surrendered. *Pillow to Post,* a farce about the wartime housing shortage on military bases, a project which Howard Hawks had intended to produce and direct after *To Have and Have Not,* his 1944 hit with *The Big Sleep* stars Bogart and Bacall, was directed by Warners contract director Vincent Sherman, and released on June 9, 1945. Another of these films was *Confidential Agent,* directed by Herman Shumlin, with Lauren Bacall, a film shot after *The Big Sleep,* and still in production as the war ended. (It was released on November 10, 1945.) With the war over, it was feared, these films would quickly lose their currency.

This anxiety was legitimate. Like those of the other studios, Warners films of the war years were loaded with refugee royalty and governments in exile (*Princess O'Rourke*), Soviet female snipers on war bond tours (*Doughgirls*), self-sacrificing defense plant workers (*Wings for the Eagle*), and antifascist diplomats (*Watch on the Rhine*), films which are culturally obscure today. The pressure on the film industry by the Bureau of Motion Pictures of the Office of War Information to make war-themed films, though privately resented and resisted by studio executives, was publicly discharged with inserted plot elements which took note of the war such as rationing and sabotage, and indeed, with entire films (*Action in the North Atlantic,* about the Merchant Marine, and *Mission to Moscow,* explaining the diplomatic maneuvers behind the Nazi-Soviet Pact and the Soviets eventually joining the Allies) which Warners made to order for the war effort.[21] Warners felt that *The Big Sleep,* as a genre piece without a specifically wartime setting, could be slotted into a less crowded post-war release calendar.

Indeed, *The Big Sleep's* few direct references to the war are so slight they pass today as merely additional instances of the film's baroquely comic dialogue and murky mise-en-scene. When Marlowe calls Bernie Ohls from the Geiger house, he announces Geiger's murder with the question, "How ya fixed for red points?" a ghoulish reference to the color of the ration stamps required during wartime to buy meat. Likewise, the film's indirect references to wartime occur near the edge of the frame, figuratively, and often literally. This is the case with the gas rationing classification stickers seen on the windshields of several cars in the film, which would have signified to postwar audiences that the film was set in the recent past.

But if Warners thought that the film was not about the war, they were wrong. Those gasoline stickers show that the war is, quite literally, taken for granted by *The Big Sleep.* The war forms a substratum of assumptions about society, crime, and sexuality which the film's complex story, with its many narrative cul-de-sacs, betrays eloquently. For a film ostensibly about crime, *The Big Sleep* displays far greater interest in the llicit than the illegal. Pornographic book stores flourish in suburban shopping districts, while casual sex occurs behind the pulled blinds of another shop across the street. Gambling and drugs are normalized in the film; far from offering a moral valuation against betting and addiction, these are presented as facts, as just things people do. We also see the illicit come out of the shadows to overtake and upend the licit. For instance, we see pillars of society like the Sternwoods revealed as a rotten and pathetic clan, while thieves like Harry Jones are incarnations of integrity. The film inverts traditional gender hierarchies, and not only by offering women like Agnes Lozier, who first appears as Geiger's assistant, meaningful roles in the film's public sphere of criminality. There is the subtle decadence of Eddie Mars' gambling club, which is a thoroughly respectable place. (The standing set Warners used for the exterior of the club, a rusticated ranch house front, would be used for suburban houses in several Warners' postwar melodramas.) Yet, with its men in flashy singing-cowboy get ups, and its matched pair of young women in riding breeches wandering through its rooms, to say nothing of the impromptu sing-a-long of "And Her Tears Flowed Like Wine" led by Vivian Sternwood, Eddie Mars' club offers something disturbing and entrancing in its veiled portrait of off-kilter (in movie terms) gender signification. The club is probably based on the Clover Club, one of several elite gambling joints in Los Angeles, which had a large gay clientele. Eddie Mars' club takes the film's disdain for puritanism to the last extreme: there is no hint in the club scenes that gambling is at all illegal, yet there is, here as in almost every one of the film's set-piece narrative episodes, a strong whiff of the illicit.

Marlowe (Humphrey Bogart) guns down Canino (Bob Steele) while Vivian Sternwood (Lauren Bacall) looks on.

But it is crime that offers the initial rationale for *The Big Sleep*. The film begins as one crime, and grows into a thicket of crimes. That it is hard to tell, by the end of the film, just who killed who, is the crux of the Owen Taylor anecdote. But the multiplicity of crimes, and their unsolvable quality, is precisely the point when finding a way to talk, symbolically, about a lived existence that had come to seem unpredictable, and fraught with both excitement and danger. The figure of Philip Marlowe does not so much investigate these crimes, as preside over their exposition, an objective and wry witness.

The film was conceived in an atmosphere suffused by wartime anxieties, and the war-related delay in release literally opened the text. *The Big Sleep* went from being a meditation on the cruelties of modern life told through the eyes of a world-weary detective (roughly, the vision Raymond Chandler offered in the 1939 novel), to a sexy, funny, violent picaresque on rationed gas through wartime Los Angeles. The process of this transformation bears recapitulation.

We know very little about the screenings to servicemen overseas of the first, 1945 version of the film. During World War II, it was typical for studios to release films to overseas military audiences before they were screened in the U.S., as goodwill advertising for the motion picture industry, but the screenings of the 1945 version of *The Big Sleep* seem to have been used as a large-scale "sneak preview," with formal responses and comments solicited from the soldiers.[22] If this is so, then the 1946 release version of the film was shaped by one of the most narrow demographics of any preview audience in the studio era, for most viewers would have been males in their late teens and '20's. We can reasonably expect that these largely heterosexual and sex-deprived audiences would have urged the filmmakers to concentrate narrative energies on scenes of sexual activity, both real (the Acme bookstore incident) and implied (the female service workers whose passing interactions with Marlowe are suffused with sex), and not on "plot," *per se*.

The film was then reshaped by a letter from agent Charles K. Feldman to studio head Jack Warner, on Nov 16, 1945. Feldman was deeply vested in the film: he was agent to both Bacall and Hawks. He complained that the insolence to Bogart which had made Bacall so popular in *To Have and Have Not,* her debut film, released in 1944, was missing from *The Big Sleep. Confidential Agent* had just been released, and reviews of Bacall, who played the daughter of an English lord in the film, were uniformly dreadful. Feldman believed that another flop would end Bacall's career, and destroy the studio's (and his) investment in her. He urged on Jack Warner a very specific pattern of retakes to make Bacall more insolent with Bogart, to reinforce the burgeoning romance the film implies they are having, and simply to give Bacall more screen time in a film crowded with memorable characters, all in an effort to make the film adhere more to the formula of *To Have and Have Not.* (Feldman's foray required considerable diplomacy, as it was Warner who had decided to release *Confidential Agent* before *The Big Sleep,* not only because of *Confidential Agent*'s topicality, but also because he felt Bacall's performance in that film was superior to her work in *The Big Sleep.*) Warner digested Feldman's letter, and then, in a November 20th wire to Samuel Schneider, a vice-president in the Warners New York office, ordered no prints to be struck on the film until further notice. The next day, November 21, Warner wired Feldman that "You must have been reading my mail," as he, Warner, had been contemplating precisely these changes...Later, on January 3, 1946, he wired Schneider again, telling him of the progress in revising the film, and ordering him to return all foreign negatives and prints to the studio, taking the 1945 version permanently out of circulation. Then, on February 9, 1946, reporting on the final sneak preview of the new version of *The Big Sleep*, Warner again wired his New York office, crowing about the improvements in the film made by the retakes and other changes, and seeming to take credit for them, although they were actually blueprinted by Feldman, crafted by Hawks with his screenwriters, and executed with great skill and further invention by Hawks.[23]

There were undoubtedly changes throughout production and revisions as a result of conversations with the Production Code Administration (PCA); although the film is not a celebrated case of Breen Office intransigence, this may be due simply to the habit of screenwriters to factor Production Code standards of social behavior and ideology into their work, and for studios to conduct much of their business over Production Code disputes informally.[24] The quota of violent deaths and the film's sexual innuendo and perversity did, however, attract PCA scrutiny.[25]

The 1946 release version of *The Big Sleep* should not be seen as merely a set of specific engineering choices made in the film's narrative. Though these were substantial (something like 20 minutes of the film was physically changed), it is the shift in narrative emphasis that the film underwent as a result of these changes that most reveals its connections to the disruptions of wartime society. The film that resulted exemplifies what Thomas Schatz has called, "the genius of the system," which is less a matter of a studio imprinting a seamless house style on a film (the studio as auteur) than it is a process of institutional negotiations carried on within the studio over aesthetic, social, and economic issues.[26] The Feldman letter and the change in release schedules exemplify these negotiations. To this list we could add other negotiations, these with the outside agencies and forces which were so much a part of wartime filmmaking: those "casual conversations" with the Breen Office, and the relationship between government agencies such as the Office of War Information Bureau of Motion Pictures, defanged by the time of *The Big Sleep*'s production, but still reflective of a widely-felt social responsibility enforced by a degree of government fiat, a situation unique in the history of the Hollywood cinema. Of all these outside negotiations, the most difficult to pinpoint, and yet also the most influential, was the relationship between the film and a disoriented wartime society.

This disorientation, of course, has its corollary in the film's complicated narrative, which, like wartime life, is adrift from reassuring linearities. Comparison between the 1945 and 1946 versions show that changes made in the film after the 1945 armed forces previews consciously and dramatically *reduced* narrative clarity in favor of the elaboration of characters within discrete scenes (just as Hawks always said later about the film), an unusual practice in the classical Hollywood cinema, and especially remarkable in the plot-driven universe of the detective cinema. These characters give us, not a direct representation of wartime society, but a gallery of characters who together portray a society of outsiders without limits on personal behavior, unmoored from traditional standards of morality and ethics. They are alternately treacherous or libidinal, but either way, they are siblings in the film's project of absurdist social deconstruction. Their epitaph might well be General Sternwood's verdict on his hot-house orchids: "Nasty things ... Their flesh is too much like the flesh of men, their perfume has the rotten sweetness of corruption."

Some of these characters, like doomed, deluded little Harry Jones, enter and exit without fanfare. Others, like soldier-of-fortune and wife-stealer Sean Regan, are somehow major characters without ever being seen on screen. The film is a chorus of noir gargoyles: General Sternwood, a shriveled shell of a man who calls himself sinister, and declares himself "a very dull survival of a very gaudy life," a life of indulgence to which he seems to have destined his youngest daughter, Carmen, a druggish nymphet addicted to the same kinds of pleasures the General probably knew in younger days. His other daughter, the older Vivian, is recovering poorly from what was then called "a broken marriage;" she "drinks her lunch out of a bottle." Then there is Geiger, the fastidiously sleazy bookstore proprietor; Eddie Mars, the shady casino owner and racketeer; Mrs. Eddie Mars, "stolen" by the dead Regan, now returned to something less than wedded bliss with Eddie, and presiding over a rural hide-out for her absentee husband; Carol Lundgren, gay companion and assassin; Art Huck, the lowlife country filling station owner and partner in a hot car ring; Joe Brody, the dumb, ill-fated hood and his treacherous lady friend, Agnes; Sidney and Pete, the goofy Mutt-and-Jeff hit men; the cruel, knife-edged Canino ... A host of others, smiling killers and gruesome butlers, stalk through the dark, rainy landscape of the film like wraiths. The Big Sleep is something other than a detective story, with the drive toward rationality that designation is supposed to represent. It is a carnival of criminality, its underworld supernumeraries crowding the film not so much as picturesque character bits, but as tiny, finely-drawn portrayals of deceit and self-interest in a tapestry of meanness.

The film's sexualized bits (Carole Douglas as the librarian, Lorraine Miller and Shelby Payne as nightclub hatcheck and cigarette girls, respectively, and most notably, Joy Barlowe as a randy taxi driver) are an Amazon chorus, affirming the film's clinical fascination with sex, a facet of wartime life studiously denied by greatest generation mythology.[27] The film turns the draft-induced "man shortage" into a satyr's fantasy, as sloe-eyed heiresses, hash-slingers with come-hither looks, and horny lady cab drivers brazenly (in 1946 movie terms) proposition Marlowe. He puts off all but one of them in the name of immediate business, but with the clear indication that he'll be back. In an extended (and, from a plot perspective, extraneous) sequence set in bookstore across the street from Geiger's pornography operation, a young Dorothy Malone as a brainy but sexually eager bookstore clerk is seduced by/seduces Marlowe.

These characters neatly allegorized the deepest fears and fascinations of wartime; sudden, violent death, and ungoverned sexuality, offering them to audiences not so much in a plot, as in a loosely constructed social setting. Robert Sklar holds that "The Big Sleep is a noir film only by the broadest definition," and he is right, but as he goes forward to remind us of the film's romantic comedy attributes, and the primacy the film gives Marlowe's wit over his toughness, Sklar perhaps forgets that that broad definition of film noir, evanescent, fluid, but insistent, is worth acknowledging as an iconic instance of film tapping deep channels of unsettling fear and desire. Or, as Siegfried Kracauer wrote (probably while The Big Sleep was playing in theaters): "What films reflect are not so much explicit credos as psychological dispositions—those deep layers of collective mentality which extend more or less below the dimension of consciousness."[28] Robert Sklar again:

> As surely, however, as the dialogue's references to `red points' and the ration stickers on car windows must have dated the film on its late summer 1946 release, *The Big Sleep* is a wartime film—in which the distinctions between good men and bad were meant to be clear, and with just cause violence was required to fight violence."[29]

But that's just it; the film's distinctions between bad and good occur almost in passing, and then only at the level of its nearly illegible plot, as the good (Harry Jones), the bad (Canino), and the ugly (Geiger) fall with equal weight. In a film without causes, how can there be a "just cause"? *The Big Sleep* is, as Sklar says, a wartime film, but not for the reasons he thinks. If there is a tragedy of wartime, it is not that there are not good causes and bad causes, but that the fact of death consumes all causes, just or unjust. In the moment of death, the cause for which one dies becomes abstract and meaningless. "What's funny?" Canino asks of Harry Jones, as the little man begins dying from the poison Canino has forced him to drink. "Nothing's funny," chokes out Harry Jones, as he topples over, and indeed, for him, nothing is funny, or sad, or suddenly, worth it.

As film critic Richard Schickel puts it in his memoir of growing up in Wisconsin during the war years and understanding the war primarily via the movies:

> Those who were obliged to support [the war] with their last full measure of devotion died mostly as soldiers from time immemorial have died—because they were in the wrong place at the wrong time. They went—if they had time to think about it at all—cursing God or fate. Or, more likely, calling poignantly for their mothers. They did not die murmuring inspiring thoughts to the folks back home. That happened only in the movies.[30]

Although he did not know it, Raymond Chandler had written the epitaph for those soldiers in 1939:

> What did it matter where you lay once you were dead? In a dirty sump or a marble tower on top of a high hill? You were dead, you were sleeping the big sleep, you were not bothered by things like that. Oil and water were the same as wind and air to you. You just slept the big sleep, not caring about the nastiness of how you died or where you fell.[31]

In *The Big Sleep*, romantic comedy sleeps side by side with a grisly murder spree, the funny with the deadly, oil with water, and the film does not care, and that is what enraged *The New York Times'* reviewer, Bosley Crowther. Unlike the "serious" films about the war which Crowther lionized, *The Big Sleep* does not offer platitudes, only "cryptic things" that arise from deep in the film's own unconscious.

James Agee's *Nation* review of August 31, 1946 summarized the oddly distancing effect of this parade of weird types and mixed genres across the screen:

> The Big Sleep is a violent, smoky cocktail shaken together from most of the print-
> able misdemeanors, and some that aren't—one of those Raymond Chandler spe-
> cials which puts you, along with the cast, into a state of semi-amnesia through
> which tough action and reaction drum with something of the nonsensical solace
> of hard rain on a tin roof. Humphrey Bogart and several proficient minor players
> keep anchoring it to some sufficient kind of reality. The picture is often brutal and
> sometimes sinister; but I can't bring myself to mind this sort of viciousness...I
> know it's a dream world...."[32]

Agee had found the truth of the film in what he thought of as a dream world, the
topsy-turvy social order of a world at war, which was so unlike the "reality" of the pre-
war Hollywood cinema. In the Andy Hardy films, in Frank Capra films, in westerns and
biopics, in star vehicles and B films, indeed throughout the popular cinema, a falsely coherent and functioning social order was maintained by cinematic devices like coincidence, mistaken identity, and a relentless cause-and-effect narration. These were finally
more contrived than anything The Big Sleep had to offer, but through repetition and
conventionalization, they had, as Paul Schrader noted, created "an American amelioristic cinema," one which salved over the wounds of class, race, and gender with reassuring narratives of common interest.[33]

III.

Detective stories are supposed to ask questions, but these are a pretext: what detective stories are really supposed to do is answer questions. In answering the artificially
high count of questions which the detective film creates, the job of the detective film
is similar to that of the classic detective novel, à la Agatha Christie and Dorothy L.
Sayers: to present what Raymond Chandler called in his essay The Simple Art of Murder
solutions to "problems in logic and deduction" as a way of offering an image of a world
which could be psychologically mastered. But as Chandler says of those stories, "they
are too contrived, and too little aware of what goes on in the world." The success of
The Big Sleep helped to quash a now-forgotten trend in American cinema toward mur-
der mysteries which were just such contrivances as Chandler viewed with disdain.
Their titles alone take us into the stilted world of deduction-and-ratiocination of
Christie and Sayers: Murder on the Waterfront, Murder in the Blue Room, Murder on the
Bridle Path, The Grand Central Murder...Among their legion were series films, including
those starring sleuths such as Nero Wolfe, Ellery Queen, Hildegarde Withers, Philo
Vance, Perry Mason, and, preeminently Charlie Chan, whose 27th film, Black Magic,
was in production at Monogram studios at the time The Big Sleep started shooting; incredibly, Monogram would crank out another seven Chans before The Big Sleep actually went into release. The contemptuous reference to Arthur Geiger's "Charlie Chan
mustache" functions as a reminder of what The Big Sleep isn't.
    What The Big Sleep is, argues Bruce Kawin, is intimately connected with its failure
to be Charlie Chan. The Big Sleep, says Kawin,

> ...is dark and violent fun. The undercurrents of perversity and amorality succeed
> in disturbing the audience because they are so rapidly and efficiently passed
> over... *The Big Sleep* blasts the genre of detection and teaches the audience how
> to 'read' a film in a new way. One follows the action because it is action; one re-
> sponds to each scene on its own terms, without probing beneath them for some
> secret, coherent structure.[34]

The Big Sleep uses its suite of ill-explained murders to effectively deny the dubious her-
itage of the detective film. But Hawks supporters' invocation of the Owen Taylor story
show that anxieties about the danger of genre subsuming auteur persist. They shouldn't,
for, in spite of the foregoing analysis, *The Big Sleep* can also be thought of as an auteurist
work. Hawks was the producer of *The Big Sleep*, and his control over certain aspects of
the film can be documented. More important, Hawks' thematic consistency, developed
across a large body of films, is still in evidence in *The Big Sleep* though somewhat
strained.[35] David Thomson, in his thoughtful study of *The Big Sleep*, has used the Owen
Taylor anecdote impressionistically, to illustrate Hawks' informal working method. The
tactic is more subtle than those who employ the story to pit Hawks against an anonymous system of production, and the result more fruitful. Thomson's account of the film
is elegant and nuanced, and shows that noir, which is less a genre than a theory of the
reciprocal action of cultural texts and the societies which produce them, can coexist
with auteurism, a theory of individual genius within a collaborative medium.[36]

But Thomson's is not the typical use of the Owen Taylor anecdote. Too often, Owen
Taylor's legacy renders impotent *The Big Sleep*'s twisted image of wartime life, perverse,
relentlessly violent and sexual, and above all unpredictable, an image that exemplifies
noir's power to offer a cynical analysis of American life all the more unexpected because it occurs in a medium which was otherwise co-opted to present archetypes of
social consensus and harmony. By withdrawing *The Big Sleep* from the realm of noir, a
cinema of social sensibility, and placing it into the realm of simple auteurism, a cinema
of personal sensibility, the film's sardonic black humor is made jokey, and a thing of
darkness becomes a thing of light.

In *The Big Sleep*, a marvelous actress named Sonia Darrin plays Agnes Lozier, the
film's most intensely cynical character. Agnes, handsome and humorless, is the picture
of unalloyed greed and underhandedness. Mere association with Agnes is fatal. She is
Geiger's hardboiled secretary in the pornography operation, until he is killed, then she
is Joe Brody's moll and accomplice in blackmailing Carmen, until he is also killed, then
she is Harry Jones' disinterested paramour and partner in the selling of information
to Marlowe, until Jones, too, is killed. She is the only woman in the film whose actions
are so consistently self-interested that they inspire a puritanical response in Marlowe.
Darrin had been considered for the role of Carmen Sternwood, a part which eventually went to Martha Vickers; Darrin is plainly too brittle and hard-edged even to play
the cruel, self-indulgent Carmen. Darrin had a reputation for being as sharp-tongued
as her character. In one version of the Owen Taylor anecdote, she was alleged to have
been present on the set when Bogart asked who killed Owen Taylor. It is said that she
volunteered, "It must have been Hawks."[37]

NOTES:

1. Bosley Crowther," 'The Big Sleep,' Warner Film in Which Bogart and Bacall Are Paired Again, Opens at Strand—'Step by Step' at the Rialto," *The New York Times,* August 24, 1946, 6.

2. David Thomson, *The Big Sleep* (London: British Film Institute: 1997), 42.

3. David Bordwell, who originated the neoformalist cinematic rhetoric these terms are taken from, subjects *The Big Sleep* to an extensive analysis. He shows that the film, like others in the detective genre, creates confusion by restricting our knowledge mostly to the consciousness of Marlowe, the film's detective, and by retarding revelation of story material through various devices (comedy, romance, and the commission of new crimes) until late in the plot. For Bordwell, *The Big Sleep* is an extreme example of retardation. I would add that the film presents some crucial plot details in such terse fashion that viewers often have the sense that a plot question has been raised and specified, but not clearly answered, a slightly different kind of cognitive retardation than those Bordwell sees as normative to the genre. For instance, the film shows us Marlowe looking at a notebook of coded entries belonging to murder victim Arthur Geiger. Later, we see Marlowe attempting to decipher the code (though we are denied a close-up of this, and rely on detective Bernie Ohls' casual reference to it to grasp what Marlowe is doing), and still later, Marlowe refers to the code book as "Geiger's sucker list" to blackmailer Joe Brody, to whom it is clearly important; yet, this is never explained. In fact, it is the list of customers of Geiger's pornography operation. (*Narration in the Fiction Film,* Madison: University of Wisconsin Press, 1985, 64–73).

4. For the record, Geiger was killed by Owen Taylor, because Taylor was angry at Geiger for blackmailing Carmen Sternwood, Taylor was almost certainly killed by Brody when Brody muscled in on the opportunity to blackmail the Sternwoods by forcibly taking the incriminating nude picture of Carmen from Taylor, Brody was killed by Lundgren because Lundgren mistakenly believed that Brody had killed his boss, Geiger, and Regan was killed by Carmen, or perhaps by Eddie Mars, because Mars thought Regan was having an affair with Mars' wife, thus beginning the chain of blackmail that the other killings in the film stem from—Sean Regan having lived and died in the film entirely off-screen. There are three other killings in the film: hit man Canino's sadistic poisoning of Harry Jones, the small-time hood whom Marlowe admires for his qualities of chivalry; Marlowe's shooting of Canino at Art Huck's hot car drop in Realito; and finally, Eddie Mars' death by machine gun at the hands of his own henchmen, back at the Geiger house, after being shot twice by Marlowe. The killings of Taylor, Geiger, Lundgren, Regan, and Jones are all explained either poorly or quickly, or their motivations left unnecessarily vague.

5. Roger Shatzkin has thoughtfully argued that the events of *The Big Sleep* can be untangled in such a way as to leave no major plot points unexplained, and indeed, this can be can done—but only after several viewings. Shatzkin, "Who Cares Who Killed Owen Taylor?" in *The Modern American Novel and the Movies,* Roger Shatzkin and Gerald Peary, eds. (New York: Frederick Ungar, 1978), 80–94.

6. See, for instance, Barry Gifford's collection of homage-essays on classic films noir, *The Devil Thumbs a Ride and Other Unforgettable Films* (New York: Grove Press, 1988), and the nu-

merous interviews with *L.A. Confidential* writer-director Curtis Hanson in which he makes it clear that *The Big Sleep* was a point of departure for him in creating his homage-noir: "There's a certain point in [*The Big Sleep*] where I stop being concerned about what happened to Sean Regan, the chauffeur they're all talking about. Instead, I'm caught up in what's going on with the characters. Not to criticize *The Big Sleep,* but it doesn't make sense. You never do understand what happened to Sean Regan. (laughs) You know? No matter how careful you're paying attention." (www.splicedonline.com/features/ in_hanson.html, accessed 11/05/03; in testimony to the film's complexity, Hanson confuses the Sternwoods' chauffeur, Owen Taylor, with General Sternwood's bodyguard-companion, Sean Regan.).

7. Joseph McBride, *Hawks on Hawks* (Berkeley: University of California Press, 1982), 104. Depending on the version of the story that is told, the screenwriters in question might have been either Faulkner and Brackett, before the film began shooting, or Furthman, once the film was in production; Hawks liked to use Furthman as an on-the-set writer.

8. Hawks may well have been basing his "recollections" on television viewings of the 1946 release print (he implied as much in some interviews), not on the screenwriting process which had at least already addressed the question of Taylor's murder or suicide before key scenes went before the cameras. It may just be that, when watching on television, Hawks had the same trouble with the film's too-hasty, too-massive exposiiton which ordinary audiences have always had.

It is remotely possible that the exchange Hawks had with Bogart occurred during the retakes necessary for the August, 1946 release; perhaps Bogart could not remember the plot line of a film he had completed more than a year previous, but Hawks would certainly have remembered shooting the scene in the D.A.'s office, and the script discussions associated with it. It is slightly more possible that the question came up during the editing of the 1946 version, but this more prosaic version is never how Hawks retailed it.

The truth is almost certainly that Hawks is correctly remembering someone asking Chandler about a plot point of a slightly different order in the novel, and then conflating that incident with the complexity of the plot of the finished film. Chandler wrote to a friend in 1949 that Hawks had wired Chandler after Hawks and Bogart "got into an argument as to whether one of the characters was murdered or committed suicide," a question for which Chandler says he was unable to provide an answer. Chandler does not tell us which character this was, or when the incident took place. He implies that it was part of a practical joke that Hawks and Bogart were playing on the notoriously ill-read Warner, and since in the novel The Big Sleep the police initially believe that Taylor committed suicide by driving the car off Lido pier before they suspect Brody of the killing, it is entirely possible that the question came up, jokingly, during Bogart's reading of the novel, rather than as a question he asked of the script. (letter from Chandler to Jamie Hamilton, March 21, 1949, Tom Hiney and Frank MacShane, eds. *The Raymond Chandler Papers, Selected Letters and Nonfiction, 1909–1959* (New York: Atlantic Monthly Press, 2000, 105).

Although the Owen Taylor story is repeated virtually every time the film is discussed (I did it myself when first writing about this film), only one analyst of the film which I am aware of, Annette Kuhn, has until now noted its ubiquitousness. *The Power of The Image: Essays on Representation and Sexuality* (London: Routledge and Kegan Paul, 1985), 76–78.

9. The Ford quote comes from Peter Bogdanovich's book-length interview, *John Ford* (Berkeley: University of California Press, 1978, 69.

10. Of the segment of the film in which Marlowe goes into Geiger's bookstore, and adopts the guise of an effeminate book collector, Hawks has himself react to a dull moment in the script by asking star Humphrey Bogart "I don't know, can you play a fairy?" forgetting that the bit was in both the Raymond Chandler novel the film was based on, and in Leigh Brackett, Jules Furthman, and William Faulkner's screenplay. Joseph McBride, *Hawks on Hawks* (Berkeley: University of California Press, 1982), 102–103.

11. Hawks' reputation was by no means uncontested during the 1960's and 1970's. In a 1962 essay for *Sight and Sound*, Peter John Dyer argues that, while Hawks is not the equal of the greatest American directors, such as Welles and Ford, he is saved from true ordinariness by his refusal to engage "serious" subject matter and topical issues in his films. On this point, both Hawks' critics and supporters agreed. To have suggested that *The Big Sleep* was anything like an analysis of wartime society would have invalidated this film as an index of auteurism. "Sling the Lamps Low," anthologized in Joseph McBride, ed., *Focus on Howard Hawks* (Englewood Cliffs: Prentice-Hall, 1972), 78–93.

12. Paul Schrader, "Notes on Film Noir," in Alain Silver and James Ursini, eds. *Film Noir Reader* (New York: Limelight Editions, 1996), 54–55.

13. Robert B. Westbrook, `I Want a Girl, Just Like the Girl That Married Harry James': American Women and the Problem of Political Obligation in World War II" *American Quarterly* 42, No. 4, December 1990, 587–614, and Lawrence R. Samuel, *Pledging Allegiance: American Identity and the Bond Drive of World War II* (Washington, D.C.: Smithsonian Institution Press, 1997).

14. Correspondents who traveled the nation during the war years reported found American society dramatically refashioned by wartime exigencies. Agnes Meyer, *Journey Through Chaos* (New York: Harcourt Brace, 1944), Mercedes Roseberry, *This Day's Madness* (New York: MacMillan and Co., 1944), and John Dos Passos, *The State of the Nation* (Boston: Houghton Mifflin, 1944).

15. Katherine Archibald's *Wartime Shipyard: A Study in Social Disunity* (New York: Da Capo, 1976 [originally published 1948], reflects the author's experience as a California shipyard worker on the West Coast, during which social stress related to race, gender, and class created massive group friction, physical strife, and production delays. Walter Mosley's novel *Devil in a Blue Dress* refers to this violent, bitter period in Southern California race history.

16. Donald DeNevi, *The West Coast Goes to War: 1941–1942* (Missoula: Pictorial Histories Publishing Company, 1998), 101–111.

17. Mauricio Mazon, *The Zoot-Suit Riots: The Psychology of Symbolic Annihilation* (Austin: University of Texas Press, 1984), Edward J. Escobar, "Zoot Suiters and Cops: Chicano Youth and the Los Angeles Police Department during World War II," in *The War in American Culture: Society and Consciousness During World War II* (Chicago: University of Chicago Press, 1996, 284–309. The quoted material is from Geoffrey Perrett, *Days of Sadness, Years of Triumph: The American People, 1939–1945* (Madison: University of Wisconsin Press, 1973), 315.

18. Gay and drag culture is included under the heading of "crime" here because this culture was proscribed by several ordinances, survived partly through pay-offs to law enforcement officials, and was publicly viewed as illegal. A lurid and useful pictorial account of this period in the criminal history of Los Angeles is Jim Heimann, *Sins of the City: The Real Los Angeles Noir* (San Francisco: Chronicle Books, 1999). Heimann's book was clearly inspired by the renewed interest in the Los Angeles underworld sparked by *L.A. Confidential*.

19. The best single source on the turbulence of the American home front remains Geoffrey Perrett, *Days of Sadness, Years of Triumph: The American People, 1939–1945*, cited above. Significantly, Perrett's work is almost never cited in the more recent celebratory accounts of the "greatest generation."

    The account of the film's production is told in Todd McCarthy, *Howard Hawks: The Grey Fox of Hollywood* (New York: Grove Press, 1997), 378–396, and the analysis of the changes between the 1945 and 1946 version given by UCLA film preservationist Robert Gitt on the DVD release of *The Big Sleep*, which contains the full 1945 version, as well as the 1946 release. An August 23, 1945 cable from Jack Warner to Ben Kalmenson, Warner Brothers' general sales manager in New York, includes Warner's ideas on changing the release schedule of Warner Brothers films to accommodate international developments is reprinted in Rudy Behlmer, *Inside Warner Brothers (1935–1951)* (New York: Viking, 1985), 248

20. Thomas Schatz, "World War II and the Hollywood `War Film'" in Nick Browne, ed., *Refiguring American Film Genres: History and Theory* (Berkeley: University of California Press, 1998), 89–128, Clayton R. Koppes and Gregory D. Black, *Hollywood Goes to War: How Politics, and Propaganda Shaped World War II Movies* (New York: Free Press, 1987), and James Myers, "The Bureau of Motion Pictures and its Influence on Film Content in World War II: The Reasons for its Failure" (Ph.D., Texas Christian University, 1998).

21. Bruce Kawin, "Hawks and Faulkner," in Jim Hillier and Peter Wollen, eds., *Howard Hawks: American Artist* (London: British Film Instiute, 1996), 146.

22. The changes for the 1946 release were done by Furthman and Brackett, together with *Casablanca* co-author Philip Epstein; Faulkner had asked in October, 1945 to be released from his contract with Warners, though he completed some revisions to *The Big Sleep* in December, 1945. The relevant documents, including the Feldman letter, the New York wires, and Faulkner's October 15, 1945 letter to Jack Warner are reprinted in Rudy Behlmer, *Inside Warner Brothers (1935–1951)* (New York: Viking, 1985). Raymond Chandler, in a letter to his friend Jamie Hamilton on May 30, 1946, wrote

23. *The Big Sleep* has had an unfortunate history. The girl who played the nymphy sister [Martha Vickers, as Carmen Sternwood] was so good she shattered Miss Bacall completely. So they cut the picture in such a way that all her best scenes were left out except one. The result made nonsense and Howard Hawks threatened to sue to restrain Warners from releasing the picture. After long argument, I hear it, he went back and did a lot of re-shooting. I have not seen the result of this. The picture has not even been trade shown. But if Hawks got his way, the picture will be the best of its kind.

    It is possible that Chandler, getting the story as hearsay, is either inadvertently making reference to the impact of the soldier audiences' feedback on the female characters, or refers to the issues voiced by Feldman, and the concerns these may have raised at Warner Bros., who were trying to raise the stock of Bacall, one of their most important young contract players. The letter appears in Tom Hiney and Frank MacShane, eds., *The Raymond Chandler Papers: Selected Letters and Nonfiction, 1909–1959* (New York: Atlantic Monthly Press, 2000), 67–68.

24. Annette Kuhn's account of censorship in *The Big Sleep* focuses less on the PCA's criticism of the film than on the climate of restraint which the PCA generated, and the ways in which the assumptions about sexuality and violence embodied in the Production Code were harmonized with prevailing ideology, a process which created considerable ambiguity in the film by citing various plot points (pornography, drug use) so indirectly that they are impossible to fathom. *The Power of the Image: Essays on Sexuality and Representation* (London: Routledge and Kegan Paul, 1985), 74–93

25. Chandler claims that he and Hawks discussed an ending which would have sent Carmen Sternwood before the machine guns of Pete and Sidney outside the Geiger house, while Hawks claimed that the existing end of the film was "written by the censors." (letter from Chandler to Jamie Hamilton, May 30, 1946, Tom Hiney and Frank MacShane, eds., *The Raymond Chandler Papers, Selected Letters and Nonfiction, 1909–1959* (New York: Atlantic Monthly Press, 2000, 68–69)), and Todd McCarthy, *Howard Hawks: The Gray Fox of Hollywood* (New York: Grove Press, 1997), 390. Their account would seem to be confirmed by documents in the Production Code Administration file on the film which Annette Kuhn discusses, which demanded that Warners change the ending to avoid making the hero of the film responsible for Carmen's death; as the film stands now, she is to be vaguely "sent away," adding another ambiguity to the film.

26. Thomas Schatz, *The Genius of the System: Hollywood Filmmaking in the Studio Era* (New York: Pantheon, 1988). Jerome Christensen, "Studio Identity and Studio Art: MGM, *Mrs. Miniver*, and Planning the Postwar Era" *ELH* 67, no. 1, Spring 2001, 257–292, presents a contextual portrait of a major studio project under roughly similar social and institutional conditions to *The Big Sleep*.

27. Page Dougherty Delano, "Making Up for War: Sexuality and Citizenship in Wartime Culture" *Feminist Studies* 26, no. 1, Spring, 2000, 33–68, Paul Fussell, *Wartime: Understanding and Behavior in the Second World War* (New York: Oxford University Pres, 1989, 96–114, and John Costello, *Virtue Under Fire: How World War II Changed Our Social and Sexual Attitudes* (Boston: Little Brown, and Co., 1985).

28. Siegfried Kracauer, *From Caligari to Hitler: A Psychological History of the German Film* (Princeton: Princeton University Press, 1947), 6.

29. Robert Sklar, *City Boys: Cagney, Bogart, Garfield* (Princeton: Princeton University Press, 1992), 174, 176.

30. Richard Schickel, *Good Morning Mr. Zip, Zip, Zip: Movies, Memory and World War II* (Chicago: Ivan R. Dee, 2003), 300.

31. Raymond Chandler, *The Big Sleep* (New York: Library of America, 1994), 763–764 [originally published 1939].

32. James Agee, *Agee on Film: Criticism and Comment on the Movies* (New York: Modern Library, 2000), 206–207.

33. Schrader's essay was published in 1972, and its analysis of the social forces reflected in film noir continue to shape understanding of the noir mode. Most appropriations of Schrader's concept of "post-war disillusionment" in writing about film noir tend toward glib statements about changed social conditions; Schrader in fact argues that much of what Americans were disillusioned with was the movies. Schrader contrasts "America's amelioristic cinema" of the late 1930's and the war years with the films of the immediate postwar period: "As soon as the War was over, however, American films became markedly more sardonic—and there was a boom in the crime film … The disillusionment many soldiers, small businessmen and housewife/factory employees felt in returning to a peacetime economy was directly mirrored in the sordidness of the crime film." Because *The Big Sleep*, with its two versions, straddles these two cultural, social, and cinematic realms, that of wartime and the postwar, it gives us an opportunity to watch the shift toward this state of disillusionment at close range, and to site its origin in the ambivalences of wartime life. Richard Maltby spells out the rhetoric of this amelioristic cinema in great detail in his *Harmless Entertainment: Hollywood and the Ideology of Consensus* (Metuchen: Scarecrow Press, 1983), 182–217.

34. Bruce Kawin, "Hawks and Faulkner", in Jim Hillier and Peter Wollen, eds. *Howard Hawks: American Artist* (London: British Film Institute, 1996), 148–150. Kawin's existential reading of the film allows him to see its descendants not only in neo-noir, but also in films "that play by no known rules," such as Godard's *Breathless*, Truffaut's *Shoot the Piano Player*, and Chabrol's *Web of Passion*.

35. *The Big Sleep* lacks several important ingredients of the Hawks' thematic: there is no tight-knit band of professionals and an attendant interest on group cohesion, there is no linkage between growing self-respect and responsibility, and there is no bonding between male characters in pursuit of a common goal. For these reasons, the film is among a small group Robin Wood counts as Hawks' "failures and marginal works." Robin Wood, *Howard Hawks* (London: British Film Institute, 1981), 163–172.

36. David Thomson, *The Big Sleep* (London: British Film Institute: 1997)

37. Todd McCarthy, *Howard Hawks: The Grey Fox of Hollywood* (New York: The Grove Press, 1997), 385. McCarthy does not list Darrin among his interviewees, and the statement is not otherwise documented, so it is not clear when the incident happened.

A fatalistic Jeff (Robert Mitchum) looks his future in the eye as a determined Kathie (Jane Greer) leads him to his doom.

"Lounge Time" Reconsidered: Spatial Discontinuity and Temporal Contingency in *Out of the Past* (1947)

R. Barton Palmer

The chief taxonomic difficulty that haunts film genre study is its dependence on circular reasoning. Discussions of genre, as Robert Stam suggests, are inevitably characterized by a "tautological quality."[1] *Stagecoach* and films that seem similar to it are westerns because they share certain conventions of setting, theme, and visual style; and these are the features we have determined westerns must have. So *Stagecoach* is a western because it is said to be one. This unavoidable circularity is a reflex of the fact that generic categories are cultural (or, perhaps better, discursive). Being stipulative, genres can hardly be made the object of either a logical or scientific analysis. A film is a western not because it possesses some essential qualities that necessitate that it be grouped with other films that can then be known collectively as "westerns."

In the absence of any unchallengeable procedures for definition, then, arbitrariness of a sort must determine what films we select as "authentic" members of a generic class and what films we exclude because they lack what we maintain are the requisite features. In fact, arbitrariness (of different degrees) figures in what genres we decide to recognize in the first place. Thus any search to determine or fix the supposedly *sine qua non* features of a genre (or a series or any grouping characterized by shared features) is bound to end in failure. But such formulations as we may devise are useful as heuristics. We may employ them as provisional frameworks to guide our mapping of intertextual relations, even as we recognize that these relations are always much too complex to reduce to some menu of unarguable propositions.

In film noir studies, the question of definition has provoked an inordinate amount of discussion because film noir is, in its classic phase at least, a post facto category. This fact lays bare the discursiveness of generic analysis. The films precede the term by which they will subsequently become known, which is thus exposed as a way of talking about artifacts that already exist. While what are now known as films noirs were being turned out by the postwar American film industry, no one in Hollywood was apparently aware that such a descriptive term existed. John Ford knew he was making westerns and had, presumably, some idea of this genre in mind during his career, but neither Robert Siodmak nor Billy Wilder knew they were making what would come to be called films noirs. If not a category of production, the term "film noir," imported from France along with the *politique des auteurs*, was, instead, and quite obviously from the very outset, a category of taste. It was introduced in American film culture as a strategy for "saving" what could thereby be claimed as the more distinguished products of Hollywood. The average American film, perhaps a largely forgettable foray into popular entertainment, was thought by some to deserve critical disdain. In contrast, the term film noir marked out an area of artistic production that could be justly valued. Hence the term style (with its connotations of an individual approach to artistic creation) was from the outset mobilized to describe this body of Hollywood films.

For many early Anglophone theorists, defining film noir thus became an issue most often approached not through some kind of empirical analysis, but through a tendentious form of evaluation. Mise-en-scène and visual stylization broadly conceived (the areas of production over which directors had most control) were declared more important than narrative materials or cultural themes, for scripts seemed the dubious products of hack screenwriters and pulp novelists that had been imposed on directors by philistine producers. But this emphasis on the visual was not universally accepted. There were those who regarded film noir as yet another genre to be defined, at least in the first instance, by shared storytelling traditions. And so was raised a central critical question, which has been variously answered during the last four decades. Is film noir a style or a genre? Or, to rephrase in terms of the cultural politics I have here sketched out, can the series be most appropriately considered the product of a group auteurism in some sense or is it, instead, essentially the transference to the screen, with a subsequent broadening, of several pre-existing literary genres?[2]

We hardly need reminding that this kind of debate has not raged around the other Hollywood genres (musicals, biopics, melodramas, etc.), and the reason is that these other forms have never been co-opted into a *politique des genres* whose purpose is to distinguish between dross and artistic gold. Aiming at the discovery of some workable essentialist formula, much of the otherwise valuable critical work done on film noir has neglected that there is, as Pierre Bourdieu puts it, "an economy of cultural goods," whose "specific logic" must be approached through a description of "the different ways of appropriating such of these objects as are regarded at a particular moment as works of art, and the social conditions of the constitution of the mode of appropriation that is considered legitimate."[3] The visual style/genre debate, we may observe, following the sociological perspective Bourdieu advocates, seems properly a matter of warring critical protocols rather than a disagreement about what the films in question could be established on some inarguable grounds "to be." Naturally, we cannot debate the truth or falsity of a "mode of appropriation," only its relative value or interest within a set of "social conditions." The reader should consider this a prefatory warning to what here follows.

Going over this well-trodden ground is worthwhile because it sharpens our appreciation for a provocatively original attempt to resolve the style/genre debate, published as part of Nick Browne's more general project of "reconfiguring" the study of American film genres: Vivian Sobchack's "Lounge Time: Postwar Crises and the Chronotope of Film noir." An implicit goal of her analysis is to render irrelevant the question that has vexed work on film noir for many years by emphasizing the mutual indispensability (or, perhaps better, inseparability) of form (style) and content (narrative patterns and themes). To do so, Sobchack has recourse to a historical commentary that attempts to "locate and ground that heterogeneous and ambiguous cinematic grouping called film noir in its contemporaneous social context."[4] This is an ambitious goal, and it is hardly surprising that her view of film noir is not without its problems. What I hope to do here is to identify these in the spirit of broadening the usefulness of her approach, focusing on Jacques Tourneur's *Out of the Past*, which has been acknowledged as one of the "key works of film noir."[5] Any understanding of a genre, it hardly needs emphasizing, must be able to explain key works, and Sobchack's view, as we will see, must be modified considerably in order to accommodate Tourneur's film.

An obvious virtue of Sobchack's approach is that it eschews the simplicities of reflection theory in exploring the connection of film noir to its historical moment. She is certainly correct in not expecting to locate untransformed in the films the prominent social themes of postwar America, such as the anxieties experienced by returning veterans, the sudden flourishing of a violent misogyny in popular culture, the political uncertainties alarmingly widespread in a post-atomic age, and, most important perhaps, a pervasive sense of rootlessness and anomie that finds varied expression, from an incredible growth in church membership to the burgeoning popularity of existentialist thought among American intellectuals.[6]

Instead, Sobchack uses the chronotope, a formal concept not hitherto often employed in film studies, whose explanatory power is that it permits the *rapprochement* of "the internal logic of the films and the external logic of the culture," causing "each to be intelligible in terms of the other" (130). In other words, once we identify the chronotope of film noir, which she christens "lounge time," we can analyze the formal ways in which cultural themes find their characteristic representational form within the films themselves. The chronotope is a unique coinage, borrowed from the Russian theorist Mikhail Bakhtin, who uses it to account for the essential differences between broadly different literary forms such as the chivalric romance and the pastoral, each of which, he argues, are characterized by a particular (and unique) chronotope.

By way of preliminary comment, which will need considerable nuancing below, the following can be said about this kind of approach. Developing an overarching scheme of different literary (or cinematic) forms at least promotes (if it does not require) a now largely discredited essentialism. Divergent genres by definition are each understood by reference to the same irreducible, determinant element. In addition, the membership of any particular text in a given genre is thus to be decided by the presence/absence of that element. Using the chronotope, in other words, certainly does not obviously avoid the taxonomic circle that haunts traditional approaches to genre description. If we accept Sobchack's argument, then film noir is to be defined by a particular chronotope, and only films with that feature can be considered truly noir.

But we can certainly agree with Sobchack that the chronotope approach is of great usefulness in pointing to a feature that seems (at least in part) to have led critics to identify the body of films now known as noir. The chronotope (a melding of the Greek words for "time" and "space"), validates, as Bakhtin puts it, the "intrinsic connectedness of temporal and spatial relationships that are artistically expressed in literature" and therefore serves to define "genre and generic distinctions, for in literature the primary category in the chronotope is time."[7] What Bakhtin means here is that the particular way time is organized in any kind of fictional representation determines other conventions, including, and especially, that of setting. Thus in the medieval chivalric romance, "the entire world is subject to 'suddenly,'" meaning that "the unexpected, and only the unexpected, is what is expected." As a result, the chivalric romance displays a "corresponding subjective playing with space, in which elementary spatial relationships and perspectives are violated" (152, 155). In the chivalric romance, space thus becomes a miraculous landscape where the customary laws of human experience may at any moment be suspended, generating both events and even forms of being that are, from the perspective of everyday experience, "impossible." But the laws that rule everyday life sometimes do apply. Knights are wounded and killed, ladies worry about defending their castles against enemies, and kings can be betrayed by their most trusted subordinates. But the limitations of human nature may be spectacularly transcended (and then as suddenly re-imposed) at any given moment. This raising of unexpectedness to a first principle shapes a world of infinite plasticity and variety in which handsome knights rightly concerned about their own mortality and green ogres who can ride off carrying their own severed heads share the same narrative space.

Departing from Bakhtin's insistence on the primacy of temporal organization, Sobchack, however, first identifies what she calls "the films' concrete and visual premises," or, roughly speaking, the story world and its manner of representation:

> These radical grounds and material premises figured concretely before us and to which we should pay heed are the cocktail lounge, the nightclub, the bar, the hotel room, the boardinghouse, the diner, the dance hall, the roadside café, the bus and train station, and the wayside motel. These are the recurrent and determinate premises of film noir and they emerge from common places in wartime and postwar American culture that, transported to the screen, gain hyperbolized presence and overdetermined meaning (130).

These "premises" are said to belong to a culture in transition between the collective, public experience of a world war that required the widest marshalling of all the nation's resources and the desired return to "the family unit and the suburban home as the domestic matrix of democracy" (131). They are the publicly accessible (if hardly socially approved) spaces of entertainment, dining, travel, and lodging, whose function is to provide for those literally, and also metaphorically, in transit. The bar and the cheap hotel, of course, substitute for what cannot be obtained in a world where nothing, we might say, is "settled." The characters who inhabit or frequent these (usually quite unwelcoming) fictional spaces feel the deprivation of the safety, security, and comfort of the bourgeois home, site of nurturing family relationships. Film noir is thus theorized as a specific response to the social conditions imposed by wartime and its aftermath: "In sum, the intimacy and security of home and the integrity and solidity of the home front are lost to wartime and postwar America and to those films we associate at both the core and periphery of that cinematic grouping we circumscribe as noir" (146). In Sobchack's view, noir films broaden their emotional and intellectual appeal by metaphorizing these settings, which are thus turned into the visual and thematic expression of a "world of existential, epistemological, and axiological uncertainty" (133).

   This description of film noir is persuasive, even though, I would suggest, it theo-
rizes the "determinate premises" of noir films at the wrong level of specificity. What I
mean is that Sobchack's analysis is too closely tied to the particular premises she anat-
omizes. As Bakhtin's discussion of the chivalric romance should suggest, a chronotope
requires a general category of setting (a miraculous world) rather than something
rather specific (say, a castle and the surrounding forest). Arguing for the usefulness of
chronotopic analysis for film study, Michael V. Montgomery has made the point that
Bakhtin's categories are often formulated at too general a level.[8] Point well taken, but

Jeff Bailey (Robert Mitchum), dazed and confused by the seductive gaze of Kathie Moffett (Jane
Greer), lingers too long in their Mexican idyll.

we must be circumspect about such re-formulations as we indulge in to adapt Bakhtin's concept for use in a different medium with narrative traditions often quite distinct from those in literature. The problem with Sobchack's anatomy of noir premises, to state it simply, is that in too many noir films the main settings are not cocktail lounges, cheap bars, bus stations, and roadside diners.

In fact, many noir films (John Stahl's *Leave Her to Heaven* and Vincent Minnelli's *Undercurrent* immediately come to mind) even avoid altogether the "dark city" where such accommodations for those "in transit" are normally to be found. Both these films are set mainly in homes of the wealthy. At the same time, no viewer of 1940s Hollywood film could fail to notice the contrast between, on the one hand, the inhospitable, dangerously permeable and anonymous spaces where the dark narratives of film noir most often (and at least in part) unfold and, on the other, the single family house that is a conventional element of film melodrama, its rooms full of family and its walls resisting any intrusion from the uninvited. And Sobchack's perception that the noir story world reflects a deep sense of both contingency and anxiety is, I believe, indisputable.

There is, however, another and larger problem with her view: it is incomplete. The unique usefulness of Bakhtin's concept of the chronotope lies not in its hardly innovative theorization of the way in which fictional settings are both drawn from the real and are then, suitably transformed, made a part of a generic story world. The chronotope is a richer analytical tool and is designed to account for the particular movement of narrative in both its senses—that is, in terms of story and storytelling time—within a given fictional genre, showing how a characteristic form of setting becomes its reflex. As Bakhtin puts it more poetically, "time becomes, in effect, palpable and visible; the chronotope makes narrative events concrete, makes them take on flesh, causes blood to flow in their veins" (250). Although she terms the noir Chronotope "lounge time," Sobchack never comments on how time is structured in film noir. We gain no sense therefore of how the represented world she describes takes shape, how time becomes "palpable and visible." Her essay briefly alludes to, but offers little comment on, the different forms of narrative time carefully anatomized by Bakhtin, and these certainly merit a closer look. But, first, some consideration of Tourneur's film is in order.

Out of the Past, so aptly re-titled from its novelistic source (Daniel Mainwaring's *Build My Gallows High*), exemplifies not only a cultural theme, but a principle of narrative structure in the body of films known as noir. Thematically speaking, noir films characteristically focus on their protagonists' "dark pasts", which are frequently explored in some form of backward turning that is motivated by a present crisis. In film noir, someone (or something) is always coming "out of the past." This backward turning may be found in the discursive arrangement of story events, whose forward movement is interrupted by the filling in of some bypassed gap; or it may figure as an element of characterization, with an intradiegetic narrator relating what has gone before and thereby demonstrating the presence of the past within his own thoughts. These two methods reflect the classical rhetorical theory of *in medias res* construction, as in, for example, Virgil's *Aeneid*. A third possibility is that the present admits the return of characters who were thought to belong to the past and who, it seemed, had been bypassed as the protagonist embarked on a "fresh start."

As *Out of the Past* demonstrates, these three forms of backward movement may be found in the same text: the film's narrative loops back to examine the protagonist's involvement in a murder, even as he narrates the events in question, explaining his innocence to the woman he now intends he marry; and this movement brings into the unfolding present the beautiful *femme fatale* with whom he had once been in love, as well as the powerful man from whom he had taken her away. The manipulative schemes and betrayals of this unholy couple are repeated as the story goes forward, but this time with even more deadly results. The past, in short, cannot be escaped and, worse yet, must find renewed expression in the present, which is often doomed, as in *Out of the Past,* simply to repeat it.

Thus the crisis the typical noir story develops can be resolved (or at least understood) only by a return in some sense to the past and to the postponed, unresolved difficulties it insistently bequeaths to the present. And so the present is always already contingent, its apparent solidity subject to a sudden, often thoroughgoing disruption that is connected somehow to what has been left behind but is not, as the story begins, in any sense "over." Such a sense of time was undoubtedly widespread in the culture, forming part of the dominant structure of feeling of the era. As historian William Graebner observes of the "culture of contingency" that was America in the 1940s, "the past was the repository of the most frightening memories—of desperate joblessness and totalitarianism, of separation and death in war" (52). If to many the present seemed marked by precariousness, this was a feeling that "flowed from being drafted and shot at, from witnessing the murder of the Jews, and from subjecting others—the populations of Dresden and Hiroshima to start with—to the possibility of sudden, undeserved death" (19).

This sense of contingency, of existential brittleness, certainly marks the experience of the characters in *Out of the Past*. In fact, "frightening memories" of what has gone before yet cannot be laid to rest provide the energy for the forward motion of the narrative after a false start marks out a quite different road not taken. A car arrives in the sleepy town of Bridgeport, California, high in the Sierras and far from the Los Angeles indicated on a road sign in one of the film's several establishing shots of mountains, sky, and empty vistas. Joe Stefanos (Paul Valentine), to all appearances an arrogant big city hood, has come for a former business "associate," Jeff Markham (Robert Mitchum), who has changed his name to Bailey and moved to the country in an attempt to escape his past. Jeff now owns and operates a service station, and he has made a new life, befriending a deaf mute Jimmy (Dickie Moore) and romancing the beautiful Ann (Virginia Huston), who has thrown over her suitor of many years, Jim (Richard Webb), even though Jim still nurtures hope of winning her away from the stranger. Despite his hard work and quiet life, Jeff has not yet attained respectability in the closed society of this isolated small town, but he is quite obviously trying to make a life for himself despite the fact that there are those, including Ann's parents, who trust to neither his virtue nor his reliability.

On the day Stefanos arrives, Jeff and Ann are trout fishing in the mountains, enjoying a romantic interlude. Like others in Bridgeport, Ann is intrigued but worried by Jeff's exoticness. He lacks the deep knowability that others have in this small community. Jeff has no past by which those in Bridgeport can measure him; he exists for them only in the present moment of his law-abiding self-sufficiency. Now quite obviously in love with him, Ann, however, needs to know more. She must be assured that the man Jeff Bailey appears to be is the man he truly is. She asks how many places has he been. "One too many," he answers. But now, it seems, his days of dangerous wandering are over. Pointing to the lake shore, Jeff says he likes "this one right here." And that one place, far from the others he has been, is the centerpiece of a vision Jeff has for the rest of his life:

> You see that cove over there. Well, I'd like to build a house right there. Marry you. Live in it. And never go anywhere else.

Ann shares his vision of rootedness and commitment, but her acceptance of this proposal (if that is what Jeff is making) is tinged with doubt. "I wish you would," she says, putting his offer and all it entails into the suspended state of the subjunctive. Her questioning becomes more insistent. Was he ever married? "Not that I remember," Jeff answers. This seems to put Ann on more solid ground. But before the couple can go any further in making plans, Jimmy arrives from the garage to announce that Stefanos has come looking for Jeff.

What makes possible Jeff's dream of a life with Ann is the solidity of his new identity, of the name he gives himself and the life he is making for himself. That life depends on hard work, on becoming a respected and contributing member of the community, on establishing meaningful relationships with others. Jeff's rivalry with Jim for Ann's affection, and the reluctance her parents later show about endorsing her romance with a "stranger," would provide themes for a melodrama that could suitably be set in the single setting of Bridgeport and whose point would be to establish the unified, domestic identity of its protagonist. As he himself suggests, Jeff would be defined by that house he would build in the cove and by the one woman he would allow to share his life there with him. All other places, all other times (and, of course, all other women) would have no part in the life, unmarked by disruptions other than the natural ones time should bring, that Ann and Jeff would live there.

But such singularity of place and continuity of time do not define the noir protagonist. Jeff's projection of a conventionally domestic future, and his inhabiting of a morally unexceptional present, are both disrupted by the arrival of Stefanos, one of many agents in the film who come "out of the past" to admonish others that they cannot refashion themselves or entertain any thoughts of a fresh start. Stefanos not only reminds Jeff who he used to be, a private eye named Markham who once got mixed up in the personal affairs of big-time gambler Whit Sterling (Kirk Douglas). He also insists that Joe must become that person again, reminding him that, now identified, he cannot escape the reach of Sterling; further attempts at evasion are useless.

On one level, then, the arrival of this even stranger stranger in Bridgeport merely externalizes what is in Markham's character, his inability to become something other than he once was. Just as Jeff is contemplating a future, the past asserts its prior claims. We sense this inner limitation in the tentativeness of his proposal to Ann, as well as in her own evident uncertainty that he can live out the vision of domestic bliss he sketches for her. On another level, however, this sudden, unexpected confrontation

represents the deadly workings of contingency. Stefanos, who does Sterling's strong
arm work, was not looking for Markham when he found him. He was simply making
his way by chance through Bridgeport some time back and happened to spot Markham working at a gas station. And now Sterling wants Jeff to drive over to his house
on Lake Tahoe, and Sterling's wish is obviously a command that Jeff cannot (or perhaps
will not) ignore. Jeff arranges for Ann to take him there in her car and, on the way, tells
her who he used to be, but (or so he thinks) no longer is. His protestations are belied
by a telling change of costume. Waiting outside Ann's house (tellingly, this is a domestic space he chooses not to enter), Jeff has abandoned the open-necked shirt and
poplin jacket suited to life in the country for a trenchcoat and fedora, the uniform of
the hard-boiled urban detective. He wooed Ann during a sunny afternoon by the lake,
but she drives him to Tahoe at night, whose shadows better suit the darker persona
he is in the midst of reassuming.

The flashback narrated by Jeff distributes his true identity over a series of places,
none of which is his home: from New York, where Markham, but not Fisher (Steve
Brodie), his partner, is hired to track down Kathie Moffett (Jane Greer), Sterling's erstwhile girlfriend who has stolen $40,000 and shot him in the process; to Acapulco,
where Jeff finds Kathie and falls in love with her, reneging on his promise to return the
woman and the stolen money to Whit; to Los Angeles, which provides them refuge
until they are discovered by Fisher at a racetrack; to a cabin in the Sierras where
Fisher, attempting to blackmail his former partner, is shot dead by Kathie, who flees
leaving her lover to bury the body; and, finally, to Bridgeport, the place Jeff seeks out
as a refuge against the crime he did not commit, the woman he still feels drawn toward, and the employer whom he had betrayed.

The soft-spoken thug Joe (Paul Valentine) watches over the perennially elusive femme fatale
Kathie (Jane Greer) in *Out of the Past.*

Some of these "premises" belong to the noir chronotope as Sobchack defines it: Sterling's "office" in New York: the "Negro" night club where Jeff gets vital information from Kathie's maid; the café in Acapulco where he hangs out in hopes of running into her and which quickly becomes "their place"; the racetrack where Fisher just happens on Jeff placing a bet ("There's wasn't one chance in a million we'd bump into our past," as Jeff says). But others do not: Kathie's Mexican bungalow; the beach where Jeff first makes love to her; and, most tellingly, the cabin in the woods where the fugitive couple lives for some time before Fisher tracks them down.

All these exceptions to Sobchack's anatomy of "premises," it might be pointed out, are domestic or, at least, proto-domestic in the sense that they serve as the reflex of Jeff's desire to transform Kathie from Whit's plaything (a homicidal gold digger with robbery on her mind who has no moral qualms about her "attachment" to the rich gambler) to a monogamous woman now satisfied to live on love and no longer in the rich style to which Whit's generosity had accustomed her. But that Kathie and Jeff can become a couple and truly inhabit any domestic space is an illusion from the outset. Both have betrayed the powerful Whit, and a fear of his vengeance drives them into a hiding from which they can emerge only to their peril. Their rejection of the criminal underworld Whit represents is thus necessarily incomplete. The life they lead is not for themselves, but in opposition to the powerful male who has a claim on each of them.

The places where they share a life are thus a form of disguise. Because it must be defined by transitoriness and deception, no home they establish could become the center of a properly middle-class existence. As Sobchack observes, referring to films such as *Double Indemnity* and *Mildred Pierce*, "the loss of home becomes a structuring absence in film noir" (144). It is not surprising, then, that *Out of the Past* contains, in a distanced and ironic form, the vision of domestic time and space it otherwise excludes. And it denies that sense of natural time (man in his "seven ages") and singular space (the concept of "home") by devising narratives that deprive its protagonists not only of rootedness, as Sobchack observes, but of any prospect for a future that, beyond the reach of contingency, will unfold unretarded by the morally ambiguous past.

These two different visions of life figure in the exchange that takes place between Ann and Jeff, his confessional flashback now at an end. Ann has listened to things that have hurt her, but she affirms that "it's all past." Eager for her acceptance, Jeff nevertheless must admit that "maybe it isn't." This conversation takes place between characters who belong, in a sense, to different chronotopes. In melodrama, the innocent but misguided can reform their ways and accept monogamy in that single space that, as Jeff points, out, looking at the cove, is transformed into a home by the embrace of marriage and the duty of earning a living.

Melodrama thus constructs time as significant in the sense that both character and space may change in the course of its unfolding. Contingency and its reflex, spatial discontinuity, characterize this form of story, but only in part. For the melodramatic notion of time centers on a moment of turning (thematically, the crisis of development that leads to growth and maturity). This turning finds its reflex in the singularity of space and character it projects for the protagonist, who, literally and metaphorically, "settles down" to a predictable and monogamous existence. The melodrama ends in an unfolding present whose uniformity can be disrupted only by the tragedies actuarial tables can measure; it is a form given to projected closure and the notion of "happily ever after."

In the film noir, by way of contrast, the innocent but misguided or obsessed man cannot escape the fatal entanglements he has, after all, chosen and which, in the end, answer better to his nature, with its impulses toward restlessness and duplicity. Lacking a moment of reformative turning, the film noir juxtaposes the false promise of a future with the reality of a present that, instead, turns back to the past, trapping the protagonist "between times" and in a multiplicity of irreconcilable spaces. As does Jeff Markham, such protagonists ordinarily come to their end "in transit," attempting to escape what they never can, which is themselves.

In the case of *Out of the Past,* what gives the story its forward movement is the possibility that Ann may be right that the past can be laid to rest, expunged from the present as the man who protests his love for her promises his relinquishing of a past self. And yet Jeff leaves her with a contradictory admission of resignation and resolve: "I'm tired of running. I've got to clean this up some way." But that, of course, proves to be impossible. At Whit's huge lake house in Tahoe, Jeff discovers that Kathie has returned to Whit, who now holds evidence (Kathie's murder of Fisher, which can be "pinned" on Jeff) that delivers Jeff back into his power. Whit dispatches him on a fool's errand to San Francisco, where he is to be made the fall guy for the murder by Stefanos of Whit's accountant, Eels (Ken Niles), who may go to the police with evidence of tax fraud that will send Whit to jail.

In the threatening city, Jeff manages to defeat this scheme and, in the process, obtain the tax records. He moves easily and readily through a series of dangerous spaces in nighttime San Francisco, even assuming for a time yet another false identity. Jeff's intention is to free himself from Whit's control by keeping the records now in his possession. Fingered for the murder to the police by Whit, however, he finds that his innocence is at present impossible to establish and returns to hide out in the woods near Bridgeport. Stefanos is dispatched to kill him there and climbs a rise from which to take a fatal shot, but Jimmy, in one of those bizarre killings that characterize film noir, hooks him with a fishing line and pulls him down to his death on the rocks below. Reassured by Ann that she still loves him, Jeff goes to Whit at Tahoe once again, and the two men, both betrayed by Kathie, decide to deliver her to the police to stand trial for Fisher's murder. As before, however, she manages to reassert her power over them, first by shooting Whit (this time fatally) and then by blackmailing Jeff to accompany her on yet another flight (her third) from a shooting. His plan to escape from Kathie's power now a failure (for only with Whit's help could he establish that she murdered Fisher), Jeff knows that his only hope for deliverance is the police, whom he secretly phones. As they speed away down the mountain, Kathie spots the roadblock ahead, realizes Jeff's betrayal, and shoots him dead before she is herself gunned down by the police.

If the film ends with a sense of projected closure, it is because Jim, with Jeff now dead, resumes his relationship with Ann. Unlike her dead lover, Ann finds she can leave the past behind. Her moment of reformatory turning comes when, questioning Jimmy about Jeff's last moments, she is answered with a saving lie. Jimmy tells her that Jeff had chosen to leave with Kathie. As not in the noir world, the past, once identified as a false start, can be left behind. In the film's closing shot, Jimmy waves goodbye to the sign over Jeff's garage, acknowledging his affection for and loyalty to a man whom he had known in his better (if hardly entirely authentic) self. The world of melodrama, we might say, reasserts its control. It is, after all, the default fictional universe purveyed by the Hollywood system with its reaffirmation of consensus values, including a distribution of outcomes for its characters based on their moral worthiness. The noir narrative is strangely framed by a melodramatic movement, whose goal is possession of Ann and the singularity of character that is suitably contained by a single fictional space. As the film opens, Jeff is the protagonist in that drama, but, as it ends, his place has been usurped by Jim. Destroyed by a past from which he cannot escape, Jeff becomes a past that the other characters can easily transcend.

Sobchack does not find a close parallel to this kind of story among the chronotopes identified by Bakhtin. But one of these is what he terms the "adventure novel of everyday life," in which the adventure time of pure romance (an unfolding of moments, not causally linked, which effect no changes in the characters who experience them), but "depicts only the exceptional, utterly unusual moments of a man's life...that are very short compared to the whole length of a human life....[but] shape the definitive image of man, his essence, as well as the nature of his subsequent life." (116) That this is a time of adventure is established by the fact that this is a "time of exceptional and unusual events, events determined by chance." Such a conception of story time results in a multiplicity of settings, drawn from real life, and a human image that is "private and isolated." (119) Correspondingly, then, time is represented as a series of separate moments, "chopped up into separate segments...deprived of its unity and wholeness." (128) With human time carefully distinguished from natural time, "the individual changes and undergoes metamorphosis completely independent of the world." (119) It is moreover "always the case that the hero cannot, by his very nature, be a part of everyday life; he passes through such life as would a man from another world." (121) In fact, the primary image of this protagonist's world is "the road." He is a character perpetually in transit, fixed in a sense of time and space that is particularly suited to "portraying events governed by chance." (244) This particular chronotope, I suggest, would be especially appealing to a culture obsessed by contingency and rootlessness, experiencing life, both personal and political, as a series of chance encounters and disconnections that do not admit of "settling down" in any meaningful sense. As Sobchack observes, film noir offers a conception of representational time/space that contrasts with the chronotope of the idyll, discussed at length by Bakhtin, which, as she points out, has "relevance to the familiarity, stability, and rootedness of home." (160) But the chronotope that structures film noir is also, I believe, connected to one of the larger categories identified by Bakhtin.

This might not, in the end at least, be a terribly important point. The noir protagonist might well resemble his predecessors in picaresque fiction of earlier eras. Like them, he is ever in transit through a series of disconnected moments as he finds himself incapable of entering into the quite different temporality of everyday life. To put this another way, the home, source of wholeness and connection, is a "structuring absence" in the story of his self-realization; it is a place that Jeff Bailey can refer to only as wish, perhaps barely as intention. And yet, to follow the line of reason pioneered by

Vivian Sobchack, his experience of time is also culturally specific, without antecedent in the general types of narrative anatomized by Bakhtin. The road on which he meets with adventure leads not forward into some ever receding future, but, instead, turns back upon itself. The path he treads is ever the same path. Like Sisyphus, he is condemned to relive what has been, in an illusion of movement that is actually a form of cruel stasis. As does Jeff Markham/Bailey in *Out of the Past,* he can only live out the division of his self between what is and what has been, glimpsing (but only glimpsing) the possibilities of rootedness and singularity, of the wholeness of everyday time, that deceptively seem within his imagination and reach.

NOTES

1. *Film Theory: An Introduction,* Oxford: Blackwell, 2000, p. 202. In *Reconfiguring American Film Genres* (Los Angeles: University of California Press, 1998), Nick Browne observes that in cinema studies older taxonomic approaches have been losing their appeal: "The implicit, ideal order of the structuralist system of genre has dissolved ... The structuralist project of the 1970s carried forward and defined this tendency [to assume an internal genetic finality] by identifying genres with distinctive patterns of narrative order and visual iconography." In place of this now largely abandoned approached, Browne advocates a view of genres as "specific assemblances of local coherencies—discrete, heterotopic instances of a complex cultural politics" (11). Browne's statement fairly characterizes the approach taken in this essay, which is opposed to any postulating of "an internal genetic finality" for the film noir phenomenon.

2. These issues are explored in more depth in my "The Sociological Turn of Adaptation Studies: The Example of Film Noir," in Robert Stam, ed., *Companion to Film and Literature* (Oxford: Blackwell, forthcoming).

3. *Distinction: A Social Critique of the Judgment of Taste,* trans. by Richard Nice, Cambridge, MA: Harvard University Press, 1984, p. 1

4. In Browne, p. 129. Further references noted in the text.

5. Alain Silver and Elizabeth Ward, *Film Noir: An Encyclopedia Reference to the American Style,* Third Edition, Woodstock, NY: Overlook Press, 1992, p. 218

6. As William Graebner observes, "the seminal events of the forties seemed to confirm that humanity had, indeed, been set adrift from its ethical moorings. Like life itself, values seemed to come and go, without pattern or reason," *The Age of Doubt: American Thought and Culture in the 1940s* (Boston: Twayne, 1991), pp. 19–20. Further references noted in the text.

7. From "Forms of Time and of the Chronotope in the Novel," in *The Dialogic Imagination: Four Essays,* trans. by Michael Holquist (Austin: University of Texas Press, 1981), 84–5. Further references noted in the text.

8. *Carnivals and Commonplaces: Bakhtin's Chronotope, Cultural Studies, and Film,* New York: Peter Lang, 1993, see esp. pp. 5–6.

The Unsuspected (1947) and the Noir Sequence: Realism, Expressionism, Style

Robert Porfirio

Most of the frames accompanying this analysis are from a sequence which has aroused considerable interest among students of film noir though the film itself, *The Unsuspected*, has remained relatively unheralded. One portion in particular (represented by Figures 12–18) has been singled out as expressing the "essence" of film noir without much regard to the rest of the film, so it seems to me that the sequence affords us an excellent opportunity to see if some of the methods of modern film criticism can help to determine why it has been termed exemplar. Indeed, though it is yet to be recognized, the whole of *The Unsuspected* is quite characteristic of the film noir in its manner of synthesizing those techniques which critics have labeled "realist" (depth of field, moving camera, location photography) with those labeled formative (expressive editing, stylized photography), a synthesis which accounts for a great portion of the cycle's distinctive idiolect.

Another cogent reason for picking a sequence from this particular film is the presence of its director, Michael Curtiz. Although Curtiz has long been regarded as one of the most "Germanic" of the émigrés (despite the fact of his Hungarian origins), with a temperament well suited to the visual flourishes of certain of Warners' "action" genres, his own prodigious output has been so eclectic and his reputation as a "studio" director so strong that he has seldom been hailed by critics of an auteurist persuastion. It would seem then that we stand in better stead of demonstrating how a personal style relates symbiotically to a broader idiolect with a director like Curtiz and a less "renowned" film like *The Unsuspected*, than with what might be regarded as a major instance of an auteur's total oeuvre. At the same time Curtiz's one major film noir, *Mildred Pierce* (1945), is more often acknowledged because of the presence of its star, Joan Crawford, and its original author, James M. Cain, though that earlier film also evidenced an adept blending of authentic exteriors with stylized studio interiors. On the other hand, the post-war trend towards "realism" (most obvious in *The Unsuspected* during the final location chase sequence) is also evidenced in two other films noirs produced at Warner Brothers during the same year as *The Unsuspected* (*Dark Passage*, directed by Delmer Daves; *The Possessed*, directed by Kurt Bernhardt), suggesting a complex interaction of stylistic inputs.

Finally, it should be noted that this film represented Curtiz's first for his own production company at Warners, so that questions of personal discretion were perhaps more crucial for him here than they had been in the past. Indeed it would seem that in selecting a successful novel by a noted authoress of crime fiction (Charlotte Armstrong) Curtiz was attempting to repeat the success of Mildred Pierce with a property that called for even more "atmosphere." This assertion is strengthened by his personal choices for screenwriter (Ranald MacDougall), art director (Anton Grot), photography (Woody Bredell) and star (Claude Rains). While the film's story appears to be a loose reworking of many of the elements of *Laura*, its plot contains ample "holes" for Curtiz to "cover" with his style.

That style is apparent immediately in the film's opening segment. A moving camera follows the shadow of a man around the walls of a darkly lit, well-furnished room, pausing with it in from of the portrait of a beautiful young woman (later identified as Matilda Frazier [Joan Caufield], the ostensibly "dead" owner of the house). There is a cut to another room as the camera follows the shadow to a closed door which is opened silently by a gloved hand to reveal (via deep focus) a young lady (Nana Bryant) typing at a desk at the far side of the study, momentarily unaware of the presence of the man or his elongated shadow on the wall behind her. The shadow indicates that the man is holding a coiled rope, and together with Franz Waxman's low-level minatory background music is sufficient to suggest that the woman is about to be killed.

Above, Figure 1. Below, Figure 2.

Even more stylized is the manner of her death which takes place while she is engaged in a telephone conversation with a blonde woman (Audrey Totter) who is inquiring after her husband's whereabouts, a sequence which alternates shots of the young lady at her desk and the blond woman in a nightclub phone booth. During the course of the conversation the young lady becomes aware of the man's presence (seen only as a gloved hand holding the rope in the left foreground of the frame) and when he refuses to respond to her entreaties she begins to scream. The alternate shot of the blond reacting to the scream, which is quite audible over the phone, allows the murder to take place off screen, and in the return shot a gloved hand simply replaces the receiver on the phone. Determining that there is no longer any answer at the other end, the blond woman oddly hides the conversation from her gentleman friend and departs the nightclub. At this point no further effort is made to conceal the killer's identity, for in tidying up after making it appear as if the woman has hung herself, his inverted reflection is seen on the shiny desk top (Figure 1, Claude Rains), and the segment concludes with his departing shadow cast on the wall next to that of his unfortunate victim (Figure 2).

In the very next segment of the film, which contains the sequence under analysis here, Claude Rains is identified as Victor Grandison, a witty bachelor and popular radio raconteur of "true" crimes (like *Laura*'s Waldo Lydecker, the character is based on Alexander Wolcott); Nana Bryant, as Grandison's deceased secretary, Roslyn Wright; and Audrey Totter, eventually, as Althea Keane, his capricious, acerbic niece. Given such an early crucial disclosure, progression of the disquieting mood established in the opening sequence would seem essential if the film is to maintain suspense. Some critics have noted that Curtiz's "Germanic" propensity for shadows and reflections seems to have been given full rein in this film, especially with respect to the character of Victor Grandison: his image is seen in a multitude of "striking" reflections (on table tops, glasses, even a shiny phonograph record) and his shadow often precedes or follows him as he enters or exits a room (with little regard for source lighting). However effective such devices may be in contributing to "mood," viewed synchronically Curtiz's characteristic tropes articulate meaning as they engage with various narrative (e.g., the hermeneutic), visual (e.g., metaphoric and metonymic), and aural "codes." What has been referred to as *The Unsuspected*'s representative noir ethos may be identified with Curtiz, but is at once the result of personal style, "Germanic" sensibility, compatibility of story and co-workers, all engaged in an on-going dialectic with a broader idiolect.

Thus Grandison's "Germanic" shadows and reflections also function as metonymic markers, for at telling points within the narrative they are juxtaposed next to the figure of each of his potential victims. In fact, the association of Grandison's shadow with Roslyn which opens the film is virtually replicated near its conclusion during Grandison's final (and unsuccessful) attempt on the life of his ward, Matilda Frazier: she too has been set up as a suicide and their reflections are juxtaposed on a shiny table top as she drinks the glass of poisoned champagne Grandison has given her. It is significant also that each of Grandison's actual or intended victims are family or surrogate family ("explained" by his greed for the Frazier estate): his personal secretary, Roslyn; his niece, Althea Keane and her husband, Oliver (Hurd Hatfield); his ward Matilda Frazier and her "husband," Steve Howard (Michael North).

The Freudian dimension of his series of relationships is complex and can only be suggested during the course of this analysis. More germane to our purposes here is the way Grandison's position in this network of relationships generates a character of real divided sensibilities, one in whom epicurean tastes so curtail genuine affection that his well-mannered paternalism is something more than a mask and less than the man. This dualism is enhanced by the quality of Claude Rains' performance (and the iconic connotations of past roles which included both angel and devil): his smooth voice and reassuring manner, occasionally offset by a patronizing waspishness. It is also contained in the symbolic connotations of the doubling effect of shadow and mirror image which, "coded" within a network of syntagmatic and paradigmatic relationships, serves to impugn a number of other characters, as we shall demonstrate. In this manner, the quickly solved mystery of Roslyn's murder is displaced by the enigma of Grandison's character, which then generates a succession of such enigmas to be worked out through the course of the narrative. The groundwork for this is established in the second segment of the film, primarily in the sequence illustrated here, which presents us with our first good view of Grandison and his radio show, which frames the diegesis, and in which Grandison poses the question that is suspended throughout much of the narrative: Who is the unsuspected murderer I am talking about?

This segment begins in a radio studio's control booth where preparations are being made for the broadcast of Grandison's show; after some initial exposition regarding Roslyn's murder, an establishing shot places Grandison behind a microphone, flanked by the announcer and studio orchestra who open the broadcast. Reading from his script, Grandison begins a tale that he assures the audience is taken from "…the files of the nation's unsolved crimes… The story of one of the most brutal and cunningly conceived murders ever committed… a murder of rare delicacy and wondrous ease, which was called… suicide." As the studio orchestra underscores Grandison's commentary with a fanfare, there is a cut to a low angle shot of him revealing the studio control booth and wall to his left (Figure 3). From this position the camera is able to truck past Grandison up to a studio speaker located on the wall to the right of the control booth (Figure 4).

One might normally expect this movement to be cued by Grandison's leftward glance toward the control booth; instead it is timed to an aural cue, pausing for Grandison to describe the psychological state of the unsuspected murderer. "But is he really free? Can he escape from the evil he has done? No. By day it follows him like a shadow [A significant moment for camera movement to start]. At night, the cold hands of death awaken him from a thousand nightmares."

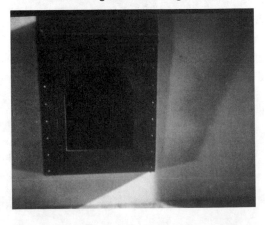

Above, Figure 3. Below, Figure 4.

At this point the camera appears to truck "into" the loudspeaker, actually fading to black in smooth visual transition to the next shot, a train emerging from the "blackness" of a tunnel (Figure 5) whose iconic congruity with the loudspeaker assists the transition. Significantly, this bridging is solely visual, for Rains' narration and the orchestral motifs behind it disappear from the sound track once their diegetic source is removed. They are replaced by the heightened naturalism of a loud train whistle, followed

Figure 5

Figure 6

Figure 7

Figure 8

by the roar of the train as it speeds by the camera (Figure 6), producing a rather disturbing aural effect. Rains' narration returns with the next cut, a compartment interior that reveals its new diegetic source, a portable radio, next to a gun, some cigarettes, and the partially obscured figure of a man (Figure 7).

As Rains' voice describes the potentially distraught and alienated condition of the killer, a reverse angle reveals an ambiguous figure (identified much later as Steven Howard, Roslyn's fiance and enacted here by an iconically "neutral" Michael North in his first film role) whose manner, especially in lighting his cigarette (Figure 8), suggests that he could be the "unsuspected" of Grandison's tale. Indeed, at this point in the narrative we have no way of ascertaining whether Grandison is glibly talking about himself or someone else who is equally unsuspected. Those aural and visual signifiers which attach enigmatic properties to Howard as well are fortified by the next shot where his images is reversed when reflected in the compartment window (Figure 9). The status of this shot as a metonymic marker of a divided personality ("reversed" image, light and dark shadowing) is further enhanced by its metaphoric connection with the earlier shot of Grandison (Figure 1) and Howard's sullen manner and rude behavior throughout a good portion of the narrative serves to prolong his moral ambiguity.

As the train slows in speed the camera begins its next important "movement" on another aural cue ("There is no escape... for one who has committed murder"): an optical effect permits it to truck "out" the compartment window and down one of the dark, deserted

streets outside-in one "take" as it were (Figures 10–12). Despite the use of exterior location footage here, a consistency of visual style allows for a smooth juncture between
two separate interior scenes (Figures 9–14) and though Rains' narration once again
goes momentarily off track, the naturalist demand for other exterior environmental
noises is not complied with. Rather, the orchestral background this time stays on track,
providing an aural bridge for the visual transition by "Mickey Mousing" the rhythm of
the train until camera movement halts on the neon sign which identifies the "Hotel
Peekskill" (Figure 12).

Above, Figure 9. Below, Figure 10.   Above, Figure 11. Below, Figure 12.

Rains' voice is reinstated with a cut to a hotel room interior (Figure 13) as a leftward pan reveals a man on a bed (Jack Lambert, later identified as Press, Grandison's
accomplice in crime) smoking and listening to the radio in the dark, his figure sporad-
ically illuminated by the sign outside (Figures 14 and 15). It is this scene whose "fundamental noir qualities" have provoked much critical attention, primarily because of its
visual inventiveness: over Rains' evocative narration Press' attention is directed to
something off screen (Figure 16), then a cut to a more subjective P.O.V. forces the audience to read a portion of the neon spelling out "KILL" along with Press (Figure 17,
compare to the more objective viewpoint in Figure 13) while another cut returns
them to another objective viewpoint (Figure 18). Of course, this is a bit of visual gim-
mickry on the part of Curtiz and his associates, but as we shall subsequently demonstrate the scene itself occupies a position of major importance within the film chain.

Above, Figure 13

Above, Figure 16

Above, Figure 14, Below, Figure 15.

Above, Figure 17, Below, Figure 18.

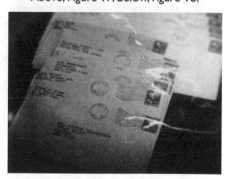

Rather obviously the flashing hotel sign can be read as a reflection of Press' inner state: the iconic value of actor Jack Lambert, who had already established a career as a "disturbed killer," and the denotative value of Rains' narration would both invite such a reading. This provides us with an important clue to the scene's centrality to the noir cycle, for its "noirness" lies precisely in the connection between mise en scene and mental states: here the connotation of entrapment carried by earlier scenes (the murder of Roslyn, the man on the train, even the iconography of the street outside) is transferred to a scene which plays upon the connotative value of certain established genre conventions (the space of a lonely hotel room, the chiaroscuro effect of a

Flgure 19   Figure 20

flashing light) and the denotative value of aural narration. Yet, unlike countless similar
scenes in other films noirs, this scene draws attention to this connection through an
unusual narration which comments on its "meaning" (similar narration could be found
in many radio dramas of the period, though the device itself goes back at least to Poe).

Beyond this simple correspondence between "outer" and "inner" states, however,
this scene provides a major channel for the passage of those enigmas which sustain the
"mystery" of the discourse. And its pivotal place within the discourse is determined
precisely by the way its aural and visual "codes" engage in a network of syntagmatic
and paradigmatic relationships. For example, though no narrative bond exists as this
point between Steve Howard and Press, a syntagmatic one does and it is strengthened
by the similarity of metonymic markers (Figures 9 and 14): each smokes a cigarette
suspiciously; each face is strobed by a bright light (due respectively to the effects of
passing lights on the train window and the flashing neon sign); each thus carries a connotation of duality which extends backward and forward into the film chain (though
the narrative will ultimately relieve Howard of any criminal guilt). Now the denotative
value of the aural cue associated with Howard (Figure 9)—that the unsuspected could
be "hiding out in some dark hole . . . listening with terror to the voice of his own conscience"—can be read with greater precision into the image of Press (Figure 14). Just
as the remark with which Grandison concludes his broadcast—that the killer will finally make one mistake and then "the lightning of justice will strike the unsuspected"—could read into either image with equal precision.

In this respect it seems significant that at the very moment Press' attention is di-
verted to the neon sign (Figure 16) Rains' voice refers to the guilty party "hiding his
evil behind the calm mask of the unsuspected" (which Grandison himself does best)
and the duality articulated in that remark evokes the important paradigmatic association between Grandison and Press (e.g., Figures 1 and 16). Press is also syntagmatically
joined, via a dissolve (Figures 18–20), to the reflection of another unknown man (Fred
Clark, later identified as police detective Richard Donovan) who is in the process of
inspecting Grandison's mail. On one level this man joins the company of the "unsus-
pecteds" quite easily, since his image is marked by Rains' oral cue that "he might even
come into my own home." But more importantly his inverted image on a table top

Figure 21   Figure 22

(Figure 19) forms a paradigmatic axis that extends backward through Press and Howard to the first such image in the opening segment (Figure 1), an axis whose articulation of ambiguity is considerably abetted by a consistency of lighting tonalities.

Indeed, the dissolve (Figure 19) which logically should have signified the conclusion of the sequence simply extends that axis syntagmatically in order to throw suspicion, at least temporarily, on several other characters. It accomplishes this by using the diegetically-grounded broadcast to motivate syntagma constructed of a number of direct cuts (not all pictured here): Donovan, listening to the broadcast as he goes through the mail; a bartender, listening to a radio prior to serving a drink to a morose man seated at the bar; Hurd Hatfield, later identified as Althea's huband, Oliver Keane (Figure 20); Press in his hotel again (Figure 21); a well-dressed party of people (Figure 22) listening to the broadcast until it concludes and Althea (identified by name and "suspicious" gesture in the film's opening sequence) shuts off the radio with the comment: "Victor is the only man I know who can turn my blood into ice water" (an apt comment since Victor literally "turns her blood cold" by shooting her). Finally, the conclusion of the broadcast, which marks the end of one segment and the beginning of another occurs in the Frazier mansion, the locale of the opening murder and the center of the diegesis, a fitting symbol for the material wealth which prompts the major series of narrative events (Grandison's chain of murders).

While the diegetic progress of Grandison's broadcast would seem to ground this sequence in a chronological order, it is quite clear that the sequence itself does little to advance the narrative, its major purpose being to create those "codes" of suspense that sustain the discourse. Despite its careful placement with the diegesis, the use of Claude Rains' voice draws upon a broad range of narrative, aural and cinematic conventions to give him the "authority" of an omniscient narrator, thereby diverting attention away from Grandison's guilt. It also manages to syntagmatically connect the lives of six major characters (Grandison, Howard, Press, Donovan, Oliver, Althea) whose ambiguities will ostensibly be worked out through the narrative. We have, for example, previously commented upon the metaphoric and metonymic functions of shadow and reflection. Their first significant use occurs when Grandison's shadow falls over the portrait of his ward, Matilda Frazier: she is ostensibly dead, so now "Grandee"

(Matilda's significant pet name for what is obviously her substitute father) has a freer hand to acquire her estate, thereby precipitating the chain of murders, all of which are marked by his shadow. When Steve Howard first arrives at the Frazier mansion pretending to be the "dead" Matilda's husband, his shadow too falls over the portrait. After Matilda is found alive but amnesiac, the mysterious Howard convinces her that he is her "husband," figuratively displacing "Grandee's" paternal role (literally also, since the two eventually do fall in love). There is a logic in Grandison's efforts to eliminate Howard that goes beyond self-interest and another which dictates that it should be Press who must subdue Howard and lock him in a trunk for later disposal (thus prompting the chase and last-minute rescue).

For Press has become Grandison's unwilling accomplice because of an event which took place prior to the diegesis: Grandison had secretly recorded Press' admission that he had taken part in a murder and has been using this record to blackmail Press into helping him. In some respects Press is the most pathetic of Grandison's victims, at one point even begging Grandison to leave him alone because he does not want to be party to any more murders. It would certainly appear as if Press were the subject of Grandison's first broadcast (this is never made explicit), and there is a strong implication that the broadcast itself is meant as a veiled threat, forcing Press back into Grandison's sphere of control (he "shows up" in Grandison's office shortly afterwards). If this is so, then the increasingly subjective series of shots which alter the hotel sign from PEEKSKILL to SKI to KILL dictates a denotative reading: it is quite literally a sign which is a command.

At the same time its placement within a scene of pivotal importance to that network of relationships which we have already sketched out bestows upon it hermeneutic status. Press of course has replaced Howard as a putative "unsuspected" in the syntagmatic chain (Grandison-Howard-Press-Donovan-Oliver-Althea), each member of which is a potential "killer" or victim ("killed"), with the possible exception of Donovan. As we have demonstrated the first four members are also closely associated by the paradigmatic axis of visual metaphors (Donovan's ambiguous "dualism," however, is rather tidily resolved). Both Grandison and Press are in fact killers, though Press is forced into accepting the "responsibility" for Grandison's acts; Steve Howard displaces Grandison as Matilda's surrogate father and he in turn is almost eliminated by Press. It seems a formal necessity then that it be police detective Donovan (whose inverted images closes that particular paradigmatic axis and who, with the deaths of Oliver and Althea, survives to "close" the syntagmatic axis) who rescues Howard at the last moment. Appropriately, the arrival of Donovan at the radio studio where Grandison is beginning another show marks the end of Grandison's career, and it is Donovan's nod of approval that allows Grandison to complete his final broadcast and thus close the narrative. Grandison is again narrating a tale of an unsolved crime and at the sight of the police he reveals to the audience that he himself is the "unsuspected" of that evening's tale. And if we "read" the gloved hands which hold the radio script upon which the opening credits of The Unsuspected are printed as belonging to Grandison, then he is constituted as the "author" of the film and his radio audience ourselves as we are caught up in the play of its discourse.

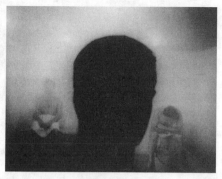

FIgure 23   Figure 24

Despite the naturalism of its diegetically motivated sound and its location exteriors, the broadcast sequence of *The Unsuspected* remains a formative exercise quite characteristic of the film noir in the consistent mannerism of exterior and interior locales and in the relationship of "setting" to "mental states." If this is typical of what are today considered to be "classical" films noirs, it is hardly less typical of those police "documentaries" which deserve to be included within the cycle, for the "realism" of their stories and settings is not at odds with the cycle's essential expressionism. It is not just in the interests of symmetry, therefore, that I have included the final two frames (Figures 23 and 24) which have been taken from *T-Men,* one of the more renowned semi-documentaries of the cycle. Indeed, the great popular success of *T-Men* helped to confirm a number of those conventions associated with this "realism," among them the use of location photography and an often unseen narrator. Such a narrator is typically the primary authority for authenticating story and setting, and while the unseen narrator here (actually Reed Hadley) does just that, his cinematic function is to bridge the visuals and to help establish "mood." Thus, aside from the fact that its source is extra-diegetic, this voice is quite similar in function to that of Claude Rains' in the broadcast sequence of *The Unsuspected:* indeed, within that diegetic world even Grandison guaranteed the "authenticity" of his tales. Typical of the work of photographer John Alton, *T-Men's* location exteriors certainly rival those of *The Unsuspected* in terms of both their expressionism and "psychological" overtones. The frames illustrated here are part of a time-compression montage in which agent O'Brien (Dennis O'Keefe) must call on a number of Los Angeles steam baths in an effort to locate the "Schemer," a member of a gang of counterfeiters. The expressionistic photography is rather evident, and together with the use of formative editing techniques (Figure 24) and Paul Sawtell's score (which is more innovative and minatory than Franz Waxman's for *The Unsuspected*) the steambath interiors are given an unmistakable infernal dimension. Indeed, a similarity of music and décor maintain this connotation in the scene in which Schemer is scalded to death. Thus the "realism" of a montage such as that illustrated here is little more than a Hollywood convention, reinforced (as here) by the presence of a voice-over narration.

Annie (Peggy Cummins) and Bart (John Dall) hiding out from a society whose rules they have transgressed in *Gun Crazy*.

Gun Crazy (1950)

Gary Johnson

> Bart, I've never been much good—at least up till now I haven't. You aren't getting any bargain, but I've got a funny feeling that I want to be good. I don't know. Maybe I can't. But I'm gonna try. I'll try hard, Bart. I'll try.

Poor Bart. He's got a thing for guns and when he meets a woman who loves guns also, he's smitten for life. But as the carnival clown tells him: "Some guys are born smart about women and some guys are born dumb ... You were born dumb." And thus starts his downward spiral in one of the greatest B movies ever made, *Gun Crazy*. Directed by Joseph H. Lewis, *Gun Crazy* is anything but typical film noir. It's a stylish, exhilarating rush of startling camera work and amazing characterizations. Its audacious visual style makes *Gun Crazy* as fresh today as it was nearly fifty years ago.

And the story is quintessentially American—a Bonnie and Clyde–like saga of two lovers who go on a robbery spree across several states. Bart and Annie Laurie Starr first meet at a carnival. He's fresh out of the Army, where he tired of the routine. Back in his hometown, he's taking in the carnival with his two old school chums, when they stop at a sideshow shooting exhibition. And Laurie struts forward onto the stage, dressed in a cowgirl outfit and firing her pistols—pow! pow! pow!—over her head. Sparks fly from the pistols and smoke curls toward the ceiling. She sees Bart in the first row, and her eyes eagerly size him up, head to toe, the way a sailor on leave might size up a woman at a bar. And she grins—a delicious, devious grin—that suggests she'd just love to eat him all up. Bart watches from the edge of his chair, rapt and already in love as she performs her shooting tricks.

He jumps at the chance to join her on stage in a shooting match. They prowl around one another like two dogs sniffing out each other's goods. In an interview with Danny Peary (*Cult Movies*, New York: Delacorte Press, 1981), director Lewis revealed his instructions to actors John Dall (Bart) and Peggy Cummins (Laurie Starr):

> I told John, "Your cock's never been so hard," and I told Peggy, "You're a female dog in heat, and you want him. But don't let him have it in a hurry. Keep him waiting." That's exactly how I talked to them and I turned them loose. I didn't have to give them more directions.

And that's exactly how they played it.

For both John Dall and Peggy Cummins, these are the performances of their careers. Dall also starred in *The Corn is Green* (for which he received an Academy Award nomination for Best Supporting Actor) and Alfred Hitchcock's *Rope*, and Peggy Cummins would star in the excellent horror movie *Curse of the Demon* (directed by Jacques Tourneur); but neither actor ever came close to capturing the same degree of devotion to character. They create two people who desperately need one another, two lovers who can't hardly survive without the other. "We go together, Laurie," says Bart. "I don't know why. Maybe like guns and ammunition go together."

The scene that best illustrates the total conviction in Dall and Cummins' performances is also one of the most ballyhooed scenes in the movie: a single take episode where Bart and Laurie rob a bank. All the while, the camera never leaves the back seat of the getaway car. Many writers have commented on the audaciousness of filming the entire sequence in just one take—and it indeed does give the sequence a documentary-like realism—but it's Dall and Cummins that really make the scene work. We watch them from the back seat as they nervously drive around the city block, looking for a parking space near the bank. It's a busy day and cars are everywhere. Dall and Cummins talk to one another like an old couple—in dialogue that must have been ad-libbed it's so spontaneous. Dall sits on the edge of his seat, his eyes groping for a parking place, while Cummins twists and turns behind the wheel. And later as they speed away from the crime scene, we see Cummins as she looks back and sees no cars are following. She grins broadly, a beautiful, deadly grin that is full of delight and danger.

Dall and Cummins are perfect for each other. Dall's innately weak and troubled Bart finds a perfect mate in Cummins' thrill-seeking Laurie Starr ("I want things. A lot of things. Big things."). Of course, no good can come from their union, but while it lasts they give each other a lifetime of thrills. And while Cummins does indeed lead Bart into a life of crime, teasing him with sex and luring him with her proclamations of love, she eventually falls in love with him.

In another of the movie's great scenes, we see Bart and Laurie after they pull a major payroll heist. Their plan calls for them to split up and meet again in three or four months. They each jump in separate cars and start to drive away, but then they look back and stop. They turn around and Bart leaves his car on the side of the road. He grabs his suitcase and runs to Laurie. They embrace like long lost lovers, and we see that wonderful, beautiful, obsessive smile of Laurie again. Pure ecstasy. It's not just love in her eyes. It's the thrill of totally possessing Bart. That's what really gets her off. To totally possess the poor sap. For Laurie, that feeling is exhilarating. Hell, it's even better than sex. And maybe that's why she loves him—because here's one poor sap that'll do whatever she wants and yet still be totally devoted to her. He might complain about their life of crime, that they can never ask anyone for help ever again, they're totally on their own, but that's part of Laurie's plan. To isolate themselves in their own world, which thrives on their need for each other in order to survive. Yes, she truly loves the guy. But it's a twisted, perverse brand of love, albeit it's all she can manage. Initially she just wants Bart for sex. And initially she probably plans to just use and discard him, the same way she used and discarded the carnival manager. (In an early scene, we see Laurie getting gussied up for a night out with Bart, while the carnival manager sits on her sofa and watches, powerless to stop her.) But eventually she comes to depend on Bart's presence and then she loves him.

For director Lewis, *Gun Crazy* remains a testament to his brilliant use of the camera (cinematography by Russell Harlan). Lewis was never satisfied with just filming two characters talking. His camera dips low in one take and then soars high in the next, constantly searching for unexpected and enlightening perspectives. In one scene, we see the young Bart as his boyhood friends are in the hills, when they spot a mountain lion. They urge Bart to shoot the cat so they can claim the bounty. But Bart isn't a killer and he won't fire. Another boy grabs the gun away from him. In the foreground, we see Bart's fist clench and tighten as the other boy, visible in the background, jerks the trigger and sends shots skittering across the rocks. Lewis uses the whole frame to constantly give us information about the characters and the situations. In *Gun Crazy,* he found the perfect vehicle for his visual style, as the stylish, kinetic camerawork captures the destructive, crazed amour of the story.

Gun Crazy is one of the great American movies, a giddily romantic story of two people who thrive off of each other and only completely come to life when in each other's presence. Some people might call *Citizen Kane* the great American movie. I might just opt for *Gun Crazy* instead.

Above, the end is near for this fugitive couple (Peggy Cummins and John Dall) in *Gun Crazy*. Below, Bart Tare (John Dall) tries once again to restrain the violent/erotic instincts of his partner in crime and love, Annie Laurie Starr (Peggy Cummins).

Violently Happy: *Gun Crazy* (1950)

Adrian Martin

Once upon a time, movies began like this: with a depopulated view of some street scene or landscape or inanimate object, just sitting there timelessly while the credits roll and the main musical theme plays. At the start of *Gun Crazy* it is raining, and we are angled toward an empty, urban corner. Then at last, after this Antonioni-esque contemplation, fiction begins with a bold, brisk stroke. A troubled, intense looking boy enters the frame. He stares at the guns in a shop window. He smashes the glass, takes the coveted object. He runs and falls and the gun skids along the ground—right up to the feet of a cop. Anguished looks. The rain on the boy's face.

It is important to stay close to the purity, and the materiality, of this magnificent, delirious film. It is a movie of "eternal moments," instants that flare up and smack you without much prior explanation. A movie of close-ups: dark brooding poems of excited faces caught in paroxysmic expressions, heads cradled together in exhaustion, mouths colliding with an urgent, desperate desire. A movie with bold, explosive accelerations of figural style, those bravura shots and long takes that buffs love to fetishize: most amazingly, the bank robbery scene filmed in one shot, an overexposed landscape flying past the front windscreen, with the camera mounted in the back seat of the car, suddenly darting forward and looking to the right for a bit while the action plays on outside the car, and then snapping back to first position. A movie full of running, falling, colliding bodies in whip-track, full-frame motion. A movie whose astonishing short-cuts, condensations, abbreviations and ellipses of plot and staging—born, of course, from extreme economy of means—today look positively Bressonian.

And once upon a time, main characters in films were introduced like this: a big intro from a sleazy sideshow barker, followed by a frame that's empty for a split second, the camera angled up at some indifferent bit of ceiling, and then a woman's arms moving forward and filling the frame, her hands shooting guns with flair and precision, and then her face, wild and passionate, frozen and imprinted on my brain for eternity in these few precious frames.

Who are the main characters in *Gun Crazy,* these B-cinema icons with the names Barton Tare (John Dall) and Annie Laurie Starr (Peggy Cummins)? They have a kind of psychology, and even a bit of "backstory," but they are mainly essential, elemental, driven, diagrammatic beings. They are both defined by their extreme emotional relation, and reaction, to guns. For Bart guns are not a means to killing; as his sister cryptically comments in an early court scene, "it's something else about guns that gets him." He loves to collect and maintain guns, and he loves to shoot mobile objects with great dexterity, but the prospect of killing any living being veritably paralyses him. (Brilliant gestural detail: the way the teenage Bart anxiously clenches his fist, in the foreground of a composition, each time his pal shoots at a nearby animal.) In a pretty straightforward way, guns order Bart's life and channel his energies in a way that seems almost normal: they are what he loves, what he does best.

Annie has a different kind of "object cathexis," one that looks a little more openly obsessive and dangerous. She clearly gets a transgressive kick out of firing guns (with only one match-head less dexterity than Bart). But the moment of murder is the crucible for her, too: she shoots to kill whenever fear overwhelms her, whenever she is seized hysterically by the threat of loss. What is she afraid of losing? Her life, her set-up, her shot at the big pay-off. And—more intensely and movingly as the film develops—her man.

It is important to say, before pop-Freudianism overtakes us too quickly, that for neither of these characters is gun craziness primarily a matter of libidinal release or phallic grandeur. Although, it is true, Bart does say that he and his beloved can't seem to ever split up, because "we go together, Laurie, I don't know why—maybe like guns and ammunition go together". And *Gun Crazy* is, no doubt about it, a fantastically sexy film. "I'm yours, and I'm real": Cummins makes the final word in that line sound like the sweetest, dirtiest thing you've ever heard in your life. And the immortal scene—whose charge is now doubled for me by its precise placement in another hot and nervy classic, Jim McBride's remake of *Breathless* (1983)—where Annie sprawls on the bed horizontally in her dressing gown, casually threatens to leave Bart, and then commands him: "Let's finish it the way we started it—on the level".

A decade ago, I used to think of *Gun Crazy* as a film about the death-drive. A film about *amour fou* and what happens to it once it cuts free from all the typical supports of "normal" society (such as the dreary nuclear family incarnated here around the figure of Bart's sister). A paean to lawlessness, and suicidal last runs, and a desire that burns around in the night until it is consumed by its own fire—if it is not, before that point, hunted down and eradicated by law-abiding representatives of the reality-principle (embodied in this tale by Bart's two boyhood chums, who only want a quiet town). More pop-Freud, of course, with a touch of normative lament or regret or nostalgia about it—the sort of sentiment that will fill many (most) subsequent "lovers on the run" movies, from *Bonnie and Clyde* (1967) and *Thieves Like Us* (1974) to *Thelma and Louise* (1991).

Gun Crazy ends up in a spooky, nightmarish swamp. But its final, gun-firing tragedy happens so fast and furiously that it disappears without the usual requiem of pained, elegiac, moral reflection. Joseph H. Lewis' masterpiece does not seem to me, today, a reflective, funereal, troubled film at all. There is something far more transparent, straighter, "on the level" about it.

What genre is *Gun Crazy*? Like many great films, it is between genres, among genres, and of no genre. It effortlessly displaces itself from the film noir properly speaking, and that genre's gothic enigmas, ambiguous femmes fatales and labyrinthine narrative intrigues. It is not a thriller or a mystery or an action film or a crime film, nor any kind of ordinary drama or melodrama.

In a way, I think it asks to be taken more than anything as a love story, the story of a couple—even more strongly and eccentrically, as a story of marriage. Annie and Bart hardly even get close to a separation or even an argument in this film. It is not a tale of betrayal or deceit, the waning of a thrill or the ending of a dream. The *amour fou* between these two burns clear and pure for virtually the entire film, and certainly unto death. There is a wildly corny scene, at a turning point in the narrative after their biggest heist, in which Annie and Bart tear off (as they have agreed) in two separate cars in two different directions along the same road. But they are both compelled to slam on the brakes, and he wheels around, drives back, abandons his jalopy and piles into the driver's seat of her car. She holds and kisses him, then, as he speeds forward, pragmatic thoughts casting no dark shadows over his beaming face. Has there ever been a simpler, more affecting picture of joy and togetherness than this?

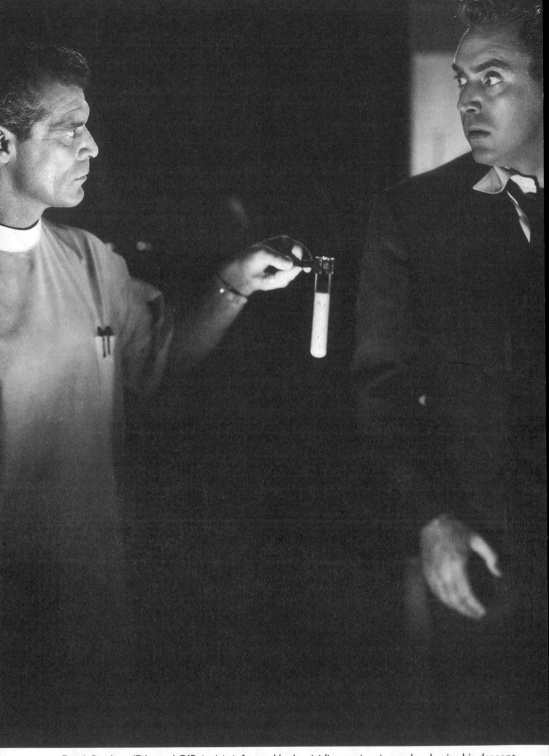

Frank Bigelow (Edmond O'Brien) is informed he has iridium poisoning and so begins his descent into the fatalistic and often absurd world of noir in *D.O.A.*

The War of the Sexes:
Men in Film Noir and *D.O.A.* (1950)

Beverley Carter

> Once masculine anxiety can no longer be displaced onto the female subject the
> prospect is indeed bleak, one might say tragic.[1]

The male protagonist in *D.O.A.* (1949, USA: Rudolph Mate) embodies the roles of both
the hero and the victim. Frank Bigelow (Edmond O'Brien) appears as the victim of a
fatal poisoning, yet he has no clue as to who committed the crime and why. He has no
longer than one week to live, meaning he must play the role of the hard-boiled detective and piece together the puzzle of his murder. He is then driven to find this faceless killer and reap his revenge. This initial break in narrative equilibrium, illustrated in
the protagonist's impending death, established Bigelow as the paranoid male. This type
of character often appears in the sub-text of noir films, due to the time in which these
films were made. During the late 1940s and early 1950s, the people of America witnessed men returning home from the Second World War (1939–1945) to a changed
society and many young men found this change difficult to adjust to. Their wives were
doing their jobs, their children had grown up in a matriarchal environment and their
country had altered. Coupled with the feelings of post-war trauma, which was discovered by the new found interest in "pop" psychology, these young soldiers came home
with an immense feeling of alienation, both towards women and other men. As Bruce
Crowther states further,

> On their return to America these young men found it less easy than they had
> hoped to fit back readily into society. Their feeling of alienation was aggravated by
> a measure of disillusionment.[2]

In a social and historical context, Bigelow's paranoia can be argued as a source of male
anxiety formed by returning to the domestic space after being at war. It can be argued
that this anxiety is illustrated in the mise-en-scène of the noir film, as "the dark streets
become emblems of alienation; a figure's unrelenting gaze becomes obsessive; the entire environment becomes hostile, chaotic, deterministic."[3]

These men of the 1940s and 1950s had changed lives, homes and wives. The death
and destruction that they witnessed during the war had altered their minds and
their place within societies clearly ordered structure. The roles that were known to

them, of husband, father and provider had been distorted while they were taken away from their home environment. The only possible way these men could cope with normal everyday life was to bring elements of the war they had witnessed into it. This war was in the form of "inter-personal" relations between men who were fighting to regain their social dominance, with the main focus on their altered gender roles.

The women in wartime and post-war America had made these men redundant from their traditional and known roles, causing their paranoid anxiety to further affect their minds and lives. This anxiety that men felt towards women in this era can be argued as being embodied in the Femmes Fatale, a common figure in the noir film. These women had taken their roles as provider (in the workplace) and father (in the home). A readjustment to normality appeared to be impossible, as the women had coped so well with their new found gender roles. However, men had the option of over-exaggeration of their masculinity and a reassertion of their patriarchal dominance. But, other men stood in their path towards rehabilitation. The older men in America's fragile post-war society, unable to serve in the war had taken over as the self-appointed leaders of the patriarchal norm. These older men represented a type of masculinity that defied law; they were controlling the law, in both normal society and in the depths of the underground. They felt somewhat superior to the men who were at war. This can be seen as "social stratification," where a person is conditioned by their cultural environment.

In D.O.A., the war of the sexes is inter-personal and focuses on Bigelow's interaction with other men. It can be argued that he is a victim of patriarchy, as older, gangster men dominate him and his environment. Therefore, the war of the sexes for men was against each other; they were fighting a battle of power and authority; and a battle against themselves.

Bigelow's anxiety is not placed onto any women in the film; therefore his paranoia is displaced onto that of the inter-personal relationships he forges with the men he encounters on his quest for personal justice through the under-belly of society. These men he meets are underground gangsters, a band of men rebelling against the known social order of rationality. They hide behind false names and the façade of business dealings, one of which is the purchasing of the poison that kills Bigelow, which remains an enigma throughout the narrative. These men have created their own "othered" group, thus placing them outside the laws that govern society. However, this group is governed by, what Jacques Lacan calls the "Law of the Father." This is when a man "identifies with the authority of the father, rather than seeking to challenge it or run the risk of refusing it by adopting a transgressive feminine position."[4] This is illustrated in the hierarchy of men involved who control the urban city of D.O.A. Majak (Luther Adler) is the man who buys the stolen "Iridium," which is the cause of Bigelow's involvement in this uncertain environment. Majak's henchman, Chester (Neville Brand), who represents his status in the world of the underground, is described as, ". . . an unfortunate boy. He's psychotic, he likes to inflict pain, likes to see blood." The character of Chester also represents how this band of gangster men are outside the law. These men, along with Halliday (William Ching) who is the ultimate villain and killer of Bigelow, causes the inter-personal war between Bigelow and the men of the underground.

Bigelow is forced into the under-belly of society, through the acts of these aforementioned gangsters. He enters a world where "men are tested."[5] A different law governs this underworld, which is a "... world of violence and lawlessness, lacking any intrinsically effective machinery of civilised order, and dominated by assertive masculine figures of self-appointed authority."[6]

Even when Bigelow is within this underworld filled with fatal women and murderous men, he is characterised as the (anti) hero. This type of character represents a shift from the hero-detective, played by Humphrey Bogart. This shift made way for the non-heroic and anxious men in these later noir films. However, the notion of being a hero in film noir is somewhat shady. "The word hero never seems to fit the noir protagonist, for his world is devoid of the moral framework necessary to produce the traditional hero."[7]

A noir hero is almost always an anti-hero, thus embodying the antithesis of the traditional, Hollywoodian style hero. "Every noir hero is an alienated hero."[8] Bigelow is alienated from his home town of Banning, which is interpreted as "suggesting the self-repression involved in such an existence."[9] He is also separated from his conventional girlfriend, Paula (Pamela Britton), in order for him to take a vacation to San Francisco, where he can be seen "... throwing himself into the hedonistic pleasures of urban high-life (signified by "hot" jazz and "available" women.)"[10] This separation can be argued as his denial to commit to a traditional relationship with Paula.

Taking it back to the beginning, the narrative commences with Bigelow staggering into a police station stating,

BIGELOW: I wanna report a murder.

OFFICER: Where was this murder committed?

BIGELOW: San Francisco, last night.

OFFICER: And who exactly was murdered?

BIGELOW: I was!

This initial statement causes immediate disequilibrium to the narrative: as we meet a fatal flaw; the protagonist is dying. The typical strong male character of the noir hero is portrayed as weak, fragile and "soft in the belly." A poison dropped into Bigelow's bourbon by the murderous Halliday, causes his weakness, his paranoia and his death. Bigelow's story is depicted in flashback, through the events that have caused his murder. He is the detective and the victim of this crime. "The moment of knowledge is simultaneously the moment of death; his triumph as detective-hero coinciding with his eradication."[11] The notion of Bigelow solving the puzzle of his murder just before his death illustrates the macabre edge that the noir film embodies. Bigelow embodies the role of the victim, due to his death sentence. However, he also plays the role of hero-detective through the solving of his own murder. As Borde and Chaumeton state, "In every sense of the word, a noir film is a film of death."[12]

The narrative travels back to the melodramatic scene, where Bigelow and his girl-friend and secretary, Paula, are discussing their business plans in the office. The character of Paula represents a radical shift for women of the 1940s. She is seen as having an equal voice to Bigelow's, while they are in the work environment. Men are usually isolated at work, in a place where they can escape the private sphere and their traditional roles. At work, men could be men. When introduced to the character of Paula, we see that she is pressuring Bigelow for a serious commitment, to conform to a "normal" heterosexual marriage in a small town for the rest of their lives. However, Paula understands his fears as she states, "You're just like any other man, you have the feeling of being trapped, hemmed in and you don't know whether or not you like it." It can be argued that Paula has a dual purpose in the narrative. Firstly, she is Bigelow's social conscience, telling him what he should do, in order to conform to society's norms. Secondly, she lets him go to San Francisco, allowing him to be free from conventionality and the restraints of a heterosexual relationship. This is not the typical scenario of a noir relationship, which normally centres on men being ensnared by fatal women, not homely, nurturing women, as Krutnik states,

> The noir hero frequently agonises about whether or not the woman can be trusted, whether she means it when she professes love for him, or whether she is seeking to dupe him in order to achieve her own ends.[13]

In effect, Frank's business trip to San Francisco can be seen as him breaking out of the traditional gender roles of husband, provider and eventually father, which is to be forced upon him by Paula's ideals for a traditional relationship. However, it is the men in this new and unstable environment he finds himself in who are the instigators of his downfall, not Paula.

The manner in which Bigelow interacts with the other characters, both male and female changes as he comes closer to death. His desperation causes him to become violent (disavowing his weak feminine tendencies) towards anyone who stands in his path and paranoid about everything that appears to be outside his normal environment. He cannot cope with being outside the norm, outside the law and out of control. While Bigelow is within the protective space of home and work, when he is with Paula, he is in the traditional role of worker and soon-to-be husband, these are gender roles that he is familiar with and knows how to control. However, when he is thrown into the underworld, filled with seductive women, murderous men, cheap (poisoned) drinks and late night Jazz clubs, he is outside the traditional gender roles and the safe domestic sphere that he recognises. The environment of the club and the Jazz music itself embodies the fear of black culture "infecting" white normality. Therefore, it can be argued that Bigelow is punished for entering into the "othered" world of dangerous Jazz music. Another site for his anxiety is by being outside the normal patriarchal society where "masculinity, as an ideal, at least, is implicitly known."[14] Bigelow's masculinity is tried and tested through the means of disavowing all aspects of femininity. By repressing any elements of femininity, such as being gentle, kind, soft and so on, he can place himself into a new gender role, the tough "masculine" guy.

> Tough guys are men who don't back down, no matter how intimidating the circumstances may be... They are winners in a world of losers; in fact they are often losers from society's perspective who prove to the audience that they are indeed winners within the context of the film's narrative.[15]

During the film, Bigelow encounters many obstacles that force him to be a "tough guy," for example, when he meets Majak and Chester. He is hit in the stomach, has a gun thrust into his ribs, yet he does not show any fear. As Majak states, "He's not scared. You can tell by a man's eyes that he's scared." However, this happens after Bigelow has discovered he has a death sentence, he as nothing to lose, he is a desperate man. The point of realisation sees Bigelow run through a crowded street, sweating, dizzy, confused and disoriented. The poison heightens his fear and paranoia, along with the busy streets filled with unfamiliar and unhomely faces. Krutnik argues that the notion of Bigelow being away from home and outside the normal social realm as being a form of escapism.

> Contemporary American society becomes something to escape from rather than to "find's one's place" within—there is a strong sense in which it can be seen as failing in its obligations towards the individual.[16]

During the period in question, there were growing fears about the impending conflict of the Cold War. It can be argued that such events caused by male insecurity, at the highest level, created a new conflict in society, in effect, causing more male anxiety, surrounding their safety in this already unstable environment.

The gender crisis that is present in the society of the 1940s and 1950s can be seen through the "dissonant and schismatic representations of masculinity, as is suggested by the sheer number of noir tough thrillers in the mid-to-late 1940s."[17] While men in the 1940s and 1950s had an underlying feeling of alienation and separation from their female counterparts, on occasions, these feelings manifest in the way the detective-hero interacts with the femmes fatales. The fears and anxieties these men experienced, due to their changed gender roles and changed environment meant that they, sometimes, displaced their anger and frustration onto these women. For example, the violent femme fatale in *D.O.A.* is Maria Rakubian (Laurette Luez), the wife of Raymond, the mysterious nephew of Majak. Maria is just as corrupt as her husband is, as Bigelow states. "You're in this up to your pretty little neck." This was revolutionary for the time, where women were deemed to be passive, weak and subordinate to men. This gender shift is illustrated when Maria pulls a gun on Bigelow and states, "Don't get any ideas, 'cause I'm not afraid to use this." This misplaced aggression, which stems from her own insecurity surrounding her new found "masculine" role, inadvertently places Bigelow in the prominent position of authority once more. He is not intimidated by her threats and her guns and subsequently disarms her by overpowering her and throwing her into a submissive position on her bed. He asserts his dominance over her, but she is still violent and aggressive towards him, "If I were a man, I'd punch your dirty face in." This statement illustrates her desire for masculine power, her desire for the phallus. Her femme fatale status allows her to be sexually dominant and manipulative, yet not physically powerful. The threat that women in the narrative pose to Bigelow is small in comparison to the threat that men pose to him. The war of the sexes, in this noir film, is between men. The fight for power and control within society, power and control over women, power and control over each other, can indeed be fatal.

NOTES

1. Pat Kirkham and Janet Thumim, eds, *Me Jane: Masculinity, Movies and Women,* New York: St Martin's Pres, 1995, p. 16.

2. Bruce Crowther, *Film noir: Reflections in a Dark Mirror,* New York: Continuum, 1988, p. 157.

3. Alain Silver and James Ursini, eds, *Film Noir Reader,* New Tork: Limelight, 1996, p. 8.

4. Frank Krutnik, *In a Lonely Street: film noir, Genre and Masculinity,* London: Routledge, 1997, p. 78.

5. Steven Cohan and Ina Rae Hark, eds, *Screening the Male: Exploring Masculinities in Hollywood Cinema,* London: Routledge, 1993, p. 19.

6. Krutnik, p. 93.

7. Robert Porfirio (1976) cited in *Film Noir Reader,* p. 83.

8. Porfirio, p. 86.

9. Krutnik, p. 134.

10. Krutnik, p. 135.

11. Krutnik, p. 134.

12. Raymond Borde and Étienne Chaumeton, "Towards a definition of film noir," (1955) cited in *Film Noir Reader,* p. 19.

13. Krutnik, p. 63.

14. Cohan and Hark, p. 19.

15. James L. Neibaur, *The Tough Guy: An American Movie Macho.* Jefferson, North Carolina: McFarland, 1958, p. 91.

16. Krutnik, p. 55.

17. Krutnik, p. 91.

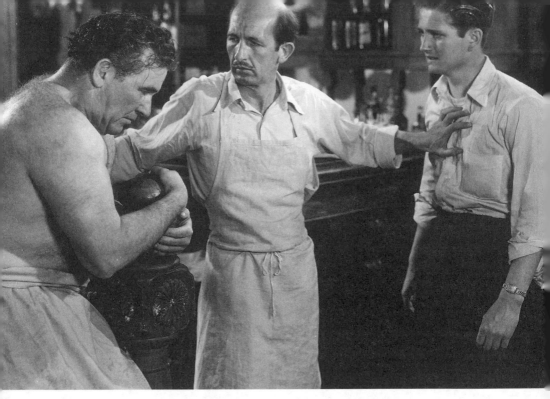

Above, the alternative nuclear family in *The Big Night*: a beaten and weak father figure (Preston Foster), a surrogate mother/mediator/bartender (Howland Chamberlain), and the angst-filled oedipal son (John Barrymore, Jr.). Below, Georgie (John Barrymore, Jr.) confronts the "castrator" of his father (Howard St. John) in *The Big Night*.

The Big Night (1951): A Naturalist *Bildungsroman*

Tony Williams

Joseph Losey's final American film *The Big Night* has not fared well over the years. Most commentators either regard it as a minor work or dismiss it preferring to concentrate on the more prestigious films Losey made after leaving Hollywood.[1] Like the director's significant reworking of Fritz Lang's *M* (1931) influenced by the plague-ridden era of the American blacklist[2], *The Big Night* is very much a film of its time. As a low-budget film noir it belongs to what British cultural historian Raymond Williams would describe as a significant "structure of feeling" defined by Thom Anderson in his essay "Red Hollywood." Anderson relates film noir to that lost opportunity of cinematic social commentary which became marginalized by McCarthyism.[3] Like Losey's *M* (1951), *The Big Night* is not currently available commercially in either DVD, theatrical, or video formats.

The Big Night was shot on a low-budget with no major stars, and suffered from the removal of scenarist Hugo Butler due to the blacklist. It was re-edited by the producer after Joseph Losey's hasty departure from America.[4] Due to these factors, the film may appear deficient and suffer in comparison with the director's more artistic European work. However, *The Big Night* is significant in several other ways. It not only represents a key example of that lost world of cinematic social possibility rejected by a Hollywood conforming to outside pressures but also another example of the diverse creative potentials existing within American film noir. As a product of collaborative authorship involving director, scenarists Hugo Butler and Ring Lardner Jr., and actors, *The Big Night* combines two significant literary and cinematic movements. It is both a key example of naturalist film noir as well as an urban *Bildungsroman* in its own right.

Despite New Critical assaults on American naturalism during the Cold War era, liberal and conservative critics were not entirely successful in their attempts to remove the radical social aspects of this tradition from the cultural landscape. Although writers such as Dreiser and Frank Norris became literary bêtes noirs within the American academy,[5] their work still flourished within the realms of a popular readership indebted to the radical cultural legacies of the American New Deal as well as reacting against the ideologically sterile conformism of the Eisenhower era. Although explicit social commentary became taboo in most American films of the 1950s, oppositional elements did exist within a literary and cinematic postwar cultural underground.[6] Film noir was just one of these elements. Furthermore, as Donald Pizer has often demonstrated, the radical aspects of American literary naturalism never died out. It was a movement inspired by the work of Emile Zola.[7] Although marginalized like the social fiction of Jack London during the Cold War era, the movement re-emerged after the demise of Lionel Trilling and other figures in Cold War New Criticism to play a prominent role in contemporary literature and film.[7] Stylistically, *The Big Night* is a film noir.

Alain Silver comments, "Although it is burdened with narrative structure that is at times self-consciously allegorical, *The Big Night* functions basically as film noir because of the relationship it establishes between the protagonist and his mutable environment. George's half-Odyssey, half-vendetta, which takes him through a series of unfamiliar settings—and metaphorically acts as a rite of passage from adolescence to adulthood—can be viewed from the same proletarian perspective as *Force of Evil*."[8]

The Big Night also shares many features common to literary naturalism. As Foster Hirsch notes, Zola and film noir may seem strange bedfellows. But there is an intrinsic connection between both.

"Noir also drew at least marginally on another literary tradition, that of naturalism as it was practiced early in the century by writers like Dreiser and Norris. Adapting to American settings and character types the philosophical premises developed in the later nineteenth century by Zola in France, the naturalist writers took a hard view of the consequences of the capitalist system. Their setting is the American city (Chicago in *Sister Carrie*, San Francisco in *McTeague*), their aim to chronicle in unsparing and minutely realistic detail the effects of the city's economic structure on its victims. Although the naturalists professed absolute detachment, their writing became feverish as it recorded their characters's inevitable corruption and decline. *Greed*, Erich von Stroheim's masterful adaptation of *McTeague*, contains both the sober, uninflected realism, and the occasional Expressionistic heightening that mark many of the naturalist novels."[9]

As noted by Silver, the film also, unconsciously, appropriates and reworks a feature common to classical literature, namely the *Bildungsroman* motif. Commonly associated with "eminent" texts such as Goethe's *Wilhelm Meister* which often focus upon the coming to age of bourgeois young males in pre-industrial society, the genre also displays more morbid and subversive patterns in works such as Stephen Crane's *The Red Badge of Courage* (1895) and Philip Caputo's *A Rumor of War* (1977). Although Henry Fleming earns his badge of "manhood," the entire novel criticizes Henry's initial perceptions as well as revealing the deadly nature of the world he now faces. Crane's message is entirely different from the Cold War Classics Illustrated version I read many years ago. It altered the original meaning to reflect patriotic conservative values in the same manner as Joseph L. Mankiewicz's 1958 ideologically appalling film version of Graham Greene's *The Quiet American*. In Crane's novel, Henry's apprenticeship will be by no means as easy as Wilhelm Meister's. By contrast, like many radical Vietnam war novels of its generation, *A Rumor of War* takes issue with the lies and mythologies which have formed part of an ideologically conservative cultural *Bildungsroman* to suggest alternative definitions. It is a process also seen in the work of Vietnam veteran writer and poet W.D. Ehrhart whose trilogy, *Vietnam-Perkasie: A Combat Marine Memoir* (1983), *Marking Time* (1986), and *Busted: A Vietnam Veteran in Nixon's America* (1995) represents another significant move in this direction. Unlike more literary minded figures accepted by the academy such as Tim O'Brien, whose *If I Die in A Combat Zone*

(1987) exhibits a conservative reluctance to depart from cherished myths, writers such as Ehrhart are never far removed from disturbing historical and political realities which often bar them from canonical acceptance.

The same thing was true for other writers such as Zola and Dreiser especially in periods of conservative reaction. Writing about the blacklist in 1970, Abraham Polonsky answered affirmatively in response to the question that an emerging social film movement was destroyed by McCarthyism in the later 1940s. "But it wasn't an aesthetic movement in the sense of surrealism as an aesthetic movement. Instead it was a generalized political awareness existing in a number of people who were trying to make films that reflected this awareness in one way or another when they had an opportunity to do."[10] This awareness need not be defined as exclusively political but may be extended to encompass a recognition of the dark side of American existence affecting many people living inside an American nightmare denied by the sentimental visions of Frank Capra and a conservative establishment. The Big Night is a "coming of age" drama. But it is completely different from certain recuperative Hollywood examples. Unlike youthful protagonists in Knock on Any Door (1949), The Wild One (1954), Six Bridges to Cross, and East of Eden (both 1955), who either reconcile their respective antagonisms to father figures by death or passive reconciliation, Georgie La Main (John Barrymore Jr.) experiences a traumatic Bildungsroman that eventually results in a more mature understanding of the adult world, his social position, and the dilemmas affecting his revered father Andy (Preston Foster). Although The Big Night may not be "radical" in a political sense, it does depart from the usual conservative climax of a "coming of age film." Georgie may finally face arrest with the possibility of prison time. But he has the advantage of living another day and gaining a much more mature understanding of complex and contradictory circumstances affecting his life than he had before. Finally, Georgie also takes responsibility for his own actions and does not allow others to again take the blame. At the climax, it is obvious that he has now become a fully mature youth who no longer needs others to conceal the grim realities of urban life from him.

Georgie experiences a personal apocalypse challenging his former naive perceptions of reality as equally devastating as the Civil War skirmishes experienced by Henry Fleming in The Red Badge of Courage. Suffering from an insecure sense of masculinity and revering his strong father Andy (Preston Foster), Georgie's world comes to a complete collapse one day when he witnesses his father's submissive compliance to a humiliating caning by local sportswriter Al Judge (Howard St. John). This traumatic event happens on Georgie's birthday. Psychologically affected by the shock of this event which radically alters his relationship to his father and his formerly secure environment, Georgie begins his "Big Night." He intends to avenge his father's humiliation and discover why this has happened. The psychologically devastated son has witnessed his father's symbolic castration before a group of people. He now embarks upon a dark psychological odyssey within the proletarian urban landscape of a New York completely different from most cinematic representations. Instead of the familiar Manhattan skyline which opens most New York films, the viewer encounters seedy diners, a ringside auditorium without any view of the big fight (which only lasts a few seconds), local bars, unglamorous nightclubs, socially alienated characters, and seedy tenements absent from most

glamorous images of the "Big Apple" in films such as *On the Town* (1949). In *The Big Night,*
New York is certainly no "wonderful town." Losey's images visually contradicts those
lines in *On the Town*'s opening chorus sung by Gene Kelly, Frank Sinatra, and Jules Mun-
shin. Georgie embarks on his own voyage of discovery which is both geographical and
psychological. But it is a threatening *Bildungsroman* which may finally undermine his fragile and insecure sense of personal identity. Traumatically cast adrift from his former relationship to his own father, Georgie encounters various "father figures" as well as
women struggling to survive in the urban jungle throughout the course of the film.
These women represent various aspects of his supposedly dead mother. Georgie also
regards Andy's missing girlfriend Frances as a substitute mother. At the beginning of the
film, neither Andy nor his partner Flanagan (Howland Chamberlin) answer Georgie's
question as to why Frances is not around any longer. During the course of the film
Georgie eventually moves from the position of naive adolescent to the mature youth
he will become at the film's climax when he learns of a family history which has previously been concealed from him. Although the film's actual climax is not as affirmative
as the traditional *Bildungsroman*, Georgie and his father eventually move towards understanding each other and resolve the conflict between them in a positive, rather than destructive, manner. It is not a happy ending in the typical Hollywood manner since both
father and son still have to face the consequences of *The Big Night.*

Andy La Main (Preston Foster) in cuffs tries to take the blame for his son's (John Barrymore, Jr.)
crime in the finale of *The Big Night.*

John Barrymore Jr.'s, character exhibits many the personal insecurities affecting him at the time of the film, Georgie also reveals many psychological traits common to that literary avenue of noir fiction represented by David Goodis and Cornell Woolrich. Rather than embodying the "tough guy" persona of hard-boiled counterparts such as Raymond Chandler, Dashiell Hammett, and Mickey Spillane, these writers focus upon elements of masculine insecurity which often originate from a confused sense of sexual identity. Although Georgie never falls into the masochistic behavioral patterns seen in Goodis and Woolrich, he appears very "feminine" and non-masculine throughout the entire film. As one character remarks, Georgie is an ideal babysitter whom baby can identify with, an unlikely role for characters such as Mike Hammer, Philip Marlowe, and Sam Spade.

The Big Night's opening shot shows a claustrophobic urban milieu. It symbolically depicts not only Georgie's adolescent crisis but also a threatening city landscape which Hirsch sees as common to both literary naturalism and hard boiled fiction. This imagery depicts the big city as a ferocious, suffocating place in which the lone person does not stand a chance due to the combined impact heredity and environmental forces.[11] A gas tank appears in the center of the frame at the end of a street dominated by two rows of buildings. Georgie enters the frame, looks back towards the camera and then moves towards the center before entirely disappearing from the image. This opening pre-credits shot associating Georgie with a gas tank suggests his future demise as a younger version of Cody Jarrett. In Raoul Walsh's *White Heat* (1949) James Cagney's Jarrett is another traumatically disturbed family victim who eventually achieves a personal apocalypse on top of a gas tank. Although Georgie does not appear to be a genetic victim of those biological forces predestinating the fates of Zola's Rougon-Macquart family group, he is, of course, the son of a father whose humiliating downfall results in a psychological crisis casting him adrift in the dark world of the big city. He is both a family and social victim. However, unlike literary naturalism whose victimized characters are unable to withstand the "collusion between personal failings—greed, lust, pride, all the deadly sins writ large—and those of capitalist society,"[12] Georgie does survive.

Like all significant works, *The Big Night* is a product of collaborative authorship. The film belonging to that group of Losey's pre-blacklist Hollywood films which all deserve detailed future analysis. But it also elicited Losey's sympathy for the psychological family dilemmas affecting John Barrymore Jr. as well as the director's own personal problems concerning his relationship to his own father.[13] Although the credits mention Losey and Stanley Ellin, author of the original source novel *Dreadful Summit*, as co-scenarists, blacklisted writers Hugo Butler and Ring Lardner Jr were actually responsible for the screenplay.[14] Actor input was also important. As Losey commented, John Barrymore Jr.'s psychological trauma resulting from "a kind of sad love affair with a father he never knew" as well as "a very ambiguous and strange relationship with his mother Dolores Costello"[15] contributed to his performance. Also, the presence of future blacklisted actors Dorothy Comingore and Howland Chamberlin resulted in fine performances suggesting a close involvement of Hollywood left wing actors fully aware of deeper meanings within the film. Like director and screenwriters, they were

conscious of the existence of disturbing dimensions existing beneath the official vision of the American Dream. Losey described Dorothy Comingore as "an extraordinary women" whose personal reaction to the blacklist was "very useful in that film."16
When her character meets Georgie she is immediately attracted by his naivete and
vulnerability as if recognizing qualities she possessed herself many years before until
the grim realities of the urban landscape finally resulted in her present cynical, hard
boiled persona. Chamberlin's Flanagan also sympathizes with Georgie's personal
dilemmas. Like Andy, he attempts to protect him from the unpleasant realities of existence as much as possible. The Big Night also contained a brief, but amusing performance, by Robert Aldrich. Although never blacklisted, his future work as director would
owe much to his formative experiences both with Enterprise Studios as well as his involvement with Losey on The Prowler and M.17 Although Losey completed the final cut
and scoring, his producer changed the original flashback structure of the film into a
"strictly chronological order" which the director felt was "very damaging to the
film."18 However, despite these reservations, The Big Night's significance is not entirely
ruined. In fact, it may work much better as a straightforward narrative since it is important to understand what motivates Georgie from the very beginning.

The viewer first sees Georgie as an awkward and shy bespectacled adolescent undergoing a humiliating assault on his fragile sense of masculinity and sexual identity.
Two boys spank him before a young girl, the blows corresponding to Georgie's actual
birthday. When they force him to kiss the girl, she refuses to comply. During this assault, Andy watches from the distance silently expressing disappointment at his son's
reaction but wisely deciding to refrain from intervening. When Georgie enters Andy's
bar, the customers tease him, "What's the matter? Tried to rush your education?" before Andy intervenes. Georgie then tells his father's employee Flanagan (Howland
Chamberlin) who has lived with them for sixteen years ("since my mother died")
about a barber's recommendation that he should now begin shaving. Andy then cur-
tails further jeering comments by his customers offering Georgie the use of his razor
any time he needs it. A bond of affection exists between father and son in spite of the
fact that many things are kept secret. Georgie notices that Andy has only bought two
tickets for a fight and remarks on the absence of Frances for over a week. Al and Flanagan exchange glances but do not answer Georgie. When the youth comments, "I liked
Miss Frances," he is abruptly told to "forget it." Andy then brings out a birthday cake.
Georgie is incapable of even performing the traditional role of blowing out all the can-
dles. One candle remains alight. Again, Andy silently expresses disappointment at his
son's failings. But the "Happy Birthday" refrains die down when sports journalist Al
Judge and two hired thugs enter the bar.

Their abrupt intrusion not only disrupts Georgie's birthday party but also represents the first of several traumatic incidents marking both an assault on the young-
ster's previous tentative relationship to his social environment as well as initiating a
successive chain of events which could result in death rather than rebirth. Prior to
Judge's entrance, Georgie had read his sports column with amusement. For him, Judge
is a successful figure in contrast to his father. However, succeeding events disrupt
Georgie's naive understanding in more ways than one. When Judge arrives at the bar,

Losey places the camera in a disturbing low angle position emphasizing Judge's cane in close up. Two threatening backs appear in the foreground at opposite ends of the frame while Georgie, Andy, and Flanagan are dwarfed in the background of this deep focus shot. Prevented by Flanagan from intervening, Georgie witnesses his father passively undergoing verbal and physical humiliation at the hands of Judge. Forced to strip to the waist and kneel down, Al meekly submits to a brutal beating, the meaning of which is a secret only shared by an adult world that Georgie has no participation in. The camera tracks in to a close-up of Georgie's head as Flanagan holds him down on the bar near his birthday cake. Georgie's spectacles fall from his eyes as the image metaphorically blurs to represent not just the collapse of Georgie's former world but also the fact that things will never be the same again. His revered father has meekly submitted to a brutal beating performed by another figure exercising a punitive patriarchal role. Since Andy refuses to reveal the reasons behind his submissive compliance as a sacrificial victim, Georgie decides to begin his "big night" to avenge both his father's humiliation as well as attempt to overcome his own insecure sense of masculinity. Advised by both Andy and Flanagan to "forget it," Georgie has no intention of doing so. He takes Andy's gun from the cash register, enters his father's room and puts on his oversized jacket and hat. Pausing briefly to taste a portion of his birthday cake, Georgie decides to use the two tickets for the fight and pursue his quarry.

By witnessing the humiliation of Andy who has fallen from his pedestal of revered Abrahamic patriarch to passive Isaac, Georgie decides to murder Al Judge's punitive father figure. Judge has exercised his own form of Judgment Day by demeaning a father before the eyes of a vulnerable son. Now the son seeks to become the father by pursuing an act of patriarchal vengeance to disavow the shameful spectacle of his actual father's symbolic castration. The way seems clear for a typical revenge tragedy involving Georgie's committing an act expected of him in a violent culture which will eventually send him to the death chamber like Nick Romano (John Derek) in *Knock on Any Door*. But the film sets up certain expectations only to eventually demolish them. *The Big Night* reveals a more challenging world of everyday reality for both hero and the audience to confront in which the expected solution proves to be not viable at all. Although the film's violent odyssey narrative may suggest a tragic end in common with the more bleaker examples of naturalism and film noir, the conclusion takes a different direction. Losey, Butler, Lardner, and their various collaborators have another goal in mind.

When Georgie visits Ehrlich's store, he finds owner and customers totally sympathetic to what has happened. Neighborhood cop Kennealy (Myron Healey) enquires about Andy and infers that he knows the real story adding that "if anything else happens, I'll know where to start looking." The customers also believe that Andy's behavior resulted from wanting to "square" a situation in "his own way." Desperate to borrow a quarter, Georgie ignores them. He wishes to play the role of a patriarchal tough guy, a performance contradicted both by his adolescent insecurity as well as his wearing Andy's jacket which is far too big for him. When persuaded by Ehrlich to baby sit for a few minutes, Georgie performs an early version of Travis Bickle's "You Talking to Me?" in *Taxi Driver* (1976) by playing a tough guy before a mirror until he awakes baby. He then clumsily cradles it in his arms along with the gun until Mrs Ehrlich arrives. Mr. Ehrlich tells Georgie that his baby "likes you" while Mrs Ehrlich remarks "You're a real father Georgie. The girl who'll get you will be the lucky one." These scenes reveal Georgie neither as a "sissy" nor a tormented gender victim from the dark galleries of David Goodis or Cornell Woolrich. Rather they show a young man of sensitivity who has other alternatives open to him other than the violent avenger he has chosen.

Searching for Judge in the boxing arena, Georgie encounters two other father figures whom will initially dominate him until he breaks away from them. The Big Night analyzes Georgie's initial inability to move away from dependence towards his eventual maturity and self-understanding. But to achieve this he must undergo a psychological odyssey in the naturalist and noir environments of seedy tenement buildings, prizefight arenas, and nightclubs. He sells one of his fight tickets to journalist professor Dr. Lloyd Cooper (Philip Bourneuf) who engages in slumming expeditions away from his family in Upper New York. Attracted by Cooper's deceptive urban sophistication, Georgie does not understand the true nature of his new-found mentor until much later. After selling Cooper the ticket, he is bullied into giving the $10 amount to Peckinpaugh (Emile Meyer) who masquerades as a plain-clothes policeman. Peckinpaugh represents the type of punitive father figure exemplified by Al Judge while Cooper embodies a treacherous patriarchal persona. When Georgie finally attends the fight, he misses the thirty-five second knock-out when searching for his father's trampled hat on the floor. Despite Georgie's wish to fit into his father's shoes (let alone, Andy's coat and hat) and avenge his humiliation, his attempts at doing so are pathetic. He really has to become his own person and The Big Night represents a tormented Bildungsroman he has to face within the naturalist and noirish dimensions of the urban landscape.

After accidentally assaulting the bullying Peckinpaugh in a restroom, Georgie again falls under the deceptive sway of the alcoholic Cooper who takes him to a nightclub and introduces him to his "girlfriend" Julie Rostina (Dorothy Comingore). Before meeting her, Georgie passes an ageing hooker who not only suggests the real nature of Julie's occupation but also symbolizes many of the "lost souls" he encounters on his "big night." We never meet Andy's girlfriend Frances. But we learn of her fate much later. The aged hooker, Julie, and black nightclub singer Terry Angeleus (Mauri Lynn) whom Georgie accidentally racially insults, represent various images of women trapped within the bleak confines of an urban environment offering no real security but only loneliness and death. When Georgie later meets Julie's sister Marion (Joan Lorring), she becomes also attracted by his naivete and sensitivity until alienated by his cruel behavior. She is also eight years older than he is and may end up like her sister. Georgie reveals his feelings of humiliation at the sight of his father's passive behavior to her. She attempts to make him understand that there are other alternatives open to him other than "to get even." Like Julie, she sees in him youthful potentials she once had and tries to influence him positively. But, traumatically affected by the spectacle of his father's humiliation, Georgie remarks, "Suppose that your father had heart and guts, that he was a real man and you were angry. Everybody just stood and laughed at him and he didn't do anything about it. What would you do?" However, during the actual beating and its aftermath, Andy's customers were certainly not laughing. They were actually shocked at the scene they witnessed. Georgie's comments reveals that he has projected his tormented feelings over Andy's humiliation to others rather than recognizing their origins within his own personal crisis of masculinity. During their second meeting, Marion tries to prevent Georgie's continuing self-destructive behavior and his inability to cope with witnessing his father's fall from grace in his eyes. When Georgie remarks, "How could he let Judge beat him," she answers, "That doesn't really matter. You can never try to make things right with a gun in your hand." However, he will not listen. As Losey remarked, Georgie's behavior towards all the women in the film result from the lack of affection he has experienced throughout his life and his relationship with a father who has never really expressed his feelings towards him.

"People who have been deprived for whatever reason, one way or another, are seeking the thing that they haven't got. In my opinion, people who are searching that way—as I am—are to a certain extent incapable of either giving or receiving the thing they want. if you want love more than anything else in the world, it's more than likely that when it's given to you, you don't know how to receive it."[19]

Despite Marion's detestation of Cooper and her feelings for the younger man, she, too, may end up like her sister (as well as the unseen Frances) by becoming a potential victim of the bleak noirish landscape. Any chance Georgie has for a continuing relationship with Marion ends when Cooper throws him out of Julie's apartment after he learns of the young man's involvement in Judge's murder. As in the lines of Terry's song, both Marion and Julie, are "too old to be lonely, too young to be loved." If Julie faces a bleak future embodied in the figure of the ageing prostitute Georgie passes in the nightclub, Marion may end up like her sister by enduring an unfulfilling relationship as the mistress of a married man by seeking to combat loneliness. Like Frances, her eventual fate may be much more tragic. All the women are mirror images in the film. As Marion tells Georgie, "We are all lonely, we've got to have somebody who knows what bothers us." Male characters are also affected by existential loneliness either as victims or victimizers. As Michel Ciment notes, Cooper initially takes Andy's place as an influential father figure. Both men also have mistresses.[20] Judge and Peckinpaugh resort to violence as if disavowing hidden personal insecurities. Judge feelings for his deceased sister appear more than fraternal while Peckinpaugh is really a grubby little grifter masquerading as a more powerful figure. Cooper performs the role of an educated sophisticated flâneur in New York's lower depths. But Marion and Julie see through his act and recognize him for what he really is. Julie merely tolerates him as a necessary antidote against urban loneliness.

Georgie's encounters with Cooper, Julie and Marion are important for his psychological odyssey. He enters a world he never knew existed but one relating to his own emotional dilemmas. Georgie not only eventually discovers the reasons why Judge beat Andy but also reaches a better understanding of his father's psychological torments as a victim of an urban landscape adversely affecting other characters in The Big Night.

Following the lead supplied by a newspaper copy-editor who hates Judge, Georgie arrives at an apartment building where he finds the name of Frances Sediasky. He then encounters Judge who not only informs him that Sediasky is the Polish word for Judge but also reveals that Frances was his own sister driven to suicide by Andy's refusal to marry her. When Georgie hears this, his desire for revenge ends. But he faces further retribution from Judge who attempts to use Georgie's accidental assault on Peckinpaugh and his intrusion into Frances' apartment to take further revenge on Andy. He intends to phone Andy to inform him of delivering his son to the police to face a fifteen year term of imprisonment for two counts of assault. Before he can do this, both men engage in a struggle for Andy's gun resulting in Judge's presumed death.

After being expelled from the Rostina apartment by Cooper whose actions echo Judge's betrayal, Georgie now returns to his real father. The camera cranes up Andy's bar and dissolves to an upstairs window showing a distraught father eager to take the blame for his son's activities during his disturbing big night. Andy removes his jacket from Georgie and puts it on to await the arrival of the police. However, despite Flanagan's pleas, Georgie finally reveals his newly-acquired mature sense of manhood and responsibility by confessing to Judge's murder. Although the arresting police officers inform him that Judge only sustained a minor injury, this revelation is less important than the final dialogue between father and son. Andy tells Georgie that he could not marry Frances because his mother was still alive. He obviously felt guilt over Frances's suicide and allowed Judge to beat him in an act of expiation. Neither Judge nor Georgie knew the full story which Andy now reveals. His wife left him for another man when Georgie was a baby while Andy was working long hours to keep his family together. Although Andy never mentions this fact, the harsh conditions of the Great Depression must have contributed towards this family trauma. Despite having grounds for divorce, Andy tells Georgie that he "kept on loving" his mother despite the fact that she was no good echoing Julie's barren relationship with Cooper. Georgie not only gains a better understanding of his father but also realizes that Andy has also shared the same type of existential despair and loneliness of Julie, Marion, and Terry. Andy also realizes his guilt in not trying to tell his son about his family history long ago. By being overprotective he has made his son more emotionally vulnerable than he would have been had he known the full story years before.

The Big Night ends on a positive note of reconciliation. Father and son walk off together with the police to face the consequences. As Alain Silver points out, this noir resolution "cannot be a simple and painless slap on the cheek."[21] Whatever happens, Andy and Georgie will still have to face the dangerous psychological world of the mean streets always ready to claim victims such as Frances and Julie. However, the son is now reconciled with the father and will not perish like those unfortunate members of Zola's Rougon-Macquart family tree in his epic series of twenty novels beginning with The Fortune of the Rougons and concluding with Dr. Pascal. Georgie has undergone his own Bildungsroman in the psychologically destructive worlds embodied within naturalistic and noir discourses influencing the film. But he survives to fight another day which is all that various characters featured in literary naturalism, film noir, and the films of Robert Aldrich can ever hope to do. For Joseph Losey, The Big Night was one of his Hollywood films which revealed his association with the radical dimensions of film noir. However, despite difference from his later work, Georgie's dilemma in The Big Night anticipate those more sophisticated personal challenges confronted by Losey characters in films such as The Sleeping Tiger (1954), Time Without Pity (1957), The Criminal (1960), Eva (1962), The Servant (1963), Secret Ceremony (1968), and The Go-Between (1970). All these films await further study in the light of Losey's formative apprenticeship within the pre-blacklist era of American film noir.

NOTES

1. Despite certain "Losey moments," David Caute regards The Big Night as being "inferior in almost every respect to his previous Hollywood films." See Joseph Losey: A Revenge on Life (New York: Oxford University Press, 1994), 95. Although Losey dismissed the film, Tom Milne expressed disagreement during his interview with the director. See Losey on Losey (London: Secker & Warburg, 1967), 93. However, Raymond Durgnat, Gilles Jacob, and Foster Hirsch found several aspects of the film worthy of admiration. See Caute, 96, as well as the sympathetic review by Alain Silver in Silver and Elizabeth Ward, Film Noir: An Encyclopedic Reference to the American Style, Third Edition (Woodstock, New York: The Overlook Press, 1992), 31–33.

2. For an excellent comparison of both versions of M, see Edward Dimendberg, "From Berlin to Bunker Hill: Urban Space, Late Modernity, and Film Noir in Fritz Lang's and Joseph Losey's M," Wide Angle 19.4 (1997): 62–93.

3. Anderson lists Losey's The Lawless (1950) and The Prowler (1951) among the thirteen films he regards as comprising a "film gris" genre distinguished from "film noir" in terms of its greater psychological and social realism. Films such as The Prowler and Cy Endfield's Try and Get Me (1951) are distinguished by their emphasis on the unreality of the American dream. See Thom Anderson, "Red Hollywood," Literature and the Visual Arts in Contemporary Society. Eds. Suzanne Ferguson and Barbara Groseclose (Columbus, Ohio State University Press, 1985), 179, 187. However, both stylistically and thematically, film noir is a fluid entity often incapable of rigid categorization. However, in wishing to break away from histories of the blacklist that comprise only directors and screenwriters to move towards a much broader picture, Anderson's remarks are extremely valuable here. 1951 appears to have been a highly significant year representing the last "gasp" of the social and psychological aspects of "film noir" before being forced underground within American culture.

4. For relevant information see Michel Ciment, Conversations with Losey (London: Methuen, 1985), 114–118.

5. For evidence of the ideological role of institutional forces such as the Hollywood industry and Motion Picture Producers and Distributors of America mobilized against the appearance of certain types of books and plays reaching the cinema screen during the 1920s and 1930s see the following two essays. Richard Maltby, " 'To Prevent the Prevalent Type of Book': Censorship and Adaptation in Hollywood, 1924–1934," Guerric De Bona, O.S.B. "Dickens, the Depression, and MGM's David Copperfield, "Film Adaptation." Ed. James Naremore, Film Adaptation (New Brunswick: Rutgers University Press, 2000), 79–105, 106–129. We must, of course, remember that such strategies were not always

entirely successful particularly in the case of low budget productions and "disreputable genres."

6. See David Cochran, *America Noir: Underground Writers and Filmmakers of the Postwar Era* (Washington, D.C.: Smithsonian Institution Press, 2000). For the legacy of the New Deal see Michael Denning, *The Cultural Front: The Laboring of American Culture in the Twentieth Century* (London: Verso, 1996), a movement in which Losey played a very significant role.

7. See Donald Pizer, *Realism and Naturalism in Nineteenth-Century American Literature* (Carbondale: Southern Illinois University Press, 1984); Documents of American Realism and Naturalism. Ed. Donald Pizer (Carbondale: Southern Illinois University Press, 1998); Richard Lehan, "American Literary Naturalism: The French Connection," *Nineteenth Century Fiction* 38 (1984): 529–557; and Charles Child Walcutt, *American Literary Naturalism: A Divided Stream* (Minneapolis: University of Minnesota Press, 1956). Gilberto Perez has also recently argued for the relevance of naturalism both to the modern novel and contemporary films such as Abbas Kiarostami's *Close Up* (1990). See Perez, *The Material Ghost: Films and Their Medium* (Baltimore: Johns Hopkins University Press, 1998), 217, 260–265.

8. Silver, 32.

9. Foster Hirsch, *The Dark Side of the Screen: Film Noir* (New York: Da Capo Press, 2001), 50. Hirsch is also aware of various currents influencing film noir such as hard boiled fiction on Albert Camus's *The Stranger*. See Hirsch, 46–47. For further evidence of the role of naturalism's influence on cinema see Dudley Andrew, *Concepts in Film Theory* (New York: Oxford University Press, 1984), 105–106, especially the case of Visconti's Ossessione (1942). Its "borrowing" from James M. Cain's *The Postman Always Rings Twice* as well as the latter's dependence on Zola's Therese Raquin is already well-known. For a perceptive essay linking an article by Zola to the blacklist era see Dalton Trumbo, "The Time of the Toad," *Film Culture* 50–51 (1970): 31–41, especially 32. "All nations in the course of their histories have passed through periods which, to extend, Zola's figure of speech, might be called the Time of the Toad: an epoch long or short as the temper of the people may permit, fatal or merely debilitating as the vitality of the people may determine, in which the nation turns upon itself in a kind of compulsive madness to deny all in its tradition that is clean, to exalt all that is vile, and to destroy any heretical minority which asserts toad-meat not to be the delicacy which governmental edit declares it. Triple heralds of the Time of the Toad are the loyalty oath, the compulsory revelation of faith, and the secret police." Trumbo's remarks not only reveal the Hollywood Left's knowledge of Zola but also apply to contemporary conditions.

10. Abraham Polonsky, "How the Blacklist Worked in Hollywood," *Film Culture* 50–51 (1970): 44.

11. Hirsch, 50.

12. Op. cit, 51.

13. Ciment, 120, 121.

14. Ciment, 116.

15. Ciment, 115. Barrymore was also the same age as Georgie.

16. Ciment, 122. See also, Dorothy Comingore's self-aware testimony before the October 1952 session of the House of UnAmerican Committee in "Dorothy Comingore Finds the Committee Cute," *Film Culture*, 65–67; Kirk Crivello, "The Second Mrs. Kane: Dorothy Comingore, *Focus on Film 9* (1972): 31–34. Well known for his "Judas" role in *Force of Evil* (1948), Howland Chamberlin refused to name names in his September 18, 1951 HUAC appearance. Investigation supposedly identifying him as a Communist Party member was not made public. See "Annual Report of the Committee on Un-American Activities for the Year 1952," reprinted in *Film Culture*, 77–79.

17. See Allan Eyles, "Films of Enterprise," *Focus on Film 35* (1980): 13–27; Edwin T. Arnold and Eugene I. Miller, *The Films and Career of Robert Aldrich* (Knoxville, Tennessee: University of Tennessee Press, 1986), 9–14; Alain Silver and James Ursini, *What Ever Happened to Robert Aldrich?* (New York: Limelight Editions, 1995), 3–9. Was Aldrich also influenced by the rehearsals Losey often made before shooting began? See Ciment, 99.

18. Ciment, 117.

19. Ciment, 123.

20. Ciment, 121.

21. Silver, 33.

Lily Carver (Gaby Rodgers) enmeshed in her reading while surrounded by menacing shapes and shadows in *Kiss Me Deadly*.

Kiss Me Deadly (1955): Composition and Meaning

Michael E. Grost

Kiss Me Deadly (1955) is Robert Aldrich's most remarkable film. Aldrich began directing in 1953, and by then, the film noir cycle had run its course as a Hollywood phenomenon, peaking in the years 1942–1951. However, film noirs were still being made steadily through the 1950's, and many of these works were classics of the cycle.

There is a remarkably detailed visual analysis of the film in "*Kiss Me Deadly*: Evidence of a Style" by Alain Silver, in *Film Noir Reader* (1996), edited by Alain Silver and James Ursini. The remarks below are simply intended to point out a few more things about this film, one of the most complex and creative of all film noirs.

3D Camera Technique

The staging in *Kiss Me Deadly* shows a three dimensional quality. Partly this is due to depth of field. Many scenes keep in focus far into the rear of the scene. This is a technique associated in Hollywood with Orson Welles. Aldrich is often considered to be a Welles disciple. There are other techniques that aid in the film's 3D quality:

1) The showing of an irregular wall along one side of the shot. When Mike Hammer's car pulls up to a gas station near the beginning of the film, we see the entire front of the gas station along the right side of the shot. The gas station facade is by no means smooth; it contains many projections. All of these are fully lit up. The gas station is shot as if it were an elaborate piece of sculpture, like one of Louise Nevelson's friezes. As the camera moves past it, it emphasizes the station's complex 3D qualities. The projections on the station all are "rectilinear": they are "box" like, with flat, perpendicular walls.

A shot with even greater depth of field shows Mike Hammer knocking on a door in the Angel's Flight neighborhood. Behind him we see first a long narrow alleyway, then a huge depth of field showing a Los Angeles cityscape. This is an astonishing shot. Both the alley and the cityscape are irregular, just like the gas station. They are full of protuberances, and show a huge amount of specialized detail. The stairs view is bounded on the left by many protuberances from the building, mainly rectilinear, although there are some angular planes as well.

A third similar shot shows the left hand side wall of Hammer's apartment. The tables and furniture form the rectilinear protuberances near Hammer's wall.

2) Aldrich often shows scenes with an L construction. For example, take the gas station, once the characters stop there and get gas. The front of the station is a long horizontal space. Then, at the left hand side of the station, we also see a walkway going straight back from the camera. The walkway is joined to the front of the station like the letter L. The front of the station forms the long part of the L, the shorter walkway the connecting stoke at the base of the L. Hammer's apartment is set up in a similar way. There is a long living room that is often shot so that it stretches from left to right, horizontally across the screen (just like the front of the gas station). Then at the left of the screen, a passage leading straight away from the camera leads to Mike Hammer's bed room (like the walkway at the left of the gas station). This is the same geometry of set design and camera set up in both scenes. The gym shows a similar L, but with the passage (the staircase) on the right hand side of the shot, not the left.

The L construction shows movement in two completely perpendicular directions. This emphasizes the 3D nature of the shot. People do move along the short bar of the L: for example, at the gas station Cloris Leachman moves first down the side of the gas station, directly away from the camera, then returns the same way straight toward the camera.

One can find somewhat similar effects in Orson Welles' *The Lady From Shanghai* (1948). Grisby's business office in the film contains both a wall with a safe, parallel to the image plane and close up, and areas of greater depth, containing the desk. Welles tracks from the deep region to the shallow, and back again. Aldrich shows a slightly different over all pattern, of revealing the geometry of the scene. Aldrich will typically start at the flatter part of the composition, showing the viewer nothing but a flat planar surface, parallel to the frame. Then a lateral track will reveal the deep area opening up: something that is visually quite surprising. Then Aldrich will typically show both parts of the L at once.

There are variations in this approach. At Carver's apartment, the deep area is in the center of the shot, not the edge. The effect is of an inverted T, not an L. At first, the door leading to the central deep part is closed, and the viewer cannot see it: the whole image looks like a flat surface. Then Hammer opens the door, and the deep well is revealed. The effect is even more startling than the tracking. Here the central area includes the complexity of a staircase, unlike the corridor like wells of the L shots, so the effect is even more complex and startling.

3) Aldrich will often include different pointing planes in the same shot. This gives a sense of 3D to the scene. For example, a two shot of Hammer and his policeman friend Pete show each near a door. Pete's door is closed, and pointing along one plane. Hammer's door is slightly open, and pointing in a different direction, at an angle to the first door. Both men are standing along the edge of their door, so that the door underlines and exaggerates the positioning of their bodies. Each seems

more macho and aggressive, with the full rectangular region of the door behind them. They also seem at slightly cross purposes. Like the directions of the doors, they seem both nearly in the same direction, but also skewed on an angle to each other. The geometry of the scene also suggests things about their personal relationship. It also helps characterize Mike Hammer: he is a man who likes to have his back scratched, like a cat. Some people like to stand so that a door is rubbing them in their back: Hammer is one of them.

The hospital scene shows an astonishing composition formed by tilting the camera. One component of this composition: a screen. The screen is placed at an angle jutting out of the wall. This is not so unusual if the scene were filmed straight on, but tilted as it is, it makes a very unusual planar projection into the surface. One is reminded of the early three dimensional reliefs of Picasso and then Tatlin, which also use a basically flat background, such as Aldrich's hospital wall, with other planes jutting out at slight angles, such as Aldrich's screen.

4) A scene in a bedroom shoots a table and its contents at an angle. The camera is turned at an angle that does not align with either of the perpendicular axes of the table. But, a clock on the table is turned so that it is exactly parallel to the plane of the shot. The clock is a very small space, but it becomes the center of the shot, because it is in such geometric alignment with the camera frame. The effect is to underline visually the various planes of the shot. It emphasizes the contrast between the camera plane, and the planes of the room and the table. The viewer becomes much more conscious of them then if the table were merely shot at a slightly off angle.

5) Aldrich sometimes sets up his camera so that Hammer is parallel to the plane of the image, but everything else in the background is at an angle. For example, when Hammer is released from the hospital, the hospital building itself is at an angle to the camera. It makes elaborate, perspectival lines on the image, similar to those often found in Anthony Mann's *He Walked By Night*. Hammer himself is at an angle to the background, but facing straight to the camera. This gives a very odd effect. In part, the viewer perceives Hammer to be at an angle to the building. But the viewer also sees Hammer face on. It is a very strange thing to watch. Here it is underlined by the fact that Hammer walks straight towards the camera. It produces another line in the image, one at angles to the background. There are similar effects in Hammer's apartment, when he is listening to his answering machine for the first time in the film.

6) Some shots in the film show simple perpendicularity. For example, there are scenes of cars, pointed not along a roadway, but turned 90 degrees from the roadway, so that they are pointing directly at its edge. This gives a 3D effect. Similarly, when Hammer leaves the night club, his car is at a 90 degree angle to the entrance way of the club.

A brutal and cynical Mike Hammer (Ralph Meeker) questions his shapely secretary Velda (Maxine Cooper) while taking notes in *Kiss Me Deadly*.

The Office Scene

In the office scene with Velda and Hammer, the perspective effect on the middle and right is enhanced by a checkerboard floor, receding all the way to the door. (1955 was a big year for checkerboard backgrounds: see also Jean-Pierre Melville's *Bob Le Flambeur*. Aldrich also used a checkerboard floor in *World for Ransom*, in the Governor's office. However, it is partially covered by a rug, and is less conspicuous than the one in *Kiss Me Deadly*.) The right and left sides of the office are associated with Hammer and his secretary Velda (Maxine Cooper). All of the business power imagery is occupied by Hammer, on the right: the fancy business desk, the file cabinets. He is sitting in a power position on the desk, as well. On the left, Maxine is stretching, in a distinctly non-business, dancing pose. She gets the empty deep space, which has the form of a lounge area, looking like the domestic space of a home. His space is filled with phallic symbols, such as the pens on the desk set, and the file cabinets. He is sitting, she is standing, and in complex motion. Hammer is in a business suit, she is in casual clothes. Throughout this scene, he is interested in business, while she keeps trying to get some romance going.

Soon Hammer will get up from the desk, and move over to a bar in the foreground.

This too is filled with phallic looking bottles and glasses. Its hard wooden surface echoes the desk.

There is a consistent depiction of men and women in these shots. Men are associated with technology and business, women with space and standing. Throughout the film, Hammer is often controlling machinery: his car, the answering machine, the telephone at the gym.

The bar scene with Friday has similar characteristics. It is not an L, but it is a corner scene, and the corner provides a 3D effect. Once again, Hammer is sitting, and occupies the bar; the woman gets the open area behind the bar. There are phallic symbols near him again, including bottles and a glass. Once again the woman is standing, and moving around some within an empty space. Once again, Hammer is in a business suit, the woman is in a party dress.

There is a similar disparity of approach at the gas station. Hammer gets the long horizontal area in the front of the station; the station is behind him, and he is sitting in control of the car. This corresponds to all the equipment and the desk in the business shot. By contrast, Cloris Leachman is associated with the deep well space receding from the left of the garage. This space is empty. She is often standing and moving in it, while Hammer is either seated in his car or moving just in front of it. Here the power might be on Hammer's side, but the mystery is on Leachman's. The long dark well of the alley is associated with her mysterious behavior, and the mystery of the plot.

There are other effects in the shot of Hammer and Velda in the office. The regularly repeating white labels on the back file cabinets echo the back and white checkerboard of the floor. The two areas both go together and clash: one is horizontal and in perspective (the floor); the other is vertical and parallel to the surface of the shot (the cabinets). The effect offers considerable visual tension. A third checkerboard element consists of the alternating whitish regions and black areas on the desk. These are less regular in their spacing than the floor squares or file cabinets, but they are similarly rectilinear. They too form a horizontal perspective element, like the floor. Such matching/clashing areas in the image give it a baroque quality, the effect of a complexly loaded image. Such shots are often associated with Aldrich's role model, Orson Welles. One also notes the X shapes sometimes assumed by Velda's body while stretching; it recalls the X shape formed by Cloris Leachman pointed out by Alain Silver in his analysis.

Lines in the Compositions

Aldrich's compositions tend to be made up of straight lines. These lines tend to be at some distance to each other. They tend to be of equal "strength": each is just as long as the other, of equal thickness, and equally emphasized by the composition. They also tend to be at wildly varying angles to each other. One reason that stairs are such a prominent part of Aldrich's mise-en-scène is that their lines fulfill all these characteristics. A staircase produces many lines: one for each side, lines along the banisters, the line where the base of the banister meets the edge of the stair itself, and lines formed by the upper and lower floors. There are also lines formed by any corners in the staircase, and also lines formed by doors.

This modern-day Pandora (Gaby Rodgers) opens the "great whatsit" box and unleashes radioactive demons upon the corrupt world of Mike Hammer in *Kiss Me Deadly*.

But Aldrich also generates straight line segments in other ways. The scene in which Nick discovers the new car outside includes some trees. These tree trunks are mainly vertical, but they are in fact tilted at slight angles to each other, a bit off the vertical. The trees are also widely spaced, so their trunks are completely separate, and at considerable distance from each other on the screen. The line segments formed by their trunks exactly fall into Aldrich's pattern: strong straight line segments, equally emphasized, widely spaced, at different angles. Aldrich must have shown some effort to hunt up exactly such a location.

The many planar segments in *Kiss Me Deadly* also tend to have straight line segment boundaries. They are doors, screens, walls. The two geometric patterns, lines and planes, make up the bulk of the compositional imagery in the film. There are a few curved surfaces, notably Hammer's cars. And there are some circles: a chair in Christina's room to the left of the table with the clock; the outdoor clock in the window during the shadowing sequence on the street. However, these circles are so rare as to look like visitors in Hammer's world, not citizens.

The separation of the lines gives a "clean" look to Aldrich's compositions. No individual section of them is cluttered. Everything is carefully spaced out into separate sections. The use of straight lines and planes also adds to the impression of visual cleanliness. No matter how wildly baroque the compositions become, they are always made up of very clear lines and planes, organized so that all of their patterns and configurations are easily visible.

Lighting

Ernest Laszlo's lighting is less "partial" than in many film noirs. In the night scenes, he tends to light up an object as a whole, and then display this white glowing area against blackness. For example, Christine's whole body is fully lit, as she stands out against the darkness of the rest of the image, stopping Hammer's car. The gas station is a glowing maze of cubes and protuberances, with the whole wall of rectangular bumps completely lit up. Later, the Whatsit and everything it touches will glow with a strong white light.

Spirals

The best images in Aldrich's previous film noir, *World for Ransom* (1954), involve shooting through the wire bed frame of the heroine's room. The frame is in the form of a spiral, and all of a sudden a spiral is superimposed on the image of the room and its occupants. It is a striking and unique image: how many films have ever displayed a spiral as part of their imagery? Aldrich creates three such separate shots in the film, the first involving camera movement behind the bed frame, showing different designs in the wire. Aldrich combines these shots with an elaborately shaped frame on a door.

The spiral and the frame together produce an elaborate masking effect. In *Kiss Me Deadly*, Hammer will encounter a wire frame chair whose back contains a similar spiral. The bed frame near the beginning also includes spiral endings, which make spiral shadows on the floor.

Social Commentary

Quite a few of the characters in *Kiss Me Deadly* seem to be remarkably intellectual. These include Cloris Leachman, a poetry loving intellectual, Hammer's secretary Velda, who practices ballet, and the opera singer in the film. All of these characters seem remarkably powerless. Leachman's character is the film's most pitiful victim of the bad guys, and both Velda and the opera singer are very small potatoes in the scheme of things, from the world's point of view.

By contrast, *Kiss Me Deadly* is full of powerful corrupt characters. These people seem to be full of a vulgar wealth: swimming pools and private clubs. These also seem to be remarkable stupid, to put it bluntly. Aldrich seems to be saying that their corruption has allowed these people to rise to the top. They have no real ability, and are remarkably lacking in any sort of virtue or accomplishment. Movie gangsters are often shown to be people of drive, dedication and talent, who are merely working on the wrong side of the law. Aldrich will have none of that. These people have no admirable qualities or accomplishments. They just seem incredibly dumb, for openers. Also, they seem lazy. The mobsters are shown sitting around a swimming pool taking bets. These are places of upper class idleness. They are not the big office headquarters of traditional gangsters, who run their crimes like a business. Aldrich grew up around rich people, and he completely deglamorizes them. One might envy these people their money, but otherwise one would hardly admire them. They seem like completely worthless pigs. Aldrich will treat other well to do people the same way in future films: *Hustle* shows a country club that is as vacuous and unappealing as the swimming pool in *Kiss Me Deadly*.

Where Hammer falls in this continuum of intellectuality is hard to guess. At the beginning of the film, Leachman's character asks him if he likes to read poetry, and he gives her a "you gotta be kidding look" that squelches the whole idea. After all, Hammer is the ultimate 50's macho man. But later scenes suggest Hammer has a hidden intellectual side. When he visits Leachman's apartment, her radio station is tuned to classical music, which he leaves on (Schubert's *Unfinished Symphony*). Later, in his own apartment, he is listening to classical music on the radio himself. Still later, in one of the most notorious anti-intellectual scenes in American film, he threatens the opera singer by smashing one of his records. Hammer in this scene behaves like a monstrous anti-intellectual thug. Maybe he is simply this. But one also suspects that he is deeply conflicted. Perhaps he is trying to suppress impulses in himself that 50's culture does not allow him to express, such as a love for culture.

Hammer is an outsider in the film, trying to be an insider. He is treated with contempt by every middle class person who knows him, other than his secretary. His quest to solve the crime is motivated pure and simple by a desire to get his cut of the take, through blackmail. He comes to a terrible end through this. But there is also a certain pathos to Hammer. He is a man from a working class background trying to better himself, in a society that just will not respect him.

Influences

The night driving scenes, and the prominence of clocks in the film, recall Fritz Lang.

The finale, with the hero shot and trapped in a burning house, trying to rescue his captive girl friend, recalls that in Anthony Mann's *Raw Deal* (1948). The fact that it is a beach house recalls Robert Siodmak's *Criss Cross* (1949).

The out-of-control cop (Cornel Wilde) violently embraces his own "obscure object of desire" (Jean Wallace) in *The Big Combo*.

Covert Narrative Strategies to Contain and Punish Women in *The Big Heat* (1953) and *The Big Combo* (1955)

Grant Tracey

In the 1930s, film gangsters were portrayed as victims of social circumstances. By the 1950s, the gangster genre, under the influx of film noir concerns and visual dynamics, turned mean, nasty and conservative. Gangsters became corporate kingpins, weaving their way into the social fabric and destabilizing the security of our communities. In the light of the Estes Kefauver hearings on organized crime, *The Big Heat* and *The Big Combo* portray the syndicate's grip on the city. In *The Big Heat,* suburban wiseguy Mike Lagana controls the police force and city commissioner Higgins. In *The Big Combo,* Mr. Brown threatens America's youth with readily available guns and drugs and hides his illicit activities behind the legitimate Bolemac Corporation. But what makes these films even more fascinating, beyond the portrayal of the gangsters, is how their covert narrative strategies reveal a fear of women and an attempt to contain them within a 1950s ideology of male dominance and gender conformity. *The Big Heat* revolves around a double misogyny. A transgressive woman fails to reveal a confessional letter that may alleviate the all-encompassing evil. Sgt. Dave Bannion attempts to uncover the evil, but in his obsessive revenge, he destroys inadvertently and directly a variety of women: well-meaning Lucy Chapman, nurturing Katie Bannion, and good-bad party girl Debby Marsh. In *The Big Combo,* Lt. Leonard Diamond also obsesses, but he worries about what goes on in the dark between former society girl Susan Lowell and her Napoleonic lover, Mr. Brown. The film's total noir style—editing, acting, shadowy lighting and mise-en-scène—is latently invested in Laura Mulvey's concepts of the male gaze, supporting Diamond's psychical obsessions by visually punishing Susan for her perceived sexual transgressions. The narrative drive, embodied in John Alton's moody photography and Joseph Lewis's direction, seeks to suspend female pleasure, to contain her sexuality and to recoup her into the boundaries of the socially acceptable.

In *The Big Heat* a woman, rather than a male detective, controls the narrative. Bertha Duncan has discovered a suicide note left behind by her husband, police officer Tom Duncan, and decides to suppress the damning evidence that indicts him, Commissioner Higgins, Lagana and his sadistic lieutenant, Vince Stone. During the first appearance of Bertha (Jeanette Nolan), director Fritz Lang presents her cold duplicity. Within minutes, Nolan brilliantly transforms through three ranges of emotion. Upon discovering Duncan's body, she first stands atop the stairs, aloof and petulant. As she reads the incriminating confessional letter, her eyebrows slightly arch and her face gleams with calculating surprise. Seconds later, she calls Lagana, her shoulders thrown back, as she confidently snaps, "Mr. Lagana. I know it's late, wake him up." After announcing herself as "Tom Duncan's widow," Bertha, through her husband, establishes her right to his kickback money. Rather than display grief over her husband's suicide, Bertha coldly weaves her way into Lagana's organization. She cares only about herself.

Bertha isn't a classic femme fatale. She isn't sexually alluring in Janey Place's sense of the deadly spider woman,[1] but she coldly portrays a woman ostracized from 1950s concepts of nurturer and familial center. She embodies the darkest of society's fears of lost stability and security in a post-World War II world.[2] Like a spider, Bertha sets a webbed trap for Bannion, using her social standing (police officer's widow), to initially deceive the detective with her mock grief. As she prepares for her first interview, Bertha works through a method-acting ritual, posing in front of a three-fold mirror, preparing for a performance. In the presence of Bannion, Bertha politely discusses her husband's death and cries. Her emotion masks what she's withholding: her husband's involvement with Lagana. "There weren't any circumstances," she lies, bravely looking at Bannion. She further adds that her husband was "clean and wholesome," before crying, again, into a curtain. Bannion, fooled by her acting, tells her "You've been most helpful." The statement is rich in irony for we know that she has been anything but forthcoming.

Bertha falsely represents her marriage and thus positions herself on the dark side of noir, the female who is neither stable or dependable. Lang counterpoints her duplicitous character in the following scene that captures the egalitarian relationship between Bannion and his wife Katie. Although for modern audiences the domestic Bannions seem overly traditional and idealized (she wears a pinafore-style apron), in a 1950's context they represent America's longing for stability in a world on the atomic cusp. Tom Flinn has called their first scene together a "short discourse on the perfect marriage",[3] and Colin McArthur sees their relationship as embodying the values of honesty, simplicity, marriage, democracy (home/parenting/sharing), tenderness and light as opposed to the outside world of Lagana/Stone/Debby/Bertha which is painted in dabs of corruption, luxury (the "mink-coated girls"), sterility, selfishness, brutality and darkness.[4] Katie and Bannion discuss parenting strategies and help each other with the dishes. And it's not just "friendly banter" that binds them, but sexual energy. When Katie discusses their daughter's behavior: "Angelic all day, but at night she's a holy terror," Bannion responds with the crackling, "That's how I generally describe you." Minutes later when he praises their partnership, how they share scotch, smokes, and steak, Katie tosses in the sexually implicit, "Among other things." But the threat of the Lagana/Stone/Debby/Bertha universe lingers and suddenly the Bannions's bliss is broken by a phone call from "B-girl" Lucy Chapman.

In part, because Lucy Chapman interrupts Bannion's domestic bliss, he dislikes her. When he visits her at the Retreat, Bannion sits away from her in the booth, leaning far to the right with rude indifference. Robin Wood rightly accuses Bannion of "self-priggishness" and class-based prejudices.[5] She's just "a B-Girl," after-all, and not a "cop's widow." Lucy informs Bannion that Tom was a "wonderful guy," but the detective

Rogue cop Dave Bannion (Glenn Ford) manipulates the wounded "bad girl" (Gloria Grahame) in *The Big Heat*.

doesn't acknowledge her genuine grief. He had, by contrast, fallen for Mrs. Duncan's false grief. Bannion even judges Lucy for swimming and lying in the sun with Tom. "That sounds very cozy. . . . What's your pitch, Lucy?" He thinks she's a blackmailer. This misreading will eventually lead to Lucy's death and the destruction of what Bannion holds most dear, his own family.

After failing to listen, Bannion returns to Bertha and indirectly sets up Lucy's death. Bertha sits primly, her shoulders back, her composure a series of forced hard lines. When Bannion questions Tom and Lucy's relationship, Bertha snaps, "She's a liar. Tom never wanted a divorce." As Bannion defends the questions, stating that he fears Lucy Chapman might try "a little blackmail," Lang drapes the scene with irony. Bannion worries about Bertha being possibly blackmailed, but unbeknownst to him, Bertha is blackmailing Lagana. In his misguided attempt to protect Bertha, Bannion finalizes Lucy's fate. As Bannion leaves, Lang frames Bertha at the window, looking callous. A dissolve conflates Bertha's overlapping image with an insert of a teletype announcing Lucy Chapman's death. The dissolve suggests that after Bannion told Bertha about the possibilities of blackmail, the Spider-lady, the film's only blackmailer, ordered Lagana to dispose of Lucy.[6]

Bertha may control the narrative by withholding Duncan's confession and ordering the hit on Lucy, but Lang clearly implicates Bannion in Lucy's death. At the coroner's office, Lang conflates images of an on and offscreen cigarette to link the unseen images of Lucy's cigarette-burned body with Bannion's discouraged gestures. Remorseful after reading the coroner's report of her body burns, Bannion butts his cigarette in an ashtray and tells the coroner that he saw "Every single one of them." As he grinds the cigarette, Lang slyly suggests that Bannion is guilty for the torture and burns that Lucy experienced.[7]

Bannion is also culpable in the death of his wife. Following a lewd, threatening phone call directed at Katie from hit man Larry Gordon (a Vince Stone hire who was brought in at the request of Mrs. Duncan to silence the police sergeant's inquiries), Bannion barges into Lagana's estate and insults the mobster: "You creeps have no compunction about phoning my home . . . talking to my wife like she was. . . ." Lagana's strong arm, George, intervenes and Bannion, in a moment of cathartic energy, Judo chops him to the ground. "You want to pinch hit for your boy, Lagana?" Bannion challenges. After his home was indirectly assaulted through words, Bannion reacts with over zealousness. But what he now fails to realize is that Lagana will react with even more self-righteous zeal to protect the sanctity of his home. "You come here to my home about a murder," Lagana snaps incredulously. "I don't like dirt tracked into it." Lagana replaces judo chops for contract killers and car bombs, as later Bannion recites "The Three Little Kittens" to his daughter, and the two of them lose a lot more than sets of mittens.

Lang follows the car bomb scene with his strongest noir moment. In terms of noir, Flinn has suggested that *The Big Heat* has little in common with other post-war noirs. There are few low-key lit or shadow scenes.[8] If anything, the film visually resembles the polished sheen of a 1940's Paramount release. But Flinn, rightly, contends that it's the film's content and character, "the ferocity of the violence," that make it a nasty noir. And nothing is more violent through its implied absence than this scene. After he resigns from the police force, Bannion stands in his hollowed-out home, and a slightly high angle, subjective point of view shot captures the all-encompassing emptiness, emphasizing the loss of what used to be present: Katie and their joyful sharing and bantering. The empty house also embodies a metaphor for the hollowness within Bannion's soul. Bannion exists in a disruptive emotional state, one of alienation and despair. Following this scene, the narrative spins inexorably to its violent climaxes, as Bannion slips into the dark realm of hate, attempting to purge his and the world's demons.

After the death of Katie, the film's empty feminine space is filled by Debby Marsh, the narcissistic party girl who enjoys wearing mink coats, drinking, and having "fun." Debby transgresses gender norms because she's not a stay-at-home nurturer. Instead, she pursues personal pleasure. But she's not a destructive spider woman. She's a hybrid of the two archetypes, a combination of the women in Place's dialectic: Debby's both dangerous and nurturing.

Debby admires Bannion because he defies her lover Vince at the Retreat. After Vince burns Doris with the end of a cigarette, Bannion grabs one of Vince's gang, mutters, "Where you going, thief?," and then orders him and Vince out of the club. Debby probably wishes that she could handle Vince and the world he represents with the same aggressive contempt that Bannion has shown, but she enjoys her luxury. Debby does use wry sarcasm to constantly needle Vince, but prior to this point she has shown no physical force toward him. Later, she'll shoot Bertha and scald Vince with coffee, thus restoring social order. Of course, the bad girl can't live in a 1950s world, but she can help maintain its status-quo. Largely, Debby uses sarcasm to be critical and yet still maintain ties with Vince's world. When she first visits Bannion's hotel room, she wryly observes about the décor, "Oh, I like this, early nothing." Her clever kibbutzing underscores her lust for comfort. Or, as she puts it: "I've been rich and I've been poor. Believe me rich is better." Similar to Bannion's critique of Bertha, who sits on her husband's confession, Debby seeks "a soft, plush life."

Debby finds Bannion sexually attractive. At his hotel room, she directly deposits herself on his bed, inviting a sexual conquest, opening up the possibility for "research."[9] But Bannion rebuffs her physical allure and inner personality. All of his communication with her centers around investigative questions, void of emotional interaction, He asks her about "Larry" and she refuses to "talk out of school." Miffed by his lack of courting rituals, Debby teases him, asking if he didn't "ever tell a girl pretty things." When she cites what those pretty things are, Bannion turns away, his head leaning against a wall. "No." Upset over his wife's death, he cruelly dismisses Debby with, "I wouldn't touch anything of Vince Stone's with a ten-foot pole." Lang punctuates the viciousness behind Bannion's words by following his rejection of her with the film's most famous scene: Vince splashing Debby's face with a pot of hot coffee.

Upon Debby's second visit to the hotel, Bannion asks her a series of systematic questions.[10] "Higgins, the police commissioner?" Who else was at the card game? Larry Gordon? Half of Debby's face is wrapped in bandages, but Bannion still refuses to empathize with her. Angry at his lack of humanity, Debby scolds Bannion, drawing him in, telling him that he's responsible: "I was followed when I came here with you. That's why I got this." Once again Bannion's actions or inaction connect him to the fate of one of the film's females (first Lucy, then Katie, and now Debby). Debby's honest pain starts to break in on Bannion, and thus Debby becomes an agent for Bannion's reintegration into society. She nurtures and helps him feel again. Her role in the narrative isn't about her own autonomy and agency, but how she is defined in relationship to Bannion, how she helps him find his way back from hate to a more even-keeled normalcy. In the film's powerful ending, Bannion finally opens up, telling Debby intimate details about his wife: "She was a sampler" and "a real Irish blow top" as he heals.

But before Bannion can be reintegrated, Debby must protect him from fully falling into the darkness. After Debby tells where Larry Gordon lives, Bannion smashes into

Gordon's home, chokes him, and forces out all the information he needs. "I'm going to spread the word that you talked. You're out of business, thief," he promises. Shortly after this scene, Stone reveals that Gordon was shot down at the airport trying to leave town. Bannion dispatched him to his death. Bannion's revenge frenzy hits an even higher transcendent gear when he visits Bertha. During this visit, Lang uses a similar medium-shot composition to Bannion's stranglehold on Gordon. Now, Bannion accuses Bertha of being on the payroll, of being delighted "when your husband blew his brains out," and he learns from her, as she gloats over Lucy Chapman's murder, that the contempt he previously held for Lucy was completely unjustified.[11] Bannion, angry over the control she holds on his universe, places his hands around Bertha's neck and quietly menaces, "But I'm not Lagana. With you dead, the big heat falls." His dark, apocalyptic words are no longer about revenge, but imply a vision of an atomic fallout in which the entire earth will be scorched. His vision echoes the image of his empty house, revealing the hollowed-out core to his being.

Fortunately, Bannion's frenzy is interrupted by the police and he's forced to leave, safe from crossing the line between good and rogue cop. He tells Debby of his frustrations. "You know, I almost killed her an hour ago? I should have." Debby, admiring Bannion and acting as his moral guide, says, "If you had, there wouldn't be much difference between you and Vince Stone." She values what he represents, but he also plants in her head the very action that he himself can't commit. Moments later, after receiv-

Dave Bannion's (Glenn Ford) idyllic home life just before it is shattered in *The Big Heat*.

ing another threatening phone call, Bannion hurries to protect his daughter, conveniently dropping a gun on the bed, and telling her to "keep that for company." Debby will use that gun, sacrificing herself for society's greater good and allowing Bannion to preserve a concept of his higher, moral self. Within *The Big Heat*'s 1950s ideology, Debby is a fallen woman, important to the hero's reintegration into society, but not important on her own terms and thus expendable.

Ironically Bertha, who dominates the narrative by controlling the men around her (Lagana, Stone, Commissioner Higgins, Lt. Wilks, and Bannion), loses her guarded control in the presence of a woman. Earlier, as she looked outside her upstairs window, she had feared the arrival of Bannion, dialing up Lagana, who in turn dispatched the police to her house. But now, Bertha underestimates Debby. As she arrives, Bertha again glances out a window, but this time without fear. Debby's good side, her non-scarred face, is turned toward the window and Bertha lets her in. "Were you in an accident?" she innocuously asks, playing the kind hostess. Debby smiles and talks about the pair of them being the "mink-coated girls," clad in the ultimate 1950's symbol of status. Bertha dislikes being grouped with the trashy Debby whom she feels superior to, and as her face hardens, she responds with a "You're not making any sense, Miss Marsh."

Debby's actions, however, make perfect sense, as she becomes an agent of patriarchy, punishing the transgressive Bertha and restoring the film's desired mode of male dominance. Bertha pays for her oversight, as Debby fires three times. In a sense, Debby, as McArthur has suggested, directly does what Bannion wishes he could do but can't.[12] This point isn't lost on Lang. Earlier in the film, Lang linked an eyeline match of Bertha looking out of a window to a teletype announcing Lucy Chapman's death. Now, Lang links Bertha's death (Debby's tossed gun on the floor) with a dissolve of Bannion standing out in the street, his back to the camera.

In the end moral order appears restored through the catharsis of Debby's violence. Bannion reintegrates with the police force, but, in its shades of noir, Lang's final imagery is covertly disturbing. Back at the precinct, Bannion picks up the phone: there's a hit and run over on South Street. As he exits, Lang shows the circularity of crime and its cost. A prominent poster on the office wall reads, "Give Blood, Now." Ultimately, Lang isn't conscious of the misogyny of his text, but structurally the need to contain and destroy women informs the noir angst of *The Big Heat*. Bannion is responsible for every woman's death, but it is *his* work that goes on (not the women's lives). Perhaps, within the film's twisted ideology, the sacrifice of women (who give *their* blood) is justified in order to eliminate male fears and to restore patriarchal dominance?

On the surface, *The Big Combo* appears to be *The Big Heat* revisited. The film has a similar pattern: a rogue cop wages a one-man campaign on organized crime. Revenge underscores both films. When Brown's hit men mistakenly kill Lt. Diamond's girlfriend Rita, the story's revenge pattern hits full force. And both films end with a mob kingpin pleading to be shot by the arresting detectives. But Diamond, according to Flinn, is much "kinkier" than Bannion. Diamond's crazed desire to get Mr. Brown isn't fueled only by hate-filled revenge, but also by a strange obsession to "save" Brown's mistress, Susan Lowell,[13] a society woman who has fallen for the gangster's charms. Diamond loves her, and his narrative quest seeks to ascertain her guilt and to reign her back into the bounds of the acceptable. Diamond's captain places the obsessions in the clearest light: "You can't bear to think of her in the arms of this hood. Forget her ...you haven't time to reform wayward girls ... she's been with Brown three and a half years. That's a lot of days ... and nights." It's the nights Diamond worries about.

Feminist-based theorist Laura Mulvey has defined the paradigmatic male gaze as cinema's means of overcoming castration anxiety.[14] Cinematic structures such as the gaze work to assuage the heterosexual male ego and contain threats to that ego's complete sense of self. The woman's lack, a constant reminder of castration anxiety, is lessened by either fetishizing the female body (as do the films of Busby Berkeley and Joseph von Sternberg) or by punishing and thereby containing her body (as do the films of Alfred Hitchcock).[15] We don't necessarily have to subscribe to the theory of castration anxiety to appreciate how Mulvey's concept of "ascertaining" the "guilt" of female characters informs the many noirs of the 1950s. The Big Combo is no exception. This brooding, seedy, Allied-Artists thriller, obsessively portrays a fear of woman and the need to interrogate and contain her sexuality.

The film opens with a strong visual metaphor of guilt. Susan, in long shot, runs in and out of slanting shadows at a boxing ring, pursued by two men. Her kinetic movement suggests a desire for self-imposed exile. She doesn't like who she is and awash in harsh splashes of white light, she seeks to escape but there's nowhere to turn except into shadows. Eventually cornered by Brown's thugs, Fante and Mingo, Susan emerges from John Alton's poetic blackness and agrees to stop running. The hit men, by contrast, remain shapeless shadows. Susan, centered in an almost noir-like spot effect, looks stark, pale and naked, a person to be observed, noted, labeled. Alton's "mystery lighting" imbues Susan's nakedness with the noir concerns of guilt and obsession.

Susan's guilt develops across scenes. Following the elegiac opening, she meets Mr. Audobon, an old family friend, at a posh restaurant. Cryptically, Mr. Audobon comments, "Well you look so different somehow, Susan. Why, I hardly recognized you." He instinctively senses that she's not the innocent woman she used to be. Susan insists that she hasn't changed, but Lewis's cutaway to Fante and Mingo sitting and eating undercuts her denials. Susan does confess, however, that she no longer has the interest in music she once had, vaguely hinting at her change from youthful, high-class innocence. Her time now, she admits, is filled with the more brooding "stud poker." As Susan and Mr. Audobon stroll across the dance floor, Susan, no longer able to run from herself, collapses: "I've taken some pills. I think I'm dying."

Later, at the hospital, Diamond forces Susan to feel worse by hounding her about Alicia (a woman Susan obsesses over—she caught Brown spelling out Alicia's name on the "moist glass" of a window pane and she's worried about Brown's past connections to the mystery woman—did he kill her?). Diamond, a representative of the law, acts as a patriarchal gatekeeper, probing her sexual history, disapproving of her perceived transgressions. Susan backs away, but Diamond hovers across the bed, attacking her personally: "You think you're the bright respectable girl you were four years ago? You're not. You attempted suicide. You're under arrest. You can be sentenced to jail for six months." Diamond's words center around suicide but his vituperative accusations concern what Susan and Brown do in the dark. And the scene ends with an even crueler comment, one reminiscent of Bannion remarking to Debby that he wouldn't "touch anything of Vince Stone's with a ten-foot pole." As Brown arrives to claim Susan, Diamond defines habeas corpus for his partner, Sam: "It's Latin. It means you may have the body. Mr. Brown may have it."

Diamond's obsession, perhaps because it is underscored with avowals of love, slowly and perversely transforms Susan. Dressed in white, Susan later tries to reclaim memories of lost innocence by listening to a private recital, but Diamond interrupts her reveries. "You think this is mink, Miss Lowell?" He grabs her furs. "These are skins of human beings, Miss Lowell. People who have been beaten, sold, robbed, doped, murdered by Mr. Brown." Diamond uses strong verbs excessively, underscoring his hatred for Brown and his distaste for what Brown, in his intimate moments, does to Susan, emotionally and physically. She turns from the truth, and Lewis and Alton reflect this mood by alienating Jean Wallace from Cornell Wilde in a wonderfully staged two-shot. The performers look ahead, through the camera, rarely at each other. Separate but together, she offers her first confession: "I live in a maze, Mr. Diamond. A strange blind and blackened maze and all of the twisting paths lead back to Mr. Brown." Earlier she had told Brown, "I hate and despise you," but his power of lovemaking captivated her with noir's transgressive promise. Brown defied her claims with kisses to her cheek, neck and then traveled down, behind her body, as the camera tracked in for a stunning erotic close-up of her complete surrender. Diamond follows her confession with one of his own. He tells her to get out, to save herself from Brown, and then admits that he, too, loves her. Susan breaks the mood of alienation. She turns and looks directly at Diamond.

Her first look becomes a more committed look following the brutal death of Rita (Diamond's on-and-off again burlesque-hall girlfriend). Susan visits Diamond at the police precinct with a photograph of Alicia. Before Diamond she abjectly places herself, apologizing for Rita's death and for failing to act sooner. "I'm sorry. Terribly, terribly sorry." Diamond, embittered, doesn't act like Bannion in his scenes with Debby by asking a series of aloof and systematic questions. Instead, his comments are personal, judgmental and mean. His mood belies his pain. He nearly scoffs at her apology, saying, "Why? Because it wasn't me?" Coldly, he tells her to say what she has to, and she reveals that she's left Mr. Brown. "You're a little late," he scolds, again ascertaining her guilt, circumscribing her within veiled words of punishment. But Susan doesn't react in anger like Debby does, sulkily exiting Bannion's hotel room. Instead, Susan acquiesces. She allows Diamond to abuse her. She also submits to the narrative's demands to contain the female body. Remaining in Diamond's office, she looks at him and confesses, "I wanted to help you if I could." She hands over the photograph of Alicia, Brown's estranged wife, and it's discovered through the photograph's details that she resides not overseas (as was thought) but in a west-coast sanitarium.

Later, after the police apprehend Alicia, Diamond forces Susan to confess her guilt in front of Alicia, the police, and himself. The scene has all of the discomfort and edginess of a revivalist cleansing. Susan tries to persuade Alicia to turn state evidence against Brown, by telling of her own implication with the gangster. "I'm a witness against Mr. Brown.... I can't do it. Haven't I humiliated myself enough?" Diamond, using the force of the law to unveil lies and deception, says no one has done enough, and Susan provides her second confession, admitting before Alicia and a group of men that she was Brown's girl. Alicia acknowledges Susan's guilt and punishes her further, "Then why did you stay four years, why did you start?" Alicia positions herself within the confines of the gaze, supporting its male, heterosexual hierarchy, working in concert to punish the desiring female. Susan fumbles for words and says, "I just wouldn't believe...." Diamond intervenes, finally helping Susan instead of forcing her to be on display. Chivalrously, he defends Susan by asking Alicia to see the connection between the two women. Susan is a younger version of herself. Alicia refuses to help and then Diamond brutally shows them a photograph of Rita's bullet-riddled body. Alicia commits and Susan, glancing at the photograph, then away at Diamond, crumples in tears. Guilty by association the two women are forced to gaze on an image of horror, an image that reminds them of their own guilt for having sexual relations with Brown.

The film's sixty-two shot closing scene is a cathartic tour de force of editing that reinforces and simultaneously troubles the gaze. Through a series of powerful eyeline matches, Lewis suggests that Susan has finally sized up Brown and, through an interpretive gaze of her own, gained power over him.

The sequence begins with an eighteen-second long take. Brown's offscreen voice frets, "What's keeping that plane? It was supposed to be here an hour ago." Brown finally walks into the frame. His momentary absence from the frame underscores his loss of power in the narrative. In *The Big Heat,* the frenzied violence escalated because Bertha withheld evidence and Bannion made a series of bad choices. In *The Big Combo,* Brown controls the world's violence, ruthlessly machine-gunning and bombing any threats to his power. But in the film's conclusion, the man who lived by the ruthless motto "First is first and second is nobody," is reduced to a nobody.

As Brown paces inside the airport hangar he reveals his loss of power. He turns from the camera, flexes his arms. "Why doesn't he come?" As Brown wonders where that "stupid pilot" is, Susan coolly lights a cigarette. Brown knocks the lighter free with a left hand, and then slaps her with his right. "Don't do that again," he threatens, but behind the violence surfaces fear. He grabs her by the neck.

A match-on-action second shot emphasizes Jean Wallace in medium close up. Alton photographs her in less shadow than Richard Conte (Brown) because she is far less dubious. "I want to be seen," she says, words that reveal her own guilt and a desire to be cleansed, redeemed.

The third shot returns to the camera position at the end of shot one, as Brown backs away, turns. He starts his self-pitying soliloquy, wondering why his pilot won't arrive, and he blurts on about his loss of control. "I've had everything figured out. Smooth as silk." Still moving, he's isolated from Susan. The mise-en-scène reflects the fallout in their relationship. The fourth shot emphasizes Susan looking at him rant. Her steady look underscores her new power. She's now interpreting him. Throughout the film Lt. Diamond's questions and Alton and Lewis mise-en-scène have rendered Susan

Susan Lowell (Jean Wallace), guarded by her gangster lover's thugs, sinks further and further into depression in *The Big Combo*.

a guilty object. Now, she's a controlling subject, rendering guilty the very man who had put her in an abject position with regard to the law.

Moments later, a police car pulls up, and Brown looks into the dark fog and re-treats. In long shot he runs, slipping and sliding into a corrugated tin wall. His hurried, clumsy actions and the camera's focal length reduce his stature. Arcing shadows engulf him. The stationary Susan, by contrast, gains in power by watching.

Diamond's disembodied voice tells Brown to "C'mon out." Brown, lit in sidelight-ing, glances in the direction of police car's blinding lights but he can't see what con-fronts him. Once again, his power and control over Susan and Los Angeles is ending. Repeatedly, Brown randomly fires into the darkness. Susan, free of Brown's controlling gaze, adjusts, beginning with shot thirty-one, the car searchlight and shines it on Brown. She now commands the mise-en-scène, and Alton's photography and Lewis's edits reflect this shift in gender power. In a series of short edits, Susan has six eyeline matches in Brown's direction. In seven shots she's shown in medium and medium-close ups hunting Brown down with the car search light. Susan reveals his guilt to all. Susan had been the object of Diamond's gaze and Brown's control throughout the film, but now she has partially inverted that control, ascertaining somebody else's guilt besides her own. Of course, this inversion isn't a complete reversal of the male gaze. Susan's gaze is inscribed within male concerns. She works within the confines of Dia-mond and the law to contain the transgressive Brown.

Brown's three eyeline matches, in this brief sequence, reveal an inability to see. As he tries to look in Susan's direction, all he can see are spots of light, and bleary arc-like shapes. Emblematically, he no longer possesses her. Framing and lighting render Brown powerless. Susan cleanses her guilt by displacing it to Brown, but she remains somewhat passive, moving from one man to another. She watches Brown empty his gun and Diamond emerges, towering over the much smaller gangster. Diamond slaps the gun away. The gesture echoes Brown's slapping away of Susan's cigarette lighter that began the sequence and now places him in the lowly position he had previously placed her. Next, Diamond seizes Brown and unceremoniously heaves him out of the frame—"Let's go hoodlum."

The film's final shots suggest a gender politic that places the woman within the confines of the gaze. As Brown slides along the wet pavement into the clutches of two awaiting police officers, he and his future disappear into the swirling fog. David Raksin's love theme begins and Diamond slowly walks to the hangar's entryway. He turns. Susan joins him. Poignantly back lit, the two exit into the fog. The sequence's final shot, a 27 second long take, book ends the final scene's opening shot, an 18-second long take. Two sets of couples are compared. Lewis fractures the Brown/Lowell pairing by moving Brown in and out of the frame and highlighting his excessive violence. With the Diamond/Lowell pairing, Lewis suggests that Susan has found the man she ought to be with, replacing Brown's brutality with Diamond's quiet resolve. Whereas in *The Big Heat*, the sexually transgressive good-bad girl, Debby Marsh, had to be sacrificed in order to maintain social order, the sexual politics of *The Big Combo* finds a space for Susan Lowell to coexist within Lt. Diamond's world. Of course, the terms are defined within his male-centered purview. He stands, waiting for her, she follows him, and as the operations of the gaze in the final scene illustrate, Susan redeems herself by subscribing to the politics of the gaze: she allows her guilt to be "seen," and she works to reveal the guilt of others.

NOTES

1. Janey Place, "Women in Film Noir" in Women in *Film Noir* (New Edition). ed. E. Ann Kaplan (London: BFI, 1978, 1998), p. 50.

2. Place, p. 50.

3. Tom Flinn, "*The Big Heat & The Big Combo*: Rogue Cops and Mink-Coated Girls" in *Velvet Light Trap* 11 (1974), p. 24.

4. Colin McArthur, *The Big Heat* (London: BFI, 1992), pp. 57–58.

5. Robin Wood, "Creativity and Evaluation: Two Film Noirs of the Fifties" in *Film Noir Reader 2*. eds. Alain Silver and James Ursini, (New York: Limelight Editions, 1999), p. 102.

6. McArthur, p. 59.

7. McArthur, p. 58.

8. Flinn, p. 25.

9. Tom Gunning, "*The Big Heat*: Circuits of Corruption" in *The Films of Fritz Lang: Allegories of Vision and Modernity* (London: BFI, 2000), p. 424.

10. Gunning, p. 427.

11. Gunning, p. 425.

12. McArthur, pp. 74–75.

13. Flinn, p. 26.

14. Laura Mulvey, "Visual Pleasure and Narrative Cinema" in *Film Theory and Criticism: Introductory Readings* (5th Edition), eds. Leo Braudy and Marshall Cohen, (New York: Oxford UP, 1999), p. 840.

15. Mulvey, pp. 840–43.

Psychic Tanya (Marlene Dietrich) predicts a bleak future for her erstwhile friend Hank Quinlan (Orson Welles) in *Touch of Evil.*

Touch of Evil (1958) and the End of the Noir Cycle

Stephen B. Armstrong

> The American cinema has been able, in an extraordinarily competent way, to show
> American society just as it wanted to see itself.
>
> André Bazin

An idea that appears frequently in the literature devoted to the film noir cycle argues that Orson Welles' *Touch of Evil* is the cycle's last, great expression. Paul Shrader, for instance, has declared that:

> By the middle of the Fifties film noir had ground to a halt. There were a few notable stragglers, *Kiss Me Deadly* . . . . *The Big Combo*, and film noir's epitaph, *Touch of Evil*.

Similarly, Alain Silver contends,

> If observers of film noir agree on anything, it is on the boundaries of the classic period, which begins in 1941 with *The Maltese Falcon* and ends less than a score of years later with *Touch of Evil*.

This highly regarded movie about police corruption and murder, however, outraged its producers when it was first screened for them in 1957 and it subsequently experienced destructive changes to its structure and content before its 1958 premiere. In fact, the film's inability to please its producers brought an end to Welles' career as a director in Hollywood.[1]

But why did all this happen? Why did the movie straggle into theaters as late as it did? Why did *Touch of Evil*—a work that stylistically and thematically matches the hundreds of "films noirs" that preceded it—ruin Welles' professional standing? And why did the producers feel the need to re-work it as they did?

To answer these questions comprehensively, we'll have to analyze the picture's history as well as the more general history of the era in which it was produced. And as we do this, we should come to realize that *Touch of Evil* was poorly received and poorly treated because it appeared too late, too long after popular taste for pessimistic crime pictures had ended. By 1958, that is, film noir had become box office poison, a development that Welles, to his great detriment, failed to recognize.

The Birth of a Disaster

In 1956, after nearly a decade of living and working abroad, Orson Welles returned to Hollywood. That year, executives at Universal-International Pictures, pleased with his performance in the studio's "modern-day" western *Man in the Shadow,* offered Welles the role of a crooked police detective named Captain Hank Quinlan in a thriller the company planned to adapt from Whit Masterson's hard-boiled crime novel *Badge of Evil.*[2] The studio also approached Charlton Heston to appear and the actor agreed under the condition that producer Albert Zugsmith allow Welles to direct as well as co-star in the film. "At that time," Heston explains, in an interview he gave to James Delson, "Orson had not directed a picture in America since Macbeth. They were a bit nonplussed, but they got back to me in a couple of days and said, 'Yeah, well that's a very good idea. A startling idea.'"[3]

Within a few weeks, Welles received the studio's existent script, which had been written by Paul Monash. Unsatisfied with it, he and a team of secretaries spent about a month rewriting in order to add momentum to the narrative and increase the film's commercial potential. Many of these changes departed significantly from Monash's script and Masterson's novel. Welles, for example, relocated the setting from San Diego to Las Robles, a provincial Mexican-American border town. He turned Heston's character, an American detective, into a Mexican narcotics official. He underscored the tragic aspects of Quinlan's fall from grace. And he introduced references to (then) contemporary American taboos like rock and roll music, marijuana use and racially mixed marriage. In fact, Welles claims in *This is Orson Welles,* a series of interviews he gave to Peter Bogdanovich, that he stripped almost everything from the studio's script except its basic scenario "about a detective with a good record who plants evidence because he knows somebody is guilty—and the fellow turns out to be guilty."

Primarily working on location in Venice, California, with a mix of celebrities and friends (like Marlene Dietrich, Joseph Cotten and Akim Tamiroff), Welles and his crew shot the film from February to April in 1957. According to Heston, "[W]e had something like a 40- or 42-day shooting schedule and a budget of slightly under a million dollars." And during production, the studio chiefs generally endorsed the director's creative decisions, praised his efficiency and considered rewarding him with future directing assignments. He told Bogdanovich:

> I was so sure I was going to go on making a lot of pictures at Universal. They went out of their way to complement me every night for the rushes, and 'When are you going to sign a four- or five-picture contract with us? Please come and see us?' Every day they kept asking me to sign the contract.[4]

After the initial shooting, however, the producers' supportiveness disappeared. Walter Murch—who participated in the 1998 restoration of the film and wrote about the project for *The New York Times*—notes that "Trouble began during editing, which wasn't unusual for Welles." A perfectionist, Welles ran a month over schedule, painstakingly arranging the film in ways that he thought would appeal to general audiences and

The bloated and corrupt cop (Orson Welles) wades through a maze of shadows and shapes in *Touch of Evil.*

cinéastes alike. "The only time one is able to exercise control over the film is in the editing room," he once told *Cahiers du Cinéma*. "Well, in the editing room I work very slowly, which has the effect of arousing the ire of the producers."

Nevertheless, the producers overseeing the project refrained from stepping in until they viewed the long awaited cut in July 1957. Unfortunately, the expressionistic style and structure of the screening copy upset them considerably. Joseph McBride explains, in his monograph *Orson Welles,* that the studio responded by firing the director and

> took the editing out of [his] hands. While the film was reworked in an attempt to make its unconventional narrative style more linear, studio director Harry Keller was called in to shoot some bland and clichéd footage.

A new editor named Aaron Stell was called in, as well, and under studio executive Ernest Nims' supervision, Stell and his colleagues pulled several scenes from the first cut, laced the famous opening shot with title credits and re-mixed the soundtrack, obscuring dialogue and sound effects with Henry Mancini's bombastic score. Other alterations followed. The working title *Badge of Evil,* for example, was changed to *Touch of Evil.*[5] And after a poor public preview, the studio cut the film further, reducing its running time to 95 minutes.

This doctored version of the picture, however, failed to attract audiences and impress critics in the United States when it was released in February 1958. The new, "linear" sequencing made the movie difficult to understand, and the addition of Keller's clarification shots could not compensate for the holes left by the deletion of several scenes shot by Welles. The following response, which appeared in *Variety* in 1958, is typical of the period:

> Welles establishes his creative talent with pomp, but unfortunately the circum-
> stances of the story suffer. There is insufficient orientation and far too little expo-
> sition, with the result that much of the action is confusing and difficult to relate to
> the plot.

But though the film flopped in America, the studio-cut copy drew acclaim abroad, particularly in France. Truffaut, for example, wrote a gushing review in a 1958 issue of *Arts*
magazine, describing *Touch of Evil* as

> a film which humbles us a bit because it's by a man who thinks more swiftly than
> we do, and much better, and who throws another marvelous film at us when we're
> still reeling under the last one.

General audiences overseas appreciated it, too. As Welles told Bogdanovich, distributors "put [the movie] into a theatre in Paris for a couple of weeks and it ran a year and
a half. It did tremendous business all over the world."[6]

For almost two decades, despite its mutilated condition, the 95-minute version of
the picture cultivated a following of highbrow critics—including the likes of André
Bazin and Andrew Sarris—who regarded it as the work of an auteur. And in the early
Seventies, when academic interest in film noir began to flourish, *Touch of Evil* came to
be recognized as one of the cycle's most important products. Appreciation for the film
increased even further in 1975, after an archivist at UCLA unearthed a lost,
108-minute copy of the film. By the way, as Terry Comito in his introduction to *Touch
of Evil* (Orson Welles, director) explains, it was hoped at first "that this was Welles'
own long lost version of the film. This proved to be not quite the case. It contains at
least one long expository scene shot after Welles had left the project by Harry Keller."

As the years passed, reverence for *Touch of Evil* grew. In journals and magazines articles continued to appear as scholars offered new interpretations of the film and in-
vestigated its production history.[7] One of the most important of these essays,
Jonathan Rosenbaum's "Touch of Evil: Orson Welles' Memo to Universal," was published by *Film Quarterly* in 1992. In the piece, Rosenbaum discusses and presents ex-
cerpts from a 58-page letter that Welles wrote to Edward Muhl, a vice president at
Universal-International, after Welles watched the re-edited version of his film in December 1957. Troubled by the 'damage' caused by the studio, Welles filled his memo
with corrections that he thought would restore the film's coherency and emotional
force; the studio, however, largely ignored these suggestions.

Then, in 1997, a producer named Rick Schmidlin, after reading Rosenbaum's article,
decided to pitch the idea of re-editing the film in a manner that would adhere as
closely as possible to Welles' suggestions. The idea was well received. In fact, Univer-

sal even supplied Schmidlin with a complete copy of the memo, and soon the producer—with Rosenbaum and editors Walter Murch, Bob O'Neil and Bill Varney—
started on the 'restoration' of *Touch of Evil*. Using the memo, the original shooting
script and the director's production notes, the restorers introduced 50 stylistic and
structural changes. Most notably, they removed the credit titles from the famous opening one-take shot, re-mixed the soundtrack and inserted more of Welles' original
footage and eliminated most of Keller's.

In addition to lengthening the running time to 111 minutes, these alterations also
improved the film's structural unity, a result which has helped to make the plot, mood
and themes more apparent and understandable. As Murch argues, in his article for *The
New York Times* (which appeared shortly after the restoration's 1998 release), the
changes "emphasize and clarify the story," making it "more in line with the director's
vision, more self-consistent, more confidently modulated, clearer. In other words, more
as it should have been." Contemporary critics have generally agreed with this assessment, as well. For example, Todd McCarthy, in a review for *Variety*, explains:

> *Touch of Evil* now emerges simultaneously as more impressionistic and more co-
> herent that it did before. The plot, always formidable in its tortured complexity, es-
> pecially on first exposure, can now be followed more easily. The initial-release
> version of the picture had a hallucinatory, feverish quality which, while still present,
> has been a tad reduced by the precise technical tweaking. On the other hand, due
> to the pristine new print, Welles' technical virtuosity and ingenious use of locations
> have never been more evident, and the entire picture moves more smoothly.

This "director's cut" copy, as interesting—and aesthetically satisfying—as it is, however, raises more questions. Why, for example, did the producers replace Welles' version of the film with one that was notably inferior? And why did Welles—who had
wanted to re-start his career with the film—endanger (and ultimately destroy) this
opportunity by delivering a product that challenged and flouted Universal-International's expectations?

Artistic Suicide

We can start to answer these questions by looking at the reasons why the film was
seized from Welles in the first place. Walter Murch believes that the producers did
this because

> they were upset and confused by the film's innovative editing and camerawork, its
> use of real locations, its unorthodox use of sound and, thematically, the boldness
> of its reversals and routine acceptance of human degradation.

Welles, as he revealed to Bogdanovich, shared similar thoughts: "The picture was just
too dark and black and strange for them."

A drugged-up Susan Vargas (Janet Leigh) screams her lungs out on the balcony of a sleazy border town hotel in *Touch of Evil*.

Indeed, without the interference caused by the studio's additions, elisions and interruptions, the film's nihilistic mood—its ability to "make the viewer co-experience the anguish and insecurity which are the true emotions of contemporary film noir"—is more present and potent.[8] Arguably, the mood is darker because one of the movie's central themes, its condemnation of abusive police power, is allowed to surge to the surface. More than before, in particular, Quinlan—the protector of American law and order—resembles a tyrant, albeit a tragic one; and his 'third degree' techniques more obviously recall tactics associated with police figures in totalitarian states.[9] That Welles wanted Quinlan and his cronies—District Attorney Adair and Police Chief Gould—to evoke Nazi Germany is obvious from remarks he made in *Cahiers du Cinema*:

> I firmly believe that in the modern world we need to choose between the morality of the law and the morality of simple justice; which is to say, between lynching someone or letting him go free. I'd rather have a murderer be free than have the police arrest him by mistake. Quinlan does not want to submit the guilty ones to justice so much as to assassinate them in the name of the law, using the police for his own purposes; and this is a fascist scenario, a totalitarian scenario, contrary to traditional law and human justice as I understand them.

However, though this 'restored' expression of Welles' point of view—this approximation of the 1957 screening copy—is caustic, similar portraits of American authority had appeared in other noir movies shot in the years prior to *Touch of Evil*. Consider, for a moment, the similarities the restored cut shares with Fritz Lang's unsparing (and commercially successful) attack on corruption, *The Big Heat* (1953). In both pictures, cops turn into vigilantes and collaborate with criminals as they place personal inter-ests before public ones. And in both, the directors' distaste for criminals is revealed constantly through the manner in which the films are constructed, from close-ups on monstrous faces to careening camera movements that emphasize the chaos that sur-rounds these characters' lives. In the 1958 and 1975 versions of *Touch of Evil*, however, these stylistic similarities are simply not as present—nor as easy to recognize. Other exemplars of film noir—as various as Siodmak's *The Killers* (1946), Lewis' *Gun Crazy* (1949) and Hathaway's *Niagara* (1953)—also resemble, if not equal, the new cut with their unrestrained renderings of violence and disorder.

But these works escaped their studios' wrath, did well in the box office and helped—or, at least, prolonged—the careers of their directors. Yet Welles' film, which embraced the narrative conventions of the crime picture (with its gangster family, gun-play and lawlessness) and the mood, tone, themes and motifs of the noir style, not only received drastic revisions, it finished him as a mainstream director. By 1957, apparently, Universal-International—and Hollywood in general—no longer wanted films of this sort. A review of the causes that contributed to this switch—from tolerance to intol-erance—may prove helpful at this point in our discussion.

A Man Out of Time

In his seminal essay "Three Faces of Film Noir," Tom Finn argues that the noir style—with its emphasis upon the dark side of human nature—emerged from "the fires of war, exile, and disillusion, a melodramatic reflection of a world gone mad." This style, which characterized hundreds of movies produced during the middle of the last cen-tury, expressed the sense of "post-war disillusionment" that had seeped into the na-tion after soldiers returned from the European and Asian theatres of World War II.[10] In *Hollywood's Dark Cinema*, R. Barton Palmer points out that the film industry recog-nized this pessimism and consciously appealed to it:

> The dark vision of American culture constructed in film noirs was acceptable to
> audiences at the time. Noir films would never have been made or attained popu-
> larity had their themes and form not corresponded to broad and insistent ele-
> ments of popular taste, elements that may have made their blackness less striking,
> less noticeable, to postwar American viewers.

A "sociological change" occurred, however, almost 10 years after Japan's surrender, fo-mented, perhaps, by advances in technology, the spread of television and the ending of the Korean War.[11] This change—a collective, national turn toward confidence about the present and optimism for the future—seems to have crystallized shortly after the U. S. Senate's 1954 censure of Joseph McCarthy, the Wisconsin politician who had aggravated the nation's anxiety about the "Red Menace" with his lists of suspected Communists, his high-profile hearings and his career-destroying accusations. Joseph Mc-Carthy was censured on December 2, 1954. With McCarthy's collapse, the appetite for cynical critiques of American institutions and mores quickly disappeared. In his article "From the Nightmare Factory: HUAC and the Politics of Noir," Phillip Kemp explains:

> The last and the darkest phase of film noir coincides with the height of the anti-Communist obsession, and the decline of the cycle follows closely on the fall of McCarthy. As the hysteria loosened its grip, the national psyche no longer needed the countervailing subconscious fantasies or, at least, not that particular kind.

As the nation moved toward 'post-post-war disillusionment,' that is, Hollywood followed, and the numbers of films made in the noir style dropped. During this period, incidentally, escapist films—ranging from romantic comedies to biblical epics—enjoyed renewed popularity and increased rates of production.

Welles, of course, was probably unaware of these developments in popular taste when he scripted, shot and cut *Touch of Evil*. And he may not have thought to note or care about the declining output of hard-boiled crime pictures after 1954. In *Cahiers du Cinema*, for instance, he professed to being a poor student of cinema: "I go to the movies very rarely, and this is not because I don't like it, it is because it procures me no enjoyment at all. I do not think I am very intelligent about films." In addition, he'd departed from the U.S. in the late Forties—during the peak years of the noir cycle—to escape professional problems wrought by his left-of-center political sympathies and a string of high-profile busts, including *Citizen Kane* (1941) and *The Lady from Shanghai* (1948). These factors, according to Terry Comito, had forced the maverick director into "exile in Europe, accepting roles in mostly mediocre films in order to finance his own intermittent and often aborted projects," a situation which distanced him from the minor and major changes that were transforming his native country's character (and tastes).

Market Forces

Thus, when Welles returned to Hollywood in 1956 and accepted Albert Zugsmith's offer, it seems very likely that he didn't understand what the studio expected from him and his movie. And as he made this movie, which David Thomson in *Rosebud* claims was "clearly an attempt at a comeback," he appears to have consciously emulated the noir style, probably because it had been so popular and profitable in the years before his departure from Hollywood, back in 1948. However, with each effort to make the film adhere to the visual and thematic conventions of noir, Welles moved closer to professional failure; formerly accepted methods and concerns, that is, were now perceived as threatening and subversive.[12] And because of this, the studio chiefs, in an attempt, it seems, to salvage the picture's commercial potential, reorganized and changed its content, muddling and muting its criticism of Americans and their socio-political institutions. *Touch of Evil,* in short, was re-worked as it was because the producers at Universal-International felt obliged to thwart its rhetorical objectives—even if this strategy damaged the movie's dramatic structure.

Nevertheless, the complacency that marked America in the late Fifties dissipated less than a decade later. As Robert Ottoson, in *A Reference Guide to the American Film Noir,* explains:

> The Vietnam War was highly unpopular and a great source of disillusionment to people who thought their country could do no wrong.... [It] brought about a mood of hopeless resignation not unlike the postwar pessimism prevalent during the 'golden age' of film noir.

And Hollywood responded to this new resignation by darkening the screen again with angry pictures—like *Madigan* (1968) and *The French Connection* (1971)—in which police characters, much like Quinlan, often regard criminals and the law with equal contempt. But these films enjoyed studio support and high receipts—a phenomenon that eluded Welles from the beginning of his movie career all the way up to its bitter end.

NOTES

1. *Kiss Me Deadly* and *The Big Combo* were both released in 1955.

2. The following summary of *Touch of Evil,* by Blake Lucas and Tracey Thompson, can be found in the third edition of *Film Noir: An Encyclopedic Reference to the American Style,* p. 293: "One night on the Mexican border, a millionaire named Linnekar is blown up along with his blonde companion by a time bomb planted in his car. At odds in the investigation are Mike Vargas, a Mexican narcotics investigator on his honeymoon with his American wife, Susan, and Hank Quinlan, a shrewd stateside detective. Quinlan believes that a young Mexican, Sanchez, is guilty of the murder and plants evidence to frame him. Discovering this, Vargas seeks to expose Quinlan. The outraged Quinlan, who has routinely framed suspects ever since he failed to bring his wife's murderer to justice, retaliates by enlisting the help of racketeer Uncle Joe Grandi, who is seeking to discredit Vargas so that the mobster's brother will not go to prison. Grandi sends a gang of punks to the American motel where Susan Vargas is staying to set her up as an apparent drug addict. To cover his tracks, Quinlan kills Grandi in the hotel room to which Susan has been brought, but Quinlan's devoted partner, Menzies, discovers Quinlan's cane in the room and is pressured by Vargas to expose Quinlan. Menzies gets Quinlan's confession, which is surreptitiously recorded by Vargas. Quinlan discovers the betrayal and shoots Menzies, who in turn shoots him. The two men die as news arrives that Sanchez has confessed to the initial bomb murder. Clear of the drug charge, Susan asks her husband to take her away while Tanya, Quinlan's old friend, has a last philosophical word to say about the once powerful cop." Although this summary is based upon the 1958 version of the film, it covers all of the plot's essential elements. The 1998 restoration copy, we should note, doesn't change the story so much as it enhances

its presentation. "Whit Masterson" is a pseudonym used by Bob Wade and Bill Miller, who wrote together as a team. Universal-International released *Man in the Shadow* in 1957.

3. RKO released *Macbeth* in 1948.

4. In 1946, Universal Pictures merged with International Pictures. The company adopted the name "Universal-International Pictures," which lasted until 1963, when "International" was dropped. Welles is referring to Universal-International, not Universal, in this passage. See Gene Blottner, Universal-International Westerns, 1947–1963, pp. 8–12.

5. See *This is Orson Welles,* p. 297: "The actual title [of the novel, the movie's source] is *Badge of Evil,* which was also what the picture was called originally. I don't know where they got *Touch of Evil* or what it means, but it sounds all right." Perhaps the studio removed "badge," a reference to the police, in order to further dilute the film's attacks on American government and authority.

6. *Touch of Evil* also won First Place at the 1958 World's Fair film festival in Brussels.

7. For instance, see John C. Stubbs' "The Evolution of Orson Welles's *Touch of Evil* from Novel to Film" and Stephen Heath's "Film and System: Terms of Analysis," both collected in *Touch of Evil* (Orson Welles, Director), edited by Terry Comito.

8. From Raymond Borde and Etienne Chaumeton's "Towards a Definition of Film Noir," collected in *Film Noir Reader,* p. 25.

9. See *This is Orson Welles,* p. 299, "Bogdanovich: Well, the theme is restated several times. Somebody says, 'It's a tough job to be a policeman,' and Heston says, 'It's supposed to be tough—a policeman's job is only easy in a police state.' Welles: Yes. I decided that, since I was doing a melodrama, I'd do one about good and evil, and it's a quite simple statement of what I considered to be good and evil." Heston/Vargas actually says: "It's supposed to be. It has to be tough. The policeman's job is only easy in a police state. That's the whole point, captain. Who is the boss, the cop or the law?"

10. See Alain Silver, "Introduction," *Film Noir: An Encyclopedic Reference,* p. 6: "[I]n the classic period, the span of years from just before World War II to just after the Korean conflict, the major and minor studios put several hundred film noir into distribution." The U.S. and North Korea agreed to a cease fire on July 27, 1953. The phrase "post-war disillusionment" appears in Paul Schrader, "Notes on Film Noir," collected in *Film Noir Reader.*

11. Silver discusses this mood swing in his introduction to *Film Noir: An Encyclopedic Reference,* p. 6. He describes what happened as "a sociological change, a shift in national preoccupations as an undirected, postwar malaise was replaced by a legitimate if less apocalyptic concern over economic recessions and foreign entanglements." See also David Halberstam, *The Fifties,* p. 505: "In that era of general good will and expanding affluence, few Americans doubted the essential goodness of their society. After all, it was reflected back at them not only by contemporary books and magazines, but even more powerfully and with even greater influence in the new family sitcoms on television . . . . However, most Americans needed little coaching in how they wanted to live. They were optimistic about the future."

Also see Tise Vahimagi, *The BFI Companion to Crime,* p. 133: "Film noir became obsolete at the end of the 50s, when post-war malaise was superseded by the optimism of the new decade." Additional reasons for the decline in the production of noir films appear in Robert Porfirio, "Introduction," *Film Noir Reader 3,* pp. 6–7. Porfirio cites the loss of the "B" film market, the increased use of color film and the emergence of "new popular genres," which enticed noir veterans like Preminger, Wise and Wilder away from crime melodramas.

12. See Alain Silver, "Introduction," *Film Noir Reader 2,* p. 3: "While it is undeniable that the film-makers of that era were most, if not all, unfamiliar with the term film noir, it seems also undeniable to us that they were familiar with the concept." See also Terry Comito, "Introduction," *Touch of Evil* (Orson Welles, director), p. 4. Comito discusses the film's adherence to the conventions of the crime film genre and the noir style: "In spite of what may appear an almost perverse abruptness, the explosive opening of *Touch of Evil* places it within a familiar narrative tradition. Crime thrillers of the thirties and forties, like the sombre film noirs of the forties and fifties, characteristically begin with a sudden, spectacular outburst of violence, whose consequences the rest of the film seeks to untangle."

Modern-day Pandora Lily Carver (Gaby Rodgers) opens the "great whatsit" box and receives her reward.

Voices from the Deep: Film Noir as Psychodrama

J. P. Telotte

My ambitions in this article are fairly simple. First, I want to suggest a trope that could be useful for thinking about the film noir. Second, I want to approach this form in what might seem a rather "spacey" way; that is, I want to talk about depth: the depth of noir's subjects, the deep recesses of the mind it commonly explored, the depth of field that was one of its stylistic hallmarks. Rather than just using this vantage to survey the form, though, I want to suggest how these varied dimensions overlap and help constitute its distinctive voice. I offer this "deep" vantage to help place noir's generic stories of crime, murder, mystery, and detection within the context of postwar American film and to model another way we might consider approaching our cinema in that era.

Certainly, the film noir of that period was fascinated with exploring the deep recesses of American culture, with the dark realms of gangsters and organized crime, as well as with the petty and even accidental criminal, with everything that seemed to threaten both the individual and social status quo. At the same time, it found new narrative material in subjects that had been repressed or, for various reasons, conveniently pushed to a cultural background in the war years—topics like juvenile delinquency (*City Across the River* [1949]), corruption in office (*Boomerang* [1947], *The Phenix City Story* [1955]), racism (*Crossfire* [1947]), and rapacious big business (*All My Sons, The Big Clock* [both 1948]). Taken together, these various cultural concerns clearly point to what David Bordwell describes as noir's "challenge to dominant values" (page 75).

With these explorations of crime, corruption, violence, and varied social failings the film noir moved into the dark recesses of American culture in a way that we had not seen since the social problem films of the Depression era. And these explorations were all the more troubling given the lack of those cultural scars—bombed-out cities, devastated landscapes, hordes of displaced people, etc.—that the rest of the world sported at the time. But noir in its own way compensates for that lack, borrowing heavily from certain cultural images of the war that our films, especially the newsreels and documentaries, had offered up and left as a disturbing legacy—images, as Jon Tuska says, "that could and did haunt the minds of Americans" (155) and left them to consider what could be in our world. Thus, to correspond to those depths, film noir repeatedly offered its own surface icons: dismal cityscapes, decaying if not bombed-out buildings, and individuals aimlessly wandering the night streets—all of which had to leave viewers hoping, like the protagonist of Maxwell Shane's *Nightmare* (1956), that these images were all just part of "some crazy dream."

Yet a recurring noir motif is the *insistence* of these dark elements, the upwelling of what 1930s crime films defined as a criminal underworld into our normal world, the connection between those icons and something deeper, perhaps outside the movies and the otherwise comforting situation of the movie theater. Noir films emphasized that those stark images were part of our own, not some distant, foreign culture, and repressing them, returning them to the depths where we might have preferred they remain, or simply containing them within the bounds of conventional generic narrative would be more difficult than vanquishing some foreign enemy, despite the efforts of a film like *The Big Heat* (1953) to suggest we think of and deal with them in the same way.

While exploring these cultural chasms, noir, as we know, proved equally adept at plumbing the individual depths of the troubled mind. Of course, the noir predilection for voice-over, flashback narratives,[1] films whose style typically implies a psyche dredging up prior events and trying to make some sense of them, already points in this direction; as do the various films in which psychiatrists and psychological inquiry play prominent roles, or in which psychotic figures are central, as in *The Dark Past* (1948), *He Walked by Night* (1949) or *In a Lonely Place* (1950). In fact, as Laurence Miller notes, approximately 260 different forms of psychopathology have been identified, all of them surfacing at various points in the noir canon (Miller). Here too we find an effort to create an iconicity that might correspond to and encode these depths: dutch angles, extended subjective shots, wide-angle distortions, and most obviously the surrealist-inspired imagery of films like *Spellbound* (1945) and *The Dark Past*.

We might also note how very near are those noir films whose subject is the traumatized psyche to the era's popular psychodramas, such as *The Snake Pit* (1948), *The Rack* (1956), or *The Three Faces of Eve* (1957). Both types of films seem intent on locating and mapping the source of trauma, although the noir works emphasize its particular face: the psychotic crimes, desires, and violence that are the surface symptoms of these deep impulses. Yet all of these films are, in a sense, stories about depth. They explore the mystery of ourselves, plumb the surface of self that we show the world, penetrate our human depths. They do so not simply to dredge up what is there, but to make some sense of what is in those depths and to help accommodate us to the repressed dimensions in our personal or cultural psyches. In effect, they remind us how those human depths connect—and at times fail to connect—with the surface or face we show to the world, to the unity we, as well as our movies, usually try to construct. In fact, we might do well to think of the noir film as always a kind of psychodrama, for this approach provides a useful metaphor for linking its cultural and individual explorations. Yet Paul Schrader and others assert that we should think of noir as "first of all a style" (63) of an unusual, even strained sort. To include this vantage on noir, I want to stretch my initial trope a bit further. By thinking of the film noir as a sort of psychodrama, or more broadly as an effort to link depths and surfaces, we might be able to retain a sense of that style as we accommodate the larger noir perspective.

A film like *Nightmare* can start us in this direction. Its protagonist is musician Stan Grayson, a performer, someone who must present a pleasing front to his audience, although that front belies his depths. For his bandmates term him "too modern" and reject his arrangements as "too progressive," and he is haunted by a recurring dream. Stan's story begins with a face rising to the surface of a dark pool as he recounts this terrifying dream in which, in "a queer, mirrored room," he kills a stranger. When he tries to escape through one of the mirrored doors there, he plummets into darkness. On awakening, Stan finds bruises, as if from a struggle; he notes blood on his hands; and on his bureau are various objects from the dream. Thanks to these tangible signs, the dream refuses to go away, despite his brother-in-law Rene's clumsy psychoanalytic effort at trying to "talk" him out of it. Like some postwar trauma—which indeed it seems to metaphorize—it haunts Stan's every moment, seemingly marking him as a murderer, burdening him with guilt, and compelling him to explore its dark depths.

His initial effort at resolving this trauma, though, is to separate surface and depth, culture and self. He feels that "out there," in the world around him, "everything was status quo"; only "in here," in the self, is there a problem. When that disconnection brings no relief, he tries to reconnect the "out there" and "in here." He wanders the streets of New Orleans, looking for someone to help put the pieces of his dream— and his life—together. Thus, he asks his friends to identify a strange, perhaps "progressive" piece of music he recalls from the dream. A montage of day and night street scenes, many shot in dutch angle and with a mobile camera, externalizes his trauma as a disturbing image field. Seeking distraction, Stan and Rene drive deep into bayou country, an area neither knows, and when a storm comes up, turn onto an unmarked road—a recurring motif in films of this period—which leads to a large, empty house where Stan finds his mirrored room, the scene of the dream murder. There, behind a series of locked and mirrored doors—surfaces that open onto dark secrets—he uncovers more of his dream's elements, including bloodstains, and finds that a murder did occur. Eventually, with Rene's help, he learns that the neighbor in his hotel had hypnotized him and used him in a plot to kill the neighbor's wife and her lover. With that solution—and the death of the murderous neighbor—Stan returns to his regular life, his girlfriend, and the stage with his band.

It is a pat ending for an otherwise rather unsettling disclosure—that we are easily manipulated by forces beyond our consciousness, control, or understanding, forces at work behind our neighbor's door and intent on frustrating our desire for unity or wholeness. It reminds us how easily we can be plunged into depths from which we might never recover. And it never recuperates Stan's "progressive" character or the fact that he did kill someone. Even that strange music he heard and that we link to his "progressive" nature is revealed to be no more than a record played at the wrong speed. But then no resolution—save for the *Dallas*-type retreat in which everything proves to be a dream—could really work here. The deaths, like those millions in the war, cannot be erased, and like our cultural psyche, the individual one, here opened up and its vulnerable nature briefly explored, could hardly be filled in like some pothole. Knowing of his manipulation, moving through those mirrored doors, seeing a link between the "out there" and the "in here" has to suffice.

Perhaps part of the problem is that *Nightmare* seems like a post-war film come ten years too late. It is, in fact, a remake of the 1947 production *Fear in the Night,* a work that does seem to direct its narrative at some sort of post-war trauma, as a way of coping with our national guilt over the massive deaths of the war and a kind of loss of cultural identity and purpose that followed. But by 1956 *Nightmare* could not make those same connections, draw very effectively on that earlier cultural climate. Consequently, its metaphoric potential never quite connects, and we are left with a trope that floats unmoored through this narrative, with what we might think of as a signifier strangely cut off from its signified.

We might note a similar problem of balance or correspondence in the film's rather un-neat style, one that involves more than just the expressionist hallmarks we expect in film noir. *Nightmare*'s already disturbing visual scheme is fitted to a narrative that moves by fits and starts: shifting into and out of flashback, offering sequences that seem like narrative blind alleys (such as Stan's meeting a blond who recalls the girl in his dream), and begging the question of causality (why Stan was targeted for this plot). The film itself, with its surfaces and depths[2] and maze-like plot, does seem almost like "some crazy dream," like the very stuff its narrative tries to repress or explain away, and that its protagonist cannot escape.

But let me emphasize that visual scheme for a moment. Its various components are ones we know well—low-key lighting, distorting close-ups, unbalanced compositions, an emphasis on oblique lines and reflective surfaces (pools of water, mirrors)—all of which conspire to make this world look strange, to distort its surface. Yet that stylized imagery shares time with starkly realistic location photography and an emphasis on depth of field—elements usually catalogued as hallmarks of film realism. In their key essay on noir style, Place and Peterson hold that one of noir's "requirements" is a "greater 'depth of field'" (31) than normal in American cinema. This emphasis on deep focus and a composition in depth, remains fairly consistent in both noir's earlier entries and its later, more neorealist examples. *Nightmare* works this combination to intriguing effect, especially in its murder room scene that plays off of the tension between deceptive mirrored surfaces and the dark depths those doors conceal. But then, as Schrader also notes, another of noir's striking traits was its ability "to weld" such "seemingly contradictory elements into a uniform style" (56). The general success of that "welding" prompts Bordwell's assertion that noir is quite conventional in its own way, that it "no more subverts the classical film than crime fiction undercuts the orthodox novel" (77). Despite its flimsy effort at closing its dreamy narrative, at shutting its mirrored doors on its disturbing glimpses of a deeper, darker world, at satisfactorily balancing surface and depth, though, *Nightmare* cannot quite pass for a classical Hollywood film, and the very clash of styles it illustrates suggests something of the hidden, the repressed in this form, as well as in the larger body of American cinema.

In this almost "contradictory" character we might begin to make out another sort of depth analysis that surfaces to varying degrees in the film noir. For these films often seem to flaunt their style, in various ways to foreground—that is, to draw up near the surface—their markedly inflected nature. Obvious examples are the frequent prologues that note how the ensuing story will unfold. For example, the subjective narrative *Lady in the Lake* (1947) begins with Philip Marlowe talking to us, warning that "You'll see it just as I saw it. You'll meet the people; you'll find the clues." The docudrama *Boomerang* (1947) opens with a 360-degree pan of a small town square, as a voice-of-god narrator notes that "the basic facts of our story actually occurred in a Connecticut community much like this one." And *Nightmare*'s dream-investigation begins with that head appearing in a dark pool, while a voice, bespeaking our own experience, recalls how "At first, all I could see was this face... floating toward me." Since this is what we too "first... see," the narration quickly points up how the film looks, how its story will unfold, and how easily we might be drawn into it. The larger effect of such openings, such initial signs, is to make us more aware, in a manner classical Hollywood films usually avoided, of narrative style itself.

What such a self-consciousness begins to suggest is an extra level of dredging up and working out, another sort of psychodrama ongoing in American postwar/cold-war films. For just as they located new subjects in what had been culturally or individually repressed, so does the film noir seem intrigued with the traditional and unremarked voice in which the American cinema spoke and with inspecting its typical inflections. In fact, in this period, we might see it as the film industry's own psychodrama, exploring the given language of the movies and holding, along with the givens of culture and self, elements of classical narrative up for examination, in the process letting us glimpse the discontinuities and gaps within the imaginary realm of wholeness and completeness classical cinema had traditionally sought to offer.

On one, very broad level, as I have elsewhere traced out (Telotte), this impulse generates a kind of reflexive turn through a focus on the various ways in which modern media wield their nearly invisible, even hypnotic powers over us. In fact, several of the best noirs analyze the inner workings of the film industry, notably *In a Lonely Place* and *The Big Knife* (1955), while others do a kind of depth analysis on elements of the larger communication industry: newspapers (*The Big Carnival* [1951], *Beyond a Reasonable Doubt* [1956]), radio (*Nightmare Alley* [1947]), television (*Trial without Jury* [1950], *The Glass Web* [1953]), and even the stage (*A Double Life* [1948], *The Sweet Smell of Success* [1957]). A film like *The Harder They Fall* (1956) is particularly exemplary, as it shows how the combination of newsreels, television, radio, and newspapers effectively create a persona—as a skilled press agent manipulates the media to turn a lumbering, unskilled Argentine giant into a supposed heavyweight boxing contender—and hints as well of how those same forces might shape or misshape our own identities, just as Humphrey Bogart's agent figure is nearly corrupted by the forces he tries to control. But probably the most famous example of this impulse is Billy Wilder's *Sunset Boulevard* (1950), which explores the shaping hold film has on us, how its seeming depths link up only with a false surface and can deprive us of any real experience of depth.

On another, less obvious level, this impulse surfaces in that strange, at times contradictory style we have described—one that constantly seems to shift between the sort of conventionally constructed reality we expect in film narrative and a rather bizarre mode of vision that cannot help but remind us how contrived film realism actually is, how much the depths it does depict are themselves but a surface construct. This problematic styling shows up most clearly in films like *Nightmare, The Dark Past,* and *Blackout* (1954), works whose use of realistic mise-en-scène, often shot on location, are filled with a dream-like imagery that reflects a character's strained, psychotic state. But the prime example is Robert Aldrich's *Kiss Me Deadly* (1955), a film that moves far afield from the Mickey Spillane novel it adapts to investigate the nature of both the popular detective and film narrative itself.

II.

Sunset Boulevard's place in this context may be all too obvious. It is, after all, about the film industry and what it can do to those who surrender to its seductive power. As such, it may have helped inspire the similar focus of *In a Lonely Place,* which appeared the following year,[3] and also suggested the viability of Aldrich's jaundiced look at the industry's destructive effects on its workers, *The Big Knife* (1955). Yet the way *Sunset Boulevard* talks about the film industry seems especially noteworthy alongside a film like *Kiss Me Deadly,* its combination of subject and style a milepost for the later film. It begins with an in-depth tracking shot, as a car moves down a Hollywood street, and it ends with death and madness—the end results of its penetration into Hollywood's depths—brought into close-up. Speaking from the point of his death—delving back into his life, as if trying to gauge the depths that led to this end—murdered screen-writer Joe Gillis describes a series of wrong turns he took as he moved deeper into this world. From a start as a promising young writer, he turned to producing simple formula stories "that would sell." When those formula pieces fail, creditors hound him, and so one day he accidentally turns into faded film queen Norma Desmond's drive-way and hides his car in her garage. From that literal turning point, Joe finds himself, almost unwittingly, moving deeper into her world: working in her cavernous living room, moving into the room above her garage, shifting to the "husband's room" ad-joining Norma's suite, and eventually, we gather, sharing her bed. When he tries to leave, Joe is shot and falls into Norma's pool, where he lies floating until the police fish him out. And Norma, thinking she is again before Cecil B. DeMille's cameras, walks into the foreground, blurring the image as she announces, "I'm ready for my close-up."

The narrative of this steady movement ever deeper into a dangerous cinematic world and its subsequent move out, ending on Norma's blurred close-up, rather liter-alizes the activity of a psychodrama. It also has a resonance in the film's visual style. For the opening tracking camera anticipates the fluid tracking and panning shots that con-stantly draw us into Norma's cluttered home, emphasizing its cavernous rooms, the jumble of her Hollywood career, and, ominously, the door to her room. That fluid movement suggests an intriguing depth to this world and mimics Joe's curious explo-ration of it. It suggests too the film's structure around the examination of these depths. Yet the doors, mirrors, pictures and portraits of Norma, even the movie screen on which the camera several times comes to rest—and perhaps the surface of the pool in which Joe's body floats—hint of something else: a lack of real depth or sub-stance in this homage to self and cinema Norma Desmond has built.

Another element of that realist style, the film's emphasis on layered images, further underscores the troubled—and troubling—sense of depth being explored here. For as Joe moves through Norma's house or sits working on her filmscript, he seems buried in her world's clutter, as tables, lamps, and pictures fill the foreground, constrict the frame, and swallow him up in the background. The same elements that help construct a sense of depth thus also work to turn it into something else, to reconstruct this world not as alluring and realistic image, but as trap, prison, burial chamber, or in an anticipatory postmodern turn, even as collage. Joe here seems placed in a far more elaborate box, but essentially of the same sort as Norma orders for her dear dead pet monkey. Even the entry to Norma's house works in much the same way; it is constructed in depth, a barred door opening onto a solid, interior one, the combination suggesting both restricted entry and entrapment, depth and depthlessness. Thus we several times see Joe framed behind the barred door in a composition that points up his entrapment here.

What the depth of *Sunset Boulevard*'s mise-en-scène ultimately reveals, then, is a world that has lost any real depth—a cinematic world that too easily renders its

Norma Desmond (Gloria Swanson) is ready for her "final close-up" as her faithful servant (Erich von Stroheim) directs in *Sunset Boulevard*.

inhabitants similarly dimensionless, flat, leaves them, in perhaps a nice metaphor for the movie star, floating on a sheer surface. This point is made, almost ironically, by a character who seems immune to this lure. Joe's co-writer Betty Schaefer takes him down the Paramount back lot and notes, "Look at this street—all cardboard, all hollow, all phoney, all done with mirrors. You know, I like it better than any street in the world." She then fleshes out this confession of her love affair with the movies by revealing how she had once rendered herself like that phoney, constructed street: doing all she could, including getting her nose fixed, to try to get before the camera—only to be rejected because she could not act.

This scene emphasizes not only how illusory the cinematic world's depth is, but also how it invites us to become like it, to construct a facade of self. In effect, it warns against investing unwarily and too heavily in the film world, lest we wind up like the principal characters at the close of *Sunset Boulevard*. Joe, shot by Norma, lies floating in her pool. Max still attends to Norma, helping sustain the fantasy that she is a movie queen beloved by her fans, while maintaining his own tangential link to the film world. And Norma walks into the foreground, into the camera at film's end, her image blurring—and in the process mocking the deep focus that has suggested this world's depths. It is, finally, just a world of movies, of film, of surfaces that, like Norma herself, have lost contact with the real depths of this world, and its tragedy is that, for all their awareness of its falseness, its facades, its hollowness, the people here almost without exception embrace it, opt to float on that shimmering surface.

III.

While *Sunset Boulevard* emphasizes subject in its psychodrama of the movie industry, *Kiss Me Deadly* more emphatically foregrounds style. It does, in a marked shift from Spillane's novel which is set in New York, place detective Mike Hammer's investigations in a Hollywood setting, thereby hinting of some connection between the film industry and the criminal underworld. But its concern is more with the nature of his movements, with the style of the detective and the detective film, through which it can better comment on films of its own type.

Like the other films discussed here, it too begins with a testimony to depth, to the realistic imperative it seemingly implies, and to the sort of activity we expect in such films, the drawing out of some deeply buried knowledge. The character Christina runs diagonally down a highway and then directly towards the camera. She seems to flee from something in the dark as she moves toward the lights of the approaching cars. As we later learn, she carries some special knowledge which, she feels, must be brought to the surface; as she tells Mike Hammer, "when people are in trouble, they need to talk." His investigation of her subsequent murder largely follows from this start, as he probes those depths from which she has come, tries to find out "why" she was in such trouble. In the manner of classical detective films, *Kiss Me Deadly* seems intent on digging up these hidden facts and bringing criminals to justice.

But the opening's style also prepares us for a swerve in a different direction—just as Hammer's car, strangely enough, takes Christina back in the direction from which she was fleeing. For the shots of Christina running are pointedly mismatched—and repeatedly so. At first she is running down the center of the highway; then we note she is running alongside the road. This shot sequence recurs several times and, in the process, serves notice—like the credits which then scroll in reverse—that something peculiar is going on here. The cinematic construction of space, which usually depends on the matching of such cuts-on-action, self-destructs, so that our experience of depth here becomes unanchored, intrudes annoyingly into our field of investigation.

That investigation includes the characters of *Kiss Me Deadly*, especially Hammer, who clearly have little human depth. As Edwin Arnold and Eugene Miller note, Ralph Meeker plays the detective in a way that shows "the emptiness inside," "his dead soul" (41). He is a private eye with all of the type's worst traits exaggerated; he is thuggish, sadistic, unfeeling, interested in fast cars, a quick payoff, and, as Christina surmises, himself. His recurring line is, fittingly, "What's in it for me?"—perhaps because there seems so little "in" him. In fact, he seems minimally suited for plumbing this world's depths, for digging up the secret behind Christina's murder and his own near death precisely because he has so little real depth or understanding. Thus he typically uses others to do his work—his secretary Velda, his friend Nick, the gangster Carl Evello's sister Friday—while his own bumbling injures and even kills those he uses.

In this way *Kiss Me Deadly* offers a rather different take on both the style and subject of the conventional detective film—a take that enables it to explore film's own depths in this period. As Aldrich described his project, "In terms of style, in terms of the way we tried to make it, it provided a . . . showcase to display my own ideas of movie-making" (Arnold 42). And they prove to be rather unconventional ideas about film and the film detective. As we have noted, one of the pillars of classical narrative, continuity editing, often disappears—or to be more precise, repeatedly fails, as in a later work like *Breathless* (1960), so that we see the seams in the narrative, the manipulations of our point of view, the mismatched fragments of the story constructed for us. Similarly, Hammer often seems a rather disjointed construct: knowledgeable and dumb, cocky yet vulnerable, and in an improbability born of many other generic efforts, brought back several times, as his friend Nick puts it, "as if from the dead" to continue his fumbling efforts.

But then the world in which Hammer and the other characters move seems to have little real depth or dimension either, despite its location shooting, save for what is transparently constructed by the cinematic apparatus. In fact, *Kiss Me Deadly* repeatedly emphasizes just how artificial or deceptive the appearance of depth here is—in both the world and its characters. Consider, for example, the trompe l'oeil effect when Mike goes to Velda's apartment and watches her exercise. Slowly, a pan of the camera reveals that we have been looking not deep into her apartment, but at a near wall covered in mirrors that reflect Velda and the apartment's interior. As other examples, we might think of the various times when a reverse angle shot puts us in a spatially illogical position, at an impossible depth, as when a car falls onto Nick and we watch from the car's point of view as it crosses an incredibly long distance. Similarly, when Mike enters Gabrielle's apartment, we see him inexplicably through the bars of her bed—a bed that, reverse shots reveal, is shoved against a back wall. When Mike slaps around William Mist, we watch the entire action from a point of view located within Mist's medicine cabinet. And when Mike finally discovers the object of his quest, "the great whatsit," we see first from Mike's vantage, as he peers into a small locker at the Hollywood Athletic Club, and then from within, behind the "whatsit" that, a reverse angle shows, fills the locker's base.

Admittedly, this last scene, offering its impossible low, reverse-angle shot four times, serves a conventional narrative function. It shows Hammer in an awkward, low-angle close-up which, with the wide-angle lens, distorts his face, emphasizes his near-manic look, and reminds us of his sadistic glee in torturing the morgue doctor and slapping around the club attendant to get access to the locker. As in the visual distortions found in many other noirs, this shot series externalizes a distortion within the central character, like the similar wide-angle close-ups of the mobster Carl Evello and his henchmen, and so stylistically links the detective and his enemies.

Yet far more important is the pattern of camera placement in such scenes that brings us up short by bringing the illusion of depth itself up short, making us aware of this world's illusory nature. Conventionally, classical narrative asks us to do a kind of "cognitive mapping" (Bordwell 59) of the world it visualizes, to imaginatively con-

Cecil B. DeMille plays himself as he comforts the delusional Norma (Gloria Swanson) in *Sunset Boulevard*.

struct the larger dimensions of a supposedly coherent world that we never see in its entirety. But here, the construction frequently fails. Thus when Hammer dispatches a thug who is following him, we cut from a high-angle shot as Hammer knocks him down a long flight of stairs to a far low-angle shot, done with a wide-angle lens. While the cut maps us in depth, the lens dissolves it by distorting and enlarging the foreground while making the background recede from view. As a result, Hammer nearly disappears from sight, while the thug appears to fall *up* the stairs. Similarly, in Gabrielle's apartment building, a series of reverse-angle shots of the stairs creates Escher-like images that flatten out the illusion of depth and leave us unsure whether we are looking up or down. Appropriately, given its name, the Hollywood Athletic Club scene underscores this constructed depth. As Hammer enters, he walks from the camera into the background, momentarily blurring the image, and when he leaves, he walks directly into the camera, again blurring the focus before the scene dissolves in but another of the film's repeated and unconventional strikes at the traditional reality illusion of Hollywood film.

Still, we can describe Hammer's investigation, perhaps with a bit of ironic justification, as a kind of in-depth exploration. As Velda describes his usual process, "First you find a little thread, the thread leads you to a piece of string, the string leads to a rope, and from the rope you hang by the neck." In the labyrinthine quality this remark suggests, *Kiss Me Deadly* recalls many other detective-type noirs, as Hammer goes from one lead to another. The frequent shots of him carefully checking the hallways of his apartment building or Christina's former rooms, walking the streets of Los Angeles, and looking through seedy buildings for Lily Carver and Carmen Trivago emphasize his efforts to thread this labyrinth in the fashion of so many of his cinematic predecessors. But much of this movement, like Stan's in *Nightmare,* seems nearly pointless, a stylized rendering of the work of detection, depth exploration as convention. The real key to his investigation is a far different in-depth movement—literally looking inside Christina's body to locate a key she swallowed. This grotesque "internal" investigation, this ultimate movement within, counterpoints Hammer's physical movement and suggests the sort of "dead" end, the morbid satisfactions to which the detective's conventional moves often lead.

That sense of our generic desires and satisfactions may be best imaged, though, in the "great whatsit," the long sought-after box that Hammer finally locates. Just what is the "great whatsit"? Aldrich never lets us see; the box's contents remain something of a mystery—and a problem for anyone who has to explain to all-too-literal-minded students what sort of unstable atomic matter it holds. All we do see when first Mike and then Gabrielle open it is a brilliant and painful light. Yet this light seems a fitting image for a film that tries to penetrate the depths of our films and our culture, for it suggests at once the blinding power of those cultural images we hide away and the potential light of the cinema, as it tries to illuminate the depths of our world. No simple depiction of fissionable matter, the "great whatsit" evokes both the corrosive norm and explosive possibility of our cinema. This surprising box of light serves up just what we desire—or deserve—or at least what Aldrich thinks we need to see.

Kiss Me Deadly closes with an appropriately in-depth image, that of a beach in the foreground and Dr. Soberin's house in the background, silhouetted against a dark sky as it explodes. The composition fits with what we generically expect and what the film's send-up of cinematic language offers. A wounded Mike rescues Velda from a locked room as the house burns, and a subsequent long shot of the house exploding seems coded to satisfy our conventional desires, to tell the usual story of background and foreground: it would establish the hero and his girl escaping, leaving the deadly house in the background, and running to the sanctuary of the beach in the foreground. But no couple enters the foreground; no one is saved; no neat resolution implausibly follows; no satisfactory coda attaches to these terrible events. We simply end with a series of long shots that show total destruction and, fittingly, a "The End" title which, in place of the expected hero and heroine, itself moves to close-up and definitively shuts the door on the sort of exploration of depth classical films usually offer.[4] In probing the depths of the mystery he stumbles upon, in trying to fathom the implications of the "great whatsit," Mike Hammer accomplishes little, partly because he is, as Arnold and Miller note, "such an obvious fraud" (40), not much of a detective.

In its efforts to investigate our modern condition, to probe our human depths, this film locates an equally unavailing and fraudulent dimension in our movies, especially our typical genre works. For they too at times get caught up with surfaces: with generic conventions and characters, with predictable plot moves, with classical patterns of reality construction. But with its own reflexive turn, *Kiss Me Deadly* manages something more, something which the film noir was moving toward. It finds its own depths to probe in the constructed space of the cinema and of generic storytelling that it has excavated for our inspection.

IV.

In bringing together this congery of cultural, psychic, and aesthetic depths that mark the film noir, I cover much ground that is probably fairly familiar. Perhaps I also prove Jean Baudrillard's accusation that "In America... space... is the very form of thought" (16). But my "spaciness," recounting the familiar and thinking not so much in typical ideological terms but in terms of depth—might be helpful. For in this way we might better see what is paradoxically on the surface and yet, thanks to its nearness, at times seemingly deeply buried and unaccounted for, a way in which, even in their familiar generic moves, our films have managed to challenge mainstream cinema. Or perhaps it might be better to think of them as a kind of primal assault on various sorts of security we have come to expect in our films: a cultural security, a psychological security, and an aesthetic security, lodged in our notions of genre and classical narrative. For while these films seem to work at the traditional task of linking the "out there" with the "in here," depth with showy surface, deep concerns with a satisfying, unifying coda, they do so in a way that interrogates the linkage, and that thus leaves us, as it were, still caught within their own depths. And if the challenging nature of these films is not quite new, the manner in which they manage this challenge deserves more exploration.

Paul Virilio has described what he terms a "crisis in the conceptualization of 'narrative'" in our time, a "crisis" that is "the other side of the crisis of the conceptualization of 'dimension' as geometrical narrative, the discourse of measurement of a reality visibly offered to all" (24). What I have done here is simply follow Virilio backwards, read his notion retrospectively—and a bit playfully. His point, I gather, is that in recent times, thanks to the increasing sense of speed of all events, our sense of space, of dimension has become distorted and problematic, and with it all that we conceptually model on that previously "sure" foundation has revealed its equally insecure footing. Architecture, the graphic arts, even narrative itself—everything that draws on a kind of spatial conceit, that we conceive of in terms of extension, dimension, and *depth* reflects this ongoing change in our sense of reality—and an increasing anxiety that attends it. That anxiety follows from a variety of uncertainties about our world and ourselves, the sort of uncertainties that have always been noir's stylistic and thematic stock-in-trade.

While Virilio's remark aims at a postmodern rather than postwar culture, the film noir, when read in this context, seems prescient. In the 1940s and 1950s it not only spoke symptomatically of postwar disenchantment and alienation, but also sensed other sorts of cultural "crisis" that still lay largely beneath the surface. Obviously, the America that emerged from the war was but distantly related to prewar society, and that of the Korean War even less so. And our ability to address that world adequately through our cinema would increasingly be called into question. That dubiousness had to do not simply with our subjects of public discourse, as we noted, but with a deep uncertainty about whether we even had a language to address these anxieties adequately, a way of measuring, articulating, or depicting them. And behind that anxiety lay yet a larger problem we would increasingly confront, the problem film always has to face, that of reality itself, its slippery and even evanescent nature, its tendency to disappear even as it seems constructed for us in such depth and affirmed by all the conventions of dimensionality.

The classical film noir responds to those cultural, personal, and aesthetic anxieties of the era, while it also points to this larger confrontation with the real that seems to power the recent resurgence of this form. In various ways, it draws much of the pattern of film narrative near the surface, thereby making us more conscious of how it works. Film's conventional armory of invisibility—cuts on action, glance-object shifts, eyeline matches, subjective shot identification, etc., all designed to help the narrative seem natural and self-revealing rather than manipulated and manipulating—begins to call attention to itself. Similarly, its conventionalized subjects and stories, like the ever so clever and resilient private eye and his beautiful girl Friday, or the mystery that is never too deep or unavailing to be unraveled or explained away, start to seem affected and calculated. In effect, a deep pattern, a cinematic repressed, if you will, rises from its depths to be seen in a new light.

While the works examined here hardly capture the full range of film noir, they do reflect a growing awareness of something that had gone repressed and that needed to be drawn up from the depths and, like Mike's "great whatsit," opened up and reassessed. That is the way in which the cinema itself had become a kind of unexamined psychic mechanism, a dark pool of dreams of the sort that *Nightmare* so effectively visualizes in its opening scene: one that defined our desires, fashioned a language through which we vaguely understood our world, and constructed us as consumers of what it had to offer. In the post-war era, we seemed to be awakening to—or from—these depths. And with the film noir, thanks to its penchant for looking into the dark, for plumbing our world's depths, for employing great depth of field, for drawing up close the very language of cinema, we had a tool that could help in such a reassessment—in a psychodrama of cinema itself.

WORKS CITED

Edward T. Arnold and Eugene L. Miller, *The Films and Career of Robert Aldrich,* Knoxville: University of Tennessee Press, 1986.

Jean Baudrillard, *America,* Translated by Chris Turner, London: Verso, 1988.

David Bordwell, Janet Staiger, and Kristin Thompson, *The Classical Hollywood Cinema: Film Style and Mode of Production to 1960,* New York: Columbia University Press, 1985.

Laurence Miller, "The Central Role of Insanity in Film noir," paper presented at the 19th Annual Florida State University Conference on Literature and Film, Jan. 27, 1994, Tallahassee, FL.

Janey L. Place, and Lowell S. Peterson, "Some Visual Motifs of Film noir" (1974), reprinted in *Film Noir Reader,* editors Alain Silver, James Ursini, New York: Limelight, 1996, pp. 64–75.

Paul Schrader, "Notes on film noir" (1972), reprinted in *Film Noir Reader,* pp. 52–63.

J.P. Telotte, *Voices in the Dark: The Narrative Patterns of Film* noir, Urbana: University of Illinois Press, 1989.

Jon Tuska, *Dark Cinema: American Film Noir in Cultural Perspective,* Westport: Greenwood Press, 1984.

Paull Virilio, *Lost Dimension,* translator Daniel Moshenberg, New York: Semiotext(e) , 1991.

NOTES

1. As one of the key components of a noir "stylistics," Paul Schrader describes the "love of romantic narration" that seems to characterize a number of the most important films of this type (57). Working from his assessment, many critics seem to assume that the voice-over, flashback style is the typical method of noir narration and have come to include it in any catalogue of noir's "generic" traits, even though it occurs in only a small portion of those films we typically label "noir."

2. We should note the complementary imagery of the conscious and unconscious mind that attends this narrative play of surface and depth. Rene, who deals in logic and rational explanations, builds a boat in his spare time. Stan, who is nearly swallowed up by his traumatized psyche, is almost drowned by the hypnotist who has been manipulating him.

3. As is also the case with *Kiss Me Deadly, In a Lonely Place*'s dissection of the film industry represents a major shift in emphasis from the Dorothy B. Hughes novel on which it is based.

4. There has always been much debate about the ending to *Kiss Me Deadly,* an ending that for many, steeped in the conventions of classical detective films, never seemed quite satisfactory or "right." The recent release of a new version of the film with a different ending restored—one showing Mike and Velda still alive in the surf—confirms that a more conventionally "correct" ending was shot, although it remains one that seems ill-paired with the rest of the narrative. And of course even that "happy" ending simply leaves unexplored the eventual fate of these characters who have "escaped" to but a few yards away from what seems a nuclear explosion.

The iconic Gilda who epitomizes the uncontrollable *femme fatale* of film noir.

Manufacturing Heroines: Gothic Victims and Working Women in Classic Noir Films

Sheri Chinen Biesen

While much has been made about the sexual "femme fatale" temptress in classic noir films, female images in many of these pictures also included "good girl" victims (or "redeemers') and "working girls" or career women. In these films noir of the classical Hollywood studio era, images of female stars were often, in fact, "manufactured" by creative and executive men who held positions of power within the motion picture production system. The screen personas of women in 1940s noir films evolved from the proto-noir gothic redeemer and the hard-boiled femme fatale, to a more multifaceted working career woman as America entered World War II. As the war progressed, these images eventually coincided with a number of women gaining greater power in creative and executive positions in Hollywood—and in many classic film noir productions.

An interesting case in point is Joan Fontaine, a female star very much "manufactured" by men, who embodied the gothic heroine in Alfred Hitchcock's proto-noir *Rebecca* (1940) and *Suspicion* (1941). Fontaine epitomized the noir redeemer "woman as victim" and Hitchcock's psychological thrillers *Rebecca* and *Suspicion* initiated the female gothic film cycle (which continued with *Shadow of a Doubt, Spellbound* and *Notorious*—an interestingly dark hybrid of the female gothic and wartime espionage thriller) that is linked to film noir. Like hard-boiled "serie noir," the term "film noir" was also derived from "roman noir," or "black novel," which 18th and 19th century French critics called the British gothic novel. As in film noir, gender distress, psychic trauma (or insanity) and misogynism were intrinsic to gothic thrillers. The gender distress of film noir and gothic thrillers crystallized amid the cultural disruption of World War II. Female hysteria and crimes of passion were hallmarks of the gothic roman noir. Both *Rebecca* and *Suspicion* cleverly used psychology and highlighted the female point-of-view of the heroine's psyche to gain endorsement from Hollywood's Production Code censors and critical Academy Award acclaim, despite a gothic premise portraying husbands committing crime—in *Rebecca* "accidentally" murdering, or in *Suspicion* "appearing" to intentionally poison, their wives.[1]

By 1941, Hitchcock and Fontaine (as well as actresses Ingrid Bergman and Vivian Leigh) were under contract to independent film producer David O. Selznick, a powerful Hollywood "talent broker" who profitably loaned his director and female stars to various Hollywood studios. After Fontaine's success as naive gothic ingenue in *Rebecca*,

RKO borrowed Hitchcock and Fontaine for *Suspicion*, then paid Selznick a lucrative $116,750 for the actress. (Selznick loaned out his contract female star and paid her a mere $17,833 salary, then noted:"I don't care . . . so much about how much she makes as I do about making sure we keep her in line."[2]—Selznick's nearly $100,000 profit from loaning Fontaine to RKO indicates he cared about both power and money.) Fontaine had lobbied Hitchcock for the role with a personal handwritten card to "Dear, darling Hitch." The actress pleaded,"*I must do that picture* . . . I am even willing to play the part for no salary, *if necessary.*"[3] Selznick retaliated to Fontaine in a nine page letter in August 1940 to a "very dear, very young Joan . . . After all . . . I have gone through to get you out of the frustrated bitplayer-and-second-lead-in-Republic-Westerns status in which you had found yourself" which regrettably most studios felt was her "maximum due. Too many people in Hollywood . . . know of your work before 'Rebecca,'" and the "unprecedented and expensive steps which I took." Selznick substantiated his "expensive investment" in Fontaine, as star commodity "developed as a result of a risk and a gamble that I took . . . against the unanimous opinion of everyone inside and outside our company, including Hitch"[4]—implying this opposition to her was held by all of Hollywood.

There, male executive authority and the gender dynamics of the production process underscored the narrative gender distress central to the proto-noir female gothic thriller. Men had power, made decisions, and determined how women were represented on screen. In fact, a *Ladies Home Journal* article,"Star Factory," traced the "manufacturing process" of female stars with photos of Fontaine being trained, groomed and refined by RKO studio as a "finished product, a masterpiece created and sold by Hollywood's master craftsmen."[5] Fontaine's depiction as feminine commodity illustrates how Hollywood studios groomed contract acting personnel to enhance performance, via a process to create "talent," produce and "construct" star persona, and promote female actresses into starlets while male actors were publicized as being "natural" and simply "playing themselves'. Male studio executive authority sculpted female stars. Fontaine (as raw starlet material) was "developed" and "made" into a star by Selznick, and her persona was constructed and "molded" by both Selznick and Hitchcock. During *Rebecca*, Fontaine's first production for the independent producer, Selznick wrote:"For months now I have been trying to tell everybody connected with 'REBECCA' that what I wanted in the girl, especially in the first part, was an *un*glamorous creature, but one sufficiently pretty and appealing, in a simple girlish way, to understand why Maxim would marry her . . . *not* glamorous."[6]

There were even turf disputes over who could rightly claim credit for discovering and developing Fontaine. Selznick explicitly warned in a September 1940 memo that Hitchcock "had better not make himself look ridiculous" by claiming to have "developed" Fontaine. Another dispute arose when RKO got wind of *Suspicion*'s potential success. In a November 1941 memo Selznick complained, "RKO has been sending out some annoying stories that would indicate that Fontaine is an RKO discovery and player and that 'SUSPICION' is the climax of her career with them. Just to make matters worse, they talk about her "free lancing," and infer that she was purchased by them as a free lance artist." The very thought of Fontaine's autonomy as a star, or any independence from his development apparatus, posed a threat to Selznick's authority as talent broker. Despite the handsome profit he made off of loaning Fontaine to RKO, Selznick took issue with the studio's attempt to cash in and take credit for the "manufacturing" efforts of his contract star. "I suggest you advise their publicity department that if they don't behave we will have to publicize how RKO threw her out as worthless before I signed her for 'REBECCA.'"[7] *Suspicion* screenwriter Sam Raphaelson also had opinions about Fontaine. "She must carry the whole finish. I think she should rise to an ecstasy unprecedented in the acting career of Miss Fontaine at the second beat when she realizes Johnny didn't kill [his best friend] Beaky." Raphaelson then conceived of her performing a "lyric dance of solemn happiness" at the film's conclusion.[8] (No subtlety here, but quite an imagi-

Illicit lovers and part-time spies (Cary Grant and Ingrid Bergman) confront cuckolded husband and Nazi collaborator Claude Raines in *Notorious*.

native variation on Hitchcock's trademark psychological ambiguity and star performance restraint.)

By the end of *Suspicion,* former comedy star Cary Grant's "dark side" and unpre-
dictably dangerous masculine charisma typifies a mysterious, potentially malignant
gothic male other, culminating in the actor's strikingly noir ascent up a shrouded spiral staircase with a deadly glass of poisoned milk to murder his young wife. *Suspicion's*
bleak climax shows an ominous Grant climbing the stairs in a pitch-black room, bringing the lethal drink (lit from inside the glass so it glows in the dark) to Fontaine's bedside. The darkness shadows Grant's face, almost in complete silhouette, lit from below
in extremely low-angle "low-key" horror style to demonize his features. Most prewar
1940s American film viewers were not ready for a menacing proto-noir lover-turned-
murderer in Grant. Based on preview audience survey cards from 1941, filmgoer reception was decidedly downbeat toward *Suspicion* portraying the actor in a sinister
role. "Why ruin Cary Grant on such a long drawn out picture as this? Please put him
in more comedies with Irene Dunne." Another viewer actually complained, "the house
maid is around the scene entirely too much for her minor position in the story" and
argued, "Anyone who has seen some number of moving pictures tends to anticipate
her having an affair with Cary Grant." Other viewers protested: "Up to the last scene
everyone thought Cary Grant was the murderer so why confuse the entire audience
by changing the impression. He should admit to trying to murder her, then after confessing, attempt to murder her."[9]

Although Fontaine's distraught ingenue does not correspond to the classic hard-
boiled gender roles of lethal femme fatale—where in a full blown noir narrative an
erotic woman would be a sexual predator killing off her male counterpart—her gothic
victim can be seen as a psychological prototype for the more passive noir "good girl"
redeemer.[10] While many were at a "loss to conceive any possible ending short of an
asylum for the heroine," several viewers thought Fontaine should have a stronger role:
"she should ... kill him in self-defense or escape and be killed during the pursuit." Another called her an "immature, driveling sentimentalist with no conception of real
love—just a sex-starved intellectualist grabbing the first man who showed any interest in her," willingly drinking the "supposed poison her husband offers, proclaiming
love for her would-be murderer. What sane woman would act that way?" Others complained, "It was a great mistake to put two such actors in a picture that was ridiculous
from start to finish ... difficult to understand ... especially after Joan Fontaine drinks
what she thinks is death potion. And how the audience laughed! Did you think Cary
Grant's promise to reform at all convincing? I don't think it fooled anyone but the
wishy-washy Joan Fontaine." They added, "She should pull a gun out" when she goes
to the cliffs at the film's finale "for the purpose of killing him."[11]

Brandishing a weapon certainly suggests crime and combat. Stronger screen images
of women would soon coincide with "Rosie the Riveter" and working females in
America's wartime homefront. Fontaine would eventually win a Best Actress Oscar
for her gothic noir heroine. Released within months of Pearl Harbor, Hitchcock's film
was a dark segue of sorts, as Depression-era screwball comedies declined in the early

1940s and hard-hitting crime narratives increased, capturing the gender distress and changing roles of women during this time, and culminating in bleaker films noir by the end of World War II. The increasing film noir style seen in Hollywood's female gothic cycle accelerated over the course of the duration as seen in Hitchcock's noir espionage thriller *Notorious* (1946). How gender (and masculinity) played out on Hollywood screens was significant. The tough, conflicted spirit, narrative corruption and hard-bitten psyche so characteristic of film noir proliferated amid the bleak paranoia and harsher realities of the wartime filmmaking climate in America's increasingly hard-boiled homefront, and—as censorship shifted—the rough and tumble world of pulp fiction detectives that Hollywood could finally adapt with a darker nuanced style during the 1940s.

Images of the hard-boiled femme fatale crystallized in such classic noir films as Billy Wilder's *Double Indemnity* (1944), Tay Garnett's *The Postman Always Rings Twice* (1945–46), Edgar Ulmer's *Detour* (1945), Fritz Lang's *Scarlet Street* (1945) and Howard Hawks' *The Big Sleep* (1945–46). Embodying the evil, alluring "spider woman", Barbara Stanwyck's deadly cool Phyllis Dietrichson calls the shots, disposes of her husband's first wife then the husband himself, manipulates and kills her lover, and generally raises the bar on female badness in *Double Indemnity*. Stanwyck's character in *Double Indemnity,* as well as Lana Turner's lethal Cora in James M. Cain's other "sordid" and censorable novel, *The Postman Always Rings Twice,* was based on a real life femme fatale, Ruth Snyder, who conspired with her lover to brutally murder her husband for insurance money in one of the most sensational tabloid stories of the roaring twenties as her unforgettable image in the electric chair splashed across the front page of *The New York Daily News*.[12] In low-budget cult classic noir, *Detour,* shot in six days at "poverty row" minor studio PRC, Ann Savage's Vera is a no-frills, lowdown venomous shrew and downright "unruly" woman. Joan Bennett's unabashedly irreverent, double-crossing Kitty in *Scarlet Street* is the ultimate duplicitous temptress. These images of women were often created and developed by men.

In *The Big Sleep,* producer-director Howard Hawks "manufactures" and glamorizes Martha Vickers' dangerous and petulant femme Carmen Sternwood to such wonderful perfection that she almost outshines her more well-behaved sister Vivian, played by sultry co-star Lauren Bacall. Hawks was, of course, key in discovering Bacall, hiring the former cover girl as a contract female star commodity for his independent production company, then grooming and manufacturing "The Look" as a husky noir siren opposite Humphrey Bogart in *To Have and Have Not* (1944). Hawks also signed another beautiful young ingenue, Ella Raines, as the major asset of his other independent production company. Like Selznick, Hawks purchased, "owned', developed and refined new feminine star talent, then sold his actresses' contract to various Hollywood studios and made a profit. Hawks sold Raines to Universal for the noir picture *Phantom Lady* (1944), then sold Bacall to Warner Bros. after her success in *To Have and Have Not,* while filming *The Big Sleep*. However, Bennett's strikingly bold femme fatale in *Scarlet Street* is not only a feminine persona and product "manufactured" by men (such as filmmaker Lang and producer Walter Wanger, Bennett's husband). The female star, in fact, enjoyed greater creative and executive influence as a business partner in the independent production company that produced *Scarlet Street.*[13]

Images of noir women also become more multifaceted. As early as 1940, Boris Ingster's modest B film *Stranger on the Third Floor* presents a noir heroine (Margaret Tallichet as Jane) who is not a sexual temptress, but rather a respectable working girl who even functions as a female detective solving the murderous crime in finding— and nearly becoming victim to—Peter Lorre's psychopathic throat-slashing murderer who turns out to be an insane asylum escapee. Even the women in Hawks' *The Big Sleep,* co-scripted by female screenwriter Leigh Brackett, are more nuanced as the noir picture showcases a variety of working girls—from taxi drivers to rare book clerks (including Dorothy Malone's film debut) to Bacall (Vivian) singing in gambler Eddie Mars' casino cabaret. In fact, in Robert Siodmak's *Phantom Lady,* Raines' working noir heroine Kansas epitomizes the female detective who not only tracks down criminals, but also takes time off her job to disguise herself and play the role of a more sexual "loose" femme fatale to solve the case and clear her boss from the chair for allegedly murdering his wife. This active female character coincided with a homefront audience of working wartime women, and was also the product of Hitchcock protege, writer-producer Joan Harrison, who co-scripted Hitchcock's roman noir gothic films *Rebecca* and *Suspicion.*[14]

Female "detective" Kansas (Ella Raines) consults police detective Burgess (Thomas Gomez) in *Phantom Lady.*

Another example of a working noir heroine is Gene Tierney's "good girl" turned advertising executive in Otto Preminger's classic, *Laura* (1944). As a successful career woman, Laura is a fascinating character that is complex, elusive, yet almost ethereal, like a ghost or supernatural spirit that seemingly haunts the narrative and whom no one in the film really understands. The film begins as Laura is perceived to be brutally murdered in her own apartment and a detective proceeds to piece together various stories to solve the crime. She turns out to be alive, but remains mysterious and absent from the first half of the film despite the fact that she appears in her painted portrait, in flashback memories and in fantasies of the male characters' imagination of her. Ultimately, we are introduced to Laura through her image as it is constructed in the minds of the men around her. She becomes an object that many different male characters (from a wide variety of social backgrounds and classes) aspire to, seek to attain and even kill for.

However, while Laura is ephemeral, there are appealing facets to her noir heroine; Tierney captures the human "every woman" quality of Laura's character, tapping in to homefront working women, while simultaneously appearing otherworldly. Yet, in many ways, she is not fully formed. As the story unfolds this absentee career girl becomes an ambiguous figure whose very nature is suspect. While Laura is characterized by those around her as a sweet, warm and earnest "all-American" girl-next-door, she demonstrates that she is secretive and is also capable of duplicitous behavior. It is not exactly clear as the film progresses whether she is a femme fatale who commits murder and lies to detectives (and whose motives are called into question), or whether she is an innocent victim with good intentions who serves as a "redeemer" for the crooked men in her life. In fact, as the film *Laura* fuses a gothic thriller narrative with a hard-boiled detective story, Tierney's noir heroine becomes all of these things: bad girl, good girl, working woman and male fantasy.

Laura's reappearance "from the dead" in the doorway of her dark apartment transpires like a dream. Dana Andrews' detective (Mark) is lost in the fragile beauty of her portrait and has drifted into unconsciousness to ponder her deceased visage. At that point, it is not even clear to Mark (or viewers) whether he is awake or in a trance, or whether the female figure before him is real or just a figment of his imagination. When it becomes clear that she is Laura "in the flesh'—very much alive and not a masculine fantasy—we realize there may be a disparity between her image, in mind and on canvas, and the real woman. Laura becomes a kind of mythic noir heroine who contradicts her mystique (while ironically adding to it) with her sudden mysterious appearance. Yet, we don't really know who she is, and neither does Andrews' detective Mark. Her entry calls every crime-solving fact (and our understanding of her character and the film's story) into question as she uproots the detective's methodical piecing together of the case. Moreover, in creating a new dilemma of mistaken identity, Laura's belated arrival implicates her for the murder of another woman (with her fiancee) in her own apartment.

Ultimately, Preminger's film is as much about deciphering who Laura is as it is about solving a murder crime. The "myth" and mystery of Laura, and of her ever-present image in the painting, reinforce the disparity between a projected female persona and the unraveling layers of who she is. Laura's character is, in fact, "manufactured" not only by the men in the narrative, but also by the male production executives involved in making the film. Twentieth Century-Fox studio chief Darryl Zanuck had very distinct and different ideas about the nature of her female gothic crime heroine than did the film's producer-director Otto Preminger. Zanuck was influential in developing Laura more fully and in removing Tierney's voice-over narration by her character that was originally in Vera Caspary's 1943 novel and in early versions of the studio's film adaptation. Zanuck urged Preminger to expand Laura's noir heroine beyond a naive gothic ingenue victim, yet maintain enough fresh innocence where she does not realize how much trouble she is in, but to avoid making her a cheap tramp or loose femme fatale.[15] Preminger considered Laura a more sexual woman of the night. The creative tension between Zanuck and Preminger added more depth and intrigue to Tierney's screen character. Laura's evolution from career woman to dream girl fantasy to deceitful femme and finally a more multifaceted variation of the gothic victim by the end of the film—almost killed but ultimately redeemed by Waldo's (Clifton Webb) murderous attempt on her life (proving her innocence)—is fascinating. Laura emerges as a contradictory noir heroine with flaws, virtues and dimensions that do not fit the classical mold of hard-boiled femme fatale, and whose feminine presence permeates the film.

Like *Laura, Phantom Lady* and *Gilda* (1946), *Mildred Pierce* (1945) is a film noir that employs conventions of "roman noir" gothic melodrama in its central "working" redeemer character. Such noir films as *Laura, Gilda* and *Mildred Pierce* revolve around a female protagonist whose presence is so intrinsic to the film that she not only structures the story, but also becomes the namesake of the entire picture. The character of Mildred, an unhappy housewife and mother of two daughters, embodies the noir redeemer and gradually evolves into a Rosie-the-Riveter style career woman when her husband leaves her and she builds her own business to support her family. The active female lead role was an ideal comeback vehicle for former-diva, Joan Crawford. A woman also contributed to the film's production. Screenwriter Catherine Turney was involved in adapting James M. Cain's novel, yet male Hollywood executives such as Warner Bros. producer Jerry Wald masculinized the story to turn it into a detective crime film.[16] Like Laura, the picture becomes a "who done it", where the noir heroine is implicated. Mildred's character is, in fact, suspected of murder through the entire picture as the film literally opens with a bang and the crumbling man who has been shot in the dark calls out "Mildred" before he falls and dies.

Mildred is presented as an amalgam of noir redeemer, working woman and a mysterious, possibly guilty, femme fatale who carries on with other (shady) men, remarries a con artist, spoils one daughter (who becomes a monster) and neglects the other (who dies). Mildred even seemingly admits her guilt when she almost attempts suicide shortly after the murder before she is interrogated by police detectives. *Mildred Pierce* combines female melodrama with a hard-boiled detective narrative to create a noir heroine that, like Laura, defies conventional notions of a gothic redeemer or femme fatale. Yet, Crawford, who won a Best Actress Oscar for the role, portrays Mildred as a humane, compassionate character who is ultimately victimized not only by the dubious men who betray her for money once she achieves success in her career, but also by her spoiled, ruthless and greedy daughter who, after running off to pursue a cabaret career and stealing her husband, turns out to be the actual lethal femme murderess (for whom Mildred is willing to take the blame).

Gilda is yet another classic noir film which is a variation of a female gothic melodrama and a more hard-boiled gangster detective crime narrative. Rita Hayworth's bold performance as wild sex siren is an exceedingly memorable character whose presence lives on well beyond the film as one of the all-time great classic femme fatales. Gilda was, in fact, a woman with much bravado accentuating her smoldering sensuality, who was also terribly vulnerable and treated sadistically. Hayworth's charismatic heroine was an erotic role that was "manufactured" and emphasized by a powerful creative executive woman involved in the production of the film, producer (and former writer) Virginia Van Upp who was also head of production at Columbia studio in 1945 (through 1947).[17] As Hayworth's real life marriage to Orson Welles

Waldo Lydecker (Clifton Webb) physically dominates the figure of career woman Laura (Gene Tierney), the woman he considers very much his own personal creation and property in *Laura*.

unraveled during the making of the film, Van Upp had a close relationship with female lead Hayworth, mentored the star and supervised the writing of the project (by screenwriter Marion Parsonnet) while producing the picture. When compared to earlier gothic heroines ('manufactured" and refined by more male-dominated film-making personnel such as Selznick and Hitchcock with Fontaine) women more actively involved in such creative or executive positions as writing or producing noir films—whether writer Brackett on *The Big Sleep*, Turney on *Mildred Pierce*, Harrison producing *Phantom Lady* or Van Upp producing *Gilda*—contributed to more fully-developed and unpredictable noir heroines who were more complex and assertive (often non-traditional "working" career women) variations on the conventional femme fatale.

Although just as Tierney's Laura is surrounded by men who find her sexually attractive and consorts with many of them, on another level *Mildred Pierce* and *Gilda* are female-centered noir stories that become sex melodramas. Mildred is having affairs with men—although they (Mildred's opportunistic suitors) are the sexual aggressors, while Mildred is reluctant and far more interested in material success for the purpose of indulging and impressing her irresponsible daughter. Gilda, on the other hand, appears to be more brazen. She is far more openly defiant and cognizant of her own sexuality, and irreverent in her active pursuit of her independence. As a dangerous femme, Gilda is deviant in using the power of her erotic female image to arouse and manipulate men for her own pleasure. Hayworth's character Gilda strives to be a "working girl" pursuing a career singing, dancing and performing strip tease in a cabaret of wildly ecstatic male patrons. Despite her transgressive behavior, however, like the female gothic ingenue, Gilda is not evil or malicious, but instead a victim of the misogynistic, violent men around her as she becomes involved in a series of bizarre, dysfunctional relationships that accentuate her gender distress. She marries a mysterious crime boss who owns a gambling casino, taunts and tantalizes her ex-lover who manages her husband's illegal business affairs, then eventually weds her ex-flame when the kingpin is suspected dead. Marital bliss is rather a wedded nightmare for Gilda as she becomes a virtual prisoner of her twisted heterosexual relations in these domestic unions. Like Laura and Mildred, Hayworth's character Gilda transcends her diva sexuality and image as a femme who men desire to evolve into a sympathetic, multidimensional noir heroine. She is human, has flaws and even exhibits self-destructive behavior.

In *Gilda*, Van Upp and Hayworth create a complex noir female protagonist who simultaneously embodies an independent woman, a victim, a redeemer, an active "working" girl pursuing a career of sorts (albeit interrupted), and a sexual femme fatale wreaking havoc in men's lives (as they battle their own demons). However, in ultimately defying lethal femme stereotypes, this dangerous classic noir woman has a heart. Like the other "manufactured" noir heroines of *Suspicion, Stranger on the Third Floor, Laura, The Big Sleep, Phantom Lady*, and *Mildred Pierce*, Gilda's provocative and alluring image as quintessential 1940s femme fatale—like Hayworth's famous wartime pin-up poster—is ultimately all for show, an act, a masquerade to save her pride (and no doubt appease censors). Her sexual exploits are allegedly not for real, just meant to emotionally hurt her tormented beau (Glenn Ford) with whom she has a history. In the end, Gilda actually turns out to be a "good girl" (despite her "bad girl" image) who is less naive than other gothic redeemers (such as Fontaine in *Suspicion*), and more comfortable with her own sexuality, but who ultimately tames her "unruly" independence, makes amends and gets together with her man—in a noir finale where the Hollywood couple disappears into the dark.

NOTES

1. "Last night I dreamt I went to Manderley again." These words, conjuring an eerie recollection of a heroine's past, opened Daphne du Maurier's gothic novel *Rebecca*, providing a prelude to the voice-over narration found in film noir. Du Maurier's story—a masterwork of infidelity, dysfunctional sexual relationships, and domestic murder—drew fire from chief censor Joseph Breen in Hollywood's Production Code office when Selznick purchased the screen rights to produce it. Disquietly embedded in these gothic thriller films was, as Thomas Elsaesser explains, an "oblique intimation of female frigidity producing strange fantasies of persecution, rape and death—masochistic reveries and nightmares, which cast the husband into the role of sadistic murderer." The female gothic film cycle developed dark stylistics and revolved around what Thomas Schatz calls "gender difference, sexual identity, and the "gender distress" which accompanied the social and cultural disruption of the war and postwar eras." Like hard-boiled detective narratives, the gothic centered on an "essentially good though flawed and vulnerable protagonist at odds with a mysterious and menacing sexual other." In the gothic, a young innocent female meets, has an affair and marries a suave enigmatic stranger. Her charming but mysterious older lover or husband, with a dubious past and with secrets to conceal, becomes an alluring but potentially predatorial sexual presence. Thomas Schatz, *Boom and Bust: American Cinema in the 1940s*, (History of American Cinema, Volume 6: 1940–1949), Scribners, 1997, pp. 233–236. Grant's menacing performance in *Suspicion* personified a masculine sexual predator. (And off-screen, as an independent freelance star with his choice of roles at different studios, Grant enjoyed significantly more control over his career than did Fontaine.) Misogynism and a masochistic self-destructive protagonist's point-of-view magnified gender and sexual distress in gothic thrillers. These psychological impulses and a subjective point-of-view extended into film noir, structuring and framing increasingly hard-boiled crime narratives on screen. Hitchcock's gothics *Rebecca* and *Suspicion* even embedded misogynism into the filmmaking process. Hitchcock put Fontaine through his "finishing school" on the set of *Rebecca*, yet she received an icy reception from the rest of the cast. Hitchcock and Selznick used intimidation tactics to make it clear that actor Lawrence Olivier wanted Vivien Leigh (soon to be his wife) in the lead female role. The verisimilitude of Fontaine's shy, naive—progressively emotive—ingenue performance on- and off-camera contributes to the gothic melodrama's narrative excess and patriarchally-coded "hysteria'. In *Rebecca*, Fontaine is a

mousy (albeit working) female companion who quits her job to marry a charming wife-murderer and costumes herself in flouncy ball gowns by the end of the film. Her character in *Suspicion* is initially a more bookish (even comparatively androgynous) intellectual at the opening of the narrative who becomes increasingly hysterical (like her role in *Rebecca*); Fontaine is gradually glamorized as the film progresses, eventually feminized in frilly diaphanous negligees by the time Grant brings "poisoned" milk to her bedside in what she imagines is an attempt to murder her.

2. David O. Selznick Archive, HRC 8-40. Drawing on 1930s horror cycles, Hitchcock's gothic *Suspicion* invoked progressively bleak film noir style. Featuring an ominous image of Cary Grant, "charming enough to make any woman love him . . . desperate enough to ruin the life of the woman he loved," publicity noted the *"terror"* Grant, "at his dramatic best," inspired in heroine Joan Fontaine.

3. Alfred Hitchcock Collection, MHL (undated).

4. Selznick, 8-40. Selznick indeed launched Fontaine's career; yet, the discourse he activated to keep his star in line was startling in its severity.

5. Eric Ergenbright and Jack Smalley, "Star Factory," *Ladies Home Journal,* 1937. See also Cynthia Baron, "Manufacturing Starlets But Teaching Actors the Tricks of the Trade: A Look at Popular Discourse in the Classical Hollywood Era," University of Southern California, Los Angeles, 1996.

6. Selznick, pp. 10–39.

7. Selznick, pp. 11–41. He added, "If they don't behave, any future deals with RKO will include a clause that we will get the same credit in publicity and advertising that we have on the screen."

8. Raphaelson in Hitchcock, pp. 6–41.

9. Hitchcock, pp. 6–41.

10. See Janey Place, "Women in film noir," in E. Ann Kaplan, ed., *Women in Film Noir* (London: BFI, 1980).

11. Hitchcock, pp. 6–41.

12. Sheri Chinen Biesen, "Censorship, Film Noir and Double Indemnity," *Film and History,* 25:1–2, 1995; Sheri Chinen Biesen, "Raising Cain with the Censors Again: The Postman Always Rings Twice," *Literature/Film Quarterly,* 28:1, 2000.

13. Thomas Schatz, *The Genius of the System,* (NY: Simon and Schuster, 1988); Sheri Chinen Biesen, "Bogart, Bacall, Howard Hawks and Wartime Film Noir at Warner Bros.: To Have and Have Not and The Big Sleep," *Popular Culture Review,* 13.1, 2002.

14. Lizzie Francke, *Script Girls* (London: BFI 1994); Sheri Chinen Biesen, "Joan Harrison, Virginia Van Upp and Women Behind-the-Scenes in Wartime Hollywood Film Noir," *Quarterly Review of Film and Video,* 20.2, 2003.

15. Darryl Zanuck, Twentieth Century-Fox Collection, USC 11-43.

16. Warner Bros. Archive.

17. See Biesen, Francke.

Philip Marlowe (Dick Powell) studies the seductive "mask" of femme fatale Velma (Claire Trevor) in *Murder, My Sweet*.

The Noir Style in Hollywood

Nicolas Saada

Europe and Other Visual Arts

The style of film noir ranks with the finest in Hollywood's history. Much has been written about noir, and many critics still contend to deliver a genuine definition of film noir: genre, school or sensibility? The Noir visual style owes as much to European cinema as to a certain tendency in other American forms, from pulp fiction to all manner of visual arts.

For some film noir is simply the fruit of the "Germanization" of Hollywood. But other influences from France, from Italian Neo-Realism, from painterly and photographic schools within the United States are also in play. Graphically, the "American look" ranges from the greatness and horizontality of the "big country" to the the verticality of the first great cities and the megalopolis. While film noir is connected to certain verticality of the American style, many visual elements within film noir (decor, atmosphere, position of the actors in the frame, use of black-and-white cinematography) combine to create the style. As more than a simple revolution in 1940s Hollywood, the "noir style" incorporates various traditions of the American visual universe.

Europeanized, yet American, the effect of the studio system is also key to the elaboration of the noir style. The strong visual motifs (street, city, lighting) and the overall unity of the noir cycle is the result of the work of craftsmen and technicians who were part of the Hollywood studio system: not merely directors but also cinematographers, art directors, costumers etc. German cinema of the 1920s is the most frequently cited prototye of the visual style of film noir. Clearly as a disproporionate number of emigres from Nazi Europe were German and Austrian-born directors (Lang, Wilder, Preminger, Brahm, Siodmak, Mann, Zinnemann) and technicians (Karl Freund, Shuftan, Theodor Sparkuhl). It is reasonable to assume that all were exposed to German Expressionism in its native environment.

Much of the literature on film noir confounds the lighting effects found in the German pictures of the era and deems such films as *M* (1931) or *Pandora's Box* (1928) "expressionist." As defined by film historians like Lotte Eisner or Rudolf Kurtz, expressionism is a distortion of reality through various plastic devices or, as Eisner says, "Subjectivism driven to extremes." It would be difficult to describe genuine Expressionist pictures, such as *Cabinet of Dr. Caligari* (1919, Robert Wiene) or

175

From Morning to Midnight (Von Morgen bis Mitternacht 1920, Karl Heinz Martin) as antecedents of film noirs such as *The Killers* (1946) or *Double Indemnity* (1944). The visual style of these two early German films is characterized by a very "personal" representation of the outside world. The bank in *From Morning to Midnight* is limited to a few painted cardboard walls (as Eisner comments, "The background is black and, like a collage, a few scenic details, a desk, a safe, a door, appear fleetingly"). *From Morning to Midnight* is considered by critics such as Francis Courtade as the ultimate expressionist picture. Why then do historians often describe American film noir as "expressionist"?

Caligari and *From Morning to Midnight* make remarkable use of light and form. In Robert Wiene's classic *Caligari,* the mad creature, Cesare (Conrad Veidt, soon a regular player in film noir) abducts the hero's fiancée, Jane. His sinister shadow on the wall, his flight on the rooftop, display a formal approach similar to that of noir. In terms of composition; the entrapment of the characters between walls, corridors, dark comers or empty rooms has a visual intensity that foreshadows film noir. It has, however, none of its realism. When Cesare is seen running across a rooftop, (like the protagonists of *Killer's Kiss* or *Naked City***)**, this rooftop has nothing to do with the architectural reality. The question of film noir as descendant of expressionism remains therefore ambiguous. The formal elements of expressionism, its use of lighting, lines dividing the screen in several areas, have been of certain influence on film noir, but few American thrillers show traces of "pure" expressionism as seen in *Caligari* or *From Morning to Midnight.*

Edward Dmytryk's *Murder, My Sweet* (1944) is certainly expressionist in style. In one of the key scenes of the film, the protagonist, Philip Marlowe (Dick Powell) is beaten up, then drugged. The scene, as seen from his point of view, is a succession of abstract images: "black pools," never-ending corridors, chaotic labyrinths, all reminiscent of the "pure expressionism" *Caligari* where reality is portrayed through a series of abstract images. This distortion of reality, though purposeful, is nevertheless the representation of the effect of drugs on Marlowe. Dmytryk's approach is expressionist in its use of odd camera angles but not expressionist in context; the director merely uses a technique to express the subjective vision of his character. "Surface" expressionism is also found in *Lady From Shangai* (1947, Orson Welles) and its Luna park scene, filled with distorting mirrors and cardboard sets, but these effects are just part of the environment of the scene (the amusement park) and therefore still connected to reality.

In the mid-1920s, German films by Lang, Murnau, Joe May, Lamprecht, Phil Jutzi or Pabst represented a new orientation, called *"neue sachlichkeit"* or "new objectivity". Films like Jessner's *Backstairs* (1921), Grune's *The Street (Die Strasse,* 1923), Joe May's *Asphalt* (1928) or Murnau's *The Last Laugh (Der Letzte Mann,* 1924) represented a compromise that anticipated the look of the early Hollywood noir: expressionist devices in lighting and composition, realism in the depiction of the social and urban background.

"Stimmung" is used by Lotte Eisner to describe the very unique atmosphere dis-

played in the films of Lang and Murnau. This "mood" was expressed through light and sets. The "*Stimmung* under the lamp," as Eisner calls it, is found in numerous films of the period and creates an atmosphere of fear, decay, and anguish: the card game in *The Street* (1923), the postman's room in *Backstairs*; the gangsters' lair in Lang's *The Last Will of Dr Mabuse* (1932) are all lit by a single lamp hanging from the ceiling. Similar images were to be found a decade later in Hollywood's noir. Victor Mature's cross examination in *I Wake Up Screaming* (Bruce Humberstone, 1942), the preparation of the hold-ups in both *Asphalt Jungle* (John Huston, 1950) and in *The Killing* (Stanley Kubrick, 1956), Van Heflin meeting a professional killer in *Act of Violence* (Fred Zinemann, 1948), racist hooligans planning their attack on the black district in *No Way Out* (Joseph Mankiewicz, 1950).

Other *physical* motifs were also in evidence. In *M*, *Backstairs, The Street,* and *Pandora's Box*, staircases divide the shot in two symmetrical areas. Staircases can sometimes establish a social relationship between characters *(The Last Laugh)* or symbolize the separation between Good and Evil (as in most of Lang's films). The staircase motif is also found in a great number of film noirs like *Spiral Staircase* (Robert Siodmak, 1945), *Notorious* (Alfred Hitchcock, 1946), *The Glass Key* (Stuart Heisler, 1942), and *The Big Heat* (Fritz Lang, 1953). The symbolic implications may vary. In Lang's *Secret Beyond The Door* (1947), Joan Bennett takes refuge at the top of a huge staircase. In Hitchcock's *Notorious* (1946), Cary Grant and Ingrid Bergman find safety at the bottom of the stairs which lead them to freedom. In Hathaway's *Kiss of Death* (1947), Richard Widmark pushes an old lady from the top of the staircase in a now famous scene. Three different films by three different directors of three different origins (Austrian, English, American) working in three different studios (Universal, RKO, Fox), all carrying the marked influence of a German motif.

The city as a menacing presence is another visual "leitmotiv" of pre-war German cinema. *The Street* describes the journey of an ordinary "bourgeois" through the nightmarish metropolis. The last shot of the film, showing the man returning home at dawn, in the deserted and dark streets is often repeated in film noir. The opening shot of Fred Zinemann's *Act of Violence* (1948) is quite similar: Robert Ryan walks in an empty street, steps into his building, then climbs the staircase that leads to his room. In Lang's *Metropolis* (1926), the futuristic sets isolate the individuals inside an "asphalt jungle". In *M*, a high angle shot isolates Peter Lorre in a deserted street as three men enclose him in the frame. *Asphalt* (1928) and Phil Jutzi's *Berlin Alexanderplatz* (1932) portray the city as a menacing and destructive environment. The preeminence of German studio shoots supported a growing use of unnatural light, which finds its origins in the theater of Max Reinhardt. The dark rooms and cellars, the menacing shadows of *M* and *Pandora's Box* are constantly replicated in Hollywood noir. In Robert Siodmak's *Christmas Holiday* (1944), the shadow of a policeman visiting the heroine is cast on the door of her home vividly recalling one of the first shots in *M*: the shadow of the murderer cast against a poster. Many German films of the era explored the theme of the double or *doppelganger* through plots in which protagonists are victims of an uncontrollable split personality and torn between good and evil, such as Peter Lorre in *M* or

Fritz Kortner in Arthur Robison's *Schatten* (1923). These ambiguous impulses are visually rendered through frequent use of mirrors and reflections.

The symbolic mirrored drawing room in *Woman in the Window* betrays the characters' moral duality, as does the mirror in the beach house of *Murder, My Sweet.* One of the most memorable examples is *Lady From Shanghai* where Everett Sloane's canes, the symbol of his corruption, appear in the mirror during his final confrontation with his wife, Elsa (Rita Hayworth). Actors in German films are often photographed behind windows or gates that cast shadows resembling prison bars on their faces. When Schraencker, the ambiguous gang leader of *M*, is behind a gate that separates him from the audience, Lang expresses Schraencker's alienated posture through mise-en-scène. A similar staging is used in the last shot of Mary Astor behind the elevator gate in *The Maltese Falcon* (1941).

The influence of the work of caricaturist George Grosz is also evident in the make-up, costuming and performance of many figures in German silent film: Lohman in *M* and *The Last Will of Dr Mabuse*, Emil Jannings in *The Last Laugh*, or Fritz Kortner in *Backstairs* and *Pandora's Box*. This taste for grotesque is also found in film noir. Ben Hecht, screenwriter of *Scarface* and *Notorious*, wrote an essay introducing Grosz's work to the American public. Grosz's "The Responsibles" (1923), "Furious Man" (1918), and "Diamond Rackeeter" (1920) are forerunners of the obese characters that would later be portrayed by Sidney Greenstreet in *The Maltese Falcon* and *Three Strangers* (1946), Francis L. Sullivan in *Night and the City* (1951), Dan Seymour in *The Big Heat* (1953) and Orson Welles in *Touch of Evil* (1958). These monsters are perfect visual answers to the asphalt jungle that surrounds them. They belong to the city and are trapped like animals in cage.

French pre-War "poetic realism" also antedates certain aspects of the visual style of noir in the work of directors like Carné, Duvivier, and Renoir. Siodmak's French films like *Pièges* (*Traps*, 1939) typifies how the German *Stimmung* was recreated in the studios of Boulogne and Joinville. Duvivier was even more noir than the "French Siodmak," especially in *La Tête d'un Homme* (1932), *Pépé le Moko* (1937) or *La Bandera* (1936). In the latter film, Duvivier opens his picture with a shadowy street comer and its lamp post, then moves inside a seedy hotel room in Spain with a characteristic light effect through venetian blinds which creates dark bars on actor Jean Gabin's face. In sordid locales like bars and nightclubs, Duvivier delineates an underworld of dark figures and dangerous outlaws, drawing from two styles he admired in German cinema and the American gangster film.

Carné was also attracted by the urban imagery. *Le Jour Se Lève* (1939) and *Quai des Brumes* (1937), both photographed by German cinematographer Shuftan, are street tragedies. Through its titled foggy docks and the final scene of the protagonist's death on a rain-splashed street, *Quai des Brumes* also foreshadows the noir style in Hollywood. In *Le Jour Se Lève*, the cramped and disordered room, the staircase filmed in high angle shots and the overall nightmarish atmosphere convey a sense of paranoia and isolation typical of American noir. (The film was remade in 1947 by Anatole Litvak, as a classic American noir piece, titled *The Long Night*.)

Long before he directed *Woman on the Beach* in the United States, even Renoir's work contained noir precursors. *La Chienne* (1932) and *La Bête Humaine* (1938) were both remade as American noir, *Scarlet Street* (1945) and *Human Desire* (1954) by Lang. *La Chienne* is full of pre-noir "motifs" such as the dark streets in which Legrand (Michel Simon) meets the prostitute for the first time or the prison cell in which André waits helplessly to be executed for a murder he did not commit. The cinematography, by German cameraman, Theodor Sparkuhl, one of the pioneers of the "noir look," establishes a world full of dark menace and violence.

Some critics have cited a final and unexpected influence on the noir style from Italian neo-realism. In the late 1940s, the noir cycle did produce a number of "semi documentary" thrillers. Nevertheless, it would be far-fetched to make a direct link between neo-realism and film noir. True, Neo-realist directors did bring drama into broad daylight and real location settings. But, as discussed later, the reasons for location shooting and a documentary-style narrator in film such as *Call Northside 777* or *The Naked City* go far beyond the neo-realist influence.

In 1929, long before the neo-realist movement in Italy, the seminal *Menschen am Sonntag* was released in Germany. Shot in location in Berlin, the film was a collaboration

Thug Vince Stone (Lee Marvin) manhandles the sensitive "bad girl" (Gloria Grahame) in *The Big Heat.*

between an impressive list of later participants in the noir cycle: Billy Wilder, Robert Siodmak, Edgar Ulmer, and Fred Zinnemann. Most of these directors contributed to the "semi-documentary" style as in Ulmer's *Detour* (1945), Siodmak's *Criss Cross* (1949). Zinnemann's *Act of Violence* (1948) and even in Wilder's *Double Indemnity* (1944). Earlier American filmmakers had introduced extensive location shooting long before film noir: Mervyn Le Roy in *I Am A Fugitive From A Chain Gang* (1932) or John Ford in *Grapes of Wrath* (1940). American photographers like Dorothea Lange, W. Eugene Smith and Walker Evans had also accustomed the American public to depression-era realism. Before that, at the beginning of the century, a group of painters known as "The Ash Can School" had emerged in the U.S. Robert Henri, John Sloan or Everett Shinn rejected the academic style of the so-called "salon" painters with dark, urban imagery. Sloan had been trained as a sketch-artist for newspapers. He and other members of the Ash Can School capture the angst of life in the big city in gray and black. Sloan's 1910 *Night Windows* is a good example of this style that anticipates the mood of film noir. Shinn often depicted the subway late at night. George Bellows painted boxing matches. These dark, proletarian settings are often the milieu of film noir. In the next decades, the paintings of Edward Hopper, often considered as a "member" of the American Scene movement, go far beyond the American taste for realism and express a despair and alienation identical to noir. *Nighthawks* (1942), *Drugstore* (1927), *Automat* (1927) and *Girlie Show* (1941) are fully noir. In their deserted bars, empty offices or dark streets, Hopper's "characters" are isolated, lost in their environment, exactly like film noir's desperate protagonists. An early sketch of his *Night Shadows* (1921) has all the visual intensity of "noir" in its high-angle view of a deserted street where a man walks alone past empty buildings. Hopper's compositions reveal a strong, almost cinematic, sense of the dramatic. Lang's *Scarlet Street* is certainly inspired by Hopper's works both in its subject matter and style: there again Lang emphasizes the total loneliness of his protagonists, who are submerged by the emptiness of the studio sets. Lang's artistic sensibility, and the fact that he was trained as a painter could perhaps explain the resemblance between his film and Hopper's paintings. In any respect however, Edward Hopper can be labelled as a genuine noir artist. One should also mention Martin Lewis, perhaps less famous than Hopper, but also a true "noir" painter. Australian born Lewis moved to New York in the early 1910s. His approach to the urban landscape is very similar to film noir, which it clearly anticipates in works such as *Giant Shadow* (1929).

As far as photography is concerned, one name stands out in terms of film noir: Weegee. Under this appellation Austrian born Arthur Fellig brought a keen sense of observation to his gritty location photographs. Not unlike a "noir" protagonist (which he became in the neo-noir *The Public Eye* [1992]), Weegee roamed New-York at night capturing on film its deserted streets, its seedy bars, and its universe of murder and rape. Weegee associated violence with the city, but his approach has more in common with the semi-documentary thrillers of the late 1940s than the sophisticated photography of the early noirs. *The Naked City* (1948) took its name and style from Weegee. Weegee's almost constant use of flashbulbs heightened the grotesque characters that he photographed. Weegee's consulting with Mark Hellinger, producer of *The Naked City*, may have helped to infuse the film with an immediacy seldom found in film noir.

The depiction of the city as a menacing and threatening environment was always a major part of noir imagery. A film noir is often identified by its first shots, particularly if the view is a high-angle of a city street evoking alienation and entrapment. The openings of *Side Street* (1949), *Criss Cross*, and *The Naked City* are typical. Whereas German films often chose a vision of the city as a nightmarish oppressive machinery, the menacing city found in film noir faithfully reflects American architectural reality. From the earliest skyscrapers to the mid-1950s, the tall, fluted structures of the American skyline created a unique physical and visual impression, "Chicago School" visionaries Daniel Burnham and Louis Sullivan and their successors, created the "naked cities" and "asphalt jungles" in the first half of the 20th century. The treatment of the urban landscape in film noir, from the New Orleans docks in *Panic in the Streets* (1950), downtown Los Angeles in *The Brasher Doubloon* (1947) or Chicago in *Call Northside 777* or New York in *The Naked City*, consistently invokes an impersonal and often hostile milieu.

American Cinema before the Noir Cycle

Most film historians identify the beginning of the noir cyle with *The Maltese Falcon* in 1941. As early as 1912, D.W. Griffith used certain visual elements later asociated with noir in his short *The Musketeers of Pig Alley*. Settings, like the back-alley in which the gangs fight to the death became a traditional milieu of film noir. As critic Michel Cieutat described it, "Pig Alley is nothing but a dead-end street enclosed by thick walls of stained bricks, the narrow locus of a life from which one's only refuge is behind the locked door of a slum dwelling."[1] *The Musketeers of Pig Alley* is not merely one of the first American gangster films but also the prototype of the thriller and of film noir, making extensive use of location shooting, more than three decades before that method was embraced by film noir.

With their high-contrast cinematography, doomed atmosphere, and evocative urban settings, many Hollywood films by Vidor, von Sternberg, Murnau, or von Stroheim anticipate the visual universe of noir. Although adapted from a naturalistic novel, Stroheim's *Greed* (1925) features a famous shot that isolates McTeague in the staircase as his wife watches him, a visual composition using low angle and depth of field that is "pre-noir". Mumau's *Sunrise* (1927), while certainly recalling *The Last Laugh,* uses the city to suggest decadence and a certain menace. Vidor's *The Crowd* (1928) introduces another noir theme: the city crushing the individual. Vidor uses the urban architecture to isolate his protagonists. Sternberg's silents are the most representative of a "pre-noir" sensibility in American cinema. *Underworld* (1927) is often cited as one of the first true noirs. *The Docks Of New York* (1928) has the same *chiaroscuro* settings and sordid characters. The dark, fog-enshrouded docks anticipate similar settings in *Nobody Lives Forever, Somewhere in the Night* (both 1946), *The Woman on Pier 13* (1950). Art director Hans Dreier, who later oversaw two dozen films in the noir cycle, designed the sets.

The evolution of the 1930s gangster film from such antecedents as *Musketeers of*

Pig Alley and *Underworld* has certain parallels with film noir. Both types of film are set in a contemporary milieu often peopled by criminal characters prone to violence. More than anything, visual style differentiates a film like Wellman's *Public Enemy* (1931) and Siodmak's *The Killers*. Deeply rooted in a social context, the sets of gangster films are indicators of the social status of the protagonists. The spatial environments of *Public Enemy* or *Scarface* (1932) are not those seen in *Side Street* or *Night and the City*. As Eugene Rosow notes, "Sets of gangster films were straightforward and relatively inexpensive, and the best work of art directors was saved for more lavish productions."[2] Nonetheless, gangster films introduced many locales that would become staples of film noir. The diner, for instance, as featured in *Little Caesar* (1931), ten years before Hopper's "Nighthawks," is reworked in *Phantom Lady* (1944), *The Postman Always Rings Twice* (1946), *The Killers, Detour* (1944), *Mildred Pierce* (1945), and *Gun Crazy* (1950) to name but a few. Despite their strong characterizations and urban settings, gangster films never attained the stylistic signature of film noir. As Rosow observed, "most of the camerawork in gangster films was simple and craftsmanlike."[3] While the low-key lighting of Lee Garmes for *Scarface* or Gregg Toland for *Dead End* (1937) may foreshadow the noir style, they serve a genre function.

Horror films of the 1930s and early 1940s were also photographed in low-key and atmospheric light. The black-and-white photography often exaggerated and heightened the monstrous features of characters such as Frankenstein's creature, the mummy and Dracula. Similar physical exaggeration is found in film noir, from the bulging eyes of Richard Widmark in *Night and the City,* the bizarre surgeon of *Dark Passage,* the battered visage of Robert Ryan in *The Set-Up,* or Gloria Grahame's scalded face in *The Big Heat.*

The baroque horrors of Universal in the 1930s was followed by the Val Lewton productions at RKO, which used atmosphere instead of the theatricality of Universal. *Cat People* (1942) and *Leopard Man* (1943) typified the pictures produced by Lewton, whose collaborators would soon direct, design, and photograph RKO noir.

The Refinement of the Noir Style

Many of the motifs of film noir, from low-key lighting to great depth of field to oblique camera angles derive from the technical evolution of Hollywood throughout the 1920s and 30s culminating with Orson Welles's *Citizen Kane.* In the 1920s Hollywood was dominated by a "soft style" in which edges and contours were blurred. The images had contrast and a certain depth of field but little sharpness. With the coming of sound, tungsten lamps replaced the noisy arcs of the silent era. The Mazda bulb patented by General Electric in 1909, was an omnidirectional, soft light designed for flat interior illumination. Fresnel lamp housings to focus the light and more sensitive film stocks like Super Panchromatic in 1931 were quickly developed, but the studios continued to reject hard light and sharp images as being "unartistic". In the mid 1930s, cinematographer Gregg Toland was already experimenting with deep-focus compositions in films for William Wyler (*Dead End,* 1937) and Howard Hawks (*Come and Get*

It, 1936). Others like Lee Garmes and James Wong Howe introduced dramatic lighting and unusual camera placement to a variety of genres. As John Alton remarked in
his classic work on cinematography, *Painting with Light:* "To create an authentic effect,
the cameraman lit the character from a low light which illuminated the face from an
unusual angle. It distorted the countenance, threw shadows seldom seen in everyday
life across the face."[3] Warners Bros. cinematographers like Sol Polito and Arthur
Edeson photographed some gangster films in this particular style but the camera
placement was quite conformist, usually straight on from the front. Most cinematographers hung lights above the set and dimished the impact of a key light on the side
with bright fill that eliminated dark corners and removed shadows.

   With *Citizen Kane,* Gregg Toland brought to bear practices developed in films like
John Ford's *The Long Voyage Home* (1940). The wide, fast lenses which permitted depth
of field also enlarged the frame and revealed the ceilings or absence thereof from a
three-wall set. False ceilings had to be built to maintain verisimilitude. The "ceiling syn-
drome" carried over into 1940s noir. The ceiling became a visual element of the frame
threatening to crush the alienated noir protagonist-within a box-like room. Deep
focus cinematography with wide angle lens was easier with faster film stock, which
also permitted low-key lighting. The opening scene of *Citizen Kane,* where journalists
argue in the projection room after the screening of "News on the March," is a good
example of this technique. By the mid-1940s, wide angle lenses were commonplace in
Hollywood.

   Because of its flexibility as a style rather than a genre, film noir could easily accommodate technical experimentation, such as the subjective camera in *Dark Passage*
(1946) and *Lady in the Lake* (1947) or the long takes in *The Big Clock* (1948) and *The Blue
Gardenia* (1953).

   Post war "realism" was marked by new experiments. Joseph Lewis and cameraman
Russell Harlan used the lighter equipment that had been produced during the war for
Gun Crazy, in the famous robbery scene, consisting of a single shot inside a car. Lucien
Ballard commented on his lighting method for director Jacques Toumeur on *Berlin Express* (1948): "We used hand-held camera in that, and it was a German camera that had
just come out: I bought one, and the results with it were excellent."[4] John Alton summarized the post-war attitude as "People are getting tired of the chocolate-coated
photography of yesterday. They have had enough of it. In the latest films there seems
to be a tendency to go realistic. This trend will no doubt have its influence upon am-
ateur, still and movie photography."[5] Significantly, one of the great specialists of the
soft style, William Daniels, adopted this "realistic" style to shoot *The Naked City* using
fast film and compact lights.

The Studio Influence from Sets to Location Shooting

During the first post-war decade film noir was also marginalized by the studios: in
1947, 30 film noirs were released by the majors, in 1955, only 12. Later films such as
Robert Aldrich's *Kiss Me Deadly* (1955), Stanley Kubrick's *The Killing* (1957) and Samuel

Fullers' *Crimson Kimono* (1959) epitomized a new emphasis on violent, anti-heroic protagonists. Whereas film noir of the early 1940s were confined to recreations of urban atmosphere from wet pavements and deserted streets to subways and bars situated on sound stages and studio backlots, technology and budget restraints set film noir out into the real world. As William Daniels remarked on the method regarding *The Naked City* "[we] shot in actual apartments. I think we only used one set. We developed some small unit lights to meet the problem."[5] From beginning to end, the style of the noir cycle was mainly influenced by the work of craftsmen and technicians who belonged to the so-called "Hollywood studio system." The studios had many contract art directors and cinematographers who were at the heart of darkness, of the noir "look." Each studio had its own approach to noir. Of course some overlooked the studio preferences (Orson Welles) or managed to blend it with their own personal style (Fritz Lang).

Paramount's early entries in the noir cycle, Wilder's *Double Indemnity* (1944) or Stuart Heisler's *This Gun for Hire* (1942), had a strong visual unity. In the 1920s, Ernst Lubitsch had brought art director Hans Dreier from Germany, a former collaborator of UFA. Dreier's work for Paramount in the 30s is ranged from the lavish interiors of Lubitsch's *Trouble in Paradise* (1932) or *One Hour With You* (1932) to the eerie sets of Rouben Mamoulian's version of *Dr Jekyll and Mr Hyde* (1933). By the 40s, Dreier was head of Paramount's art department and supervised *Double Indemnity,* where the luxurious villa interior of the Dietrichson house contrasts with the shabbily appointed apartment where she and Walter Neff plan the killing of her husband. In the George Marshall/Raymond Chandler collaboration, *The Blue Dahlia* (1946), the "Dreier look" is again manifest: upscale interiors of the hero's pre-war household are counterbalanced by seedy hotel rooms where he must take refuge when falsely accused. Dreier's ability to create an unreal, nightmarish atmosphere is epitomized in Fritz Lang's *Ministry of Fear* (1943) and is still evident in one of his last assignments, *Union Station* (1950), despite the film's "semi-documentary" approach.

Warner Bros films often relied on art-director Anton Grot, designer for *Mildred Pierce.* The opening scene of the film is "pure" noir: Wally Fay (Jack Carson) is caught alone, in the spiral staircase of a deserted Malibu beach house. Warner films noirs offered a strange mix of large scale Hollywood filmmaking and touches of pure American Gothic. Before he came to Warners for *The Unsuspected* (1947), cinematographer Woody Bredell had teamed with Robert Siodmak at Universal on *Phantom Lady* and *The Killers.* During a short period, Universal noir films also bore the influence of a few skilled technicians. Producer Mark Hellinger, who had previously worked for Warner, finished his short career at Universal with *The Killers, Brute Force,* and *Naked City.*

Under the post-war influence of Darryl Zanuck and Louis de Rochemont, producer of the **"March of the Time"** series, Fox specialized in doing "social" dramas. As early as 1940, Ford's *Grapes of Wrath* (1940) contains many visual elements that anticipate the documentary noir at Fox. Talented cinematographers such as Lloyd Ahem (*The Brasher Doubloon* [1947]) and Joseph McDonald (*Call Northside 777* and *Panic in the Streets*) combined location shooting and deep focus, as in the final chase of *Panic in* the Streets. The art direction, exemplified by Lyle Wheeler's work, blended with actual locations and studio sets. Wheeler's heavily influenced the overall style with such designs as the warehouse in Panic in the Streets, the fruit market of Thieves' Highway (1949), the pier in Pickup on South Street. "The underworld milieu has rarely been as well depicted as in Lyle Wheeler and Chester Gore's sets for William Keighley's Street with No Name (1948)," Eugene Rosow notes in Born to Lose, "with its flophouses and cheap rooms near the bus depot, the penny arcade and boxing gym, the gang's warehouse hideout and hidden arsenal, the cops' office and the night club."

Despite the "Crime Does Not Pay" series of edifying shorts in a semi-noir mode, MGM's reputation was for a high key look and far removed from the shadowy universe of film noir even in its "B" pictures. "Naturally, you didn't have as much time to spend on one of the [lower budget] films," recalls MGM cameraman Harold Rosson, "but I remember Mr. Mayer saying to me, 'If it's an MGM film, it has to look like an MGM film,' regardless of the fact that it was officially a 'B' picture."[6] One of Rosson's early noirs was Johnny Eager (1942), a film noir with a soft photographic style. Under Cedric Gibbons' authority, the art department provided sets that sometimes clashed with dramatic intent of certain films. "One scene took place in a bookie joint," director Mitchell Leisen recalled regarding Young Man in a Hurry(1952). "We used some tacky real estate office in Washington Boulevard for the exterior but when Gibbons did the interior, it looked like something out of House and Garden. He had copper lamps with plants growing out of them. In a bookie joint? He wanted it a certain way. That was the MGM style, and that's what you got."[7]

When former RKO executive Dore Schary took over at MGM, he instituted new policies under which cameramen began to "deglamorize" their style. Joseph Ruttenberg, known for his use of "soft-focus," shot Mann's 1949 Side Street with a gritty, semi-documentary look. Harold Rosson turned "noir" for Asphalt Jungle (1950). MGM's evolution within the noir style is typified by The People Against O'Hara (1951). Photographed by John Alton, who had been brought to the studio by Anthony Mann, and designed by James Basevi, who had previously worked for Fox, the resulting film fully embraces the visual style of noir.

Under the influence of Citizen Kane, no studio produced a more consistent noir look than RKO. Directors Jacques Tourneur, Edward Dmytryk, Nicholas Ray, Anthony Mann, Robert Wise, and Robert Siodmak all worked there at some point. It was the arrival of Welles that precipitated changes in the orientation of the art department run by veteran Van Nest Polglase, designer of the Astaire-Rogers musicals. Toland and art director Perry Ferguson had to accommodate budget problems with partial sets, mattes, and other special effects. This economic approach to mise-en-scène was continued and perfected by Val Lewton. More than half of RKO's noir films were designed by one of Citizen Kane's set decorators, Darrell Silvera. Cat People directed by Jacques Tourneur also featured the work of cinematographer Nicholas Musuraca and art director Albert S. D'Agostino. Musuraca later worked on many noir films such as Out of the Past (1947) and Blue Gardenia. D'Agostino was a former art director at Universal and was fascinated by staircases which are are found in Mann's Desperate (1947),

Brahm's *The Locket* (1947), Dmytryk's *Crossfire* (1947), Hitchcock's *Notorious* (1946) and *Murder, My Sweet*. Many elements of "decor" in these films recall the Lewton period, such as the police headquarters of *Murder, My Sweet* which echoes the architect's darkened office in *Cat People*.

Five Prototypes of the Noir Style

Murder, My Sweet, completed in July, 1944 and released in March, 1945, is a film noir "malgré lui" largely influenced by the studio and its technical crew. Director Edward Dmytryk's visual style relies heavily on the first-person narrative of Raymond Chandler's novel, *Farewell, My Lovely,* and has a reputation as one of the most imaginative early noirs, much of which is based on a few significant scenes. *Murder, My Sweet* is certainly dark, with few scenes shot in daylight and most of the action set inside dimly lit rooms or at night. Still most of the staging is "frontal": medium shots and close-ups of the protagonists. The hallucinatory sequence after the beating and drugging of its protagonist Philip Marlowe does contain a series of visual devices seldom found in films of the period. Keyed to a voiceover narration, distorted images, odd angles, even

Avaricious morgue doctor (Percy Helton) angers the abusive Mike Hammer (Ralph Meeker) while the duplicitous Lily Carver (Gaby Rodgers) looks on.

fade-ins and fade-outs, convey a feeling of fear and anxiety that is uncommon for a non-fantasy film. But Dmytryk did not actually direct this scene with the mentality of the expressionist artist. Rather he used some devices to express the point of view of a single protagonist. As an RKO production, *Murder, My Sweet* also partakes of that tradition. When Marlowe visits the lavish Grayle mansion, one shot frames him sitting on a table in the hallway with an impression of depth that recalls *Citizen Kane* and Xanadu. Both Darell Silvera and Vernon Walker, who created *Citizen Kane*'s visual effects, certainly had significant influence on on the design and other aspects of *Murder, My Sweet*.

While Elia Kazan's association with film noir is marginal, *Panic in the Streets* exemplifies the use of locations and semi-documentary style. Three years earlier, Kazan had collaborated on *Boomerang* with Louis de Rochemont, pre-eminent producer of that style of noir at Fox. *Panic in the Streets* benefits from a great number of different sets and locations, which exploit the architectural background of New Orleans and the diversity and complexity of its different districts to create a noir universe. Even with de Rochemont, the influence of 20th Century Fox is clear. Under art direction by Lyle Wheeler the bars and restaurants of the Turkish district in *Panic in the Streets* clearly echo the Chicago locations of the Polish neighborhood that figured prominently in *Call Northside 777*. Remarkably, Kazan's experience on *Panic in the Streets* colors his later, better-known work. In *A Streetcar Named Desire* (1952), Kazan re-explores the New-Orleans atmosphere. The card game between Kowalski and his neighbors mirrors the card game which opens *Panic in the Streets*; and Kazan makes the use of the *Stimmung* in his lighting scheme. As a milieu, the port of New Orleans anticpates the visual universe of the docks in *On the Waterfront.* (1954). As Kazan himself noted, "From a visual perspective, I could never have succeeded as well with [*On the Waterfront*] without the experience of *Panic*,"[8]

Unlike Kazan, few directors are as closely associated with film noir as Fritz Lang. At the time of its release, the critical reception for *The Big Heat* was tepid at best, reflecting perhaps a bias towards the more flamboyant style of Lang's silent German films. *The Big Heat* is photographed "flat," typical of 1950s films noirs, especially those made at Columbia. The location shooting is limited and the overall visual tone of the film is uncluttered, far removed from the *chiaruscoro* of *M* or Lang's earlier American films. It seems that Lang deliberately chose this flat style for his technique had always been one of simplification. The brutality of both the "good" and "evil" characters in *The Big Heat*, the "raw" emotion marks a transition from the stylized 1940s noir of *Woman in the Window* and *Scarlet Street* to the character studies in the 1950s *Beyond a Reasonable Doubt* and *While the City Sleeps*. The gray tones of *The Big Heat* are a particular choice. Visually, Lang's characters are still often isolated in "blank sets": naked hallways, deserted apartments, empty corridors. Like his character emotions, Lang's style could be described as "raw." In *The Big Heat*, to achieve such an impression, the director would forego on the dark frames of the earlier thrillers for a more visceral violence, and an almost geometrical approach to each frame. The use of long takes allows Lang to work with more emphasis on mise-en-scène and performance that matches characters who are realistically drawn. Departing from the

baroque atmosphere of *Woman in the Window* and *Scarlet Street,* Lang adapts different elements of the noir style in *The Big Heat* and turns a classic thriller story into
a dark tale about moral corruption.

The opening of *Kiss Me Deadly* is typically noir: a deserted highway, a naked woman,
and night. But from the first director Robert Aldrich introduces the concept of light
itself as menacing. It is from the glare of the headlights and the policeman's torch, that
the fleeing woman recoils. Danger and violence occur in broad daylight: the bomb
placed in Hammer's sportscar, the fight on the beach, the struggle near the swimming
pool. An underlying chaos is implied because there is no safety, in light or in darkness.
Classic film noir often alternate light and shadow as representatives of security and
peril. Gangsters and thieves take refuge in darkness; but there is no such equation in
Kiss Me Deadly.

The scene in which Hammer opens the box, the "great what-zit," in the lockroom
uses a growling beam of light as its most sinister image. When Lily Carver opens the
box, it leads to detonation. *Kiss Me Deadly* uses most of the visual elements of noir
(from the dark streets and seedy locations) and adds them to those of 1950s science
fiction, a paranoid viewpoint which finds menace in the ordinary and everyday.

Whereas *The Big Heat* may be a search for visual simplification, *Touch of Evil* is an expressive opposite. As the culmination of Welles' work in the noir style, it builds on his
previous noir pieces, *The Lady from Shanghai* and *The Stranger.* As with Kazan, *Touch of
Evil* relates visually to the non-noir work as well from the deep focus *Citizen Kane,* to
the architecture of *Othello* (using the arches and columns of the Venice district of Los
Angeles to create a strange and dreamlike urban landscape). With its long takes, the
odd angles, and the larger-than-life characters, *Touch of Evil* also relates to *Kiss Me
Deadly* and the cynical end of the noir cycle in which corruption underlies all. Although
it may be remembered for its characteristic noir atmosphere, its prototypical locations inside motels and bars, its narrative paranoia, Welles' noir canvas is inclusive
rather than exclusive. Almost every shot of the film is filled with different elements and
pieces of information. This mise-en-scène is a formal choice by Welles that was at the
opposite of Lang's late noir and provides a striking example of the wide range of the
noir style.

Just as it emerged from Hollywood the noir style was subsumed back into it. As an
amalgam of influences, so too its influence on other films and filmmakers has been
sustained through new generations. There is no singular mode of expression in film
noir, just as there is no single element which defines it. As a cycle of films it is easy
enough to delineate. As the various examples have demonstrated, Noir remains elusive as a style: obvious on its surface but subtle in its particulars.

NOTES

1. "Naissance du thriller," *Positif* 171/172, July–August, 1975.

2. *Born to lose: The Gangster Film in America,* New York: Oxford Univerity Press, 1978.

3. *Painting with Light,* New York: McMillan, 1948

4. Quoted in Leonard Maltin, *The Art of the Cinematographer*, Mineola, New York: Dover, 1978.

5. Quoted in Charles Higham, *Hollywood Cameramen*, London: Thames & Hudson, 1970.

6. Quoted in Maltin, *The Art of the Cinematographer*.

7. Quoted in David Chierichetti, *Hollywood Director: the Career of Mitchell Leisen*, New York: Cutis Books, 1973.

8. Quoted in Michel Ciment, *Kazan par Kazan*, Paris: Ramsay Poche, 1973.

Many thanks to Alain Silver, James Ursini and Kent Jones.

I dedicate this piece to the loving memory of my friend and film noir enthusiast Yann Crenn.

Irena (Simone Simon), to whom emotions can be a dangerous trigger, caresses her doting husband (Kent Smith) in *Cat People*.

The Noir-Horror of *Cat People* (1942)

Eric Somer

After serving as David O. Selznick's apprentice for eight years, Val Lewton was ready to go it alone as a hands-on producer for RKO studios in March of 1942. Faced with the challenge of making horror films around predetermined titles, Val Lewton produced horror films that shared few traits with the competition of the day. With heavy emphasis on suggestion and atmosphere, the films Lewton's horror unit produced for RKO between 1942 and 1946 transcended horror genre conventions of the 1940s. Robin Wood observes that "... they strikingly anticipate, by at least two decades, some of the features of the modern horror film."[1] Though horror was bouncing back as a commercially viable genre in the late 1930s, the glory days were over.[2] Film noir, on the other hand, was in its prime period when the Lewton films were released. In fact, standard film noir visuals[3] abound in the Lewton horror cycle with emphasis on darkness, chiaroscuro lighting, entrapping shadows and cage-like imagery. These "horror films," I suggest, are equally at home in the film noir genre.

Though primarily indexed as horror films, the Lewton films have been afforded some attention by writers interested specifically in film noir. Gifford was one of the first to categorize several Lewton films as film noir works. He considers *Cat People* (1942), *I Walked with a Zombie* (1943) and *The Leopard Man* (1943) to be in good company with films like *Gilda* (1946), *The Big Combo* (1953) and *Kiss Me Deadly* (1955).[4] Without using the noir term, Telotte refers to the Lewton films as *vesperal*. Offering a definition of his term, he "... refers to the labyrinthine, indeterminate, and dark perspective on the modern world and its rule of reason ... [the films] repeatedly deconstructed our normal vision of things and our usual methods of formulating or narrating the complexities of human experience."[5] It seems the difference between Telotte's *vesperal* film and film noir, if any, may be merely one of degree.

The term "film noir" is credited to French critic Nino Frank, who first used the term in print in 1946, though it probably was not his original term. Film noir is, in one sense, a term used by critics, as opposed to a studio tag, i.e. "romantic comedy" or "Western." It is doubtful the words, "you're gonna star in a film noir" were uttered by studio brass at the time films like *Double Indemnity* (1944) and *The Blue Dahlia* (1946) were in the works. However, since the film noir has evolved from a stylistic phenomenon of the '40s and '50s into a proven, money-making formula, one would assume that film noir is an accepted genre at this point, yet some critics remain vehemently opposed to the notion that film noir is in fact a genre. Of course, the genre (or not a genre) argument invariably must be rooted in the critic's flexible definition of the term. Historically speaking, the film genre was developed by the Hollywood studio system in the hope of guaranteeing formulaic but profitable mass entertainment. The success of a genre film, then, to at least some extent depends on the mass audiences' ability to perceive it as such. That identification process was first operationalized by the development of specific iconography that extends from the genre film's content to the poster and other materials necessary for the film's promotion. Furthermore, if genre is defined by certain assumptions in storyline and style that lead to box office bankability, as well as being cyclical in nature, the unity of film noir as a genre cannot be ignored easily, nor would it be convincing to suggest filmmakers did not consciously create film noirs. I have to disagree with the Palmer assertion that "No studio, director, screenwriter, or art designer set out to make a film noir..."[6] The absence of the term film noir did not appear to preclude the evolution and proliferation of noir films in any way. As Silver and Ursini helpfully point out:

> Whether they had a name for it or not, whether they called their pictures thrillers
> or mysteries, actioners or mellers, it would be fairest to assume, particularly for
> those who did so again and again, that the filmmakers of the noir cycle were well
> aware of what type of motion picture they were creating.[7]

It would seem equally fair to extend the same courtesy to Lewton. All of his films—whether with elements of the horror piece, mystery, or period film—are marked by the same visual style and sense of fatalism that was so noteworthy in the noir film, especially during the noir peak from 1946 into the early '50s.

If film noir is a genre, then, it can mingle with other genres, as explicated in Wood's oft-quoted article *Ideology, Genre, Auteur*. If the Lewton horror films indeed share noir elements as well, it seems the cross-genre fertilization that Wood sees as intrinsic to the Hollywood system is at work: "The close juxtaposition of genres has implications that reach out through the whole generic structure of the classical Hollywood cinema."[8] Wood's concept of genres as symbiotic helps to explain the nuances of the Lewton films, i.e. mystery/noir *(The Leopard Man)*, horror/noir *(Cat People)*, horror/noir/period film *(Isle of the Dead* [1945], *Body Snatcher* [1945], *Bedlam* [1946]), and so on. Similarly, Dale Ewing appears to take the cross-genre paradigm as a given: "From horror films, such as *I Walked with a Zombie* and *Cat People*, film noir gained a mise en scène of repulsion and dread."[9] In yet another comparable line of analysis, horror film analyst Newman sees film noir as an extension of the 1930s horror film:

> The film noirs of the 1940s deal far more effectively with the underlying horrors
> of the decade—war traumas, alienation, psychological imbalance, social up-
> heaval—than any of the contemporary outings of Boris Karloff, Bela Lugosi or
> Lon Chaney Jr. Val Lewton led the way by taking horror themes into noir terri-
> tory in *Cat People*...[10]

Though Leifert sees the noir film as a "tone" that can be "applied" to any film genre, he agrees on the connection between the two:

> Besides the horrific nature of these films, noir and horror also place style and at-
> mosphere on the same level of importance as content. In short, the manner in
> which the stories are told is as important as the stories themselves.[11]

In his exhaustive survey of Lewton's career, Bansak explicitly recognizes the close relationship between the noir film and the horror film:

> ...a surprising number of noir elements were already present in the horror genre.
> The noir protagonist, almost always a down-on-his-luck male, was a tragic hero
> with a tragic flaw, a character usually beset by hasty decisions, obsessive behavior
> (often entwined with the lure of a femme fatale), and well-intended ambitions that
> go awry, a man in a trap of his own making. The noir form was further character-
> ized by both its narrative and visual style; often flashbacks were used, sometimes
> with accompanying voice-overs, and there was usually an abundance of night
> scenes characterized by expressionistic camerawork and chiaroscuro lighting.[12]

Bansak continues to draw the connection between the Lewton horror productions
and the film noir of the 1940s:

> The Lewton RKO films have strong associations with the early 1940s examples of
> noir melodrama, which is what sets them apart from the horror fare of the previ-
> ous decade. The prototypical film noir is a modified horror film, one which ex-
> ploits adult concerns and discards the fantastic elements...both genres are the
> stuff of nightmares.[13]

That the Lewton productions have advanced the horror genre has been well documented.[14] My analysis of *Cat People* will identify prevailing film noir motifs, iconography and themes, and also examine the displaced family that is so common to the noir
library of films.

(Noir) Horror Films to the Rescue

Upon his arrival at RKO in 1939, the illustrious Orson Welles developed a reputation for
exceeding budgets and ignoring the demands of his executives. After almost two years of
delivering no product for his employer, his first two films, *Citizen Kane* (1941) and *The Magnificent Ambersons* (1942), though revered by critics today, were dismal box office flops that
incurred significant losses upon RKO, prompting RKO President George J. Schaefer to re-
sign. His position was eventually filled by Charles Koerner, who wasted no time in doing
away with Orson Welles and his Mercury Productions. Planning a return to the black for
RKO, Koerner took note of the profitability of RKO "B" budget movies, while noticing a
resurgence of Universal horror product, especially the commercial success of *The Wolf
Man* (1941). The RKO "B" horror unit would be headed by Val Lewton, who would be
granted decidedly less artistic freedom from Koerner than Schaefer afforded Welles.

Fresh from his experience gained working with David O. Selznick, Lewton was ready to produce films on his own. Koerner's RKO paid Lewton $250 per week and allowed him to set up a "B" horror unit with the understanding that:

- Each film had to come in under a $150,000 budget.

- Each film was to run less than 75 minutes.

- Lewton's superiors would supply the title for each film.

Val Lewton himself is generally acknowledged as the dominant creative force behind the RKO horror unit, even though critics tend to regard the producer as an individual who impedes rather than facilitates the creative process of filmmaking. In *From Cyd Charisse to Psycho,* Thomajan recognizes Lewton as "...the sole argument on behalf of the producer-as-artist notion."[15] Not all critics, however, have felt inclined to champion Lewton's status as an auteur.[16] Assigning credit for creative contributions, especially for films of so many years gone by, is always a shaky proposition. Nonetheless it is hard to believe films worked on by a variety of writers, directors and actors could turn out so similar were it not for Lewton's presence. In fact, Lewton's horror-by-suggestion approach was already in place by his mid twenties at the time he wrote the short story "The Bagheeta," originally published in Farnsworth Wright's *Weird Tales* magazine in 1930. In his analysis of the story, Bansak concludes, "Lewton's characteristic phobia of cats and his fear-the-dark horror techniques are to be found, intact, in 'The Bagheeta.'"[17]

A great deal has been written about the Jacques Tourneur-directed *Cat People,* the first of the titles produced by the reputed ailurophobe Lewton. Focussing on the suggestive rather than the explicit to create psychological horror, *Cat People* must have come as a startling wake-up call for audiences accustomed to the Universal-style "monster" horror titles that had dominated the genre. Where Universal preferred a Frankenstein monster or a Wolf Man, Lewton's horror unit relied on the suggestive power of the darkness, the elaborate use of oppressive shadows, and pessimistic themes. As Telotte writes, "Although devoid of the traditional monstrous figures of cinematic horror, [Lewton's] films explore the very source of those well-known images..."[18] Still, as noted by Bansak, the transformation sequences in *Cat People* owe an obvious debt to those in Universal's *The Wolf Man.*[19] To the delight of Koerner, *Cat People* was a commercial success, grossing $4 million dollars internationally on a well under-budget investment of $134,959.[20] Thus the debut from Lewton's horror unit immediately helped bring RKO out of the financial gutter.

Critical response to *Cat People* has been plentiful, particularly since the release of director Paul Schrader's rather exploitative remake in 1982.[21] Though the remake inspired some critical analysis, the original continues to draw the most attention. Berks identifies psychoanalysis as the critical method film scholars have found most useful in the pursuit of explaining Irena Dubrovna's (French actress Simone Simon's) alter ego, "...and even those critics who reject psychoanalysis or find fault with its basic problematic seem to take it as a given that their own readings must differentiate themselves from a psychoanalytic one."[22] Craig and Fry were among the first to employ the psychoanalytic approach:

Lobby card for Cat People.

> The supernatural clap-trap of the story line is a veneer for yet another story—the gradual deterioration of a woman's psyche into schizophrenic violence. Through patterns of visual symbols and symbolic imagery, Lewton and Tourneur show the story of a girl who is the victim of severe sexual repression and who, because of her repression and jealousy, develops a personality split that ultimately destroys her. The transformation of Irena into a cat in the conventional horror plot is a metaphor for a more deeply moving story.[23]

Through the hermeneutics of psychoanalysis, it is possible to explain away Irena's disorder. I would add that film writers who draw from psychoanalytic critical methods tend to treat the studio-imposed footage of Irena in her panther form as somehow disconnected from the film. The convenient omission of the panther footage certainly adds weight to a psychoanalytic interpretation of *Cat People*. But a concession to RKO studio brass or not, that footage many critics have deemed "unnecessary" to what Tourneur and Lewton "intended" is indeed part of the film we know today, and therefore should be treated as such. In fact, the transformation sequences serve the noir film well; as a foreign world of unspeakable evil collides with the "decent" American setting of *Cat People,* Irena's mutation into a predatory panther confirms her suspicions that an ominous force has closed in on her for reasons beyond her control.

The Haunted Noir Protagonist

> "I'm backed up in a dark corner and I don't know who's hitting me."
> Bradford Galt in *The Dark Corner* (1946)

A quick recollection of famous noir characters may prompt one to label film noir concerns as primarily masculine, with males pushing the narrative along and women in secondary roles. On the other hand, Cowie argues against "...the tendency to characterize film noir as always a masculine film form."[24] Cowie cites noirs that were written by women, as well as those that center on a female character, including *Shadow of a Doubt* (1943), *Mildred Pierce* (1945), *Sorry, Wrong Number* (1948) and *Sudden Fear* (1952), among others. Though the private detective in particular is generally a man in the noir film, the lead protagonist, especially in other noir permutations, need not be. Prolific director Fritz Lang, on whose behalf "...it could easily be argued...invented the genre that would come to be called "film noir,"[25] made a number of noir films with female protagonists, including *Secret Beyond the Door* (1948), *Clash By Night* (1952), and *The Blue Gardenia* (1953).

In their description of the noir protagonist, Silver and Ward cite obsession and alienation as recurring motifs.[26] The past that ineluctably haunts Irena exemplifies the predicament of the classic noir protagonist. She rightly believes she is the descendant of Balkan Satanists and will metamorphose into a murderous cat at the height of arousal or sexual jealousy. This obsessive fear controls Irena's life to the extent that she has cut herself off from virtually everyone. Even her work is done in isolation at home; never is she shown in the traditional workplace. According to Cowie, "Characters feel compelled by forces and passions beyond their reason to act as they do..."[27] As an individual oppressed by a dark, omnipotent force, Irena can be linked to the alienated lead protagonist in a prototypical noir film like *Detour* (1945), in which the character Al Roberts closes the film with this statement:

> Fate, or some mysterious force, can put the finger on you or me—for no good reason at all.

Like Roberts, Irena is confined to the uncertain noir environment, a diegetic world of corruption, darkness and omnipresent shadows. "Cut off in some way from the normal world, noir characters inhabit a terrain of bleak and often terminal isolation..."[28] Tied closely to Irena's isolated state, then, is the oppressively dark imagery. According to Telotte, "...the ominous and ubiquitous dark patches...shoulder a heavy structural and thematic weight. They generate a pervasive dreamlike atmosphere, that of a world in which the individual seems to have little autonomy..."[29]

Monster or not, Irena may well be the most moral character the film presents. The time her husband Oliver Reed (Kent Smith) spends with Alice Moore (Jane Randolph) outside of the normal workday only serves to strengthen viewer identification with Irena. Dr. Lewis Judd (Tom Conway) is pretentious, condescending and lecherous. Given such a cast of characters, Irena wins our complete sympathy. Many scenes frame her in a sympathetic portrait: weeping in the bathtub, the target of Judd's strenuous advances, displaced by Alice, and so on. According to Bansak, "She is a female version of the classic noir protagonist: obsessed, alienated, haunted, ill-advised, and doomed."[30]

Women and Marriage

> She may appear pure and beautiful on the outside but evil may, nevertheless, reside within. It is this stereotype of feminine evil—beautiful on the outside/corrupt within—that is so popular within patriarchal discourses about woman's evil nature.[31]

More often than not, it is her sexuality that gives the noir woman definition. The seductress, or femme fatale, is a primarily sexual woman with devious intentions. Her antithesis is the nurturing woman, who represents the restrained sexuality that her opposite lacks.[32] Of course, the virgin/vamp dichotomy is not unique to film noir. One need only look to the Western to find evidence of the same feminine polarization at work, and of course plenty of evidence exists on film that women always have been, and continue to be, similarly stereotyped in the majority of motion pictures. What is unique to the film noir is the special weight given to these female archetypes; particularly the sexually strong woman, and in no other Lewton film is the sexuality of a female character and its influence on males more pronounced than in *Cat People*. The role of the woman in noir vacillates between victim and victimizer, but quite often she is both.[33] In the words of Palmer, ". . . women often appear as victims of fate or circumstance who frustrate male desire."[34] Such a definition suitably describes both of the major female players under consideration here, as we shall see.

However, to dump Irena into the same category as the femme fatales seen in films like *Murder, My Sweet* (1944) and *Out of the Past* (1947) could be wrongheaded. Never is the viewer led to believe that Irena is motivated by greed, nor does she desire the destruction of the man who falls in love with her. Even so, Irena represents feminine sexuality at its most violent and self-defeating; if not a femme fatale, she is at least something of a temptress best avoided by wanton males. Ultimately she is condemned to die because of her own sexuality. In her discussion of *Cat People* and *The Lady From Shanghai* (1948), E. Ann Kaplan notes ". . . Irena expresses . . . what 40s American culture was unable to address and which thus found indirect expression through film noir narratives."[35]

If one accepts Irena as a noir temptress, there are further complications that need to be addressed. Although the monstrous nature of Irena's sexuality may seem to exemplify the dangerous libido of the femme fatale, or perhaps even antedate the best examples of the noir seductress, Irena's refusal to sleep with her husband is also characteristic of the noir housewife, who fails to provide her mate with sufficient sexual satisfaction. Because of this lack felt by Irena's husband, he finds himself more and more attracted to his co-worker (whose function in the narrative I will return to). The deep sense of dualism (cat/woman, temptress/housewife) that can be ascribed to

Irena in some ways transgresses the usual feminine dichotomy of the noir film, though her non-productive marriage strikes one as distinctly noir, and provides the strongest impetus for a discussion of *Cat People* in terms of noir conventions.

In the noir diegesis, sex and marriage are not concomitants but dialectically at odds. Marital sex is seldom depicted as healthy or even possible in the film noir. Instead, one must look outside the marriage for sexual satisfaction; an alternative family must be created. In *Cat People,* the man who makes the mistake of marrying the temptress must seek redemption from a woman more suitable for a conventional relationship. In this light, the post-wedding celebration at The Belgrade is prophetic, with Irena framed between Oliver and Alice at the dinner table, as if she already is driving a wedge between them; already it seems sex is more likely to be found outside the confines of marriage. By the film's conclusion we witness the destruction of the traditional marriage and its replacement as formed by the "healthy" heterosexual union of Alice and Oliver.

Sylvia Harvey's article, "Woman's Place: The Absent Family of Film Noir" provides the means to achieve an understanding of the odd marriage that superficially bonds Irena and her husband. Harvey writes:

> It is the representation of the institution of the family, which in so many films serves as the mechanism whereby desire is fulfilled, or at least ideological equilibrium established, that in film noir serves as the vehicle for the expression of frustration.[36]

Harvey goes on to note that married couples are de-eroticized,[37] and that film noir is centered on the impossibility or elimination of romantic love in the family.[38] With Harvey's assertions in mind, we are now set to examine the problematic marriage in *Cat People,* from beginning to end.

For purposes of stressing the importance of the film's exposition, it is important to recall that libidinal excess often leads to death in the film noir. As the male dupe led astray by the noir woman, marine architect and self-described "good plain Americano" Oliver does not possess the worldliness needed to properly assess the dangerousness of the woman he so quickly falls for, his obvious self-confidence notwithstanding. Oliver first spots Irena at the Central Park Zoo, where the pretty Serb is sketching a black panther. This particular animal becomes Irena's symbolic *other*. Her wardrobe seems to have been inspired by the animal's color and texture, and she visits the caged cat frequently, the embodiment of her predatory, sexual side, or *bête noire,* as perceived by Craig and Fry.[39] The reading offered by Wood further explains the panther "…as an alternative potential mate."[40] Such a possibility emphatically raises the level of Irena's animalistic sexuality, and confirms her disconnectedness from other people.

A fashion designer by trade, the sexually repressed Irena sketches the zoo animal with a huge sword through its torso. The drawing, which Irena refuses to show to her new admirer, performs several meaningful functions. First of all, the sword, an obvious phallic symbol, foreshadows violent, coital death. Secondly, and perhaps most important, the drawing defines Irena's sexual need, which can be explained further as her need to be destroyed. Although she fears sex, she desires it at the same time, as her attempt to toss a failed sketch into a wastebasket indicates. Oliver, on the other hand, does not fear his quite normal sexual drive. With ease and confidence, he shows Irena how to throw her unwanted art into the basket. He will learn to his dismay that placing Irena's sexuality into the context of marriage will be an impossibility.

Irena's carefree littering has still deeper implications. When Oliver notices her failure to properly dispose of the unwanted sketch, he alerts her to a sign:

> Let no one say,
>> and say it to your shame.
> That all was beauty here,
>> until you came.

These stringent words allude to Irena's culpability for Oliver's ensuing frustrations and blazes a trail to another film noir component: the female's sexual dominance over the male.[41] After walking Irena home like a true gentleman (who most likely wants more than stimulating conversation from Irena), she invites him into her apartment for a cup of tea. Once inside the building, Oliver comments on the vastness of the interior[42] before ascending the huge staircase that leads to Irena's apartment. The confusing staircase that points to a dangerous situation is a recurring noir motif, as Hirsch (among others) contends.[43] Moreover, the door to Irena's dwelling is blocked by entrapping shadows that at first seem to stand only for her self-imposed isolation (she tells Oliver he may be her "first real friend"). On another level, the cage-like shadows could be construed as a device meant to keep others out; a warning signifier disavowed by a naive man not equipped to decode it. Once inside the apartment, Irena stresses her connection to darkness and evil, as she continues to do throughout the narrative. Oliver laughs it off and leaves, after setting up a dinner date for the following evening with his new romantic interest. As he descends the huge staircase, the frame composition and camera angles comment on his powerlessness. Oliver, the helpless naïf, is photographed from Irena's elevated point of view above. We then see Oliver's subjective view from a location significantly beneath her. This set-up anticipates the famous sequence in *Double Indemnity* (1944), in which Phyllis Dietrichson, atop a staircase, meets Walter Neff (an obvious homophone for naïf), who gazes at her from below. In both cases, the woman's superior placement alludes to her power and control, while the man's position connotes vulnerability.[44] The sexual dominance of Irena over Oliver heightens with Irena's repeated refusal to consummate the marriage, as the two are repeatedly separated in terms of mise en scène. On the couple's wedding night, Irena locks herself in her bedroom, leaving both parties frustrated and unfulfilled.

In his Frommian analysis of *Cat People,* Poindexter concludes that Irena's fear of domestication best explains her sexual problem, based on the notion that she must relinquish her autonomy in order to enter a relationship with a man successfully.[45] There is a fair amount of evidence to support his assertion that Irena is afraid of losing her independence through marriage. Oblivious to the danger of attempting to contain

Oliver Reed (Kent Smith) gazes with awe and confusion at his psychologically conflicted wife (Simone Simon) who may or may not turn into a panther when aroused in *Cat People*.

Irena in a relationship, Oliver's hope to trap his new love is perhaps best illustrated when he purchases a house cat for her, with predictably disastrous results. Before presenting the cat to Irena, Oliver shows the boxed feline to his pretty colleague Alice, who briefly plays with the friendly creature. As the cat already has been linked to the feminine, Alice's favorable response to Oliver's purchase seems to confirm her willingness to be contained by a man; to relinquish the autonomy she has gained in the workplace and replace it with subservience to the male in the patriarchal symbolic order, as she presumably would have to do after the war anyway. Hence, the domestic cat becomes a metonym for the "safe" sexuality of Alice. Irena, on the other hand, attempts to make a connection with the cat that never could be possible. Already linked to the wild black panther, she is dialectically opposed to the domestic cat. The house cat's reaction to Irena can only be one of instant fright. The same holds true with the other domesticated animals at the pet store, as well as the bird that ostensibly dies of fright after standing in for Oliver's intended surprise gift. Significantly, Irena places the dead bird in a box that recalls Oliver's original gift, the boxed-domestic cat. She throws the bird to the carnivorous panther at the zoo, in testimony to her feelings about domesticity. The panther, Irena's symbolic *other*, will consume the bird Irena would like to feed on herself. After this sequence, the viewer should recall the commotion Irena caused at the pet store. Following the chaotic intrusion of Irena, the lady who runs the store comments that the last time her animals became similarly alarmed was when an alley cat got in the store and devoured one of her finches. Again, Irena is linked to the predatory, the wild; that which cannot be domesticated.

Alice, Sweet Alice

The marriage between Irena and Oliver is marred by its artificiality. At the risk of obviousness, the following list of contrasts may help summarize the clash between the diegetic marriage and the ideologically satisfying one:

> *loneliness / togetherness*
> *unhappiness / happiness*
> *unconsummated / consummated*
> *no children / children*

Though not the obvious anomaly of the text, Alice alludes to her *otherness* when she declares herself "the new type of other woman." Opposed to the monster Irena, Alice is positioned as a healthy alternative to Oliver's unconsummated marriage. In the museum sequence, Irena is excluded and treated like a nuisance. It is Irena who is the outsider in the company of her husband and Alice, and it is Irena's jealousy of Alice that first releases Irena's feline form. Irena first kills several sheep to ventilate her hatred of Alice, and later claws Alice's robe during the swimming pool sequence. The close juxtaposition of Irena's sexual rage and the Alice character emphasizes the disparity that accounts for Irena's actions. Faced with the "good egg"[46] Alice, as Oliver calls her, Irena cannot help but reveal her true monstrousness. However, our identification and sympathies lie with Irena as Alice not too surprisingly sought more than friendship with Oliver all along.

The key scene to feature Alice takes place in the workplace, where she fulfills ideological needs dictated by the war-time economy. She has a conversation with Oliver that is prompted by his inability to concentrate on his work. As a metaphor for sex, the two smoke cigarettes. It turns out Oliver's marital problems are beginning to affect his job performance. He says, "I've never been unhappy before. Things have always gone swell for me... That's why I don't know what to do about all this. I've just never been unhappy." It is worth noting that Oliver claims he never experienced unhappiness before he took a wife. After being moved to tears, Alice declares her love for "Ollie," who continues to question his bond with his wife. "It's a different feeling," he says. Perhaps that "different feeling," from the very beginning, was lust for Irena, not love. To borrow an old idiom, Irena is not the type of girl you marry. In *Cat People,* though, we identify with Irena anyway; one feels no wish for Oliver and Alice's happiness after Irena is eliminated at the film's conclusion.

It can be said, then, that there are two types of women in *Cat People*: those suitable for containment and those who are not. The violent, "wild" sexuality of the foreigner, Irena, and the domestic, pro-creative sexuality of Alice. Because his marriage offers him no release for his sexual need, the despondent Oliver increasingly finds himself drawn to his place of employment, where Alice is always waiting beyond the purview of his chaste wife. The Alice character is interesting in that she poses a threat to the institution of marriage, which has been designated unproductive for both parties involved thus far, yet provides the possibility for a replacement marriage, which would reach fruition in *Curse of the Cat People* (1944).[47]

Admittedly, the abundance of phallic imagery (the cane/knife, the key to the cage, swords) that horrifies Irena would seem to be putatively at odds with the film noir theme of male impotence,[48] but the patriarchal power of the phallus in *Cat People* is disputable. Irena refuses to allow the males she turns on to derive sexual pleasure from her. Though such an arrangement dictates her sexually repressed state, it also allows her a considerable amount of emasculating power.

Just as Oliver never connects physically with Irena, so is the lecherous Dr. Judd, who always uses a walking stick, symbolically impotent. Though his cane may be construed as a symbolic phallus, especially the hidden knife inside, it proves to be a useless one.[49] The viewer will note that it is finally the released panther that does in Irena, apparently at her own will. In much the same way, the zookeeper, who appears to have no other area of the zoo to maintain apart from the panther's quarters, exhibits no desire to control the key that symbolically unleashes Irena's sexual rage. Her control of that key, which is of chief concern in the noir context, underscores her control of the phallus, which is precisely why she must be contained to re-establish the patriarchal status quo. After Irena's sexual power is demonstrated, she must be destroyed.

Existential Recognition

> Existentialism is an outlook that begins with a disoriented individual facing a confused world that he cannot accept.[50]

The film's concluding scene also summarizes another level of film noir meaning: existential recognition. The motif of existential recognition recurs in many noir films, including, *The Killers* (1946), *The Postman Always Rings Twice* (1946), *D.O.A.* (1950) and *The Killing* (1956), to name just several. According to Silver and Ward, " ... this moment of realization, this resignation to being annihilated by a relentless, deterministic abstraction, is the only, bitter solace that the noir vision permits."[51] In the case of *Cat People,* Irena's voluntary release of the caged panther evinces her acceptance of the only way out of her predicament. Fittingly, her symbolic *other* dies shortly after she does. Following the symbolic coital death of Irena, with Judd's knife driven through Irena by her *other*, comes the death of the panther, the embodiment of her evil (sexual) side. The implication is that Irena's sexual threat has been vanquished, which " ... allows the creation of the new all-American couple, Oliver and Alice, who move into the night and fog in the film's penultimate image."[52] Irena makes the supreme sacrifice that will permit the union between Alice and Oliver; it is Irena's own recognition of the inescapable evil she represents that finally forces her to give up. As for Judd, never is the viewer encouraged to mourn his apparent passing. His broken phallus stands for his attempted seduction of the noir temptress, which often leads to death for both parties involved in the film noir.[53] But like most monsters who appear in money-making movies, both characters would be resurrected in ensuing Lewton productions.

NOTES

1. Robin Wood (1979), "An Introduction to the American Horror Film," in Wood and Richard Lippe, editors, *The American Nightmare: Essays on the Horror Film,* Toronto: Festival of Festivals, p. 18.

2 See David Soren (1977), *The Rise and Fall of the Horror Film,* Baltimore, Maryland: Midnight Marquee Press, 1995, pp. 59–64 for a brief overview of 40s horror.

3. See Paul Schrader (1972), "Notes on Film Noir," reprinted in *Film Noir Reader,* editors Alain Silver and James Ursini, New York: Limelight, 1996, pp. 52–63 for an overview of the origins and characteristics of film noir.

4. Barry Gifford, *The Devil Thumbs a Ride and Other Unforgettable Films.* NY: Grove Press, 1988.

5. J.P. Telotte, *Dreams of Darkness: Fantasy and the Films of Val Lewton,* Urbana and Chicago: University of Illinois Press, 1986, p. 186.

6. R. Barton Palmer, *Hollywood's Dark Cinema: The American Film Noir,* New York: Twayne Publishers, 1994, p. 6.

7. Alain Silver, Elizabeth Ward, and James Ursini, editors, *Film Noir: An Encyclopedic Reference to the American Style,* Woodstock, New York: The Overlook Press, 1992 (3rd Edition), p. 398.

8. Robin Wood, "Ideology, Genre, Auteur." *Film Comment, 13,* 1 (Jan/Feb, 1977), p. 50.

9. Dale E. Ewing, Jr. (1988), "Film Noir: Style and Content," reprinted in editors Alain Silver and James Ursini, *Film Noir Reader 2,* New York: Limelight, 1999, p. 74.

10. Kim Newman, *Nightmare Movies: A Critical Guide to Contemporary Horror Films,* New York: Harmony Books, 1988, p. 211.

11. Don Leifert, "They Collide by Night: Film Noir Meets the Horror Genre. *Midnight Marquee,* 48 . (Winter, 1995), p.57.

12. Edmund G. Bansak, *Fearing the Dark: The Val Lewton Career,* Jefferson, North Carolina: McFarland, 1995, p. 117.

13. Bansak, p. 118.

14. See Phil Hardy, editor, *The Encyclopedia of Horror Movies,* New York: Harper & Row, 1986, pp. 78–79; Donald J. Skal, *The Monster Show: A Cultural History of Horror,* New York: Penguin Books, 1993, pp. 218–221; and Leonard Wolf, *Horror: A Connoisseur's Guide to Literature and Film,* New York: Facts on File, 1989, pp. 39–40.

15. Dale Thomajan, *From Cyd Charisse to Psycho,* New York: Walker and Company, 1992, p. 160.

16. See Robin Wood, *Personal Views: Explorations in Film,* London and Bedford: The Gordon Fraser Gallery Ltd., 1976, p. 212 and Telotte, pp. 10–11, who both stress the collaborative structure of filmmaking.

17. Bansak, p. 20.

18. Telotte, p.7.

19. Bansak, p. 117.

20. Bansak, p. 128–9.

21. See Carrol L. Fry and J. Robert Craig, "Track of the Cat: Freudian Symbolism and Values Transmission in Two Versions of Cat People," *Journal of Evolutionary Psychology,* 8 (August, 1987), pp. 269–277.

22. John Berks, "What Alice Does: Looking Otherwise at the Cat People," *Cinema Journal, 32,* 1 (Fall, 1992), p. 26.

23. J. Robert Craig and Carrol L. Fry, "Patterns of Symbolism in Val Lewton's Cat People," *Illinois Quarterly,* 42 (Fall, 1979), p. 7.

24. Elizabeth Cowie, "Film Noir and Women," in editor Joan Copjec, *Shades of Noir: A Reader.* New York: Verso, 1993, pp. 135–136.

25. Bansak, 1995, p. 34.

26. Silver and Ward, p. 4.

27. Cowie, p. 130.

28. Foster Hirsch, *The Dark Side of the Screen: Film Noir,* New York: Da Capo, 1981, p. 78.

29. Telotte, p. 22.

30. Bansak, p. 137.

31. Barbara Creed, *The Monstrous-Feminine: Film, Feminism, Psychoanalysis,* New York: Routledge, 1993, p.42.

32. See Janey Place, "Women in Film Noir," in editor E. Ann Kaplan, *Women in Film Noir,* London: British Film Institute, 1978, pp. 35–67 for a more complete discussion of the woman's role in film noir.

33. See *Double Indemnity* (1944) and *Scarlet Street* (1945) for examples of this feminine duality.

34. Palmer, p. 139.

35. E. Ann Kaplan, "The Dark Continent of Film Noir: Race, Displacement and Metaphor in Tourneur's *Cat People* (1942) and Welles' *The Lady from Shanghai* (1948)," in *Women in Film Noir,* p. 198.

36. Sylvia Harvey, "Woman's Place: The Absent Family of Film Noir," *Women in Film Noir,* pp. 23.

37. Harvey, p. 24.

38. Harvey, p. 25.

39. Craig and Fry, pp. 8–9.

40. Wood (1976), p. 217.

41. We never see the woman's face who is standing next to Oliver when he first notices Irena. Is it Alice whom Oliver is at the zoo with? If the unidentified woman is indeed Alice, one might further explain the zoo sign as an intimation of the sexually potent woman's power to lure Oliver away from Alice in the first place.

42. The set was leftovers from *The Magnificent Ambersons* (1942) RKO production.

43. Hirsch, pp. 95–96.

44. See Place, pp. 42–50, for a detailed analysis of the compositions used to denote the woman's power in the film noir.

45. Mark Poindexter, *Beyond Libido: A Frommian Analysis of Cat People.* Unpublished Paper, 1994.

46. The egg, of course, connotes feminine reproduction, which the text posits Alice as quite capable of.

47. In the course of persuading Irena to marry him in *Cat People,* Oliver ignores the possible validity of the "fairy tales" Irena takes seriously. He suggests she could tell them to their future children, which oddly prefigures her role in *Curse of the Cat People* (1944).

48. See Harvey, pp. 29–30 for more information on male impotence in film noir.

49. The character Ballin Mundson's cane has strikingly similar thematic connotations in *Gilda* (1946).

50. Robert Porfirio (1976), "No Way Out: Existential Motifs in the Film Noir," reprinted in *Film Noir Reader,* p. 81.

51. Silver and Ward, p. 4.

52. Tom Gunning, "Like unto a Leopard: Ffigurative Discourse in *Cat People* (1942) and Todorov's The Fantastic," *Wide Angle,* 10, 3 (1988), p. 37.

53. See *Double Indemnity, Gun Crazy* (1949), *The Killing* (1956), *Scarlet Street.*

Ellen Graham (Veronica Lake) is abducted by a hit man named Raven (Alan Ladd), who is humanized by his relationship with her in *This Gun for Hire*.

The Rise and Fall of the War Noir

Daniel M. Hodges

Film noir typically has been studied across a twenty year span, 1940–1959, and the categories used to describe or explain it consequently have stretched over most or all of this time. These categories have different names, such as "character types," "existential motifs," and "subheadings [for a] family tree." What they have in common is that they are *ahistorical*. The period of film noir, in short, has not been well periodized.

Ahistorical categories have been derived from a single element, such as a kind of crime or character. What I want to introduce, in contrast, is a time-based film noir category. Its distinctiveness is due to a variety of recurring plot elements. In other words, this category is a plot *formula*. It is historical because the specific combination of its plot elements only existed for certain years and then ceased.

I call this formula the *war noir* and date it from 1940 to 1944. Clarification of the plot elements of the war noir and the meanings they encode in the formula is the subject of this article.

As a shorthand for referring to *all* of the film noirs released from 1940 to 1944, I use the phrase *film noirs of the war noir period*. However, the term *war noir* refers only to the film noirs of this period that have the explicit formula, the complete combination of plot elements.

Additionally, it must be emphasized that my analysis can be applied to other crime movies made during these years. Although not necessarily appearing in any of the published encyclopedias of film noir, many have the film noir "look." As they were released in the same period, they shared the same historical context as the referenced film noirs. Thus, their plot elements were similar to, rather than different from, those of referenced film noirs of the war noir period.

The chief rule about film noirs is that they involve crimes. (I do not intend to pursue the will-o-the-wisp of trying to define film noirs. I accept their existence as given; and I take as given that the movies I discuss are film noirs.) The kinds of crimes, of course, vary. Yet these differences are, in a fundamental sense, the result of changes in historical period. For instance, these changes can be observed in terms of what thing is stolen and why someone is killed. In the war noir the variation is especially and significantly limited.

The main cause of crime in film noir (as well as all other forms of crime stories) is *property*: people try to enrich themselves through theft and/or murder. However there is a key contrast between the kind of property for which crimes are committed during World War Two and then after. In the war noir property is **personal**. In the immediate postwar years it is increasingly **public**, and nearly always so after 1949.

I consider personal property to be what is intimately associated with a person: his or her existence and riches. Examples of personal property in film noir include: Thomas Mitchell and John Qualen's savings (Out of the Fog); the landlady's house in the country (Ladies in Retirement); the insurance on Joan Fontaine (Suspicion); the blackmail demanded from William Powell (Crossroads); the bookmaker's bankroll (Christmas Holiday); and the jewels of Ingrid Bergman's aunt (Gaslight).

I want to emphasize that personal property crimes do occur after 1944, but their frequency diminishes, and almost vanishes by the end of the decade.

In contrast, public property is bound up with society at large. There are a couple of rare examples in the war noir period, both of which are embezzlements (Angels over Broadway and Suspicion). Other instances of public property crimes must be taken from postwar film noirs: Marvin Miller's robbery of gold bullion (Johnny Angel, 1945); Ray Collins' swindle of original paintings (Crack-Up, 1946); Tyrone Powers' "spook racket" (Nightmare Alley, 1947); Vincent Price's sale of counterfeit bonds (The Web, 1947); Howard da Silva's illegal immigrant smuggling (Border Incident); and Burt Lancaster's various heists of a hat factory (The Killers, 1946), an armored car (Criss Cross, 1949), and African diamonds (Rope of Sand, 1949).

I have given a lot of examples to show the variety of public property crimes and their differences from personal ones. It is unnecessary to name movies with the most blatant public property crimes: bank robbing, racketeering, etc. These crimes are frequent in film noir but, crucially, only in the years after the war noirs.

As the kind of property crime is different in the war noir, so too is the nature of homicide. For instance, in Angels over Broadway and Suspicion, no one is killed for the embezzled money. Murder for public property in the war noir period is rare. Murder to get hold of public property is a key element of postwar film noir formulas, but in the war noir formula homicide occurs for other reasons.

To be sure, someone is often killed for personal property, in the form of personal savings or other wealth. But there are also many victims of maniacs who have no interest in monetary gain (for instance, Stranger on the Third Floor, Among the Living, Bluebeard, Experiment Perilous, The Lodger).

More pathological than even Jack the Ripper's multiple murders is the death of Robert Montgomery in Rage in Heaven. He is deluded in the belief that his wife, Ingrid Bergman, is having an affair with his best friend and idol, George Sanders. After failing to kill Sanders himself, he schemes to have him executed for murder by the state. Montgomery arranges his own suicide to provide the incriminating corpus dilectus!

There are also murders committed in the war noir period because of espionage (e.g., Man Hunt, Saboteur, This Gun for Hire, The Fallen Sparrow, Journey into Fear, The Mask of Dimitrios). Insofar as national security is threatened, espionage is not concerned with either personal or public property. Instead, it deals with "possessions" of the state: documents and weapons, the lives of spies and statespersons. This type of film noir is gone, not surprisingly, by 1946.

It is a commonplace throughout the years of film noir that crimes of the heart do not concern property. In the war noir period, when public property crimes were absent, the most common reason for murder is a personal feeling, *passion* (either anger or jealousy). The following are examples.

Bette Davis kills her lover for dumping her *(The Letter)*; Ida Lupino kills her husband, Alan Hale, to try to make George Raft her lover *(They Drive by Night)*; Betty Field kills Howard da Silva for refusing her *(Blues in the Night)*; Elisha Cook, Jr. kills Carole Landis for refusing him *(I Wake Up Screaming)*; Ida Lupino kills Isobel Elsom for wanting to evict her two dotty sisters *(Ladies in Retirement)*; Ona Munson kills Gene Tierney, her daughter, for insulting her *(The Shanghai Gesture)*; Moroni Olsen kills his son, albeit accidentally, while arguing with him *(The Glass Key)*; Franchot Tone kills his best friend's wife for not running away with him *(Phantom Lady)*; Clifton Webb kills the wrong woman, thinking she is Gene Tierney, for not loving him as much as he loves her *(Laura)*; and Edward G. Robinson kills Joan Bennett's lover, Dan Duryea, in self-defense—and in a dream *(Woman in the Window)*.

In sum, most of the murders in the war noir period do not involve any kind of property. Of those that do, it is personal property. This attention to the kind of crimes that occur is to help make it clear who the **criminal-catchers** are.

The persons in postwar film noirs who solve crimes and eliminate criminals (by arresting or killing them) are law enforcement officials. Whether they are local cops, state police or federal agents, they are *public* defenders of the law, and of property. In order to verify the Hollywood "saw" that "crime does not pay," they have to be competent. In order to get their man or woman, they have to be correct. But in the film noirs of the war noir period they are neither.

In postwar film noirs public law-enforcers go after public law-breakers. But the absence of public crimes, namely of public property, in war noirs accordingly leads to the recurring absence of the police. And even when cops *are* on the scene, they bungle and fail. Much of the war noir formula, and its social meaning, hinges on the missing or mistake-making police. Furthermore, it is not only the cops who cannot fulfill their responsibilities; it is the whole justice system, the apparatus to provide *public order*. The following are failures of law enforcement in the war noir period.

James Stephenson, an attorney, wrecks himself, if not his career, by arranging a bribe to clear his guilty client, Bette Davis *(The Letter)*. Elisha Cook, Jr., and then John McGuire, are falsely arrested by the police. In Cook's trial the judge and jury doze off; the mise-en-scene of McGuire's trial is cinematic Daumier *(Stranger on the Third Floor)*. Albert Dekker is arrested and nearly lynched for a couple of murders; no one believes that his twin brother did not die long ago but is alive, insane, and responsible for the killings *(Among the Living)*. Laurence Olivier, though innocent of killing his wife, nonetheless does dispose of her body and then is found to have had no connection with her death and disappearance by a town inquest *(Rebecca)*. Elisha Cook, Jr. is guilty of murder, and chief detective Laird Cregar knows it but is obsessed with convicting Victor Mature *(I Wake Up Screaming)*.

George Sanders is convicted and sentenced to die for killing Robert Montgomery, who in fact staged his own death *(Rage in Heaven)*. Robert Cummings is wrongly arrested for murder and arson of an aircraft plant *(Saboteur)*. Detective MacDonald Carey tells Teresa Wright that, since one suspected Merry Widow killer has died, her uncle, Joseph Cotten, is no longer under suspicion *(Shadow of a Doubt)*. New York's finest falsely arrest for murder Dean Jagger *(When Strangers Marry)* as well as Alan Curtis *(Phantom Lady)*.

Over in Britain Ray Milland has served two years in prison for committing a mercy killing of his wife. However, she actually committed suicide. Upon release he is soon arrested again, this time for murdering a private investigator who was in his employ. The detective was in fact killed by Nazis, but Scotland Yard doesn't believe that there are any Nazis on its side of the Channel *(Ministry of Fear)*. Nor will Scotland Yard allow Joseph Cotten, one of its own men, to reopen the murder case of Ingrid Bergman's aunt *(Gaslight)*.

Cotten goes ahead anyway and discovers the killer. This, at first, might seem an exception to the failure of law enforcers in the war noir period. However, Cotten conducts his investigation against the wishes and the orders of his superior. Most significantly, he acts as a private citizen, not as a member of Scotland Yard.

Other crimes are dealt with in the virtual or actual absence of the police. After Betty Field guns down Howard da Silva, Wallace Ford takes her for a car ride and intentionally crashes to kill himself and her *(Blues in the Night)*. That Evelyn Keyes is on her way to tell the police she overheard Ida Lupino confess murder to Louis Jordan convinces Lupino to go (off screen) to meet them and turn herself in *(Ladies in Retirement)*. Shakedown racketeer John Garfield falls off Thomas Mitchell and John Qualen's boat and drowns; their neighborhood cop turns a blind eye to the possibility they have pocketed Garfield's bankroll *(Out of the Fog)*.

Except if they come around for payoffs, cops will never bother casino owner Ona Munson, although she gunned down her daughter, Gene Tierney *(The Shanghai Gesture)*. Conrad Veidt's scheme to kill a child, his rival heir, ends when, chased by Melvyn Douglas and Joan Crawford, his sleigh plunges over a precipice *(A Woman's Face)*. Although a policeman urges Kim Hunter to file a report on her sister with the department's bureau of missing persons, she is never contacted. Later, when she wants to report a murder, Hugh Beaumont contends that the police won't believe her *(The Seventh Victim)*.

A plot to take possession of Merle Oberon's plantation results in the capture of the mastermind, Thomas Mitchell, by Franchot Tone; Elisha Cook, Jr., who has murdered three persons, is swallowed up in quicksand *(Dark Waters)*. Hedy Lamarr and her son are rescued by George Brent just before her townhouse explodes. When it blows up, her husband, Paul Lukas, who has murdered his sister among others, is in it *(Experiment Perilous)*. Off camera the Turkish police check out a corpse on a beach and declare Zachary Scott's character is dead. But mystery writer Peter Lorre, in his own research about Scott's life, comes face to face with the truth that escaped the police *(The Mask of Dimitrios)*.

These examples point to a key question, as well as suggest its answer. In the war noir period, "Who solves the crimes?" We know that law enforcement officials do not. The actual criminal-catchers are almost unique to these years; they are rare in postwar film noirs. They are rapidly replaced by first, local police and then by various kinds of federal agents. Postwar "official" law enforcers are a far cry from their fellows in the war years: they are competent and correct.

But, between 1940 and 1944, as the absence of public crimes leads to the absence of public investigators, the presence of personal ("private") crimes leads to the presence of private investigators. They are not professionals, however. Of all the movies which would be likely to appear on consensus list of war noir, only two have the well known hardboiled dicks *(The Maltese Falcon and Murder, My Sweet)*. The criminal-catchers in the war noir are private through and through. They are private citizens, male and female *civilians*.

Very often it is a man and a woman who work together to solve the crime. Nearly as often one of them starts alone, then he or she is joined by the other to finish the case. The second partner I call the **ally**, and in general the ally in a war noir is a *woman*. Yet, in analyses of film noir, this special female "character type" has been missed. She is neither a femme fatale nor a woman in distress, and she is not a Goody Two Shoes. As an ally, she is at least the match of the man she is teamed with, in courage and intelligence.

"There are also many victims of maniacs who have no interest in monetary gain as in *The Lodger*": the sympathetic "Ripper" (Laird Cregar, center) gazes down on Kitty Langley (Merle Oberon).

The significance of women in war noirs relates to their growing independence as workers, their contributions to the war effort, as well as their numbers at the box-office. But of all the war noir elements to get jettisoned after World War Two, none goes out faster than the woman who is an ally, if not an equal. She is all but finished in 1946. In view of American women's postwar social experience, it is self-evident why this character was, unfortunately, eliminated from movie plots. Yet when film noir starts in 1940, she is on hand, present at the creation. Her appearances are a roll call of war noirs.

After Margaret Tallichet's fiancee is jailed for his neighbor's murder, she leaves work early and scours the neighborhood until she finds the real killer (*Stranger on the Third Floor*). More than once Betty Grable outwits the police to help her lover stay at large and discover the murderer of her sister (*I Wake Up Screaming*). Joan Bennett refuses to tell Nazis the whereabouts of a man she befriended. Her loyalty costs her her life (*Man Hunt*). Ingrid Bergman is "the only intelligent witness [who] at least suspected that [her] late husband was insane," according to the psychiatrist who helps her prevent in the nick of time the execution of her lover (*Rage in Heaven*). Priscilla Lane sees to it that the saboteur of the film's title fails to catch the ferry from the Statue of Liberty and escape capture.

Veronica Lake is asked by a Senator to work undercover to penetrate a business network which is providing chemical formulas to the Axis. Her ally is a hit man who is humanized by his relationship with her (*This Gun for Hire*). Dolores Del Rio has a Nazi assassin kept occupied so that his room can be searched by an endangered friend (*Journey into Fear*). With three male companions Kim Hunter takes on a murderous sect in search of her older sister (*The Seventh Victim*). Marjorie Reynolds saves her lover's life and prevents a microfilm of the layout of the minefields in the English Channel from reaching the Nazis (*Ministry of Fear*).

In three war noirs, based on novels by Cornell Woolrich, the criminal-catchers find out their ally is false. Ella Raines doggedly and bravely tracks down leads to exonerate her boss of murder. His best friend is her ally, the real killer (*Phantom Lady*). Kim Hunter first helps her husband elude capture by the police. After he is found and jailed for robbery and murder, she figures out the killer is her ex-boyfriend, who has pretended to be her ally. Then she cannot convince the chief detective of the truth. It is not until the killer becomes wild-eyed and frantic that he can see what she deduced (*When Strangers Marry*). Because she believes they have a romance, Claire Trevor reluctantly gives a man whatever assistance he wants so that he can prove himself innocent of murder. However, she is the killer, and he is married. Moments after their mutual discoveries she is shot by a police detective. Before dying she clears him of the killing, for he has pretended again to love her (*Street of Chance*).

An aside, but an illuminating one, is that the Hollywood screenplay makes Trevor's character a false female ally, whereas in Woolrich's book, *The Black Curtain* (1941), she is a true one. She helps the man she loves solve the mystery (the same ways as in the film), then is unintentionally shot to death by the book's killer. The man never reveals to her that he is married. After the smoke has cleared, the man says to the police detective, "She was a great kid. Without her—" And on the final page, as he is returning by train to his wife,

> [He] caught a fleeting glimpse of a familiar mound. He saw the small headstone that had been his only gift to Ruth Dillon. Ruth who had given him so much, the past and the future. He raised two fingers to his temple, brought them out again in salute. Salute and farewell. [Quotations are from the 1982 Ballantine edition, p. 137 and p. 148, respectively.]

A *salute* indeed, to his ally.

Not only are the criminal-catchers in war noirs private civilians, they are also **working class**. Moreover, their class character is the key to grasping the double meaning of the war noir formula.

In *Saboteur* Robert Cummings tries to fight off some county police who, on a tip from Nazi spy, Otto Kruger, have arrested him. He is outnumbered and will certainly be rearrested. However, a passing truck driver, who befriended him earlier, misleads the cops to allow Cummings to get away. This is a minor example of a man who is a working class ally. The significant allies in war noirs, women, are not only shown as being of the working class, they are clearly established as *workers*.

Margaret Tallichet is a secretary/stenographer *(Stranger on the Third Floor)*. So is Betty Grable *(I Wake Up Screaming)*. Joan Bennett's character is a prostitute in the *Atlantic Monthly* article, "Rogue Male," which is only hinted at (by the stress on money exchange) in *Man Hunt*. Ingrid Bergman is a private secretary before marrying ne'er-do-well industrialist Robert Montgomery. After she marries George Sanders, she will be the wife of an industrial engineer *(Rage in Heaven)*. Priscilla Lane is a photo model for billboards *(Saboteur)*. Veronica Lake is a nightclub entertainer with an eye-tricking magician's act *(This Gun for Hire)*. Delores Del Rio is a nightclub dancer with an eye-catching leopard's costume *(Journey into Fear)*. Marjorie Reynolds is a staffer for a non-profit organization, The Mothers of Free Nations *(Ministry of Fear)*. Ella Raines is another secretary destined to marry an engineer *(Phantom Lady)*.

In its most basic form the plot for allied or lone civilian criminal-catchers is a **puzzle**. In postwar film noirs, when women no longer help figure out mysteries, the intelligence to solve them is men's. After law enforcement officials take center stage from civilians, puzzles exit altogether. The private detective, of course, has achieved status as a film noir icon. Yet it is actually rare for a hardboiled dick to be a central character. He may rule in a few renowned movies, but the two superpowers of film noir are civilians and cops; and which one is in charge in the formulas depends on whether the movie was made before or after 1945.

A **social context** always conditioned the plot elements of film noir, thus the need for periodization. The key elements of the war noir gave way to other ones after the war, such as crimes about public property, masterful law enforcement officials, femme fatales, or women in distress. Understanding this transition means reviewing the connections between film noir and society from their start.

Film noir began under the storm clouds of war, when armies were already marching in Asia and Europe. Exactly a year before the release of *Stranger on the Third Floor,* the Nazis invaded Poland. In the intervening time the Axis was formed, lend-lease ratified, and the Atlantic Charter signed. Although there was opposition to entering another war, there was mainly widespread anxiety that U.S. involvement was inevitable. Then came December 7, 1941. The rise of film noir, therefore, belongs to the decline and fall of national peace and isolation.

The guarantor of such conditions of "national security" is the state. However, once at war, things change. Above all, national defense is achieved by the people, especially the working class, who make the weapons and fire them. These points suggest an explanation of the relationship of cops to civilians in war noirs.

Crime stories are a **displacement** of class conflict in the real world. The usual root of struggle is property. Insofar as true class struggle is not waged around the house but rather throughout society, the property at stake is in the public arena. Al-

"Mother" Gin Sling (Ona Munson) later kills Victoria "Poppy" Charteris (Gene Tierney), her daughter, for insulting her in *The Shanghai Gesture.*

most all property, of course, is possessed by the capitalist class. On the other hand, the working class is essentially propertyless. In the class struggle, workers aim to advance their material position; capitalists try to constrain them. Therefore, workers, as displaced in crime stories, are *criminals*.

State power, through law enforcement among several means, serves to protect the propertied against assault by the propertyless. Law enforcement officials, therefore, are the displacement of state power, standing for the interests of capitalists.

Social disharmony is, by definition, a constant feature of the crime story; yet the underlying social tension in it can vary. U.S. entry into World War Two radically affected the "normal" crime story's focus on public property. Common cultural representations of class conflict were abandoned as the social context made it desirable instead for representations of cross-class ceasefire, if not cooperation. For example, the no-strike pledge contributed to forming this context. Film noir, consequently, *began* without public property in plots because displaced "normal" class struggle was not appropriate for wartime crime stories.

Being appropriate means attracting an audience, making a profit, and meeting the propaganda needs of the state (which Hollywood would never have blatantly and constantly contradicted). Thus, although they are structured as crime stories, war noirs convey a coded message that is consistent with the same win-the-war line of battlefront movies. The latter, of course, lack displacement and coded messages about winning the war because they intentionally approach overt government propaganda.

In war noirs the message deals with mobilization and commitment to the war effort. By showing characters compelled to involve themselves as a last resort (after the collapse of law enforcement), war noirs indicate that extraordinary public engagement and sacrifice is urgent. To be sure, while trying to solve crimes, war noir allies endure dangers and anguish. Nonetheless, it is the mettle to succeed of their celluloid civilians that the film makers, in service to Washington as well as Mammon, wished their patrons to match. The "all's well" endings of war noirs are displaced promises to the audience of a happier, better America after Victory.

The plot elements reviewed so far are appropriate in the context of the war, but they do not establish a full formula. Other elements exist, which are not combined by accident. In the circumstances of the time, a certain set of plot elements "fit" together for a marketable crime story. The war noir formula is the approximate sum of these appropriate elements.

To elaborate the point, if the film noirs of the war noir period are considered *ahistorically*, then there is no way to explain the calculations by the studios to use these elements. There are no grounds for justifying how these elements *per se* would have produced better or more popular crime movies than using markedly different ones (such as those that *were* used in postwar crime movies). But the fact of the repeated use of a discernible and exclusive formula in a specific number of years shows that the Hollywood studios thought they were giving audiences, the government agencies monitoring their scripts and final releases, and their expected return on investments what was called for. The fact is shown, that is, only when these film noirs are considered historically.

For instance, in the real circumstances of the people having lead responsibility for defeating the Axis, it became appropriate for civilians instead of cops to solve crimes. The personal nature of the robberies and murders attests to the shift away from social property relations as the claim on audience interest. Insofar as personal problems are a displacement of the war crisis, for a historically given period civilians themselves overcome their adversities and adversaries.

Complementing the distinctive crimes and criminal-catchers of the war noir period is a different kind of "criminal." Indeed, these film noirs' most defining plot element is the suspected lawbreaker who is an **innocent** man. Examples include: Elisha Cook, Jr. and John McGuire *(Stranger on the Third Floor)*; Albert Dekker *(Among the Living)*; George Raft *(They Drive by Night)*; Victor Mature *(I Wake Up Screaming)*; George Sanders *(Rage in Heaven)*; William Powell *(Crossroads)*; Brian Donlevy *(The Glass Key)*; Robert Cummings *(Saboteur)*; Burgess Meredith *(Street of Chance)*; Ray Milland *(Ministry of Fear)*; Alan Curtis *(Phantom Lady)*; and Dean Jagger *(When Strangers Marry)*.

Similarly, although Joan Fontaine suspects Cary Grant of killing Nigel Bruce and planning to murder her, she is wrong *(Suspicion)*. And, although Joan Bennett and Edward G. Robinson think he has killed her boyfriend, they are wrong *(Woman in the Window)*.

While serving time in jail, civilian men are taken out of the story of the movie. Soldiers were similarly out of the picture during their military service. (Furthermore, in film noirs released after the war noir period, male characters tend to "come back" after varying lengths of absence. Some are explicitly veterans, such as Alan Ladd in *The Blue Dahlia*. But usually the war is displaced. They return from trips, hospitals, prisons, and bouts of amnesia.)

While these men are on the run or behind bars, women dedicate themselves to disproving the guilt and ending the persecution. So too, people on the home front sacrificed and worked to win the war and bring the boys home. The romantic ending when the wrongly accused man is freed to the embrace of his wife or girlfriend played to the hopes that when the fascist nightmare ended, friends, relatives, and lovers would be safely reunited.

However, even before the armistices film noir's plot elements begin to change, signaling the finish of the war noir formula. Some key changes have already been mentioned—crimes become committed for public property, and criminal-catchers become law officers instead of civilians, especially women. In addition innocent civilian men become guilty outlaws, either for crimes committed before the start of the movie or during it. By the end of the decade their crime stories are not about individual citizens but of organized gangsters. The causes of these changes were the conditions of postwar America.

The impending conclusion to international hostilities meant the end of the national cross-class ceasefire. Labor militancy was but one dramatic factor in making it appropriate for film noirs to turn to public property. But even a great strike wave would not necessarily have made law enforcement appropriate. However, over the course of the America's period of greatest worker "unrest" (late 1945 to early 1946) public opinion shifted. Perhaps it was due to a multi-million dollar business sponsored public relations campaign. At any rate, respondents to a survey indicated they had become less favorably disposed to unions and slightly more so to business. "In Taking the Risk Out of Democracy: Corporate Propaganda versus Freedom and Liberty" [Urbana: University of Illinois Press, 1997, p. 35], Alex Carey quotes a State Department public relations officer.

> The public opinion climate changed completely in America. While the rest of the world has moved to the left, has admitted labor into government, has passed liberalized legislation, the United States has become anti-social change, anti-economic reform, anti-labor. It is not moving to the right, it has been moved—cleverly—to the right.

In the fall of 1946 the Republicans took control of both houses of Congress. Passage of more pro-labor reforms (such as "full-employment") stopped, and anti-labor legislation (such as Taft-Hartley) became the laws of the land instead.

In these circumstances the return of the police would have been appropriate. Yet by then the advanced level of U.S. industrialization was mirrored in large-scale division of labor in the organizations of law enforcers. Keeping up with these changes outside the Bijous and Roxys, inside on their silver screens the familiar local police department, not to mention the infrequent freelance private eye, gives way to bureaucracies, especially federal agencies. Generally introduced by a stentorian "Voice of God," it seems by the late forties that everywhere in film noirs there are uniformed and plainclothes operatives of the FBI, Secret Service, Coast Guard, and the departments of Justice/Immigration, Post Office and Treasury.

The bureaucratization of "justice" is paralleled in crime. Thus Hollywood flatfeet and G-men confront city-wide rackets and national syndicates. Their job is not to discover a mob, but to secure evidence and witnesses (usually women) to indict it. This plot change means puzzles give way in the late forties-early fifties to police procedurals. Furthermore, the film noir parallel to the blow by blow of cops busting gangsters is the step by step of crooks pulling capers. The appearance of procedurals, whether showcasing heroes or villains, is in the same period because they were two sides of the same coin, generated by an identical social context.

In the immediate postwar years the social context influencing film noir is still weighted to civilian anxieties (e.g., war, demobilization, unemployment, infidelity). However, the representation of these anxieties is typically through gender conflict. For example, male anxieties seem related to women, whose great entry into the wartime job market resulted in changes in economic and sexual relations. Through the mid- to late forties film noirs are generally displacements of those anxieties. Thus civilians, innocent or guilty, are the dominant characters.

The next transformation of plot elements and formulas corresponds to the transition from the Second World War to the Cold War. As demobilized men get jobs and deindustrialized women get mops, the incidence of film noir's displacement of anxieties of working class civilians falls while displacement of anxieties of non-working classes rises. Returning to their "normal" existence in crimes stories as criminals, working class people are replaced as the central characters in film noirs by law enforcement officials. Whereas the focus of film noirs began on the hunted in the war noir period, it logically turns to the hunters in the cold war period. Lots of men with many types of badges combat threat upon threat to the social order. Overall, Hollywood's often semi-cinema *verite* cataloging of their crusades relates to containing if not rolling back the extremists invading, undermining the polity: communists, mobsters, rogue cops, psychopaths, white supremacists, juvenile delinquents, and ever on.

In retrospect it seems predictable rather than paradoxical that new elements in film noir are frequent in 1945, and even first appear the year before. The armistices did not mark the shift from war noir to postwar formulas. The process of transition, like others later, took place as follows: the appearance of new elements, coexistence with old ones, dominance of the new, and (virtual) disappearance of the old. New elements were appropriate during the late war years because the postwar social context began *before* the victory.

In the summer of 1944 the Normandy invasion ended the long delayed second front in Europe; U.S. air strikes started against Japan's home island cities; and the postwar economic order was planned at Bretton Woods. Military success abroad led to industry layoffs at home. This and government-ordered pay limits provoked strikes, mostly wildcats, which surged to a tidal wave two years later. The class struggle did not end during the war, but it was muted, even suppressed in the culture industry. The coming of the end of the war not only intensified class conflict, it necessarily marked the appropriateness of using new elements which pertained to the displacement of class struggle in crime stories. In other words, changes in the national and world scene relatively promptly impacted the plots in film noirs.

The first key new plot elements are introduced in *Double Indemnity* (released in 1944 and shot a year before). Most important of these is film noir's first full-fledged femme fatale, Barbara Stanwyck. Two earlier female killers brook no comparison with her.

Bette Davis opens *The Letter* by emptying a chamber of bullets into her lover because he intended to stop an affair with her. She does not spin a web. She reacts spontaneously, and then spends most of the rest of the film trying to beat her murder rap. Nor is Mary Astor a spider woman in *The Maltese Falcon*. Only at the end of the movie does Humphrey Bogart unravel the puzzle for us and reveal that she did his partner in. Though he is the leading man, she is no threat to him. They are in love, and he will wait twenty years for her until she is let out of prison.

In *Double Indemnity* there is no puzzle, and the investigation is conducted by a bureaucratic institution, an insurance corporation. The property involved can be considered "transitional." The insurance policy is personal because it belongs to Stanwyck's husband, but it is paid out by a public enterprise.

The second most important new element of the movie is Fred MacMurray's guilt.

There is male guilt in three earlier film noirs, but none of the characters remotely resembles Walter Neff.

In *Angels over Broadway* John Qualen's boss blames him for embezzling $3000. With the help of several friends (Thomas Mitchell, Douglas Fairbanks, Jr., and Rita Hayworth) he cons some racketeers in a card game and is able to square the debt. However, he was never guilty of the theft in the first place. His wife took the money when she ran off with another man. After making amends, Qualen can have his job back.

In *Suspicion* Cary Grant embezzles some company funds and is discovered. But his employer is his cousin, who hesitates to press charges. His efforts to raise enough money for the payback successively fail. His wife, Joan Fontaine, starts imagining he intends to murder her (and that he has already killed his best friend). As he drives recklessly on a cliff road, her door flies open. He grabs her arm to save her, but she pulls away. He holds on and stops the car. A heated argument begins.

He is incensed that she has stopped sleeping with him and now wants to visit her mother. He announces she won't have to put up with him anymore. *"I won't bother you again."*

Suddenly she sees why he wanted to know about an untraceable poison: he planned to commit suicide because of his debt. Explaining that he had realized it would be *"the cheap way out,"* he says, *"I'm going to see it through, prison time and everything."*

Fontaine's response is significant as example of class being the key to unlocking the secrets of the war noir formula.

> "Oh, Johnny, if I'd only known. This is as much my fault as yours. I was only thinking of myself, not what you were going through. If I'd been really close to you, you could have confided in me. But you were afraid to. You were afraid to come to me. Oh, if I'd only understood! Oh, Johnny! But it'll be different now. We'll make it different."
>
> "People don't change overnight, Lena. I'm no good."
>
> "Let's turn back. Johnny, let's go home and see it through together."
>
> "No. It won't work. I'm driving you on to your mother's."
>
> "It will work. I know it will. Oh, Johnny, please!"
>
> "This isn't your problem, Lena."
>
> "But it is! You can't shut me out! Johnny, turn the car around and let's go home. Please, Johnny, please."
>
> "No, Lena, no." [*Grant goes to the car.*]
>
> "My darling!" [*Fontaine goes to it too.*]

For a moment they drive forward, then he turns around the car. *Suspicion* ends. Which means her suspicion ends. The significance is that until the final scene she refuses to be his ally. The explanation for it is her class difference. He is broke, propertyless, a displaced proletarian. Despite being madly in love with him, she did not fully accept him; thus he could not, would not, confide in her. Social leveling, on his terms, means that now they really can *"see it all through together."* It also implies that an overnight change in people to effect a cross-class alliance, with pride of place given to the working class, can see through the trials of the future.

In *Shadow of a Doubt* Joseph Cotten makes ends meet by robbing and knocking off widows. (The fact that there were so many war widows is played on; in a macabre way the victims are "appropriate.") The property Cotten takes is theirs personally. He is a killer and a thief, and yet how guilty is he? After he dies (trying to murder his niece, Teresa Wright), there is a crowded church service given to commemorate him. Wright and her boyfriend, police investigator MacDonald Carey, stand outside and promise to keep what he did a secret. So, in the final analysis, on the public record that is, the Merry Widow murderer is an innocent man!

On the other hand, by killing to defraud a business, Fred MacMurray initiates a critical change in film noir crime *and* character. Simultaneous with one transformation of hot property from personal to public is the other of the hunted man from a law abider to a transgressor, from a victim of injustice to a deliberate outlaw.

As befits transition, although the place of property in *Double Indemnity* is public, it is also as personal as a house or purse rifled by Joseph Cotten. The explanation is that this is a crime story about an inside job: MacMurray works for the firm making the payout to Stanwyck. That is why the chief claims examiner, Edward G. Robinson, gets taken in. Uncharacteristically sensitive, Robinson listens as the man who was more than just his favorite insurance agent, but is now nearly dead from bleeding from Stanwyck's gunshot, cracks wise once more.

> "You know why you couldn't figure this one, Keyes? I'll tell you. 'Cause the guy you were looking for was too close. Right across the desk from you."
> "Closer than that, Walter."
> "I love you, too."

That *is* personal. For later criminals, however, the place of property would be public and impersonal.

The transition from wartime to postwar film noirs is complex because there is no one-to-one switch in formulas. In the first years of film noir there is a relatively limited range of plot elements and only a single formula, the *war noir*. But after the war there is a much wider range of elements and several formulas emerge (to be joined or replaced by different formulas in later years). One of the principal postwar formulas concerns the *other* lead female character, the woman-in-distress.

A telltale blindspot in the history of critical writing on film noir is that, while the femme fatale is a standard topic of interest, the woman-in-distress has been largely ignored. (Similarly, hardboiled fiction, whose novels and pulp stories were targeted to a male audience, is always cited as a "source" of film noir. However, melodramatic fiction, whose novels and popular magazine articles were aimed at a female readership, has been overlooked as a key "source" of film noir.) This oversight is especially unjustifiable because, in the twenty years of "classic" film noir (1940–1959), there are more appearances of the woman-in-distress than the femme fatale. It is additional evidence of transition taking place in 1944 that it is the year of first film noir with a full-fledged woman-in-distress.

In the war noir a working woman goes about the city to prevent the capture and/or execution of her husband (to-be). The reversal of these plot elements begins in *Gaslight*.

Instead of holding a job, Ingrid Bergman is a housewife, with inherited wealth. Instead of voluntarily searching through the streets to solve the puzzle of a crime, she involuntarily wanders upstairs downstairs, and is puzzled about her mind. Instead of using her intelligence to reject and disprove the word of official authorities, she doubts her sanity when confronted by her husband's "proofs." Instead of trying to end the threat to her husband's life, hers is threatened by him. Meanwhile, instead of being a man who is innocent of murder, Charles Boyer is guilty of it (killing her aunt). Instead of finally being released from prison, he is at last sent there. And when

Det. Mark McPherson (Dana Andrews) questions Waldo Lydecker (Clifton Webb), who kills the wrong woman, thinking she is Laura, for not loving him as much as he loves her.

her ordeal is over, instead of embracing the man she rescued, Bergman embraces Joseph Cotten, the man who rescued her.

At first glance, two of Alfred Hitchcock's movies released before *Gaslight* might seem to be woman-in-distress film noirs, but are they not. In *Suspicion* Joan Fontaine imagines Cary Grant wants to do her in, but she is mistaken. In *Shadow of a Doubt* Teresa Wright has more in common with the woman of the war noir formula than a woman-in-distress.

Wright is, indeed, imperiled. However, it is not from simply being in the way of a man getting rich or taking up with another woman. Rather, her danger comes from intentionally getting in the way, going outside the house, and figuring out what the police across the country have failed to: her beloved uncle is a murderer hiding out in her family's home. By using her wits Wright compares to the women in film noirs with the war noir formula, which were made at the same time as *Shadow of a Doubt*. If Wright would mind her own business, Cotten would gladly, merrily, leave her alone.

But no such situation exists for the true woman-in-distress. She willingly *does* nothing, other than to marry the wrong man. Thus, as the basis of this formula, the woman-in-distress, who expects security homemaking in her rooms, is menaced although she is passive. In contrast, the woman (ally) of the war noir formula, who accepts risks venturing in the streets, is threatened because she is active. Teresa Wright is not an ally, and *Shadow of a Doubt* is not a war noir. But, as she hurries through traffic to get to the public library before it closes so that she can read the page of a newspaper Cotten has manipulated her from seeing, Wright is the kind of woman, for the reasons I have argued, typically represented by Hollywood in these special years, which I call the war noir period.

The concurrent appearance in 1944 of the femme fatale and the woman-in-distress reinforces my earlier point that this is *the* year of transition of film noir plot elements and formulas. The social context of drastic changes in women's role in society and their relationship with men made it appropriate that plot elements alter.

The war noir's displaced representation of an alliance between the sexes transformed to an anxiety about hierarchy in each gender toward the other. For men it was confronting and competing for jobs with independent women. This anxiety was experienced "outside." In film noir it is displaced in terms of the femme fatale and the renewal of crime stories with public property.

For women it was losing their independence, economic if not also sexual, by leaving their jobs, staying at home, and raising a family. This anxiety was experienced "inside." It is displaced in terms of crime stories about personal property, and the woman-in-distress, separated from postwar city life by way of place (confined within a house, often rurally located) as well as in time (the nineteenth or turn of the twentieth century). When she is ultimately rescued by her next husband, the inference is that their marriage will strike a balance between the demands of the social structure of postwar America and *her* needs. However, these needs are framed by two conditions, her banishment from the job market and her placement in the kitchen.

To recapitulate, these are the key elements of the war noir formula: absence of public property; absence or failure of law enforcement officials; presence of personal property; innocence of a male civilian, considered guilty by the law enforcers; vindication of his innocence by his own efforts and those of a woman's; or, if he is jailed, restoration of his freedom by the efforts of other civilians, especially a woman's; solution of a mystery puzzle by these civilians; revelation that the real killer is another male civilian, the "unsuspected;" romantic coupling of the innocent male civilian and the female ally.

Although they were hardly ever frequent in peacetime, downbeat endings were especially unacceptable in wartime. The Roosevelt administration, the military services, the Hollywood studios, and the audiences wanted upbeat endings. That the film noirs of the war noir period do not deviate from this may explain why they have not been given much attention. Film noir fans may prefer characters in the formulas developed after the war. At any rate, however much I enjoy postwar film noirs, the appeal of the war noir is just as strong, not only because of its mise-en-scene, but because of what is signified by its plot elements.

To begin with I enjoy watching clever and courageous women in war noirs. There may be excitement when femme fatales deceive and doom the opposite sex or women-in-distress flee their homicidally inclined husbands, but both these character types are deeply flawed. Women in war noirs, of course, are not flawless role models; for instance, they must always get a man. But they have the guts and smarts for a good cause (justice, freedom). They are not so materialistic as to be murderous to men, nor so vulnerable as to be victimized by men. They go shoulder to shoulder with men.

Then, too, I enjoy watching working class people do for themselves what cannot be done for them by official authorities. This theme is typically forbidden. I do not mean working class people winning something; I mean their resolving something. After all, a boxing match or a fortune can be won without implying power relations between classes have changed. They, of course, have not. It may mean that hard work pays off, or America is strong (again), or women and people of color deserve equal treatment and respect. But it does not mean the working class is more capable than the ruling class and its agents to solve crises.

Crime stories are displacements of crises. In postwar film noirs one force is shown for solving crimes, for resolving crises, and it is law enforcement authority.

But in war noirs innocent people are repeatedly chased, jailed, and sentenced to die. What do the authorities do? They are responsible for the persecutions. How do they make things aright? They don't. Either they are disappeared from the plot or they encumber those trying to restore order. What takes place in war noirs to solve crimes, to resolve crises, is the appearance of another force, and it is the working class.

A dialogue in *I Wake Up Screaming* is revealing.

Laird Cregar, the police department's chief detective, already knows Elisha Cook, Jr. is guilty of killing Carole Landis, but he wants to pin the rap on Victor Mature. Betty Grable, Mature's girlfriend and Landis' younger sister, has just been arrested.

Mature comes up behind Cregar on a street corner and pokes a Tootsie Roll in his side, as though it were a gun.

> "You've taken Jill. She hasn't got anything to do with this. Let her go and I'll give my-self up."
>
> "You've turned into quite a Lochinvar, haven't you? Self-sacrifice and everything. Well, it's no use, Frankie. I don't have to make bargains with you. I'll get you even-tually. If not tomorrow, next week. If not next week, next year. Time's nothing in my life, it is in yours. Each minute is an eternity to a man in your shoes."
>
> "You've got the wrong steer this time, Cornell. They told me at headquarters that you're a pretty sure thing. But this time you're trying to convict an innocent man."
>
> "That's what you say. But you can't sell me on it. I'll follow you into your grave. I'll write my name on your tombstone."
>
> "You're not a cop looking for a murderer. You're crazy, Cornell. You oughta be put away."
>
> "Sure. Why don't you call a policeman?"

Law enforcement, then, is not simply unallied with the working class, it is pitted against it. This point is made in the text of Cornell Woolrich's *The Black Curtain,* on which the war noir, *Street of Chance* is based.

A hunted and confused man, Frank Townsend, had had another identity, "Dan Near-ing," while he was an amnesiac for three years. (In the film his amnesia has been for a much shorter time, in fact not much longer than the U.S. had been at war.) Going to a library, he discovers in an old newspaper article why he is being pursued. He is wanted for murder. The police believe that, while he was an invalid's guardian at a sub-urban mansion, he was caught robbing a safe by his employer. The police hold "Near-ing" responsible for killing this old man with a shotgun. (1982 Ballantine edition, pp. 78–79).

Although the absence of public property alters the terms for plotting crime stories in war noirs, it does not remove the representation of class struggle. This holds true despite the separate representation, discussed earlier in terms of propaganda, of an-other kind of struggle: marshaling popular commitment to the war effort. Multiple meanings therefore coexist in war noirs, and they are related to each other. That is, specific historical conditions led to certain plot elements that were appropriate for conveying, albeit through displacement, a win-the-war message. However, and the point is key, the logical consequence of having *these* elements to offer a politically cen-trist message was to imply at the same time another, politically leftist one.

Because of the World War Two context (demanding win-the-war movie themes, displaced or otherwise), there was a shift toward favorable representation of the working class, in crime films as well as battlefront ones. Due to the same conditions the ruling class lost favorable representation. Then, in the circumstances already de-scribed, in postwar and especially cold war period film noirs the ruling class regained favorable representation, as shown by law enforcement being successful and good to the innocent. But in war noirs displacement shows us again and again that the working class *by itself* can overcome physical and psychological threats to its well-being. Chief among these threats is official authority.

What is wonderful about the war noirs is that they consistently show the side of the underdog—instead of the overlord—victorious. In this way, these B movies reveal A politics.

The corrupt world of crime and capitalism, Doc (Sam Jaffe) foreground and Louis Ciavelli (Anthony Caruso) in *The Asphalt Jungle*.

The politics of crime and the crime of politics: Postwar noir, the liberal consensus and the Hollywood Left

Reynold Humphries

> If you want fresh air, don't look for it in this town.
>
> —*The Asphalt Jungle*

The starting point of this study is the now famous remark made by the lawyer Emmerich in *The Asphalt Jungle* (1950). Discussing his work with his bed-ridden wife, he replies thus to her question about the criminals with whom he comes into contact: "There's nothing so different about them. After all, crime is only a left-handed form of human endeavor." I wish to discuss this remark in the context not only of the film but of that of post-war Hollywood, the Cold War, the increasingly repressive climate of fear and Red-baiting, and the function of film noir and the gangster/crime film within that period. I shall highlight pertinent points in a number of films of the period 1947–50, before returning in more detail to *The Asphalt Jungle* and to the film which seems to me to bring together in the most complex fashion what was at stake for the Hollywood Left in those years: *The Prowler* (1950). To do so, it will first be necessary to dwell in some detail on recent research dealing with certain questions germane to my argument. In particular, I am indebted to the work of Thom Andersen and Noël Burch, Lary May, Brian Neve, James Naremore, Jonathan Munby, Paul Buhle and Dave Wagner.[1]

Introduction

Jonathan Munby presents his analysis of the evolution of the gangster movie of the 30s and 40s as "the story of how the concerted efforts to contain the subversive potential of this Hollywood film form were resisted and countered."[2] He goes on: "The postwar crime cycle we now call film noir was received as an awkward reminder of problems whose resolution had been postponed by the need to prosecute the war," adding that his purpose is to "to reveal how 1940s deviance...was deeply indebted to a socially antagonistic cinematic tradition allied to lower-class and ethnically marginalized American interests in the 1930s"[3]. This juxtaposition of the war and memory on the one hand and class and "deviance" on the other has produced a book of considerable importance whose complexity and subtlety I cannot hope to do proper justice to here. Certain points, however, must be highlighted at the outset, notably the creation of a "liberal consensus" anxious "to shift Hollywood away from Depression-era socio-political associations" and to make of its movies "forces central to hege-monic regulation."[4] By this Munby means something that most certainly does not go without saying, namely the objective alliance between the House Committee on Un-American Activities (HUAC) and Eric Johnston, President of the Motion Picture Asso-ciation of America (MPAA), formerly the Motion Picture Producers and Distributors of America (MPPDA), to which Johnson came in 1945 "espousing the ideals of liberal corporate consensus." These ideals demanded the elimination of class rhetoric and, by extension, of any reference to the New Deal in favor of a systematic championing of capitalism: "Paradoxically, HUAC's function was to do the dirty work for the emerging political order of liberal consensus, which actually had much to gain from the vilifica-tion of certain more centralized aspects of the New Deal legacy, those that militated against the belief that capitalism could service a democratic mandate."[5]

Johnston was perfectly clear about Hollywood's new objectives:

> We'll have no more *Grapes of Wrath,* we'll have no more *Tobacco Roads.* We'll have no more films that show the seamy side of American life. We'll have no pictures that deal with labor strikes. We'll have no pictures that deal with the banker as villain[6].

This declaration of faith partakes of the same ideology as that of Ayn Rand, a "friendly wit-ness" in 1947 and member of the right-wing Motion Picture Alliance for the Preserva-tion of American Ideals (created in 1944, the same year as the publication of Johnston's *America Unlimited,* a defense of "the principles of full production"[7]). A further, crucial link between the Hollywood hierarchy and Red-baiting is furnished by the late Nancy Lynn Schwartz who points out that J. Parnell Thomas (Republican chairman of HUAC in 1947) drew explicit parallels between the New Deal and Communism. By so doing he was sim-ply continuing the tradition set by Martin Dies, Democratic Chairman at the time of the Committee's earlier foray into Hollywood territory in 1938.[8] It is hardly a coincidence that 1947 "was also the year of the Taft-Hartley Act (forbidding communists in the labor unions)" and "of an executive order from the White House requiring government em-ployees to take loyalty oaths."[9] Brian Neve has quoted an article written by Darryl F. Zanuck in 1945 to the effect that American movies sold not only such key consumer goods as telephones and automobiles but also the "American way of life" and goes on to refer to the State Department frowning on film noir "as likely to give foreigners precisely the unflattering view of America that it wanted to redress."[10] Which brings us back to the liberal consenses, Red-baiting and the main thrust of Munby's argument.

Eric Johnston, the Motion Picture Alliance, HUAC, the Hearst press, the *Los Angeles Times,* old uncle J. Edgar and all had a simple outlook on life: Reds got propaganda into movies and thus corrupted the American way of life and acted as a new fifth column within the country. Munby is less concerned with proving or disproving that thesis—the books of Andersen and Burch, Buhle and Wagner show beyond a doubt the bit-terly ironic fact that the Left did succeed in putting over pro-socialist ideas, before, during and after the Second World War—than with insisting on something far more disturbing for the cut-and-dried ideologues of the Cold War, namely that certain movies of the period 1945–1951 maintained a link with the past that kept alive certain ideologies indicating a slippage from endorsement to criticism: "The crime film was a primary example of the kind of socially dysfunctional Hollywood both McCarthyites and consensus liberals wanted to eradicate. The crime film was a problem not because it could be tied to any specific ideological agenda (e.g., Communism) but precisely *because it could not.*"11 Buhle and Wagner adopt a similar standpoint:

> The subject of film noir opens wide the Pandora's box of film's social, artistic, and political meaning. ... What *was* the point of the protagonist's disorientation, alienation, or betrayal? The deeper political meaning often remains hermetic and distinctly secondary, especially in the auteur perspective. But in real-life Hollywood, film noir perhaps more than any other film genre expressed the artists' political worldview and the politics of contemporary film production.12

This calls for some explanation.

The reader will have noticed that I am conflating the crime movie (the subject of Munby's book) and film noir. Basically, I am in complete agreement with the argument of Munby when he draws our attention to the fact that certain gangster movies—he cites *Force of Evil* (1948) and *The Asphalt Jungle,* both of which are generally considered as examples of noir—"connected psychological distortions to the realm of determining and corrupting social values. These films' impact lay in their dramatization of the sociopsychological disintegration of everyday life, not in their portrayals of law/criminal confrontation."13 Munby earlier makes a crucial distinction between early Cagney (*Public Enemy,* 1931) and late Cagney (*White Heat,* 1949). In the former, the central character's "criminal motivations stemmed from understandable desires to overcome the sociocultural barriers that condemned him to poverty," whereas in the latter "Cody's propensity to violence and crime, however, are rationalized as a matter of mental aberration." Evoking *Kiss Tomorrow Goodbye* (1950), he points out that "the ethnic and class component that informed the actions of Cagney's 1930s gangster is absent."14 Having set up an apparent binary opposition, Munby promptly proceeds to deconstruct it: far from suggesting a complete break with the past, *White Heat* insists on "the gangster as alienated social fugitive" and "the appeal of Cagney's performance rests in part on his rejection of the sinister aspects of a conforming culture embodied in Edmond O'Brien's faceless (and duplicitous) undercover FBI agent."15 We can say, then, that radical gangster movies incorporated negative aspects of noir and transformed the conservative notion of "fate" into an interrogation of social and psychic alienation. It is this notion of alienation I wish to discuss now.

Alienation, the American Way

In a recent essay on the place of class in film noir, Paul Arthur states: "rarely are noir protagonists exempt from some existing structure of economic social power directly inflecting the course of their exploits."16 He proceeds to give the example of *Double*

Dix Handley (Sterling Hayden), the "hooligan" of the gang, finds a soft spot for Doll Conovan (Jean Hagen) in *The Asphalt Jungle*.

Indemnity (1944) and refers to the opening where the wounded Walter Neff returns during the night to his office to dictate his confession to his superior Keyes: "The nocturnal world [Neff] has accessed is a ghostly version of the commercial middle-class bustle abandoned as the day closes, and it is redolent of a social category all but suppressed by the narrative...."[17] Two words interest me here: "ghostly" and "commercial." Georg Lukacs opens the first section of his study "Reification and the Consciousness of the Proletariat" with the following statement:

> The essence of commodity-structure has often been pointed out. Its basis is that a relation between people takes on the character of a thing and thus acquires a 'phantom objectivity', an autonomy that seems so strictly rational and all-embracing as to conceal every trace of its fundamental nature: the relation between people.[18]

Put "ghostly" in the place of "phantom" and you have the situation obtaining in *Double Indemnity*, between Neff and Keyes on the one hand, Neff and Phyllis Dietrichson on the other. Keyes is the perfect paradigm of that "calculation" which sums up for Lukacs the "modern capitalist concern," [19] which helps explain Neff's refusal to be other than a salesman. If he accepts Keyes' offer, then he submits to that world of facts and figures he wants to escape but cannot as he is unable to grasp consciously the nature of his alienation. Neff believes that by driving around Los Angeles and making contact with people by selling policies he can remain human and independent, although his relationship with Phyllis—based on an attempt to alienate the female by turning her (body) into a commodity to convince himself human relations are possible—obviously betrays that very alienation he is striving to overcome. If we juxtapose the scene in the offices of the insurance company and the couple's encounters in the supermarket, we can glean some notion of what, wittingly or not, *Double Indemnity* is criticising. The people cleaning up are indeed "ghostly," workers without existence as far as the rest of the world is concerned, yet signifiers of the effects of that very exploitation Neff suffers from but cannot understand. The supermarket is the *locus classicus* of commercialism, the ultimate signifier of the consumer society, a place where one can spend money without having to think where the goods come from (nor the money, provided one has money to spend). The alienation here is both social and psychic, with shoppers as divided subjects, subjected to hidden economic forces which turn them into objects destined to consume. [20] The supermarket is indeed a perfect meeting-place: one can go about one's business (buying food, plotting murder) without coming into genuine contact with anyone. Neff's alienation is such that, like any petty criminal or gangster, all he can do is repeat the ideology on which capitalism is based by turning to robbery and murder in the name of social success and getting out from under.

Double Indemnity is neither a postwar work nor one associated with the Left. It does, however, correspond to the type of film soon destined, as we have seen, to be looked upon as subversive: it cannot be tied down to a particular ideology, radical or consensual. Conceived in 1943, released in 1944, but set in 1938, it thus suggests a certain continuity between the 30s and the 40s, while at the same time creating a sense of anxiety, frustration and general social breakdown very much associated with postwar noir. Particularly relevant are two movies of 1947. Both evoke and create precise links with the 20s and 30s, their plots setting up as antagonists characters representing either the past or the new corporate consensus: *The Gangster* and *I Walk Alone*.

The Gangster was directed by Gordon Wiles from a script written by radical novelist Daniel Fuchs. [21] *I Walk Alone* was directed by Byron Haskin from a script based on an adaptation by John Bright, a future blacklistee and author of several early Cagney vehicles, including *Public Enemy*. Both films "feature the problems of old-styled 'ethical' gangsters failing to adjust to the new order. All tell tales of alienated individuals up against the faceless organization that has usurped the "faced" gangster of the pre-war era." [22] The gangster of the title, called Shubunka, cannot accept that things are changing and that it is possible for a syndicate or corporation to move in, take over and squeeze him out. He has spent six years getting control of the seaside town where the action takes place, taking a percentage of people's businesses by offering protection and ensuring they have the financial means to stay in business and build up their trade. The opening shot shows us his apartment, complete with a painting, assorted ornaments and a substantial wardrobe, signifiers of wealth but not (as in *Laura* [1944] and

The Dark Corner [1946]) of sexual decadence as well. One person who counts on him and is his most trusted collaborator is Jammey who owns an ice-cream parlor where much of the action takes place. One shot shows us Shubunka and Jammey sitting together, with two customers strategically placed to suggest loneliness and an employee in the background. It evokes Edward Hopper's painting *Night Hawks,* but also such places as the diners in *Detour* (1945) and *The Killers* (1946), where are to be found those lonely and alienated individuals who people post-war noir.

Of particular interest is the scene where Jammey is "persuaded" to have lunch with the boss of the syndicate who intends to coerce him, by force if necessary, to abandon Shubunka and thus create an atmosphere of fear where others will follow suit, thus ending the gangster's control. A number of contrasts are set up here, the first of which is fundamental to film noir from *Double Indemnity* on: private space versus public space.[23] Whereas Shubunka surrounds himself in his private space with signifiers of success that ultimately mean nothing because he is about to be deprived of the economic and social power necessary to maintain that standard of living, Cornell the boss eats out in plush restaurants, openly escorted by his thugs. In other words, Shubunka acts as if it is essential to keep criminal activities secret and private, whereas Cornell does not hesitate to act as if his function in society were completely normal and the order of the day. Which is precisely the point: Cornell has invited Jammey to a matter-of-fact *business* lunch where he intimidates verbally the unfortunate victim while preparing a salad with all the care an art lover like Shubunka might devote to choosing one of his *objets d'art.* Cornell is really proposing a merger, where Jammey has no choice because Cornell is involved in a "big investment" and cannot allow individuals to stand in the way. The implications are clear: this is the new capitalism, that of the liberal consensus, based just as much on rationalization as strong-arm tactics.

Cornell corresponds to Big Jim Colfax (Albert Dekker) in *The Killers*[24] and to the characters played by Kirk Douglas in *Out of the Past* (1947) and *I Walk Alone.* In this last film the Burt Lancaster character corresponds to Shubunka, except that he survives and gets the girl, whereas Shubunka is shot down in a rainy street. In *I Walk Alone* Frankie Madison (Lancaster) returns to New York after spending fourteen years in jail, only to discover that his former partner at the time of Prohibition, Noll Turner (Douglas) has not only turned his new club into a flourishing business but has no intention of sharing the profits with him. Turner considers he owes Madison 50% of what he sold their old business for and not a penny more. Clearly Turner is the new-fangled sort of "self-made man," a product of corporate business: "we deal with banks and lawyers," he tells Madison, just to show him where the real power lies. As he is driven up Broadway by his brother Dave (now Turner's accountant), Madison is as excited as a child: "fourteen years and it's just the same," to which Dave replies: "it only *looks* the same." When Frankie tries to take over, backed up by several hoodlums he has hired, Dave explains the new corporate set-up: Turner's club is owned by three corporations "on account of the taxes." Madison's hoods change sides at once: they have understood. Like *The Gangster, I Walk Alone* evokes the war only implicitly, but whereas Shubunka used that period to consolidate his individual power, Turner has put it to another use: seeing the writing on the wall, he has thrown in his lot with banks in order to have power and money within a set-up where the individual is meaningless, except as an ideological ploy, a lie to hoodwink the victims. Dave has settled for a situation where one is a willing victim in exchange for security and status: "I'm my own boss as long as somebody is my boss." Thus he submits to the new authority and draws up Turner's contracts. Theirs is a business approach—how can you calculate the "value" of fourteen years in prison?—which is not without points of contact with *Double Indemnity*. The explicit foregrounding of economic power moves both *The Gangster* and *I Walk Alone* into the new territory of alienation favored by the Left to replace the conservative and alienating notion of the *femme fatale*.

Waging War on the Liberal Consensus

In my discussion of *The Gangster* and *I Walk Alone* I have chosen to highlight also the function of the Second World War, the way certain groups took advantage of it for reasons of ideology and power and the henceforth indissociable links between crime and business.[25] One such group was the Motion Picture Alliance which, under cover of an attack on totalitarianism, launched the campaign against radicals, unions and the New Deal at a time (1944) when the Soviet Union was America's ally. We must not forget that the MPA encouraged HUAC to take up its investigation of Hollywood Reds. In this context it is instructive to look at a film which uses the war to engage with and resist post-war political orientations: *Key Largo,* directed by John Huston and written by him in collaboration with Richard Brooks.[26] Referring to the compromises imposed on the script by the Breen Office, Brian Neve has written of the final version: "... there are rather lame references to the return of prohibition, and the object of liberal anger is merely the familiar and villainous 'gangster'—with Robinson's presence recalling the character's past glories rather than any powerful post-war stature."[27] This summary misses the film's meaning.

   That the use of Robinson refers back to *Little Caesar* is clear: his character in *Key Largo* is not called Rocco by chance. If that certainly constituted the censorship problem—the clear evocation of a past form of film making which the consensus was determined to keep off the screen[28]—it in no way enables us to grasp the film's political and historical thrust. This is summed up by Rocco himself when denouncing his deportation (he has re-entered the States illegally in the hope of taking things up where he left off). Evoking with undisguised outrage that he was called an "undesirable alien," he says he was thrown out after thirty years "as if I was a dirty Red." We are surely entitled to interpret this as a criticism by Brooks and Huston of Hollywood's recourse to gangsters when it came to opposing such subversive (= Communist) elements as unions.[29] Similarly, we can take the formula "undesirable alien" as an elliptical reference to radical unionist Harry Bridges (an Australian) on whom the State Department and Hoover waged their own little war for a generation in an unsuccessful attempt to deport him.[30]

   The fact that Bogart, Bacall and Robinson joined forces with Huston at the time of the Committee for the First Amendment—set up to defend Hollywood against the repercussions of the HUAC hearings launched against the Hollywood Ten—provides a complex background to the film. Bogart plays a former Major who has come to Florida to inform the characters played by Lionel Barrymore (confined to a wheelchair like Roosevelt) and Lauren Bacall of the heroic death of his son (Bacall's husband) in Italy. It is crucial that Rocco's reference to "the good old days" (by which he means Prohibition) be taken up by the other three to designate the New Deal period and the war years: the notion of social progress and meaningful collective action stemming from an opposition to tyranny. If the father simply wants to return to the past, Bogart uses the return of Rocco to comment ironically on postwar America, while simultaneously championing values that need to be kept alive. He evokes a time—the 30s—when the United States thought it could do without Rocco, adding that now all is forgiven: the Roccos of the world are in power, even if Rocco himself is not. It is here that he talks of the war as a time of sacrifice so that people would not return to the life they had after the First World War. Just as real gangsters profited from the political climate in force in the 20s, so symbolic gangsters (the MPA, HUAC, etc.) were exploiting that of the late 40s to put the clock back economically and socially.

There is, however, a certain irony present in the use of Bogart who quickly climbed down from his prominent position as defender of free speech in the wake of the October 1947 hearings. The character he plays has the opportunity to kill Rocco, but would be instantly shot down himself. He defends his backing down with the argument that it is not worth dying to rid the world of Rocco. That the father and widow disagree would seem to indicate a representation of the stance taken by Huston in the late 40s as opposed to that of Bogart, not to mention the refusal of the Ten—and large numbers of other Hollywood personalities between 1951 and 1953—to answer questions and name names. From this standpoint, what once struck me as a particularly corny ending—Bacall throwing open the shutters to let the light in ("let there be light," so to speak) after the victory over the gangsters and Bogart returning to the mainland in the boat where the final confrontation has taken place—now takes on a quite different meaning. That the sequence refers to Bogart the star is manifest: the boat is called "Santana," the name of his production company. In which case Brooks and Huston are both criticising him for abandoning the Ten and the Committee for the First Amendment and expressing wistfully what might have been: men returning from the war to keep alive the progressive values of the 30s and the collective spirit of the war years as weapons against alienation. The ending of the film can perhaps best be seen as corresponding to Freud's description of a dream: what the subject wishes is represented as *having actually taken place*.

The dream had turned, of course, into a nightmare: not what the subject wished but what he or she feared above all else: the victory of forms of fascism over democracy. Two films in particular are extended considerations of this victory, representing as they do lynching as both figurative and literal: *The Underworld Story* and *The Sound of Fury*, both directed by Cyril Endfield in 1950. I shall return briefly to the latter when discussing *The Prowler* (the characters played by Lloyd Bridges in the Endfield and by Van Heflin in the Losey are remarkably similar in ways crucial for appreciating the full extent of the criticisms made by the Left in the period 1949–1950). *The Underworld Story* is exemplary for the ways it shows the quite frightening power and influence of the press when it comes to practising the art of character assassination, central to the fate of the Ten and those (like Endfield) marked out for blacklisting in the McCarthy era. Such lynching by the media had started as early as November 1946 in a series of articles written by Frank Hughes for the *Chicago Daily Tribune*[31] and was carried out systematically from 1947 by the venomous columnist Westbrook Pegler and George Sokolsky of the trade paper *The Hollywood Reporter*. What is so striking and revealing about *The Underworld Story* is that, although it sports a particularly nasty gangster (played to manic perfection by future blacklistee Howard Da Silva), the "underworld" of the title has little to do with gangsterism but refers rather to the life-style, values and activities of the wealthy bourgeoisie. They include a newspaper magnate (Herbert Marshall) and sundry citizens of the little town where journalist Dan Duryea ("blacklisted" for writing an article embarrassing his paper's editor and said magnate) has settled to co-run a local paper and save it from bankruptcy. The magnate's son has murdered his wife and he and his father decide to pin the crime on the wife's servant, a young black woman called Molly Rankin; after all, who's going to take "the word of a nigger against ours?" asks the son.[32]

However, the film does not make the mistake of turning itself into an anti-racist tract, but concentrates instead on the effects of the press—all the national papers try and convict Molly without benefit of jury—on citizens, local and national. "The verdict's in," says a lawyer contacted by Duryea to defend the victim and, to prove his point, calls over the waiter and tells him the journalist believes Molly innocent. The man replies: "Don't you ever read the newspapers? That's the trouble with people. They never know what's going on." The bitter irony of this unconscious truth will not have been lost on the besieged liberals and radicals of the time and its impact is strengthened by the lawyer pointing out that, even if white, Molly would lose. Even more pertinent is the way the film resorts to newspaper headlines in order to communicate just how news is made and lives unmade. Thus spectators are shown a headline where a Senator demands a "Finger print law for servants," which nicely evokes the loyalty oath demanded of civil servants by President Truman and foregrounds the question of class where fear and exploitation overdetermine each other.[33] A psychiatrist comments on Molly's "deep-rooted criminal instincts"; racial prejudice and a refusal to countenance any social dimension to crime converge. Most telling is the call for the investigation of the "Save Molly Committee," a reference to the smear tactic whereby all those supporting a cause defended by the CP were automatically tarred with the Red brush. I would suggest that this can also be interpreted as representing the attack on Huston and the Committee for the First Amendment. *The Underworld Story* does not hesitate to refer to "witch burning" by drawing parallels between the Seventeenth century and the contemporary period. Thus a wealthy local citizen, called simply "the Major," denounces Molly as guilty because she is poor; people like her want handouts and the more they get, the more they want. (Implicitly the film makes the same comment on the press magnate in the context of power, money and influence). A woman points out that, for the Major, one is an interloper if not a descendant of the original witch burners, adding: "I hate these wild accusations." It would be difficult to be more limpid.

By showing the shared vested interests of businessmen and hoodlums, the underhand deals and the scare tactics of both in sharp contrast to the frankness of Molly and her supporters, *The Underworld Story* is an explicit example of that "deviance" referred to by Munby. Its designation of a press magnate as chief villain—beside the gangster—would seem to be a reference to William Randolph Hearst, but it is just as likely the film had in mind the owners of the *Los Angeles Times*.[34] However, the magnate in the film finally kills his own son rather than go along with murder and submit to the law of the gang boss. *The Underworld Story* thus has a happy ending, commensurate with those of *Force of Evil* and *Key Largo,* an indication that hope was necessary. *Quicksand* (1950), directed by Irving Pichel (one of the original Hollywood Nineteen), is instructive here.[35] An openly Marxist critique of the credit system, the film presents an implacable and totally realistic representation of how a naïve and well-meaning young man can get caught up in a life of crime. He starts by borrowing (= "stealing") $20 from his stingy employer, goes on to commit such crimes as car theft and grand larceny in his desperate and increasingly futile attempts to pay back what he owes, and finally attempts to murder his boss, who refuses to listen to him.[36] The ending has him arrested and certain of a light sentence, whereas the logic of the script could have led to the employer's death and the hero being shot down by the police (the way Pichel shoots the final sequence on Santa Monica Pier presents this as possible, indeed more than likely). The co-presence of a real happy ending and a potentially tragic one condenses perfectly the need for hope on the Left and the realisation (especially in 1950) that more than hope was needed. From that point of view both *Quicksand* and *The Underworld Story* stand apart from the other major examples of film noir made in 1949–50: there is nothing remotely optimistic about *Caged* (directed by future blacklistee John Cromwell), *Gun Crazy* (written by Dalton Trumbo using a front), *The Asphalt Jungle, The Prowler* and *The Sound of Fury*. On one point, however, there is a fascinating continuity between *The Underworld Story* and *The Sound of Fury*: the magnate in the former and the journalist responsible for the story that triggers off the lynching hysteria represented in the latter are both called Stanton. Of particular relevance to understanding *The Sound of Fury* is the use of an anti-fascist Italian doctor to draw attention to the return in American society of thought and behavior patterns he had opposed in the past. The ways crime, class and money are intimately tied up with politics and history are central to these films, which brings us back to the remark by Emmerich with which I opened this investigation. It is time therefore to turn in some detail to *The Asphalt Jungle* and *The Prowler*.

Class, Economics, Masculinity

The title of *The Asphalt Jungle* refers to city life and I wish to point out a parallel between the postwar career of Huston and that of Jules Dassin.[37] Each director made four movies in three years, each brought out his major achievement in June 1950 (*Night and the City* in Dassin's case), each saw his career threatened at this juncture: Dassin left for France, Huston was forced to turn to less controversial fare.[38] By what can only be an extraordinary coincidence as far as textual influence goes, but which is arguably very much dictated by a common political desire to criticize contemporary American society, a shot of Dix Handley walking through the streets portrays the town as being almost as dilapidated and rundown as London after the war in *Night and the City*. Given that the town in *The Asphalt Jungle* is not named—which is curious: we are usually told the action is taking place in New York, Chicago, Los Angeles, etc.—but is situated in the mid-West, west of Chicago, we can perhaps conclude it is being set up as the signifier of modern American urban society. In which case, the film is already critical—or "deviant"—before it has hardly started.

"Crime is only a left-handed form of human endeavor." As the term "endeavor" can be replaced by, say, "enterprise," the script is manifestly drawing a parallel between crime and big business.[39] Discussing Doc Riedenschneider's plan with him in the presence of middle-man and money-lender Cobby, Emmerich says: "I know some pretty big men around here. Highly respectable men, I might add," a remark which is followed by a knowing look between him and Cobby. Towards the end of the film, when he asks his mistress (Marilyn Monroe) to give him an alibi, he explains this awkward request as follows: "good old dirty politics." Rather than interpreting these two scenes as indicating that the "pretty big men" are politicians, it might be more in keeping with the subtleties of the film to suggest that they could be both businessmen and politicians: businessmen involved in politics and politicians in business. I have chosen to split hairs because of the way Huston's direction sets up resonances throughout the film. In one scene, both Emmerich and Cobby are wearing bow ties. Both Emmerich and Lieutenant Ditrich wear double-breasted vests, a fact Huston draws attention to by having both men fasten them at different points of the film, hardly essential for the story. The safe-cracker also buttons his vest at one point, but it is not double-breasted. Thus at one and the same time Huston creates parallels between characters and stresses the class element that is so important. Brannom, the private eye who works for Emmerich, is dressed like a businessman and Doc carries the attaché case containing the jewels as if he were on his way to a business appointment. Where does this get us?

The sequence where Doc, Emmerich and Cobby start to plan the robbery and discuss whom to hire and what funds are necessary takes on the form of a boardroom meeting from which the workers and their representatives have been excluded. Significantly, Doc and Emmerich are in favor of keeping the hired hands in a state of ignorance.[40] The roles would seem to be distributed thus: Emmerich as banker, Doc as the "mastermind" who needs money to finance his operation, with Cobby in the role of foreman. This, however, is too easy: I am forgetting the fence, who takes at least 50%. In which case, the latter is the capitalist or banker, making a fortune without doing any work, with Emmerich rather in the role of "middle man," using his position to get things moving. This is an example of Marxist economics and one that turns capitalist logic upside down. Whereas the logic of capitalism is to hide all traces of labor so as to justify fixing wages and making profits, here the real situation obtains: the downright exploitative nature of the enterprise—starting with the fence and extending to Doc and Emmerich—is foregrounded, along with the class identity of the hired help, paid what Doc considers them worth, irrespective of the size of the booty expected. In such a context, the close up of the safe-cracker's wife rocking the baby's cradle in an attempt to lull it off to sleep turns into a genuine cry of revolt on behalf of those who work so that others can live off the surplus value thus created.

Emmerich, of course, is a classic instance of this; by overspending drastically, he has simply fallen victim to the ideology he unconsciously upholds. Thus he can offer himself a beautiful young mistress, presented very much as a possession, like his second home, called "another place to hang his hat." Women are certainly treated like so many goods and chattels, but not by the film itself which makes a valiant attempt to oppose sexism through the character of Doll, the one totally sympathetic person. Although Dix accepts to put her up, he is far more interested in brooding over his bad luck, a formula which he recites like a mantra; it's difficult to know if he's trying to exorcise it or just wallowing in self-pity. Ultimately he has a totally alienated view of society: everything is reduced to the misfortunes that befell his family, then himself, which simply comes down to being a negative version of the "self-made man" ideology: the latter means "I got to the top all by myself," whereas Dix is saying "it wasn't my fault." His desire to earn enough to buy back the family farm—which he returns to just in time to die there—is clearly "a tragic metaphor for the end of pastoral idealism before the forces of consumerism and urbanization."[41] Another way of putting it would be to suggest that Dix's flight is both a flight from history in an attempt to deny change and the futility of a Southern vision of society; and an unconscious rejection of those very forces that Dix has been submitting to over the years: money, success, extreme individualism.

I would suggest his flight takes on further meaning in the light of Doc's ambition to settle in Mexico, live off the fat of the land and offer himself the services of the senoritas; and of the mistress wanting Emmerich to offer her a trip to Cuba. Cuba reminds us that Huston had just made We Were Strangers, a film about an attempt to eliminate corruption, remove the apostles of big business and give the country back to the people. The film also portrays politicians backing down on the question of free speech in a manner uncannily like that being practised in Hollywood and by the country's representatives. Doc's colonialist vision of Mexico is also prophetic of the move there, for diametrically opposed reasons, of numerous blacklist victims. Perhaps more than that is at stake, however, or, rather: we need to express ourselves differently. The whole question evokes the extraordinary ending of Dark Passage (1947). Bogart, who is on the run, arranges to meet up with Bacall in Peru, if possible. He leaves San Francisco by bus—the bus station is yet another of those alienating spaces so brilliantly analysed by Sobchack—and the camera tracks in to concentrate on his pensive look. Cut to him, in a white tuxedo, in a luxury nightclub in Peru; then Bacall enters. Whether we take this as reality or Bogart in the bus imagining what might be—the ending looks forward to that of Key Largo analysed above—it is surely an eloquent testimony to a general despair, a feeling that only by flight can the abjection of contemporary American be overcome, that the only other solutions offered are prison, even death.[42] It is in this context that The Prowler, a more historically and politically oriented movie, is so bleak and powerful.

With The Prowler Losey and Trumbo crafted what is perhaps the most subtle and far-reaching representation of the relations between masculine self-assurance and class resentment Hollywood has given us.[43] I am thinking in particular of the marvellous way Losey directed actor Van Heflin (patrolman Webb Garwood) in the opening sequences where Garwood and his partner (a much older married man) come to investigate a call: the heroine Susan (Evelyn Keyes) has reported a prowler outside her

Noll Turner (Kirk Douglas) with gun and Frankie Madison (Burt Lancaster) play crime partners who end up sworn enemies in *I Walk Alone*.

bathroom window. Making himself at home by walking into the living room (whereas his partner remains more discreetly in the hallway) and picking up and looking at a framed photograph, Garwood generally acts as if he owned the place or were an intimate friend of the wife's. Suddenly, looking smug and sure of himself, he hitches up his pants as if he saw himself as God's gift to women. Visibly fascinated by the wife but also contemptuous—he questions her sincerity by suggesting she imagined the prowler— he returns after dropping his partner off to begin his seduction. When she leaves the room to fetch him a drink, he starts leafing through various personal documents of her husband's left lying open upon a desk. If this is important from the point of view of the story-line—he discovers the husband's life-insurance policy—it is perhaps more pertinent to interpret it as a form of surveillance, where a law-enforcement officer takes advantage of his function to pry into a person's private life in a way formally forbidden by law (he's off duty, has no warrant and the wife is not a suspect).

Garwood is the perfect paradigm of resentment; he is also—and this is fundamental to the film's political project—incapable of the slightest analysis of the situation, still less of any self-criticism. He assumes the wife failed to become an actress due to lack of "pull," whereas she replies with dignity: "no, I had no talent." We are light years away from the usual anti-Hollywood Hollywood movie which shows starlets sleeping around with producers to get work. Her remark insists on the importance of work, whereas Garwood is scornful of it, especially of manual labor. Thus his father was content with his "one buck twenty an hour, union scale," as if this were wrong. For Garwood it was: individual success is his only aim in life. The reference to a union is hardly innocent in a film involving Marxists like Losey, Trumbo and Butler; it evokes at once the notion of class interests and the collective, not to mention the role of certain members of the Ten in the Screen Writers' Guild and the struggles for union recognition. Significantly, Garwood lost his basketball scholarship to University for punching the coach who felt he lacked "team spirit" or a sense of working *with* others for the success of the game, rather than *against* them for his own self-aggrandizement. Similarly, when she tells him there's "nothing wrong with being a policeman"—not an idle compliment from a woman who has just called on the police to protect her—he answers that he wants to turn up at work at 10 a.m. after arguing with himself over which car to take that morning. Garwood makes everyone but himself responsible for his social status and can only combat alienation by reinforcing it: turning himself into a capitalist exploiter living off the labor of others (his reference to expensive cars and his jealousy over the luxury home whose owners he is called upon to protect).

This is beautifully hinted at at one point where Garwood is enjoying his new status as the wife's lover. As usual, the radio is on so that the wife, Susan, will be able to tell her husband about his programme that night. We hear the husband talking of "leaning back and taking that first puff at a cigarette," which is precisely what Garwood is doing that very moment. Several factors converge here: Garwood's desire to occupy the husband's place, both in the marriage bed and as a social success; and the husband's own good fortune in being able to enjoy moments of leisure and pleasure, something that comes with his job. George Lipsitz has called the husband "right wing," whereas there is superficially no indication of politics whatsoever.[44] He is surely justified, given the husband's constant reiteration of the remark that "the cost of living is going down," a form of mantra destined to underpin capitalism and the liberal concensus at a time of political difficulty and controversy. Of equal significance, but with a very different purpose, is the way Garwood settles confortably into an armchair and literally puts his feet up as he discusses, with the pride that comes less from talent than from narcissism, his basketball career. Here we have another manifestation of that masculine self-assurance to which I have already referred, one that creates a striking link with the exactly contemporary *The Sound of Fury* which presents us with an even more extreme version of Garwood.[45]

The character of Jerry Slocum, who ropes the unwilling but desperate Howard Tyler into his robberies prior to involving him in a kidnapping and a murder, is the most explicit political denunciation of aspects of masculinity in postwar film noir. Slocum took advantage of his status as a soldier in the liberating forces in Europe in 1944 to sleep with as many French and German women as possible. His only comment on this is that all women are partial to money. Unable to understand either the power exerted by American troops in Germany or the relief felt by the French at being liberated, Slocum is so alienated that he assumes his phallic status is something natural—phallic "power" as an ideological discourse—and that a woman's body exchanged for money is just another piece of merchandise circulating within a market economy. Which is exactly the attitude of Garwood within the parameters of a consumer society that stimulates desire, the ideological ways of (mis)representing one's own place within the economic circuit and the ways such desire can be satisfied. The way Endfield films Slocum—combing his hair endlessly, showing off his athletic body,

getting Tyler to admire his silk shirts (purchased with the money he's stolen from people too old to defend themselves and even less able to withstand such financial loss)—
points up clearly what sort of man Slocum is. His hatred of the rich, his exploitation
of women in a socially inferior position that is historically determined, his drive to obtain wealth and pleasure without letting anything stand in his way makes of him a
working-class fascist, an American version of that fascism the film's Italian doctor
fought before the war and which this truly terrifying movie shows returning implaca-
bly like the repressed in the final lynching sequence.

Slocum's "muscular" ethos is represented in *The Prowler*. Garwood is seen reading a
body-building journal. Just as Slocum prowls around town in a car driven by Tyler in
search of easy prey, so Garwood preys upon Susan and turns himself into a prowler in
order to justify killing the husband. Nor should we forget that a "patrol car" is called a
"prowl car." Other little details insist on the links between Garwood and the act of
prowling. As Susan is explaining to his partner how she came to notice the man through
the bathroom window, Garwood suddenly appears outside the window in a shot that
produces as big a shock in the spectator as the prowler did in Susan. Losey films Garwood in the garden in such a way that he seems to be spying on Susan, turning him into
a Peeping Tom and neatly introducing the twin themes of sex and the commodification
of the woman's body. It is here that the script is particularly revealing of the overall political project of the film. The partner suggests to Susan that she make every effort to
keep her body covered when in the bathroom and makes a fascinating—and seemingly
irrelevant—comparison to a woman and money. Just as in a Bank the money is hidden
so that the customer's gaze not be drawn to it and he will not be tempted, so Susan
should cover herself up to avoid being looked at. This at once suggests it was really
Susan's fault and shows the good-natured partner falling unconsciously for the same ideology as Slocum when dealing with woman in Europe; and that female beauty, like money,
is something desirable. This in turn brings us back to the thrust of modern capitalist society, based as it is on consumption, success and private property. The partner is really
saying to Susan that, as one of her husband's prize chattels, she must not be shared by
other men, which is not a moral argument but a purely economic and patriarchal one.

If there can be no doubt about *The Prowler*'s Marxist politics, the film is also central
to any discussion of postwar noir for its vision of American history; the final scenes in
a ghost town are not there just to offer us a change of scenery. Garwood's partner has
already evoked ghost towns in the context of an attempt to discuss history with him,
but Garwood can show interest only in the woman he has just met. We must not allow
the film's history lesson to pass us by unnoticed. A ghost town in California perforce
conjures up the Gold Rush and mining, the scramble for easy money and the concomi-
tant colonization of the State. It is therefore revealing that Calico, where Garwood
hides out with the pregnant Susan in a pathetic attempt to keep their affair hidden, was
the place of the "worst Indian massacre" in the region. The very evocation of Indians
in the context of whites taking the country over, full of the frontier spirit and the lust
for gold (replaced in the film by the lust for women *and* gold), is already eloquent, but
the formula used is nicely ambiguous. Normally—i.e. in a way ideologically determined—it refers to Indians massacring whites, but why not interpret it the other way

round? The repression of the past represented by ghost towns suggests a past one is not proud of. What is crucial here, I would suggest, is the shot of Susan inside the cabin where she and Garwood had taken refuge. We see her shocked face looking out of the window off-screen right, exactly as in the film's opening shot where she catches sight of the prowler. It is as if *The Prowler* were explicitly linking Garwood to this unknown and unseen man, with Garwood condensing fetishism in the Freudian and Marxist sense. The female body as object of fascination is transformed into a commodity to be bought or else fought for by the male whose fetishization of his own body can only lead to war, the extermination of the other or to an everyday violence extolling force, whether it be emotional, physical or economic.

In which case crime has become the norm within the system set up by the "liberal consensus." Already implied by Robert Rossen's great script for *The Strange Love of Martha Ivers* (Lewis Milestone, 1946), the theme was to become central to the films written and directed by the Left in that brief period when political and intellectual freedom was still possible.

NOTES

1. Thom Andersen and Noël Burch, *Les Communistes d'Hollywood. Autre chose que des martyrs*, Paris: Presses de la Sorbonne Nouvelle, 1994; Lary May: "Movie Star Politics: The Screen Actors' Guild, Cultural Conversion, and the Hollywood Red Scare" in editor May. *Recasting America. Culture and Politics in the Age of the Cold War*, Chicago and London: University of Chicago Press, 1989, pp. 125–153; Brian Neve, *Film and Politics in America. A Social Tradition*, London and New York: Routledge, 1992; James Naremore, *More Than Night. Film noir in its Contexts*, Berkeley, Los Angeles and London: University of California Press, 1998; Jonathan Munby, *Public Enemies, Public Heroes. Screening the Gangster from Little Caesar to Touch of Evil*, Chicago and London: University of Chicago Press, 1999; Paul Buhle and Dave Wagner, *Radical Hollywood. The Untold Story behind American's Favorite Movies*, New York: the New Press, 2002.

2. Op.cit., p.1. I shall return in due course to the political implications of the relation between the terms "gangster movie" and "film noir" in the context of the post-war period.

3. ibid., pp.7, 10.

4. ibid., p.148.

5. ibid., pp.169, 150.

6. May, p.145.

7. Munby, p.169.

8. Nancy Lynn Schwartz, *The Hollywood Writers' Wars*, New York: Alfred A. Knopf, 1982, pp.135–7. Dies, of course, is notorious for accusing Hollywood liberals and radicals of "premature anti-fascism" for their filmic and political activities in the 30s, an accusation that took in just about everyone from John Howard Lawson to the Warner Brothers.

9. Naremore, p.106.

10. Neve, p.91. To a certain extent, of course, such consumer goods *are* the "American way of life."

11. Munby, *op.cit.*, p.173n30 (emphasis added).

12. op.cit., p.324.

13. op.cit., p.179n34.

14. ibid., p.116 and footnote 1.

15. ibid., pp.118, 119.

16. "The Gun in the Briefcase; or, The Inscription of Class in Film noir." in editors David E. James and Rick Berg, *The Hidden Foundation. Cinema and the Question of Class,* Minneapolis and London: University of Minnesota Press, 1996, p.94.

17. ibid., p.97.

18. In *History and Class Consciousness,* London: Merlin Press, 1971, p.83.

19. ibid., p.96.

20. The great modern version of this vision of the consumer society is Romero's *Dawn of the Dead* (1978), where the zombies' mechanical and repetitive gestures symbolize those of people who misrecognize their real place in society by assuming they are acting freely when buying.

21. I know nothing about Wiles, except that he was Production Designer on *Gun Crazy* (1949) and Art Director on *The Underworld Story* (1950).

22. Munby, p.130n17.

23. See on this and related matters Vivian Sobchack: "Lounge Time: Postwar Crises and the Chronotope of Film noir." In Nick Browne, editor, *Refiguring American Film Genres.* Berkeley, Los Angeles, London: University of California Press, 1998, pp.129–170.

24. One of his hoodlums is played by Charles McGraw, one of the killers in the Siodmak movie of 1946.

25. The key film here and one that figures prominently in all discussions is *Force of Evil.* See Reynold Humphries, "When Crime Does Pay. Abraham Polonsky's *Force of Evil.*" In *Q/W/E/R/T/Y,* No.11, University of Pau, France, October 2001, pp.205–10.

26. Brooks had just written *Crossfire* (which used the war as a form of collective action to combat anti-Semitism), the last film on which Adrian Scott and Edward Dmytryk collaborated prior to the prosecution of the Hollywood Ten.

27. op.cit., p.111.

28. For a discussion of these matters, see Munby, pp.156–8.

29. The literature on this is considerable. See Dan Moldea, *Dark Victory. Ronald Reagan, MCA and the Mob,* Viking, 1986; Mike Nielsen and Gene Mailes, *Hollywood's Other Blacklist. Union Struggles in the Studio System,* London: British Film Institute, 1995; Gerald Horne, *Class Struggle in Hollywood. Moguls, Mobsters, Stars, Reds, and Trade Unionists,* Austin: University of Texas Press, 2001.

30. The Hollywood Right did the job for them textually by basing the character of the vicious CP boss (played by Thomas Gomez, obviously atoning for playing Garfield's elder brother in *Force of Evil* and one of Rocco's henchmen in *Key Largo*) on Bridges in *The Woman on Pier 13*. The film takes place in San Francisco and portrays inter-union strife on the waterfront as fomented by Communists. Similarly, Frank Lovejoy, who played the desperate Howard Tyler in *The Sound of Fury,* was called upon in 1951 to portray FBI undercover agent Matt Cvetic in the scurrilous *I Was a Communist for the FBI.* See Reynold Humphries: ""Investigators, undercover men and the FBI: from gangsterism to Communism and back again." In Pierre Lagayette and Dominique Sipière, editors, *Le Crime Organisé à la ville et à l'écran (Etats-Unis, 1929–1951),* Paris: Ellipses, 2001, pp. 212–24.

31. Jack L. Warner Papers, Box 43, folder 1. Special Collections, University of Southern California. My thanks to Ned Comstock whose knowledge of the Warner Papers proved invaluable.

32. I assume that naming Molly after the viciously anti-Semitic and segragationist pro-lynching Dixiecrat John Rankin (a member of HUAC) was a bitter private joke.

33. In 1942 the War Department directed that workers employed on war contracts be fingerprinted; within two years the FBI "had built up a fingerprint dossier on some 37 million workers, prints which were freely provided to employers engaged in detecting or busting strike leaders." David Caute, *The Great Fear. The Anti-Communist Purge under Truman and Eisenhower,* New York: Simon and Schuster, 1978, p. 116.

34. On the union-bashing and Red-baiting activities of this paper, not to mention its owners' avid—and eminently successful—scramble for power and money, see Robert Gottlieb and Irene Wolt, *Thinking Big. The Los Angeles Times, Its Publishers and Their Influence on Southern California,* New York: G.P. Putnam's Sons, 1978.

35. Thanks to Noël Burch for lending me a tape of this little-known and essential movie.

36. His reason for borrowing this trivial sum is symptomatic: to impress a young woman he has met. We shall return to the question of masculinity in the next section.

37. See Reynold Humphries: "Jules Dassin: Crime and the City." In John Dean and Jacques Pothier, editors, *Le Crime Organisé de la Prohibition à la Guerre Froide,* Nantes: Éditions du Temps, 2002, pp. 145–58.

38. We must not underestimate the problems Huston had with the Right, both inside and outside Hollywood. *We Were Strangers* in particular was controversial. On May 9 1949 the representative of the California Federation of Women's Clubs, Los Angeles District, wrote to Harry Cohn, President of Columbia which had produced the film, denouncing it as "cleverly disguised propaganda to advance the Communist party line." She went on to refer to

the praise for the film by the CP press and to the director's "consistent support of Pro-Communist causes and programs." None other than the Vice-President of Columbia replied just one week later to defend the film, pointing out that Louella Parsons had praised it in the *Los Angeles Examiner*. John Huston Papers, Special Collections, Margaret Herrick Library, Academy of Motion Picture Arts and Sciences, Beverly Hills, California. My thanks to Barbara Hall for her help in researching the Huston Collection.

39. This presumably did not escape the attention of the Ohio censor who cut the line. See Naremore, p.293n8.

40. There are no unions in this business.

41. Munby, p.136.

42. The other solution, imposed on Cobby by the corrupt Lieutenant Ditrick, is to "squeal." The terrified Cobby accepts: "once I start singing, I won't stop." The reference to naming names is patent and it is ironic that Marc Lawrence did just that when called to appear before HUAC in 1951, as did Sterling Hayden (doubly ironic: Lawrence named Hayden). Other members of the cast were blacklisted: Sam Jaffe, Dorothy Tree (Emmerich's wife) and, of course, scriptwriter Ben Maddow. *The Asphalt Jungle* thus marks the end of an era in more ways than one.

43. Future blacklistee Hugo Butler fronted for the proscribed Dalton Trumbo. The writer's widow, Jean Rouverol Butler, has confirmed that the script was mainly Trumbo's, although Butler did make contributions. See the interview with Jean Rouveral Bulter in Patrick McGilligan and Paul Buhle, *Tender Comrades. A Backstory of the Hollywood Blacklist*, New York: St. Martin's Press, 1997, p.165.

44. *Rainbow at Midnight. Labor and Culture in the 1940s*, Urbana and Chicago: University of Illinois Press, 1994, p. 301n17.

45. What makes *The Sound of Fury* so utterly despairing is not simply the lynching but the character of Slocum: totally negative and destructive from every standpoint. Garwood, on the other hand, comes over at the end of the film as more pathetic and alienated, despite his ruthlessness. He forgets that the only people who do get away with murder (literally or figuratively speaking) are businessmen evading taxes (a theme mentioned briefly in *Out of the Past* and central to *I Walk Alone*): they have the wherewithal and the contacts necessary to hire smart lawyers.

The sadomasochistic lovers in *Duel in the Sun*: the violent, unpredictable Lewt (Gregory Peck) and the exotic half-breed Pearl (Jennifer Jones).

Noir Westerns

James Ursini

> *Pursued*... a noir western, apparently a contradictory hybrid both in terms of narrative and visual style. [1]
>
> Martin Scorsese

The above comment by director Martin Scorsese neatly capsulizes the seeming paradox of this "hybrid" called "the noir western." The western genre since its inception, but particularly during the classic period stretching from the teens until the 1950s when revisionists like Anthony Mann and Budd Boetticher began to twist the conventions of the genre, has been characterized by clearly definable themes, rigid archetypes, and expansive visual icons which most audiences could identify within a few minutes of the opening credits. In their appendix entry on "The Western" in *Film Noir, an Encyclopedic Reference to the American Style* (third edition, 1992), Alain Silver and Carl Macek also concur with director Scorsese in his analysis of apparent contradictions between film noir and the western genre: in their words, "the claustrophobic atmosphere of many noir films and the emphasis on open spaces in the Western," along with the "simple moral conflicts" in the latter, made the two seem incompatible. Although Silver and Macek do eventually come to the conclusion that this hybrid called "the noir western" does exist, they believe that it came to fruition in only a handful of films.

In this study I have chosen to concentrate on six westerns (*The Ox-Bow Incident* [1943], *Duel in the Sun* [1945], *Pursued* [1947], *Ramrod* [1947], *Blood on the Moon* [1948], and *Devil's Doorway* [1950]) which most clearly evidence this grafting of noir onto the western genre. These films were all produced between 1942 and 1950, the height of the noir classic period. Three were directed by men noted for their other more mainstream noir films (Anthony Mann, *Devil's Doorway*; Andre De Toth, *Ramrod*; Robert Wise, *Blood on the Moon*) and two were shot by cinematographers also heavily associated with the noir period (John Alton for *Devil's Doorway* and Nicholas Musuraca for *Blood on the Moon*). But whoever the director or cinematographer, all six films share with classic noir films, like De Toth's *The Pitfall*, or Mann's *Raw Deal* or Robert Wise's *The Set-up*, archetypes, themes, and visual iconography which are unmistakably in the noir style.

Archetypes

Conflicted, alienated protagonists: "The word 'hero' never seems to fit the noir protagonist, for his world is devoid of the moral framework necessary to produce the traditional hero. He has been wrenched from familiar moorings . . . "[2] All of the protagonists in the six films of this study reflect the sense of alienation Robert Porfirio describes above. Further they are in direct conflict with the traditional western hero, with his strong code of right and wrong and his inherent sense of justice.

The Ox-Bow Incident introduces its protagonist, Gil (Henry Fonda), in a dimly lit saloon drinking himself into oblivion while staring longingly at a painting of a reclining, semi-nude woman. The audience learns from the dialogue that he and his friend Art (Frank Morgan) are drifters and that Gil has been jilted by the town "prostitute," Rose (Mary Beth Hughes), who has recently left town with a wealthy, older husband. In his despair he picks a fight with another customer and has to be knocked out and restrained by the bartender with the aid of Art. Although the tone is somewhat comic and ironic, the pain the character feels is no less real. This is no traditional western hero. He is unshaven, dirty, drunk and ornery. In fact he resembles more the traditional villains of the classic western.

But what is even more disturbing is his lack of interest in "doing the right thing," a necessary characteristic for a classic western hero, but a common failing among noir protagonists from Double Indemnity on. Throughout most of this tale of mob "justice" and the necessity of moral commitment, Gil goes along with the majority. He rides with the posse on its pursuit of the individuals they believe to be murderers and cattle rustlers. He never speaks out during the initial deliberations within the posse itself about the legality of their plan. When the African-American minister, Sparks, tries to convince him of the immorality of this rapid pursuit of justice without legal proceedings, Gil replies by spitting and saying, "It's a way of spending time."

Gil finally has his metanoia after it becomes clear that the evidence against the three men they eventually capture is just too flimsy and that the posse has simply become a bloodthirsty mob, symbolized by the raucous and cackling laugh of Jenny (Jane Darwell), the posse's own Greek fury. When Major Tetley (Frank Conroy) finally calls for a vote, Gil is one of the seven who steps across the line and votes against the lynching. He even physically tries to stop the illegal execution but is restrained by the others. Finally, in the resolution of the movie, it is Gil who reads the poignant letter of one of the victims to a row of shamefaced cowboys who are lined up, heads down, against the shadowy bar. By the end of the movie this alienated drifter has found a purpose and heads off to deliver the letter to the dead man's wife.

In Pursued, written by Niven Busch who also worked on the scripts for The Postman Always Rings Twice and Duel in the Sun, the protagonist is, as the title indicates, haunted. In this case the pursuers are both human, Grant Callum (Dean Jagger)—dressed most often in black and looking like an avenging demon—as well as psychological. Like so many noir heroes (e.g., The Killers, Cornered, etc.) Jeb Rand (Robert Mitchum) cannot truly love ("I couldn't even return love. Is there something the matter with me?" Jeb to his foster mother) or even be happy until he can understand his past, his temps perdu, as Proust called it. The film is told in flashback with a first person narration by Jeb, a common technique in noir films such as Double Indemnity and Sunset Boulevard as well as countless noir novels. This technique does not only establish a strong bond between the viewer and the narrator, as the audience is forced to see the story from his point of view, but it also creates a deterministic fatality to the events which are strung out in the narration and which lead almost inexorably to the end-point where the film began. The symbol for Jeb's "un-recovered memory" which so alienates him from others as well as himself is a pair of boots with jingling spurs which haunts his dreams as well as his waking hours. In a clas-sic Freudian catharsis Jeb finally frees himself when he remembers that the boots be-longed to his father and that he had witnessed the murder of his entire family by Grant Callum, his pursuing demon. With that knowledge and the death of Callum, Jeb is able to reunite with his wife Thorley (Teresa Wright) and move towards a brighter future

In *Ramrod,* based on a story by Luke Short—noted noir western writer, the death of his wife and children leaves the protagonist Dave Nash (Joel McCrea) a shell of a man, an alcoholic with very little will of his own who is humiliated and initially dis-counted by the antagonists of the piece, especially the villain, Frank Ivey ("I see you, drunk," Ivey to Nash). In fact Dave spends most of the film bounced back and forth be-tween the two female pillars of strength: the angelic Rose (Arleen Whelan) and the driven yet sympathetic femme fatale of the story, Connie (Veronica Lake). Both tend to his psychological and physical wounds in several scenes and protect him from the land-grabbing, ruthless Ivey (Preston Foster) and his henchmen. Even his best friend, Bill Schell (Don Defore), loses his own life protecting Dave as he leads Ivey and his men away from Dave and then is shotgunned in the back by Ivey himself. Even though Nash shows his potential for strength on several occasions, most notably in taking over the henchman's line camp as a residence for Connie when her ranch house burns or killing Virgil (Wally Cassell) whom he believes murdered his friend Sheriff Jim Crew (Donald Crisp), his true redemptive act comes at the end when he decides to stop running and face Ivey. Although he confronts him in the street and kills him in a shootout, the final scene of him being helped by Rose into her house tempers his heroics as the audience sees him once again in a dependent state.

Blood on the Moon, again from a story by Luke Short, directed by Robert Wise, and photographed by Nicholas Musuraca—all important figures in noir, presents another noir icon, Robert Mitchum, as Jim Garry, an uninvolved drifter and gun-for-hire who finds him-self enmeshed in a range war over beef and land between the Luftons and Tate Riling (Robert Preston), Garry's friend. Initially, Jim goes to work for Tate partially because he needs the money and partially out of a sense of loyalty, even though Tate has told him about his plans to cheat the Luftons. Jim participates in several of Tate's nefarious acts, in-cluding the stampeding of the Luftons' herd which causes two deaths. The deaths and his growing romantic involvement with the tomboyish Lufton daughter Amy (Barbara Bel Geddes) become a moral turning point for Jim. The objective correlative for this change of heart is the climactic violent bar fight between Jim and Tate. Like most noir protago-nists Jim ends up in the film both psychologically and physically damaged, in this case he is knifed by one of Tate's henchmen, and is forced to kill his once close friend, Tate.

Devil's Doorway, directed by noir innovator Anthony Mann and photographed by John Alton—Mann's favorite cinematographer during his noir period, mixes socially aware themes (racism) with noir themes of determinism. Broken Lance (Robert Tay-lor) returns from the Civil War with the Congressional Medal of Honor and a faith in the country and people he bled for. "Why should anyone want to bother me?"

Broken Lance tells his father who replies ominously and prophetically, "You are home. You are again an Indian." Over the years Broken Lance acquires land, cattle and wealth while Wyoming becomes a territory and begins enforcing anti-Indian laws. This begins the downward spiral of Broken Lance's fortunes along with his sense of optimism. He is shot at and humiliated in a bar where he now cannot drink. His land is divided up by incoming sheepmen. He tries legal methods at first, hiring a lawyer—Orrie Masters (Paula Raymond)—but all to no avail. "You are a ward of the government," she tells the distraught but stoic Broken Lance. Egged on by a bitter, racist lawyer Verne Coolan (Louis Calhern), the town turns further against him. In a series of battles Broken Lance's friend, Sheriff Carmody (Edgar Buchanan), is killed and Lance shoots one of the sheepmen. Coolan organizes a posse to go after Broken Lance and his people. They are surrounded and decimated. Orrie, who is now infatuated with him, appeals to Broken Lance to surrender once the army arrives but he is now so filled with anger and pain that he cannot see beyond it. He bends to kiss her but cannot even allow himself that, "A hundred years from now it might have worked." He has accepted his fate, a common theme in noir films. In a telling touch of irony, he puts on his army uniform and congressional medal and walks out shooting, knowing he will be killed by the members of an army he once fought for.

The femme fatale: "The film noir world is one in which women are central to the intrigue of the films, and are furthermore usually not placed safely in any ... familiar roles. Defined by their sexuality, which is presented as desirable but dangerous to men, the women function as the obstacle to the male quest."[3] Although the "good girl/bad girl" dichotomy informed the western as well as other genres in American film, the "bad girls" of classic period westerns, e.g., Linda Darnell in *My Darling Clementine* or Claire Trevor in *Stagecoach,* were tame compared to the noir femme fatales. Western "bad girls" were generally just misunderstood females yearning to be supportive "good girls" who could be transformed by a little love and kindness, which is exactly what happens in both *Stagecoach* and *Clementine*. This is not the case for noir femme fatales. They are truly subversive characters, intent on turning the patriarchal paradigm on its head.

Duel in the Sun is an excellent film for seguing from conflicted protagonist to femme fatale, another key archetype of film noir. For in the character Pearl Chavez (Jennifer Jones) we have both archetypes combined. Like Broken Lance in *Devil's Doorway* racism dogs her trail and creates an almost deterministic chain which will result in tragedy as it does for the protagonist of *Devil's Doorway*. Pearl, after the execution of her genteel Southern father for murdering her Indian mother and her lover, goes to live with her father's cousin and former paramour Laura Belle (Lillian Gish), Laura Belle's overbearing and racist husband Senator McCanles (Lionel Barrymore) and their two sons— Jesse (Joseph Cotton), sympathetic and somewhat weak, and Lewt (Gregory Peck), the wild and dissolute favorite of the Senator. Pearl's entry into this family's life causes disruptions which are deep and long-lasting. She initially tries to be a "good girl" and not offend anyone in the family. But the senator's hostilities coupled with the seductive yet deceptive charms of Lewt cause her to throw off the strictures of their Southern gentility and be herself. She indulges her own sensuality with Lewt while swimming naked at the water hole and at night in her room during a violent storm. At the same time she

Pearl Chavez (Jennifer Jones), the femme fatale of *Duel in the Sun,* combines sensuality with child-like innocence. Here she is summoned by the household servant (Butterfly McQueen).

pursues Jesse whom she romanticizes as a purer form of Lewt, although in reality he seems nothing more than a weaker version of his brother, afraid to stand up to their father, at least initially. Like the traditional femme fatale from Phyllis Dietrichson in *Double Indemnity* to Anna in *Criss Cross,* her presence is subversive to the patriarchal structure. Both her sexuality and her force of personality cannot be controlled by the men in the dramatic piece, no matter how hard they try. The filmmakers emphasize her subversive sensuality throughout the movie: half-dressed and bathed in the light from a lamp while Lewt lusts after her in her room; kneeling child-like, wrapped sensually in an Indian blanket while a hypocritical minister prays for her soul; swimming naked in the local water hole. Most of the action of the plot, in fact, stems from conflicts surrounding her and the male characters' desire to possess her. Pearl's affection for Jesse as well as her tempestuous affair with Lewt gives Jesse the strength to break with his father and side with the railroad against the senator and his autocratic control of the land. Her reactions to Lewt's betrayal of her, by refusing to acknowledge her largely because of her half-breed status, causes her to marry a much older man, whom Lewt kills, and then to side with Jesse which leads Lewt to shoot and wound his own brother. In addition, Pearl also exemplifies many of the characteristics of the traditionally male protagonists of other noirs. She is haunted by racism as well as by the exploitative acts of men like Lewt. And as much as she tries to break with her past, she is drawn back in. At the end she finally tries to make a clean break by killing Lewt herself, not only in order to protect Jesse but also to exorcise her own demons. In the famous duel in the rocks Pearl and Lewt end up shooting each other, which guarantees Jesse's safety. But it is obvious that Pearl is still not free of her own demons as she crawls across the rocks in order to touch once more the man who has caused her so much pain.

Next to *Duel in the Sun, Ramrod* presents probably one of the most complex and sympathetic femmes fatales among noir films in general. Connie Dickason (Veronica Lake) is a woman in the old West surrounded by weak men. Her fiancee leaves town in the first scene, afraid to fight for her ranch against the villain Ivey, the only strong male in the film. Her attitude is summarized visually in one shot as she throws herself on the bed in anger and clenches her fists in foreground. Her father calls her "hard" and "headstrong" (words often used to describe women who take on traditional male roles in classic American movies) for refusing to compromise with the greedy Ivey who desperately wants Connie as his wife. In fact, in the early parts of the movie, she is the only one who stands up to the villain of the piece. When she finally convinces the alcoholic Dave Nash to be her foreman, she implies that she is "strong enough" for both of them. She is also, like any true femme fatale, not above using her sexuality to obtain her ends. She seduces a young cowpoke into silence with just a touch of her hand. She manipulates Schell into stampeding her own herd in order to shift the blame to Ivey. She serves Ivey and her father cookies and drinks like a submissive daugher/fiancee while plotting their ruin. In one particularly memorable scene Ivey shows up at the ranch and beats up one of her workers for helping her take over his line camp. In response she slaps him repeatedly and forcefully, an act no one else in the film had dared to do at this point. Connie again and again defies the patriarchal structure and ultimately wins, even though as the "good girl" Rose says, "[her battle] is costing too many lives." And even when she is left alone in the town street after Nash shoots Ivey and puts an end to the conflict over her land, an audience cannot help but feel admiration for the strength and subversive power of this woman in a man's world.

Pursued features a female character who begins and ends as a traditional helpmate to the protagonist but shifts in midstream to a femme fatale. Thorley is Jeb's adopted sister whom he grows to love. But when he kills her brother in self-defense, she refuses to believe his story and begins to give credence to the rumors about him, namely that he is descended from "bad blood" and can only "do evil," rumors that Jeb himself partially believes. Her sense of betrayal is heightened even further when he kills Prentice, her new suitor, in a shootout. So like any self-respecting noir femme fatale she decides to take her revenge. She allows him to court and marry her, in a series of scenes which emphasize her cold and devious passivity while underlining his stoic acceptance of her no matter the consequences. Acting on his instinct that Thorley is planning to take revenge on him, he brings her, on their wedding night no less, a platter with cookies, wine and a revolver. The filmmakers had just given the audience a glimpse into Thorley's mind in a mirror shot so common to film noir, a shot in which she prepares herself for her new husband while she stares with wicked intensity at her own image, an image constructed to deceive this man. So when she takes the revolver and faces the man she hates, in a scene quite similar to the final confrontation between Walter and Phyllis in *Double Indemnity,* the audience is not surprised. But, of course, neither is Jeb. She shoots but misses and he tells her, "Your hand shook not because you hate me." Unable to deny her love for him any longer, she breaks down and embraces him passionately. Although this love-hate relationship ends on a positive note with Thorley helping Jeb remember his past and shed his sense of shame, it is still a prime example of the kind of conflicted love in which the femmes fatales of film noir often find themselves embroiled.

Both *The Ox-Bow Incident* and *Blood on the Moon* only flirt briefly with the femme fatale character. In the former it is Rose, the town prostitute, who has jilted the protagonist and married a rich, older man. She is seen luminously and briefly in a stagecoach scene in the mountains. In *Blood on the Moon,* the tomboyish Amy has all the strength and sassiness of a noir femme fatale, shooting at the protagonist when he first enters their land, dressing in men's clothes, berating the rustlers for their actions. But ultimately she becomes secondary to the story and does not maintain the subversive quality necessary for a true femme fatale.

Themes

Existentialist angst: "The concept of alienation is crucial to most existentialists from Kierkegaard to Sartre. For them, man stands alone, alienated from any social or intellectual order, and is therefore totally self-dependent." (Porfirio, *FNR,* p. 85) Although the classic western hero is often a loner, he is usually a loner out of choice, the rugged individual who has consciously decided the live his life in the sparsely populated landscape of the West. For the noir protagonist there is often no choice. He is haunted, pursued, guilty, usually for a variety of reasons but with the same effect—alienation and anxiety.

In all six of the movies in this study the protagonists demonstrate the classic noir symptoms of angst and alienation. In *Pursued,* the protagonist Jeb tries alternately to recover and then to push out of his consciousness a traumatic childhood incident, the murder of his family. But his struggle only leads to violence (he kills two men) and the hate of his foster sister/wife Thorley and his foster mother. Even his love for Thorley is tainted in his mind by incestuous overtones while his affection for his adopted mother, who had rescued him from the family massacre, is muted and eventually turns to hate on her part after Jeb kills her son. But Jeb's severest critic is himself and his fears about his own iniquity, about, as he says, standing over the grave of his second victim, "some badness locked up inside me."

In *Ramrod,* Dave Nash fights his own demons, the memory of the death of his wife and children. His burden of the past, as pointed out earlier—a common motif in noir angst, like that of Jeb's in *Pursued* cannot let him rest. He is racked by shame and guilt and so turns to alcohol. He no longer has the respect of the town and can only find strength in others, mainly in the arms of the two strong females in the film: Connie and Rose.

In *Duel in the Sun,* Pearl also has a past to deal with. She too, like Jeb, begins to believe that she has "bad blood" inherited from her wild Indian mother. In the first scene Pearl, as a young girl, witnesses her mother dancing sensuously for a crowd of aroused men in a casino and later in silhouette sees her mother and her lover shot by her beloved father. She too vacillates. At times she puts on the "uniform" of the good girl, dolling up in buttoned-up, proper white dresses given to her by her doting cousin Laura Belle. But when disappointed by men like her fickle lover Lewt or ridiculed by the racist Senator McCanles, who calls her "Pocohontas" derisively, she defiantly dresses in the "uniform" of the "bad girl," the femme fatale: tight blouses off the shoulders, Indian blankets half-draped over her body, or even totally naked as in the water hole scenes. She never really resolves this conflict, unlike Jeb in *Pursued* who finally recalls and purges his childhood memory or even Nash in *Ramrod* who goes off with Rose at the end. She instead performs an act of bravery by protecting Jesse from his dissolute brother Lewt but in the end cannot resist her passion for the "bad boy" and crawls to him so they can die in an embrace of passion.

In both *Blood on the Moon* and *The Ox-Bow Incident* the protagonists are presented initially as amoral drifters who have very few deep emotional ties. Their angst centers around their inability to make commitments, to choose a side, to do "what seems right." This is significant in terms of Sartre's view of existentialism which posited an absurd universe with no inherent meaning but also called for individuals to make commitments, to choose sides in order to impose meaning on this meaningless universe. And as existentialism, along with Freudianism, was a major influence on noir it is not unusual that these two noir characters would reflect this thread of Sartrean philosophy. Both protagonists, of course, do make commitments by the end of the movie, Jim Garry in the first movie by joining forces with the Luftons against his own friend who is persecuting them and Gil in the second film by voting against the lynching of the three innocent men.

Devil's Doorway presents a unique situation in that Broken Lance begins the movie as an optimistic, even naive individual, ready to forget the past oppression of his people and live side-by-side with the Whites in harmony and peace. But gradually the dominant culture wears away his positivist attitude with their new anti-Indian laws, their humiliations, and their legal chicanery. Slowly his demeanor changes as does his personality. The close-ups of him are no longer of a bright, smiling face but of a stoic, saddened one. Society, rather than psychology, turns him into an angst-ridden noir protagonist. *His* demons are not internal, they are external. But the result is the same. As he and his people are penned in and gradually massacred by a posse of Whites, he loses the will to live and sees only "assisted suicide" as an honorable option. In the final scene he walks into a volley of bullets with a look of anguish and pain and then drops out of frame, released physically and visually at last from his torment.

Determinism: "But while Camus's fictional characters experience an 'existential despair' that is based on the consequences of choosing and the operation of free will, the choices of noir protagonists are most often overwhelmed by an underlying determinism that is neither benign or indifferent."[4] Although most noir films, including noir westerns, do endorse the existential mandate to make choices, there is, as Alain Silver notes above, a sense of inexorable doom that tempers the concept of individual choice and freedom.

As pointed out earlier, Pearl in *Duel in the Sun,* Jeb in *Pursued,* and Nash in *Ramrod* all carry burdens of the past on their back, psychological burdens they cannot seem to shake. Pearl's conflict resolves itself in death, in a shootout with the man who symbolizes both the sensual love she deserves and the disdain she feels for herself as the daughter of a "loose half-breed." Dave Nash takes action and faces down the villain of the piece, the man who had called him "a drunk" and murdered his best friend in cold blood. But he seems in the final scene as weak as ever, as he limps away held up by Rose. Jeb is the only one of the three that seems to totally escape his burden. He finds his complete regeneration in the arms of a woman, his wife Thorley. After finally recalling the murder of his family, which he had witnessed hidden under the floorboards, and realizing that he was not responsible in some way, he feels released and able to love. It is also significant that the human personification of his guilt and shame, his avenging demon, Grant Callum, is killed by Ma Callum in the same scene. Thus, he finds his release on both a physical and psychological level.

In *Blood on the Moon, Devil's Doorway* and *The Ox-Bow Incident* it is society which dogs the three protagonists. For Jim Garry in *Blood on the Moon,* Gil in *Ox-Bow Incident* and Broken Lance in *Devil's Doorway* are not marked by deep psychological scars. The source of their angst is a corrupt society. All three films posit a social determinism, rather than a psychological one. Jim Garry is caught between warring cattlemen who battle over the price of beef. He wants to make a living and "to get by" but he finds himself involved in murder, including the killing of his own friend, and the destruction of property. His existential angst centers entirely on making a moral choice, on not being led by the forces or the factions around him but to make his own decision. With Gil it is even more definitive. He is caught up in the mob fury and becomes part of a posse bent on executing the men responsible for the supposed murder of Kincaid, a local rancher. As the posse becomes more bloodthirsty and bent on seeing their three suspects hang, Gil's indifference changes to anguish. The social determinism of *The*

Ox-Bow Incident, along with *Devil's Doorway,* is the most emphatic of all six movies. Gil cannot change the course the posse has chosen. He is restrained physically when he tries and even his vote against the lynching is almost perfunctory as the audience knows the majority of these men and one woman are set on seeing a "true triple hangin'." Broken Lance's fate is probably the most determined and inexorable. Once he has attained wealth, land and cattle, the White power structure begins to flex its social muscle and proceeds to dismantle his holdings as well as his sense of self-esteem. The audience can only watch helplessly as his situation worsens and this inherently brave and good-natured man become embittered and bent on self-destruction, "They're set on dying. Then let's make it count."

Visual Iconography

> A dark street in the early morning hours, splashed with a sudden downpour. Lamps form haloes in the murk. In a walk-up room, filled with intermittent flashing of a neon sign from across the street, a man is waiting to murder or be murdered…shadow upon shadow upon shadow…every shot glistening low-key, so that rain always glittered across windows…faces were barred deeply with those shadows that usually symbolized some imprisonment of body or soul.[5]

Joel Greenberg and Charles Higham's rather poetic narrative above manages to summarize neatly many of the visual icons associated with noir: low-key lighting, night (or day for night) exteriors, storms, faces in shadow, low camera angles, canted angles. All of these techniques help create an ominous, oppressive world where so much is hid-

In *Blood on the Moon,* alienated loner Jim Garry (Robert Mitchum) joins up with his old friend Tate Riling (Robert Preston) in his criminal operations.

den—psychologically, emotionally, physically—that the protagonists are often at a loss to know what is real or not, what is true or not. Where most traditional westerns concentrated on bright, hot, dusty exteriors and flatly lit interiors, with notable exceptions like *Stagecoach* and *My Darling Clementine,* noir westerns revel in darkly cloudy skies, rainstorms, horsemen riding through the night, chiaroscuro interiors with oppressive ceilings and shadowy figures. Five of the six films analyzed in this article exemplify this visual style. The only exception is *Ramrod* where the director De Toth has chosen to remain faithful to the more naturalistic look of the traditional western. Then why is the film part of this study? As evidenced earlier, *Ramrod* so forcefully fulfills the other criteria of a noir film that it would be critically irresponsible to eliminate it simply for not adhering to all the prerequisites. Even among mainstream noir films that kind of variation is allowed, most notably in films like *Laura* and *The Big Heat* where Preminger and Lang respectively have also chosen a flatter visual style to document their characters' journeys into the noir underworld.

Night on the plains: In the other five films of this study the directors have opted to show their characters most often on the plains at night. The majority of *The Ox-Bow Incident* takes place on a mountain pass at night, with its deformed tree bent over the pass, foreshadowing the lynching to follow. The setting visually exemplifies the darkness of this lynch mob's purpose while at the same time symbolizing the Dante-esque "dark woods" Gil finds himself in as he tries to determine for himself what the truth is and whether he has the courage or desire to stand up to this bloodthirsty mob. When the sun finally does rise over the mountain pass, it only brings death as the three innocent men are lynched without mercy or even a trial.

Duel in the Sun, even though in color, also favors exterior settings at night when trying to set its mood of doom and dark sensuality. It opens at night with the murder of Pearl's mother by her father and punctuates the narrative with erotic scenes between Lewt and Pearl which take place initially outdoors at night and then move onto darkly lit interiors. The filmmakers even stage one of the major action scenes in the evening as Lewt blows up a train.

Blood on the Moon opens on the protagonist riding across the plains at evening with stormy skies in the background and ends in the woods at night as a wounded Jim is forced to kill his friend Tate in order to protect himself and his newfound love. In the final scene the camera follows Jim through the shadowy woods, creating even more suspense by limiting the view of the audience as well as the characters. After Jim has shot his friend, he bends down to him and there is an exchange of grief-stricken expressions in shadowy close-up which summarizes the pain of both men whose affection for each other was never the issue, only the paths they had chosen.

Both *Pursued* and *Devil's Doorway* have their share of night exteriors but each has one that is particularly evocative and suspenseful. In *Pursued* Jeb tries to escape one of Thorley's beaus (Prentice) who believes Jeb has insulted "his girl." The scene is set in a dark alley, a familiar icon of noir movies. Jeb does not want to kill again and so weaves in and out of the shadows and around buildings. But Prentice spots and shoots. Jeb returns the fire and kills him. In *Devil's Doorway* there is a series of night attacks on the Indian encampment which are particularly striking and ominous in terms of the

resolution of the movie. The posse uses dynamite to destroy the buildings and deci-
mate the tribe. Soon the night is lit by fires and smoke from the explosions as the
small band led by Broken Lance try to defend their land and property. This scene is followed by a guerilla counterattack by the Indians in which a now desperate Broken
Lance throttles the leader of the posse.

Claustrophobic interiors: One of the most distinctive visual markers of a noir film
remains to this day the manner in which interiors are shot. Noir movies favor for
the most part interiors which feature chiaroscuro lighting, low angles which often include the ceilings, and faces shot in half-shadow—all creating a claustrophobic, ominous, and mysterious mood. In *Pursued* the key memory scene, which is seen several
times in bits and pieces, is shot at night as the boy Jeb hides under the floorboards
and witnesses the murder of his family. The point of view is his so it is by necessity
at a low angle. All of this of course heightens the suspense as well as the mystery,
particularly as the audience and the main character never put the pieces of this
memory together until the final scene.

Blood on the Moon stages one of its key turning points in a darkened bar where Jim
Garry finally takes a moral position and refuses to go along with his friend Tate's
newest scheme. A lamp is knocked over and a fight ensues in the now shadowy saloon. It is a violent brawl which goes on for over five minutes, leaving the combatants
as well as the bar in tatters. Although *Ramrod* opts to tells its noir story with a traditional western high-key look, there are a few notable exceptions. The most important
is a particularly erotic and tense scene in a cave where Nash, Connie, and Nash's
friend Schell, who is in love with Connie, are hiding out from Frank Ivey. In a single
mise-en-scène, bathed in shadows, De Toth externalizes the emotions and conflicts
of all three characters. The director positions the three in a rough triangle with Schell
attending to the fire, while Connie, her luxurious hair flowing to her shoulders, caresses the wounded (psychologically as well as physically) Nash who lies in her lap.
At one point she looks up from her putative lover and smiles at Schell. Schell tries
not to look but instead goes about tending to the fire, but the expression of angst on
his face is unmistakable.

Duel in the Sun sets several key scenes in darkened interiors. The sexual encounters between Pearl and Lewt take place inside her room, with only a lamp as the light
source, creating a Rembrandt style interior evoking a sense of eroticism as well as impending doom. The murder of Pearl's husband (Charles Bickford) by Lewt occurs in
a large, almost deserted, shadowy saloon, shot in wide angle with a lengthy bar bisect-
ing the frame, as Lewt instigates a gunfight he knows he will win. The night interiors
in *Devil's Doorway* are probably the most claustrophobic. Director Mann and cinematographer Alton in their mainstream noir films had often favored very low angles
which serve to heighten the drama of the scene while highlighting the oppressive
ceilings. In this film the set itself visually symbolizes the gradual narrowing of Broken
Lance's universe, as the White world begins to encroach more and more on his land
as well as his sense of worth.

Noir as a style was undoubtedly the single most important influence on American
films of the forties and early fifties. And so it is little wonder that it is not confined to

the detective/mystery genre or even the western. Traces of its dark mode can also be seen in period films, the gangster film, the science fiction film, even the musical. The style's ability to express the dark side was adopted again and again by filmmakers no matter the genre. This may in fact explain why the style has experienced such a resurgence in the last decade with a generation of filmmakers who were not even born when most of the classic noir films were made.

NOTES

1. In his introductory remarks for the 1994 Republic video release of the UCLA Film and Television Archive restoration of *Pursued*.

2. Robert Porfirio, "Now Way Out: Existential Motifs in the Film Noir," reprinted in *Film Noir Reader*, editors Alain Silver, James Ursini, New York: Limelight, 1996, p. 83.

3. E. Ann Kaplan, "Introduction," *Women in Film Noir*, London: British Film Institute, 1978, p. 2.

4. Alain Silver, "Introduction," *Film Noir, An Encyclopedic Reference to the American Style*, New York: Overlook Press, 1992 (3rd Edition), p. 4.

5. Joel Greenberg and Charles Higham (1968), "Noir Cinema" (from *Hollywood in the Forties*), reprinted in *Film Noir Reader*, p. 27

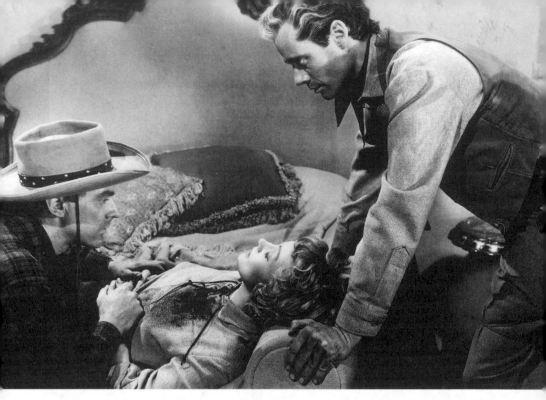

Above, Altar Keane (Marlene Dietrich) cared for by her two lovers: Vern Haskell (Arthur Kennedy), right, and Frenchy Fairmont (Mel Ferrer) in *Rancho Notorious*. Below, "entrepeneur"/femme fatale Altar Keane (Marlene Dietrich) dominates most of the men who come to her ranch by the force of her intelligence coupled with her seductive charms.

Rancho Notorious (1952): A Noir Western in Color

Robin Wood

If I begin by correcting yet another misrepresentation of my work, this is not merely for my personal satisfaction: the correction provides a useful and relevant starting-point for some of the things I want to say about *Rancho Notorious*.

In a review of Andrew Britton's *Katharine Hepburn: the Thirties and After* (*Screen*, September–October, 1985), Simon Watney remarks: "He accuses [Richard] Dyer and Robin Wood of effectively setting up a descriptive theory of discrete genres, as they present themselves, whereas he argues that the differences between genres are far from absolute."

Britton "accuses" me of no such thing: in fact, precisely the opposite: his reference enlists me on his side in his argument against Richard Dyer. The passage to which he refers (it occurs in an article entitled entitled "Ideology, Genre, Auteur," published in *Film Comment*) runs as follows: "One of the greatest obstacles to any fruitful theory of genre has been the tendency to treat the genres as discrete. An ideological approach might suggest why they can't be, however hard they may appear to try: at best, they represent different strategies for dealing with the same ideological tensions... In the classical Hollywood cinema motifs cross repeatedly from genre to genre."

I don't see how I could talk plainer than that. For somebody (like, presumably, Watney) who had not read my article, Britton's reference to it might appear ambiguous. Any ambiguity—the possibility that I might be granted the benefit of any doubt, or that it might be worth at least checking—clearly passed by unheeded, and I am credited within *Screen*'s prestigious pages with an opinion that I regard as extremely stupid and which happens to be the precise opposite of the one I put forward. *Screen*'s hostility to my work (necessary and justified, up to a point, in the days when the magazine was committed to constructing alternatives to primitive auteurism) remains, apparently, unmodified, and I must not expect any just consideration from its contributors.

The relationship (in many respects a close one) between *Rancho Notorious* (1952) and *The Big Heat* (1953) proves the intricate interrelatedness of the Hollywood genres, a further proof of the foolishness of regarding them as discrete and fully autonomous on the grounds of their defining iconography. It also proves, however, that they are not merely interchangeable, that, for all the overlap of themes, character-relations, there remain important distinctions to be made between the two films that are traceable to their generic categories.

First, however, the resemblances. My argument is that (a) in their basic patterns these belong to narrative structures deeply enmeshed in the ideology of western pa- triarchal capitalist culture, but (b) in their particular inflection within the films, they be- long to Lang—the reader is at liberty (is indeed encouraged) to see in this assertion a succinct restatement of auteurist principle.

1. "Good" Woman/ "Bad" Woman

At the heart of both films is our culture's archetypal, fundamental, binary opposition of women: on the one hand "good"—chaste-virgin-wife-mother; on the other "bad"— sexual-immoral-whore: an opposition that, as we know, echoes back through the his- tory of patriarchy, crosses all the Hollywood genres, and founds the structure of literally thousands of our films. *Rancho Notorious* and *The Big Heat* are marked off, how- ever, by a complex of specific inflections.

a. The "good" woman is violently killed, in an act of extreme brutality, near the be- ginning of each film. There are differences: Beth/Gloria Henry is the hero's fiancee, Katie/Jocelyn Brando is the hero's wife; the former is deliberately raped and mur- dered, the latter killed by a bomb intended for her husband (and at a point con- siderably later in the film). But in both cases the death provides the pretext and impetus for the film's major action and the hero's motivation.

b. The "good" woman is never replaced, neither film moving towards the restora- tion of the "good couple"; there is no one with whom the hero can settle down and re-establish the domesticity that was so brutally shattered. Again there is an important difference, the index of the wider differences between the two films: the hero of *The Big Heat* has a young daughter, so that some degree of continuity and domestic stability (however incomplete) is guaranteed.

c. The "bad" woman moves to the centre of the narrative. At this point it becomes necessary to qualify the term "bad woman" which is in certain respects mislead- ing here. Both Altar/Marlene Dietrich and Debbie/Gloria Grahame are involved in criminality (the former centrally, the latter marginally—for her "complicit" might be a better word than "involved") but both differ markedly from the archetypal femme fatale of film noir, an archetype whose range one might define by reference to the Rita Hayworth of *The Lady From Shanghai,* the Joan Bennett of *Scarlet Street* and the Jane Greer of *Out of the Past,* all three characters being crucially revealed as betrayers, as consistently unreliable and when necessary for their own ends treacherous. Altar shares one major characteristic with the typical noir woman: the acquisition (whether attempted or realized, but in either case central to her motivation) of power in the form of money. Debbie does not even have that, being a mere "kept woman" with no more power than a plaything and little apparent de- sire for it (beyond a pleasure in expensive clothes and other gifts).

d. In the course of the film, each woman falls (genuinely) in love with the hero, commits herself to him, and is morally redeemed by this. The "redemption" is, as we shall see, not without its bitter irony, and its function is not to convert her into her opposite, the "good woman, or make her a possible marriage partner for the hero. We might say that she reverses the typical trajectory of the noir woman but is cruelly subjected to a similar fate. The noir woman initially commits herself to the male protagonist, but this proves to be ambiguous (in *Scarlet Street*, not even that): she is constantly ready to manipulate and betray him, and her death is a punishment for her duplicity. Altar and Debbie begin in the criminal world, gradually learn to commit themselves to the male protagonists (whom they perceive as figures of superior morality and purity) and their deaths are the direct consequence of that commitment.

e. The woman's commitment to the hero necessitates that she disengage herself from a prior relationship with another man, a representative of the criminal world which, for the hero's sake, she has decided to repudiate. Again, the difference between the films is as important as the parallel. Frenchy/Mel Ferrer is genuinely in love with Altar, indulges in wild romantic gestures for her sake (risking his life to get her perfume), and is accorded the status of the romantic outlaw-hero (though this, like every other apparent "positive" presented within the film, is rigorously undercut). Altar's commitment to the hero, then, links her again to the noir woman as it is experienced as a sort of betrayal, though a very different sort as it is not motivated by the desire for power/money (rather the reverse—Altar will lose her status and prestige by leaving the gang). Vince/Lee Marvin, on the other hand, is a brutal, violent psychopath with no redeeming features whatever, and Debbie is not so much "betraying" him as getting her just revenge for her disfigurement at his hands.

2. The Revenge Hero

"Hate, murder and revenge"—the refrain of the "Ballad of Chuck-a-Luck" that runs through *Rancho Notorious* as Brechtian commentary—has been taken as a kind of motto for Lang's work; certainly, it points to a preoccupation that recurs throughout it, from *Kriemhild's Revenge* (1924) to *Der Tiger von Eschnapur* (1959) and seems particularly prominent in the American period (e.g. besides two films discussed here, *Fury, The Return of Frank James, Scarlet Street, Man Hunt,* and even *The Blue Gardenia* in which, while revenge is not the central concern, it turns out to be the motivation for the murder in the culminating revelation). The theme and its most obvious message (that revenge, however apparently justified by moral outrage, eventually destroys the soul of the avenger) is by no means unique to Lang: the western offers dozens of examples *(Winchester 73, The Searchers, Nevada Smith...)*, and there are many more within film noir, the gangster genre, and the "ultra-violence" horror film *(Witchfinder General, Last House on the Left)*. One specifically Langian inflection is suggested by the ballad itself:

its association of "Hate, murder and revenge" with "the gambler's wheel," "the Wheel of Fate." I shall return to Lang's preoccupation with "Fate" later. What particularly connects *Rancho Notorious* and *The Big Heat* is the way in which Lang pinpoints the revenge hero's moral decline in his treatment of women: if Lang is one of the cinema's strictest and most uncompromising moralists, the highly idiosyncratic and subversive nature of his moral sense receives here a defining embodiment. Lang was able to pursue this theme far more rigorously and unambiguously in *Rancho Notorious* than in *The Big Heat*.

3. The Gang and the Law

Law and outlawry are essential components of most westerns and all gangster films. Lang's are not the only films that place the hero in an ambiguous position between them (or against both), but the narrative strategy is central to the projects of both films. The difference here is crucial: Vern/Arthur Kennedy never aligns himself with the Law; Bannion/Glenn Ford is (at the beginning and end of the film, though not throughout its middle) himself, as a policeman, a representative of the Law. Both films, of course, operate within the venerable and still potent (e.g. *Cruising, Year of the Dragon,* DePalma's *Scarface*) tradition that presents the law and outlawry in terms of either interchangeability, complicity, or both.

It is expedient at this point to return to my opening remarks about genre. *Rancho Notorious* and *The Big Heat* share the same structure; the differences between them largely are dependent on the genres to which they belong. "Dependent on" rather than "determined by": it is necessary to insist on the distinction, in these days when the author is denied not only intention but intelligence, reduced to (Stephen Heath's phrase) "an effect of the text." The genres may well have a determining influence on the work of commercial hacks; for an artist like Lang they not so much "determine" what he does as offer specific possibilities for his use (which of course also implies limitations).

There are numerous period films with noir elements (a phenomenon made possible by the ambiguous nature of film noir, occupying an indeterminate space between a style and a genre); the typical film noir—those fully embodying what we think of as the noir world—is strictly contemporary. A Hollywood movie can suggest that certain aspects of contemporary society are in need of reform; if it wishes to go beyond that and attack its basic structures and premise, it has to proceed with much caution and circumspection, covering itself by means of ambiguity and deviousness. Lang's problem with *The Big Heat* (supposing that at some level, conscious or unconscious, he had the intention of producing a radical critique of patriarchal capitalism—and the prior instance of *Rancho Notorious* seems to confirm that such an intention existed) was compounded by the nature of the material: organized crime vs. the law, with a policeman as protagonist. A western, on the other hand, is (allowing for the intermittent attempts at "modern" westerns like *Lonely Are the Brave*) by definition a period film. But it is also, potentially, more than that: despite the costumes, it can become in some hands virtually *period-less*. I would distinguish roughly here between the historical western and the stylized western—while acknowledging that most examples of the genre contain elements of both. The former (one thinks at once of Ford) is (while not necessarily committed to historical "fact") deeply involved in a sense of the American past which may of course be largely mythical. But the genre, as it evolved, developed an iconography and set of conventions and stereotypes that can be used as more or less neutralized "counters" through which a filmmaker can express a personal thematic that has little or nothing to do with "period" or "history." If *Drums Along the Mohawk* and *Fort Apache* are the closest to "pure" examples of the former category, *Rancho Notorious* is an unusually pure example of the latter. (Anthony Mann's westerns are perhaps the clearest instance of a "middle ground" between the two.)

Most of us have a general sense of the distinction between "realism" and "modernism," despite the fact that both terms are somewhat slippery and no two critics' definitions of either are likely to be identical. Most would probably agree that one defining component of modernism is stylization. One might describe the classical Hollywood cinema (among the most stylized of all art forms) as a modernist cinema that passes itself off as "realist" (and fools most of the people most of the time): we have become so acclimatized to the stylization that we don't (or are not supposed to) be aware of it. If we accept Colin McCabe's definition of the "classical realist text" (which includes everything from Tolstoy to Donald Duck), then *The Big Heat* and *Rancho Notorious* both fall within this elastic category. It seems to me, however, worthwhile to make distinctions, and it seems meaningful to assert that (given the Hollywood film's pervasive modernist/realist dichotomy), *Rancho Notorious* belongs more to modernism and *The Big Heat* more to realism.

I must at once forestall a possible misunderstanding of what is to follow: it may well appear that I am valuing *Rancho Notorious* over *Heat* because (as a—relatively—modernist film) it is the more ideologically pure. I think the last clause is true but valuation does not follow from it. I see *Rancho* as a Brechtian parable about patriarchal capitalist culture, *Heat* as a complex and contradictory realist/psychological drama with fascinating subversive implications. For me the greater "purity" of the former is bought at a certain cost, to define which would require words like "richness" and "complexity." I want to make it explicit here, then, that I am not preferring one film over the other, although the primary purpose of this article is to celebrate *Rancho's* remarkable—perhaps unique—achievement. I would add also that I find the obviously "modernist" elements of *Rancho* (the painted backdrops, the ballad, the use of deliberately "corny" images like the fire that blazes up when Altar and Frenchy are reunited) somewhat awkward and uneasy, though they contribute so much of the film's interest: the awkwardness is clearly a product of Hollywood's overall commitment to "realism" and the difficulty of incorporating obtrusively Brechtian elements in a "classical realist text."

The difference of mode between the two films is analyzable within every aspect of the common structure outlined above. We may begin with presentation in each of the "good" woman and the value of domesticity. *Heat,* committed to psychological real-ism, offers us a series of domestic scenes for husband, wife and daughter. We may find the marital relationship a trifle precious, cozy, and superficial, but it is easy (with our conditioning in the conventions of Hollywood representation) to accept it as "typical," and sanctioned by the familiar values of American family life. We may also feel invited to perceive (a) the precariousness of this "perfect" family life, surrounded by the vio-lence and corruption of a very powerful and threatening outside world (the obsceni-ties over the phone by which Mrs. Bannion is so shocked and disturbed), so that domestic security, the sanctity of the home, may come to seem something of an illu-sion and (b) the ironic reflection of the family values of the Bannions in the family val-ues of the Laganas (both foreground the devotion of a father to his daughter). But nothing compels us to accept this invitation even if we become aware that the film is offering it.

To move from this back to *Rancho* is to receive an object lesson in Brecht's distinc-tion between representation and presentation, a distinction that might be roughly summed up as that between saying "This is the way things are" and saying "*Look* at the way things are." The distinction becomes extremely problematic with regard to a styl-ized/realist medium like the classical Hollywood cinema, where scenes may slip subtly from one to the other and where many moments may operate on a borderline be-tween the two: *The Big Heat* itself would provide many examples, of which I shall cite but one, the close-up of Debbie just before she dies. Her head is cushioned by her mink coat, her right profile presented to the camera, so that the image resembles that of a posed fashion model from a glossy magazine. We know, of course, not only that she is dying, but that the concealed side of her face is hideously disfigured, and the fur coat has been established earlier as the reward for prostitution. The whole notion of "glam-our" is foregrounded and undercut. *Rancho* opens with the close-up of a romantic kiss, without benefit of their situation. In the ensuing scene we learn that the couple are en-gaged but will have to wait for eight years before they can afford their ranch. The woman has thought of the perfect name for it: "Lost Cloud Ranch"; the man responds by pinning on her a somewhat gaudy brooch which he has been assured comes from "Paris, France." If in *Heat* domestic security can be felt to be *represented* as illusion here it is unambiguously *presented* as illusion. More: the illusoriness not only colours the do-mestic bliss of the future but the romantic love of the present—a romantic love whose emblems are a lost cloud and a piece of false jewelry, and which can exist and be be-lieved in only outside of any reference to present social reality. (Douglas Pye discusses a similar treatment of romantic love in his article on *The Blue Gardenia*.)

The deaths of the two women in their respective films are perhaps equally devas-tating (it is crucial to Lang's purpose that our sense of outrage should initially mirror and validate the hero's). But the actual effect and the means by which it is achieved are very different. The death of Katie has behind it our knowledge of the character and a fairly detailed, "realist" depiction of the marriage which, whatever criticisms of it we may feel to be implied (complacency, conventionality, a slight sense of familial self-congratulation), seems attractive in its stability, in the couple's mutual supportiveness

and their open affection, for each other and for the child. The death also has an immediate dramatic context that heightens its shock by contrast: as Katie goes out to start
the car, Bannion is telling their daughter her bedtime story ("The three little kittens
who lost their mittens"). The scene threatens to become cloying in its sweetness and
its sentimental appeal—at which moment comes the explosion that kills and shatters
Bannion's domestic security forever.

Given the extreme conventionalization of the character, the brief screen time allot-
ted her, and the drastic undercutting of the ideology of romantic love, Lang has no opportunity (if he had wanted one) of providing Beth's death in *Rancho* with an
equivalent context. Instead the sense of outrage is evoked by a single extraordinary
image: Beth, kneeling before Kinch and staring up at him with a look of supplication as
she holds open the door of the safe. Up to that point, Kinch has been interested only
in the availability of money; it is the (completely innocent) suggestion of sexual invitation that immediately precipitates the rape.

The greater ruthlessness of Lang's treatment of the revenge hero in *Rancho* is made
possible by two factors, of which genre is prime and casting secondary. Arthur
Kennedy never achieved permanent "star" status, hovering for most of his career
somewhere between second male lead and character actor: he could play villains (*The
Man from Laramie*) or moral weaklings (*The Lusty Men*) as readily as heroes. Glenn Ford
was another matter: his star image was fairly consistently centred on notions of "nice-
ness," decency and moral integrity. It is perfectly possible to sit through *The Big Heat*
without questioning the hero's actions and motivations. Besides the casting, of course,
there is the question of Bannion's relation to the police force and the relation of the
police to America's national image. Here, as I suggested earlier, one cannot go too far.
The film opts (out) for a liberal-populist compromise: the higher echelons of the police force are corrupt, complicit with "dirty" capital and criminality, but the "ordinary
guys" (who initially chickened out) come through, and Bannion, forced out of the official Law to "go it on his own," is finally exonerated and reinstated.

Far more interesting is what the film does with Bannion as "revenge hero." It is important for the film's compromise position on America that his motivation is ambiguous quite unlike Vern in *Rancho,* he is introduced at the outset as a disinterested
crusader, without personal motivation, determined to contribute to the collapse of
organized crime. The personal motivation creeps in with the obscene phone call, and
becomes dominant with his wife's death, but the disinterested crusader element is always there: he can remain throughout a "hero" in the full sense, not just the sense
that has become synonymous with "male protagonist." But Lang subtly undercuts this.
When Debbie, her face disfigured by Vince's boiling coffee, seeks refuge in his hotel
room, he explains to her (a) that everything now depends on Bertha Duncan's death
(her letter spilling all the dirt is to be opened on her death) and (b) that he cannot
possibly shoot her himself (because he still sees himself as a cop, because he has been
a good husband and father, because he must remain the hero of the movie, because
he is Glenn Ford). He then leaves Debbie a gun with which to defend herself. She
takes the hint.

The audience, however, doesn't necessarily have to. If Bannion gives Debbie the gun so that she can shoot Bertha Duncan for him, we must assume that this motivation is unconscious (though perhaps not too far beneath the surface). The naïve spectator (and Glenn Ford fan?) needs make no connection between the gift of the gun and what Debbie does with it—it is perfectly reasonable for him to leave it with her for her own safety, and the decision and initiative are all hers. But if one reads the film carefully it is clear not only that Debbie risks (and loses) her life for Bannion but that he subtly encourages her to do so (her disfigurement, already, was the direct result of her contact with him). Her death, from his viewpoint, is more than merely convenient—it is necessary. He can sentimentalize over her as she dies, but (to put it brutally) he won't have to be embarrassed by any expectations she may have formed. The film can then rise to the complex irony of Bannion's (and its own) last line: "Keep the coffee hot."

The stylization and schematization made available by the western permits Lang in *Rancho* to expose nakedly what in *Heat* is covered and rendered ambiguous. From the moment of his discovery of Beth's death and its circumstances, the obsessiveness of Vern's question is underlined, and the film charts his progressive dehumanization. Two factors can be felt to contribute to the intensity of Vern's outrage: the idealized, illusory nature of the relationship (the loss of an illusion is always the most difficult to get over, as the illusion is essentially a part of one's inner self, product of the "ideal ego"); and the fact, guaranteed by generic convention, that Beth is a virgin (Kinch has had what Vern will never have). If Lang makes it possible to sit through *Heat* without ever questioning Bannion's moral rightness, he begins the process of alienating us from Vern very early in *Rancho*. I am thinking of the scene where Vern forces information from the dying Whitey by withholding water from him. Some might want to justify this in terms of "seeing things realistically": it is the only recourse Vern has if he is to learn what he needs to know before Whitey dies. But the reason the moment jars so gratingly on most sensibilities has more to do with generic convention than "being realistic": this is simply not the way a western hero behaves. Lang underlines the point by having Whitey, after he divulges the name "Chuck-a-Luck," die before Vern can give him the water that might have eased his last moments: the "hero" is not let off the hook.

But our ultimate revulsion from Vern is provoked by his treatment of Altar. Unlike Bannion with Debbie, it is clear that Vern encourages Altar to fall in love with him, as a means of manipulating and using her. The climactic moment of their relationship, when Altar, in the middle of what she has been led to expect as a tender love scene, inadvertently reveals that Kinch was the rapist/murderer of Vern's fiancee, is marked by one of Lang's bitterest and most disturbing ironies: Vern's gesture in savagely ripping off the brooch (the one from "Paris, France") from Altar's dress echoes Kinch's violation of Beth. Altar, of course, is not Beth. Neither is she Debbie: there are important distinctions to be made. Beth is "pure," Debbie is "innocent," Altar is neither. Debbie's innocence is compromised (she might be seen as a midpoint between Beth and Altar); she the kept woman of a hoodlum. What she is "innocent" of, in the first part of the film, is moral sense: her moral sense is awakened by Bannion, and the awakening leads first to her disfigurement, finally to her death. If Altar has preserved any innocence whatever, it is a very dubious commodity: she doesn't know how her gang acquire so much cattle and money, what acts they perform to get it, because she *chooses* not to know, insisting that such things are not mentioned within the fences of Chuck-a-Luck. She is also, unlike Debbie, a woman of power, although (because she is a woman) her power is always precarious, its foundation (sexual allure) unstable (she is entering middle age).

This does not exhaust the comparisons between the two films, but I find it convenient at this point to abandon systematic comparisons in favor of exploring *Rancho Notorious* from a number of loosely connected angles: hopefully, this will illuminate the film without seeming to reduce it to a single coherent, "definitive" reading (such a reading is always a matter of "seeming").

4. Lang, Dietrich, and Brecht

One might reasonably claim *Rancho* as the most Brechtian film ever to be made in Hollywood (in some obvious ways and others less obvious but more important). The connection between Lang and Brecht is a matter of fact and well documented. Lang actually brought Brecht to Hollywood to collaborate on *Hangmen Also Die* (with heavily qualified success: all the more extreme Brechtian elements were eliminated from the film). I know of no evidence connecting Dietrich and Brecht, or Brecht and Sternberg (Brecht is not mentioned in *Fun in a Chinese Laundry*), but even if no direct, factual connection exists one can still argue for the Brechtian nature of the Sternberg/Dietrich collaborations. It is quite possible that Sternberg reached a very similar aesthetic by an entirely different route; yet his interest in, and cinematic appropriation of, German culture is well known (it seems that the influence of Expressionism on his films has been as exaggerated by critics as the "influence"—from whatever source—of Brechtian practice has been neglected). As for Dietrich, her artistic development took place within the same environment and period as Brecht's: she was appearing in Berlin cabaret (and in German movies, e.g. *Joyless Street*) prior to Sternberg's "discovery" of her. A film such as *Blonde Venus* strikes me as exemplary of the possibility of a Brechtian Hollywood cinema: each of the roles through which Dietrich passes, from water-nymph in a "lesbian" Garden of Eden, through housewife, night-club star, mistress, fugitive mother, prostitute, human icicle, is "presented" rather than represented, the object being the foregrounding of male construction and the woman's resistance to it. Dietrich's performance style is itself Brechtian: as Marina Vlady tells us at the beginning of *Deux ou Trois Choses que Je Sais d'Elle*, Brecht said that actors should speak as if they were quoting. Hawks and Sternberg have both laid claim to the brilliant inspiration of dressing Dietrich in male attire for her first stage appearance in *Morocco*; but it is on record (there are photographs to prove it) that she was already wearing men's clothes in her cabaret performances prior to *The Blue Angel*. Her appropriation of the signifiers of male domination seems to me to have very little do with fetishization and everything to do with a Brechtian "presentation" of the social construction of gender.

I have suggested already that Hollywood "realism" resists the incorporation of the more obvious—I think superficial—elements of Brechtian practice. The painted back-drops of *Rancho* (which Lang in any case repudiates, attributing them to budget re-strictions) are more distracting than distancing, though the ballad (which almost became a western convention—witness *High Noon,* made later the same year) works well enough, fulfilling its Brechtian function of reducing suspense and emotional in-volvement and concentrating the spectator's analytical intelligence by telling us what is going to happen in advance of the event. The fundamental Brechtian principles, on the other hand—distancing the spectator, the refusal of identification, the encourage-ment of analysis, use of interruption and contradiction—are by no means incompati-ble with classical Hollywood Cinema, of which developed techniques and conventions offer themselves readily to Brechtian appropriation. I think it can be argued that, with the Sternberg/Dietrich films as forerunner, an ideal of Brechtian cinema came closer to being realized in the Hollywood of the 1940's and early 50's than has ever been ac-knowledged, notably in the work of European emigres—Lang, Sirk, Preminger, even Ophuls. (Whether Brecht would have acknowledged it is another matter). Many crit-ics have explored this in the melodramas of Sirk, but the rigorous refusal of identifica-tion in the films noirs of Preminger seem equally relevant here (see Richard Lippe's article on *Angel Face* in this issue for a development of this). Ophuls is a more compli-cated case, but his characteristic and pervasive irony can associate quite easily with Brechtian principles of presentation and distance. The last scene of *The Reckless Mo-ment* is exemplary: the carefully composed ("staged") family group around the tele-phone; the son, his resistance to bourgeois cleanliness and decorum vanquished, in an adult-style suit; the daughter inheriting her mother's fur coat (established earlier in the film as the reward for services rendered interchangeably of housewife and pros-titute); the camera lowering to frame Mrs. Harper, acquiescing once again in her do-mestic imprisonment, behind the bars of the banisters.

Distanciation, interruption and the refusal of identification are Lang's guiding prin-ciples throughout *Rancho.* Identification with its most obvious magnet, the male pro-tagonist, is, as I have suggested, undermined very early in the film and completely lost as it progresses: by the end, he is probably for most viewers the least sympathetic of all the leading characters. Altar is consistently "presented" throughout: the flashbacks, discontinuous fragments, that recount something of her past, constitute a series of Brechtian "gests" foregrounding issues of money and gender rather than establishing her as any sort of identification figure. The film could have built Frenchy Fairmont/Mel Ferrer as a romantic outlaw-hero, but conspicuously rejects the possibility: his sense of his age, and fear of his loss of prowess (and of Altar), undercuts the convention of such a character's automatic charisma.

The strategy of distanciation—its means and its function—can be analyzed very precisely in Lang's treatment of Altar's song, "Get away, young man, get away." Distan-

ciation ("alienation," as Brecht's *verfremdungseffekt* has traditionally been rendered—
the principle of "making the familiar strange") is concerned not with the puritanical
denial of pleasure (as is often assumed) but with something much more complex: the
simultaneous experiencing of pleasure and awareness of it, so that its premise and
sources are called into question. The song is clearly there because this is a Dietrich
movie and the audience will wish to have her perform. Lang at once permits and frus-
trates our satisfaction. Dietrich exerts her customary fascination, but any simple, un-
interrupted pleasure is heavily qualified: as she sings, Vern recognizes the brooch that
was torn from Beth's dress when she was raped and murdered. Lang then gives us a
series of quasi point-of-view shots (they are too close to be literal POV) as Vern stares
at the other men trying to decide (granted his first concrete evidence) which of them
is the killer. Pleasure in Dietrich's performance is countered by another form of cinematic pleasure, suspense, the two jarring discordantly. But this second pleasure is also
undercut: if we have been sufficiently observant, we (unlike Vern) know that the killer
is Kinch. We are forced to share the hysteria of Vern's agonized and penetrating gaze,
but cannot identify with it, as we already know what he is trying to find out. The dis-
cords on which the sequence is composed jar us into awareness of: (a) Dietrich's status as performer, both diegetically and extra-diegetically the aging woman continuing
to sing erotic and seductive "numbers" addressing the "young man"; (b) the obsessiveness of Vern's revenge drive, which we are forced to share (through the POV shots)
yet cannot share; and (c) (perhaps) the mechanisms of Hollywood convention itself,
through the collision of incompatible conventions.

5. Dietrich's Star Image

Some years ago, in an article on *Blonde Venus* (*Film Comment,* March–April 1978), I suggested that the "meaning" of Dietrich as star could be summed up in a question: "How
does a woman assert herself in a male-constructed and male-dominated culture?" The
formula is of course too simple, too non-specific: it could apply almost equally to Davis
or Crawford, for example. Yet I think it has a special resonance in reference to Dietrich: the Sternberg films, in particular, are more single-mindedly, more explicitly, more
consistently, and finally more bitterly (culminating in the heartbreaking alienation of
The Devil Is a Woman) about that than one can trace through the careers of Crawford
or Davis: perhaps because the theme is foregrounded through Dietrich's Brechtian
performance-style and Sternberg's Brechtian distanciation.

Lang said of *Rancho,* "It was conceived for Dietrich... I wanted to write a picture
about an aging (but still desirable) dance hall girl and an old gun hand, who is not so
good on the draw anymore. So I constructed this story," (in the Peter Bogdanovich interview-book, *Fritz Lang in America,* Praeger, 1969). As a Dietrich vehicle, *Rancho* takes
up (again with Brechtian foregrounding—the flashbacks) the theme that I have suggested and proceeds to adapt it to the fact that Dietrich was now 20 years older: Altar
has achieved power, in a man's world and on men's terms, in the form of money,

through the use of her sexual charisma, but the stability of her situation is becoming increasingly precarious. Lang describes his problems with Dietrich: "Now Marlene resented going gracefully into a little, tiny bit older category; she became younger and younger until finally it was hopeless." And later: "She was still very much under the influence of Sternberg. She would say, 'Oh, look, Sternberg would have done so and so.' 'Well,' I said, 'but I am Lang.'" It wasn't hopeless: one can watch the battle on the set being fought within the finished film and Lang won. The more makeup Dietrich applies, the harsher, more unmerciful, and more anti-Sternbergian becomes Lang's lighting, so that one is aware throughout of an aging woman trying to look much younger than her age, greatly increasing the character's (and the film's) poignancy.

6. Money, Dirt and Purity

Freud, followed by (among others) Norman O. Brown, noted an intimate psychoanalytical association between money (originally gold: see Aesop's fable about the donkey that could shit gold coins) and excrement: money as the "dirt" of capitalism. Brown cites the phrase "filthy lucre" as an unconscious acknowledgement of the connection. Even more resonant (though more localized, as far as I have been able to determine) seems to be the euphemism employed for the act of shitting in the British middle-class milieu in which I grew up in the '30's: "Doing one's business" (rather charmingly abridged, within my own family, to the succinct "biz," as in "showbiz"). One may also adduce a familiar and seemingly permanent graffito on a Toronto wall: KAKAPIPITAL-ISM. This is why money matters were not discussed in the Victorian home: the "dirt" of "business" must not sully the purity of the family. One thinks of Bannion's unsuccessful efforts in The Big Heat to preserve his domestic purity from the contamination of organized crime, or of the invasion of blackmail into the Harper household of The Reckless Moment (at Christmas-time, no less), as against Mrs. Harper's obsession with cleanliness. The impossibility of purity in a world dominated by money values is a leading concern of Rancho Notorious. At the outset, the realization of the (illusion of) romantic love is shown to be dependent on eight years of saving; and for Kinch, Beth's holding open of the safe door instantly identifies one form of lust with another.

But the theme is developed most extensively through Altar (whose name, in association with her moral situation, inevitably evokes a notion of an artificially constructed, false purity). There is a remarkable juxtaposition of images (one verbal, one visual) in an early flashback, that can stand as another marvelous instance of Brechtian "presentation": as Frenchy, after their first meeting in the gambling house, escorts Altar to her hotel, he tells her how he once saw her ride up a staircase on a white horse; as he speaks, Altar steps down from the boardwalk into ankle-deep mud. Altar's whole life (as I suggested earlier) is built upon a false purity, an attempt to deny contamination: she both knows and doesn't know that her position as owner-manager of Chuck-a-Luck, secret hideaway of a gang of outlaws, involves her in complicity with robbery and murder, and that the money she claims as her cut is as "dirty" as money can be.

7. Lang and "Fate"

"Fate" is taken to be a common theme of Lang's cinema, and what finally links his American films to German Expressionism. The concept of Fate in Expressionist cinema (and in the American noir films it influenced) is not monolithic, but it can often appear as a metaphysical principle, a pessimistic apprehension of an inescapable and inexplicable doom before which the protagonist can only prostrate him/herself: from this viewpoint Nosferatu is a key text (Murnau's vampire can certainly be explained psychoanalytically but that is another matter). Already in his later German films (M, for instance), Fate for Lang is becoming more a matter of social mechanism than of metaphysical principle: the individual is still trapped and ultimately helpless, but the entrapment can be subjected to analysis and explained. If the protagonist is trapped, the spectator is set free: a central principle of Lang's American films, and one that absolutely demands distanciation and the refusal of identification as the prerequisites of its realization. Here, "Fate" is the end result of a set of interacting social conditions/ideological assumptions and the men whose actions are determined by them (women are, by and large, its victims rather than its agents).

The "Ballad of Chuck-a-Luck," over the opening credits, identifies the "gambler's wheel" as "the Wheel of Fate," Lang comments on this in one of the early flashbacks, when he reveals that the Chuck-a-Luck wheel in the saloon is controlled, not by metaphysical principle, but by the foot of the owner's henchmen. "Fate" in Rancho Notorious—the Fate that destroys all the significant characters, without exception—is constructed by the ideological assumptions of patriarchal capitalist society: idealized romantic love, the revenge drive, the greed for money: in short, by the whole dichotomy of illusory purity and dirt that characterizes our culture.

8. Lang as Radical Moralist

The preceding commentary will have suggested that, if Lang is the Hollywood's cinema's most rigorous moralist, the moral system embodied in his work is far removed from that of capitalist orthodoxy. What is ultimately denounced in the films as immoral is patriarchal capitalism itself—the "Fate" that traps and destroys the characters and makes successful human relationships impossible. This must not, however, be seen as offering the characters some kind of general exoneration: Lang's view of Fate, I have argued, is by no means naively deterministic. If his characters are trapped, it is partly by their own actions and their own decisions, and they are viewed as having at least a relative moral responsibility for these.

While never being permitted to become identification-figures, Altar and Debbie—unarguably, I think—are the emotional centres of their respective films. This happens for two reasons: (a) because they are women; (b) because they are morally redeemed by their love for the hero. The former is relatively unproblematic: as women, born into and kept in a subordinate position, we cannot attribute to them the moral responsibility which the men—victims of ideology yet also its agents—cannot entirely evade. Neither woman is in the least sentimentalized (in particular, Altar's complicity with crime, the fact that she in a sense condones, say, the rape and murder of Beth by refusing to know about such things, is held by Lang in very sharp focus), but the sense that they are more victims than agents (even Altar, with her assumption of power) is never lost sight of. The moral redemption is another matter, the locus of Lang's bitterest irony: in both cases, the woman is morally redeemed by falling in love with a man whom she perceives as her moral superior when in fact he is using her in the most opportunistic manner for his own ends, and in both cases she dies for what is simultaneously her moral salvation and her fatal misunderstanding. The corollary of this is that, as the woman becomes the film's emotional centre, the morally righteous (from the conventional viewpoint) hero becomes its most reprehensible character. Not true, of course, of *The Big Heat:* Bannion, however, compromised, retains something of the charisma of the disinterested crusader against organized crime, and while it is possible by the end of *Rancho* to prefer even Kinch to Vern, one can scarcely find Bannion morally inferior to Vince or Lagana. But it is entirely true of Vern, whose treatment of Altar is mercilessly exposed by Lang in all its ugliness. He is even denied the hero's privilege of the generically guaranteed successful showdown with Kinch.

9. The Ending

The end of *Rancho Notorious* fully confirms our sense of the film's ruthless, almost schematic logic. It is an extreme example of closure (certainly closure has never been so complete), but not the kind to which the Hollywood cinema has accustomed us: no happy ending, no formation or restoration of the heterosexual couple. In fact, no survivors: the mechanisms of "Fate" that Lang has analyzed culminate in the deaths of all the principal characters. I have found that many people miss this (perhaps because they are reaching for their coats, perhaps because they can't believe their ears), but the final verse of the ballad is quite unambiguous about it: the two men who ride away from Chuck-a-Luck die under a hail of bullets before the day is over.

10. Lang as Closet Marxist

Lang's politics, as expressed in the Bogdanovich interview-book, seem to have been, on the level of "intentional" utterance, hopelessly confused: a melange of vague metaphysical assumptions about "the human condition" and equally vague "liberal" sentiments. But "never trust the artist—trust the tale": the best of his American films come as close to being Marxist deconstructions of capitalism as has ever been possible within the Hollywood cinema. One might point here to Lang's succinct summation of American politics: when Vern first meets Frenchy in jail, the next cell is occupied by the leaders of the Law and Order party, jailed for corruption in the current election and expecting any moment to be lynched by the opposition. The films cannot of course go further: they cannot propose a Marxist alternative. Lang was blacklisted, but only briefly. The ultimate irony is that, throughout the McCarthy period, he continued steadily to produce movies that are far more devastating and radical critiques of American capitalism than the "socially conscious" works of the major victims of Mc-Carthyism, and that this went apparently unnoticed despite his known associations with Brecht: "Entertainment" is a wonderful and indispensable cover.

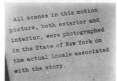

The Noir Title Sequence

Robert Porfirio

The accompanying pages of stills provide some illustration of the important development of the credit title sequence throughout the noir cycle. They are presented here to support my assertion, that the film noir was the primary avenue of transition between the conventional graphics of the studio style and the highly conceptualized, diegetically integrated graphics of the contemporary cinema. I have selected the following examples to indicate the cycle's progression from rather standardized studio graphics to those diegetically related superimpositions which culminated as links in a proairetic chain. During the course of my analysis I also hope to illustrate another assertion, namely that in certain instances these credit sequences can be used as hermeneutic guides to the body of the film.

Figure 1 (*The Maltese Falcon*, 1941). This credit sequence looks backward to an older tradition, with Max Steiner's familiar brass fanfare behind the Warner Brothers logographic, followed by relatively conventional studio graphics. Still, this fanfare segues immediately into Adolph Deutch's slightly dissonant overture as the credits are superimposed over a highly expressionistic shot of the same falcon statue present in the film. Its slightly oneiric effect is heightened by the ripple dissolves which punctuate the graphic succession and this connotation carries over into a roll-up prologue which describes the early history of the statue. Thus the deno-

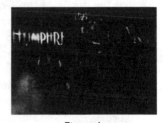

Figure 1

tative authority of a written prologue designed by the director to present the origin of the statue as factual (unlike the novel whose historical source was Casper Gutman) is undermined by the connotative value of its signifiers.

Figure 2 (*Shadow of a Doubt*, 1943). Following the Universal logographic these credits are superimposed over a group of dancers whose "period" costumes mark the action as outside the diegesis. But Dimitri Tiomkin's otherwise perfunctory overture incorporates familiar stanzas from "The Merry Widow Waltz" and the extra-diegetic insertion of both the song and this shot at key points in the narrative become a metaphoric sign of Uncle Charley's covert identity as the "merry widow killer." Moreover, the diegetic use of the song (for example, when Uncle Charley tries to mislead

Figure 2

277

his family as they attempt to identify the tune) extends the enigmatic function of a character whose hostility to older women and bizarre behavior is passed off as the result of a "childhood" accident. Finally, the blurred, slightly distorted rendition of the waltz during the credits also functions as a metonymic sign of Uncle Charley's disturbed psyche.

Figure 3 (*Double Indemnity*, 1944). This film begins with Miklos Rozsa's score immediately behind the Paramount logographic and its major motifs continue through the

Figure 3

credit titles which are superimposed over the shadow of a man on crutches walking toward the camera position. This background is as expressionistic as that in *The Maltese Falcon* but the surface naturalism of the shadow itself (which bears a marked physical resemblance to actor Fred McMurray) makes it a non-diegetic index of Walter Neff's later impersonation of the murdered Mr. Deidrichson. And Rozsa's title score segues quickly into the frenetic background of the film's opening shot (a

car careening through the streets of downtown Los Angeles), suturing the title sequence more closely to the diegesis.

Figure 4 (*Murder, My Sweet*, 1944). The background here is the cycle's first to be extended directly into the diegesis: a bird's eye shot of a table around which are seated Marlowe and some policemen (their figures barely perceptible at the outer edges of the frame), it is part of the décor of the film's opening sequence. The credits are superimposed as the camera moves downward until, with the fading of the last title, the camera is so close to the table that the reflection of the desk light

Figure 4

on its surface completely washes out the frame. This in turn provides the transition for the first shot of the film's introductory sequence which does not, however, carry over Roy Webb's credit title background score.

Figure 5 (*The Spiral Staircase*, 1945). In *The Spiral Staircase*, the credits are finally superimposed over an action which, though not directly linked to the proairetic chain, partakes

Figure 5

of the diegesis in its mixture of motivated and unmotivated signifiers, that in turn provide an important clue to the meaning of the film text. Here the opening emblems of a David O. Selznick Production—the logographic, the fanfare, the "beautiful" shot of the neo-classical building, all marks of a "quality" film since the late 1930's—quickly fade into a nocturnal long shot of a gothic mansion set behind a clump of trees where the motivated noise of a strong wind almost masks the strings of Roy Webb's

score. After the superimposed credits of the film's three stars there is a rapid dissolve to a bird's eye view of the staircase itself, over which are presented the remainder of the credits. Here Webb's subdued score initiates its theremin (whose value as a signifier of suspense had previously been established by Miklos Rozsa) to coincide with the effect of the thunder and the flashes of lightning visible through the window (upper left of frame). The singular action of this shot involves a young girl (Dorothy McGuire) who enters the frame from the lower left corner and begins to descend the staircase, revealing her anxiety by her circumspect manner and a brief attempt to cover her ears with her hands. Since the body of the film begins "elsewhere"—in town, during the day, while the girl, Helen, watches a silent movie—this action is excluded from the proairetic chain. Yet, the care taken to place its action within the diegesis affords us a good opportunity to test the credit sequence's usefulness as a hermeneutic guide to the filmic text. Naively, of course, the staircase itself represents the film's title but the diegesis establishes it as the principal locus of peril for its young heroine, Helen, whose muteness makes her a potential victim of its mysterious killer: it connects the upstairs bedroom of Mrs. Warren (Ethel Barrymore), Helen's enfeebled protectress, with the cellar where a young girl is murdered and a potential rescuer, Steven Warren (Gordon Oliver), is imprisoned; it provides hiding space for the mysterious killer (revealed at length to be Professor Albert Warren [George Brent]) whose presence is indexed by the sinister eye and the sound of the theremin; it is the area where Helen attempts to elude Professor Warren and where he is finally killed by his stepmother. The credit sequence therefore provides the initial conjunction of those elements through which the film text is articulated and which include staircase and girl, girl and storm (Helen's two most critical encounters occur during thunderstorms), theremin and motivated sound, and, most importantly, sound and silence: Helen's muteness prevents her from crying for help, she tries to block out sound by covering her ears, her first narrative action is to watch a silent movie while a girl is being killed in a hotel room upstairs, her reflection in a staircase mirror as perceived by the killer lacks a mouth, and so on.

Figure 6 (*The Unsuspected,* 1947). The title sequence here does not progress the form much as a pair of hands turns the pages of a "script" containing the credits and as Franz Waxman's overture recalls some of Adolph Deutch's motifs for *The Maltese Falcon.* Still, the gloved hands are the metonymic marker of Victor Grandison (Claude Rains), whose radio voice enunciates a key sequence of the film and whose final broadcast identifies himself as "the unsuspected" of the title. In fact, the

Figure 6

diegesis presents Grandison composing his own radio script on various occasions so that the conjunction of hands and "film" script here extends Grandison by metaphor as enunciator of the filmic discourse and stand-in for the film's true "authors."

Figures 7–12 (*The Killers,* 1946). This entry's title sequence is the first wholly "modern" one, for with the exception of Universal's logographic (Figure 7), the credits are superimposed over a visual background that is not only part of the diegesis but directly connected to its proairetic chain: it depicts the approach of the two killers (Charles McGraw and William Conrad) to Brentwood, an action whose consequences include the murder of Ole Anderson, which in turn prompts the remainder of the narrative. It is also significant for a Miklos Rozsa overture that begins immediately on the opening logographic and serves to suture the action of the credit sequences with that

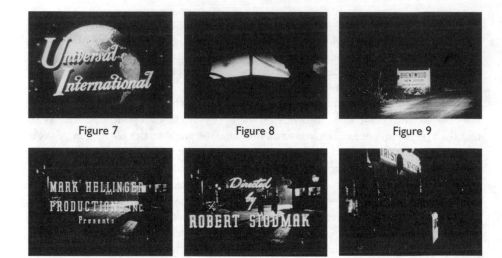

Figure 7   Figure 8   Figure 9

Figure 10   Figure 11   Figure 12

of the main body of the film, where it finally fades out. In double counterpoint with another melody this overture introduces the "killers' theme" which functions as an aural signifier of the killers of the film's title and accrues with narrative progression. Its connotative value here is just beginning since the status of the two men remains uncertain, until later in the opening segment when they identify themselves to Nick Adams and the café's owner. In fact, the first shot of this sequence is a semi-subjective one, from behind the two men in their car (Figure 8) and this is followed by a more purely subjective POV of the advancing highway and a roadside sign announcing their arrival in Brentwood (Figure 9). A dissolve connects this with a more objective shot of the town (Figure 10) during which the two men emerge on foot from behind the diner in the right background and advance toward the left foreground of the frame. The credits are superimposed over this shot as the title music fades in louder until the appearance of the final credit (Figure 11) when it begins to diminish. With the fading of this credit the camera begins to pan left with the killers as they inspect a darkened service station (Figure 12). When they realize it is closed for the evening they move toward the center of the frame, pause for a moment, and then begin to walk toward the lighted diner as the camera pans back right with them before a fade out ends the sequence as they enter. Since the first shot of the body of the film picks up the two men as they enter the diner, there is no break in the proairetic chain.

Figure 13 (*In a Lonely Place*, 1950). Much in the mold established by *The Killers*, the credit sequence here opens immediately on the relatively subjective POV of a nocturnal driver (Humphrey Bogart), his face partially reflected in the rear-view mirror. A portion of the credits are presented over this shot and the remainder over a succeeding shot "out" the car window from a semi-subjective position behind Bogart's back. One indication of the growing tendency towards naturalism is the use here of authentic Los Angeles locales "outside" (probably back-projected) whereas the roadside vista of *The Killers* had been filmed on studio grounds. By 1950, Bogart's established persona lacked much of the ambiguity of the figures of Charles McGraw and William Conrad, who portrayed the two killers at the very start of their film careers, yet the iconic values of his eyes and their framing in the mirror here initiate the ambivalence of his character, Dixon Steele. This ambivalence is articulated further as the credit sequence proceeds into the first scene of the film, bridged by a dissolve and the fading of George An-theil's background score: while paused for a red light

Figure 13

Steele jokes at the expense of an adjoining motorist but when the man reacts badly Steele loses his temper and challenges him to a fight. This ambiguity establishes the enigma which is not resolved until the film's conclusion when Steele is cleared of the suspicion of murder.

Figure 14 (*Kiss Me Deadly*, 1955). The modernism of an opening which underscores the ability of the film noir to direct a naturalistic tendency towards its own expres-

Figure 14

sionistic ends locates *Kiss Me Deadly* at the close of the cycle. Here an important pre-credit sequence dispenses with both company logographic and background score, using only motivated sounds of someone running and panting, the roar of a car, and the squeal of tires behind its visuals: a young girl (Cloris Leachman) clad only in a raincoat and running down a deserted stretch of high-way attempts to wave down Mike Hammer's (Ralph Meeker) sportscar, forcing it off the road. After Hammer angrily orders her into the car and proceeds on his way, the credits are then superimposed over a semi-subjective shot of the highway from behind the two occupants. The only unmotivated element in this sequence is the credits themselves, for the background music (Nat "King" Cole singing "I'd rather have the blues than what I've got") is justified by Hammer's car radio. And even the strained naturalism of their graphic design (they are roll-up titles which must be read "backwards" as if they were signs painted on a highway) will become a fitting analogue for the confused diegetic world ahead. In this location sequence, as in much of the body of the film, a profusion of naturalistic sounds (the noise of a car, the song on the radio, a girl's heavy breathing) and sights (headlights and roadside vistas looming weirdly out of the darkness) create a fabric so dense that it is clear that verisimilitude is not an issue. What is at stake is an ethos to which these early sequences are related in ways too complex to explain here. Let us simply summarize by asserting that the estrangement of familiar surroundings here represents the appropriate milieu for the enigma which advances the narrative and which is posed in the film's opening scene: it is epitomized in the quotation from the Christina Rossetti poem "Remember Me" which the girl, Christina, gives to Hammer as a clue and which takes him finally to the very brink of atomic destruction.

Figures 15 and 16 (*Where the Sidewalk Ends*, 1950). Beginning with *I Wake Up Scream-ing* the noir series at Fox had a veritable matrix for its credit title sequence: credits superimposed over some of sort of urban vista (most often of New York City) and backed by Cyril Mockridge's rearrangement of Alfred Newman's "Street Scene" theme. By 1950 the Fox noir series was in decline and what had been a conventionalized opening for the

Figure 15

Figure 16

urban crime film was now modified and ostensibly modernized. This meant relating the credit sequence more directly to the diegesis and giving its signifiers a more naturalistic rationale. After the traditional fanfare and Fox logographic, star credits and main title here are designed as sidewalk graffiti and presented in linear order while the camera trucks along the sidewalk as if following first one, then another, pair of male legs. The music is nothing more than "someone" whistling the "Street Scene" theme, its intensity increasing as the second pair of legs approaches the edge of the sidewalk and the camera (Figure 15). The theme itself is truncated in the very middle of its third stanza when the legs step off the curb and the camera tilts down, terminating its movements on the dirty water at curbside. Over an aural bridge of environmental ambience a dissolve provides the transition to an establishing shot of a major New York thoroughfare at night, followed by a direct cut to a trucking, medium close up of a police car over which the credits resume (Figure 16). The succession of credits then continues over a montage which effectively "moves" the police car through various New York locations to its destination at precinct headquarters where the credits conclude and its two occupants (soon identified as Mark Dixon [Dana Andrews] and his partner Paul Klein [Bert Freed]) emerge and enter the building. Throughout this montage the sound track presents only the environmental sounds of the traffic and the voice of the police radio dispatcher. One can see here an obvious attempt to bring an "older" convention more in line with a popular police series. But the sequence may also be read as a guide to the text, for the unusual truncation of a familiar melody metonymically "points" to Dixon himself: at the film's conclusion he terminates his career when he reveals to his superior that he has accidentally killed a man and thrown the blame on an innocent party. Ironically, the sidewalk ended for Dixon as it had for his father, a criminal who was shot down in the streets of New York.

Figure 17 (*T-Men*, 1947). Though the graphics here function more as prologue than as credits this frame is included to demonstrate how the title sequence can be used as a signifier of "authenticity." The denotative function of the graphics—warning an implied viewer—is probably less important than the connotative one which insures the complicity of the federal government in the film's production. Since this shot is followed immediately by location shots of Washington D.C. over which can be

Figure 17

heard the "reassuring" voice of an unseen narrator (Reed Hadley), its value as "authenticator" is enhanced by a prologue whose syntagmatic chain culminates with the figure of an actual official of the Treasury Department (Elmer Lincoln Irey) directly addressing the implied viewer.

Figure 18 (*Kiss of Death*, 1947). Although Eleazar Lipsky's original novel, *The Kiss of Death,* claimed to have been based on his experiences with the District Attorney's Office of New York, the producers of the film version make no such claim for their scenario. Instead they use graphics to guarantee the authenticity of their film's settings so that its "realism" is defined in photographic rather than narrative terms. Thus the appellation "semidocumentary" attached to certain films of the noir pe-

Figure 18

riod became more questionable as it was ambiguously applied to include films whose only ostensible connection with reality was the visual "guarantee" of actual locales.

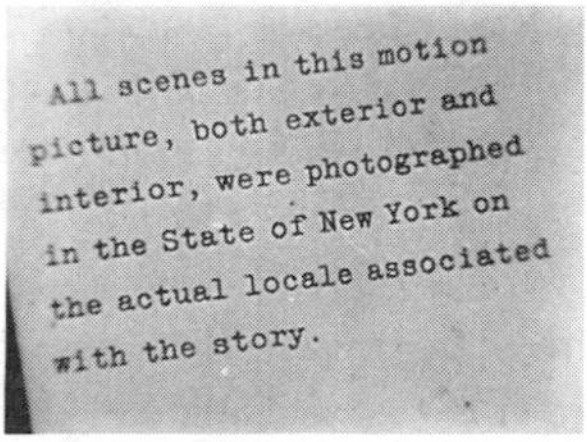

Figure 19 and 20 (*The Naked City,* 1948). Released in March, 1948, and borrowing its title and conceptualized use of the New York locales from Arthur Fellig's book of the

same name, *The Naked City* must be regarded as a major semi-documentary, despite the fact that its story was not based upon a so-called "case study." Rather its authenticity was based on a novel convention: over a series of aerial shots of New York City (see Figure 19) the voice of the producer, Mark Hellinger, identifies himself and some of the film's major contributors (the credit titles themselves do not appear until the end of the film) and proceeds to assure the viewer of the film's uniqueness by virtue of the fact that it was shot entirely on location in New York. Thus, in an unprecedented move for a Hollywood film of that era, a producer used the authority of his voice and position to guarantee the "realism" of a film based upon the naturalism of its settings. This same gesture would be repeated by producer Herbert Leonard in a television series (1958–1960) based on the film that would also conclude with Hellinger's tag line: "There are eight million stories in the naked city,

Figure 19

Figure 20

and this has been one of them" (establishing an important aural convention of authenticity). Certainly, *The Naked City* was unusual for its time in its total avoidance of studio settings, but whatever its claim to "realism" its style and ethos were quite consistent with the noir cycle: all aleatory elements (aural and visual) were rigidly controlled and William Daniels' photography, despite a few simplifications in lighting, displayed a characteristic mannerism and closed form. This adept manipulation of the real is already quite evident in the opening montage which succeeds the aerial shots (and during which the naturalistic noise of the helicopter is displaced by Frank Skinner's subdued background music): a tableau of nocturnal urban vignettes cued by Hellinger's voice-over commentary. This tableau adroitly mixes a series of candid scenes "discovered" by an independently motivated camera (for example, a washerwoman at work, a reporter in a newspaper office, an all-night disc jockey-each one contributing an appropriate voice-over comment) with a few "staged" ones designed to introduce some of the diegetic characters. In fact, the camera seems to be guided in its choices by Hellinger's voice, and as he indicates that one of the city's inhabitants is "at the close of her life" the camera, from its objective position atop a crane, trucks up to an apartment window and from this voyeuristic POV "discovers" two men inside struggling with a woman (Figure 20). A cut to the apartment interior modifies the "candid" objectivity of the previous shots, positions the viewer within the proiaretic chain, and displaces Hellinger's voice with that of the diegetic characters. Finally, the stylized brutality and eroticism of the scene—the two men "finish the job" by placing the girl's body in a tub filling with water—confirms the voyeurism of the camera as well as the position of the viewer within the hermetic world of the film noir.

Figures 21–24 (*Touch of Evil,* 1957). The two and a half minute sequence shot which opens *Touch of Evil* is certainly the most notable credit title sequence of the noir series although Orson Welles himself has denied any intention of placing the credits there. While the graphics seem to fit well enough pictorially (see Figure 22), the action described by the visuals is so complex and integral to the narrative that the frame is overloaded with information, making an intelligible reading of both impossible in a single viewing. Whether or not this confirms Welles' assertion, it places *Touch of Evil* among a small group of contemporary films where the relationship between the credit sequence and the diegesis has been constructed to overwhelm the viewer. In any event, enough has been written on the significance of this opening sequence in posing the "problems" which structure the body of the film text that I hardly think it necessary to demonstrate its hermeneutic value here. Therefore, interpretation will be put aside in favor of a description of its action. Briefly then, a complex trucking shot involving ascending and descending crane movements depicts a man in such a way that is impossible to make out his face, as he sets a time bomb and plants it in the trunk of a car (Figure 21) before running off. An older man and young blonde who emerged from a bar quickly enter the car and drive off, but the height of the camera allows the viewer to keep track of their progress as they make a series of left turns which points the car back towards the camera position. Over this portion of the shot the credits begin, and the camera now trucks backward ahead of the car (Figure 22), staying with it as it turns right and passes a young couple on foot (Charlton Heston and Janet Leigh). The young couple in turn pass the car as it waits in line at the Mexican border station, only to arrive simultaneously with it at the American border station (Figure 23). At this point the

Figure 21   Figure 22   Figure 23

overlapped dialogue identifies Heston as Mike Vargas, a
Mexican official who recently broke up a drug ring, Janet
Leigh as his new wife, Susan, and the older man as Rudy
Linneker, a prosperous American. Vargas and his wife depart first, while the young blonde, who is obviously not
Linneker's wife, keeps complaining of a ticking noise. The
camera follows the car as it departs to pick up the new-
lyweds again and it stays with them as they chat and
start to embrace. Their embrace, however, is interrupted

Figure 24

by the sound of an explosion (Figure 24) which prompts the first cut, a shot of the
burning car. Obviously, a very complicated title sequence, but one that is a fitting epitaph to the noir cycle: the tension engendered by the conjunction of the music (here
a raw, vaguely Mexican jazz piece which might have been inspired, though not precisely
diegetically motivated, by one of the strip-bars) and a nocturnal setting of car and highway places it in a tradition which extends back to *The Killers*, while the baroque use of
naturalistic elements (here the city of Venice, California "doubles" for the Mexican border town) exceeds even that found in the opening of *Kiss Me Deadly*.

The lovers/enemies in *Double Indemnity* (Barbara Stanwyck and Fred MacMurray) about to break out into a witty repartee.

It's Déja Vu All Over Again:
Double Indemnity Resonates with Generation X

Ginny B. Schwartz

Double Indemnity, a 1944 film from the classic noir era, is undergoing a renaissance with 90's movie audiences. Recent articles from popular magazines illustrate this resurgence in popularity. *Newsweek* magazine identified *Double Indemnity* as one of the "Ten Best Noir Rentals," and adds, "Stanwyck burns."[1] In an article about "the ten best films noirs of all time," *Premiere* magazine listed *Double Indemnity* as number 1, because "it's got everything: style, sex, murder.... Who wouldn't kill for Barbara Stanwyck in this one? Even Fred MacMurray did."[2] *Entertainment Weekly's Guide to The Greatest Movies Ever Made* identifies *Double Indemnity* as one of its top 25 Dramas and describes it as

> Grade-A sleaze.... Fred MacMurray has the role of his life as the small-time insurance salesman, and Barbara Stanwyck is all brass and cheap perfume as the bored tootsie that persuades him to kill her husband. It's not the murder that's the meat here; it's the way these two so willingly jump at the chance for moral degradation. A million movies have ripped off the plot, but none of them—not even 1981's *Body Heat*—has captured the original's seamy erotic thrill.[3]

However, this revived interest in *Double Indemnity* goes beyond movie critics and film experts. Perhaps it is more significant that this black and white classic noir, with no special effects and no graphic sex or violence, is very popular with today's college students.

As evidence of this recent interest in film noir, a film noir course has been available to undergraduate college students at a northeastern liberal arts college for the past five years. This course begins with a study of the classic noir films, then uses this knowledge of classic noir as a basis for studying neo-noir films. The class is always filled to capacity with young traditional-aged college students who are very experienced film viewers. They have grown-up watching movies on widely available cable TV movie channels. In their lifetimes, they have always had access to VCRs and video rentals, and they live in the era of the movie multiplex, where several film choices are always available. They watch movies frequently, and movies are an important part of their social life and recreation. Although these students might not be familiar with the classification of neo-noir films, they are familiar with their favorite filmmakers, many of whom are known by film critics for their exceptional neo-noir films. In fact, many "of our most talented young film makers began in the noir mode: the Coen brothers *(Blood Simple)*, Quentin Tarantino *(Reservoir Dogs)*, John Dahl *(Red Rock West)*, and Bryan Singer *(The Usual Suspects)*."[4] Some of these young film buffs are familiar with the term film noir. However, few have seen very many of the black and white classic noir films of the 40s and 50s.

Each year, the students in this film noir class, who are also members of Generation X, put aside their experiences with and expectations for color films, with explicit sex and violence, and stunning special effects, and thoroughly enjoy these classic noir films. One film, which always appears early in the course, is Billy Wilder's 1944 *Double Indemnity*. It is always interesting to see that consistently, year after year, this film gets an incredibly positive response from the students in this course. In fact, in the words of one student, "Of the various noir films that we watched throughout the semester, *Double Indemnity* was definitely my favorite." Additional student comments demonstrate their affection for this film. "Sometimes the best entertainment comes out of something that is out of the ordinary or unexpected, and this can make a movie great. The movie *Double Indemnity,* directed by Billy Wilder is that type of movie. The story line, characters, and mood of the movie are different and they really make you think about what is happening and why." Another student commented, "the type of film that is popular today very often resembles *Double Indemnity*. It does not have typical heroes and villains and it has twisted plots."

These types of comments are not unusual for *Double Indemnity*. It typically emerges as one of the students' favorite films. This preference remains even after the students watch *Body Heat,* a 1980 film that is widely recognized as a remake of *Double Indemnity*. Students virtually always prefer *Double Indemnity* to *Body Heat*. This comes as a surprise, particularly given the fact that *Body Heat* is a color film, it features actors they recognize, and the movie contains scenes of graphic sex and violence. But this student response raises an interesting question: Why does classic film noir in general, and *Double Indemnity* specifically, strike such a resonant chord with these intelligent, film savvy, and cynical members of Generation X? The answer is that *Double Indemnity* is popular because many of the issues that come to life in this film resonate with the lives of these Gen X students. In other words, the issues of the post-World War II era have a remarkable similarity to the issues, stresses, struggles, desires, frustrations, values, and fears of the post-Cold War era of Generation X. Moreover, *Double Indemnity* connects strongly with Gen X because: it is an intelligent film, they see this movie as realistic, it speaks to their interest in gender and relationship issues, it resonates with their dark perspective and mood, and it confirms the Gen X belief that you should "trust no one."[5]

Generation X is the name given to the Americans who followed the baby boomer generation. This group was identified in 1990 in by Douglas Coupland.[6] Authors Neil Howe and Bill Strauss have defined Gen Xers as the 80 million people born between 1961 and 1981.[7] Various publications have identified defining characteristics of this generation of Americans. Gen Xers have been described as "educated young people who are purposeless, apathetic, and usually work in a dead end job;"[8] who are "pessimistic, alienated, and angst-ridden;"[9] who are "cynical, lazy, and always seeking fun and immediate gratification."[10] These young Americans have grown up in a world where sex and relationships are dangerous and even life-threatening, for example the dangers of AIDS and other sexually transmitted diseases. They are "the most media-savvy generation ever;"[11] they are "defined by a media culture... which appeals to... "glamour, violence, [and] desire."[12] They have grown up in a world where you can "trust no one" and they have lived in an era that has seen the "collapse of virtually every mainstream institution."[13] Lastly, some people would argue, "Generation X is a term that defines not a chronological age but a way of looking at the world."[14]

As mentioned earlier, movies are very popular with Gen X, and are an important part of their recreation and social life. In "Marketing Madness," Ted Rall goes one step further when he states, the "notion of Gen X as a socio-cultural movement reached its zenith in the cinema...."[15] He goes on to identify one film director in particular, Quentin Tarantino, as an important director of Gen X movies. Rall also identifies two Tarantino films, *Reservoir Dogs* and *Pulp Fiction* as important contributions to the cinema.[16] The fact that Rall has identified Tarantino and these two films as examples of the zenith of Gen X cinema is significant because this director, and these two films, have been classified by many film critics and scholars as film noir. In fact, some of the most popular films with the Gen X students in this film noir class include the following neo-noir films: *Red Rock West* (1994), *Pulp Fiction* (1995), *Fargo* (1996), *LA Confidential* (1997), *Wild Things* (1998), *Go* (1999), and *Memento* (2001). All of these popular neo-noir films reflect issues and themes that resonate with Generation X. Interestingly, many of these same issues and themes appear in the classic noir film, *Double Indemnity*.

Both Gen X and film noir have several characteristics in common. For example, noir films are often described as complex narratives with dark moods. These films have characters who are ambiguous heroes; the characters are cynical, flawed, and angst ridden, and they have an ambiguous morality. These characters feel trapped; they live in a world where the desire for money, sex, and power take precedence over values and morals, where nothing or no one can be trusted, where gender issues cause distress, disrupt, and dominate their lives, and where relationships are doomed and obsessive. In the introduction to the *Reference Guide to the American Film Noir,* Robert Ottoson describes film noir with terms such as angst, hopeless, no control, fate, despair, alienation, disillusionment, moral ambiguity, pessimism, corruption, and deceit.[17] It is interesting to note that many of the same terms are used to describe Generation X, film noir, and *Double Indemnity*.

Double Indemnity is a movie about Walter Neff, a competent but bored nice guy insurance salesman. The movie starts with Walter dictating a confession into a Dictaphone. The story continues in a flashback, which shows Walter making a routine stop to renew a lapsed insurance policy. When he reaches the beautiful L.A. house, Mr. Dietrichson is not at home. However, Walter meets Dietrichson's bored housewife, Phyllis, a dazzling blonde wearing a "dandy" anklet, white bath towel, and not much more. She is beautiful, smart, and sexy, and it is immediately obvious that Walter is obsessed with Phyllis. They flirt with playfully suggestive banter, which is full of double entendres. Mrs. Dietrichson suggests that Walter return another time. When Walter returns the next day for Mr. Dietrichson's signature, he is pleased to discover that once again, the husband is not home. As they continue to talk, Phyllis asks Walter if it is possible for her to buy a life insurance policy for her husband without his knowledge. Walter immediately recognizes that Phyllis wants to kill her husband and collect the insurance money; he lets her know that he is aware of her scheme and that he will not be involved. After a few days of obsessing about Phyllis, Walter decides he will use his expertise as a crack insurance agent to help Phyllis kill her husband and defraud the insurance company by collecting on the double indemnity policy. Walter reasons that this will allow him and Phyllis to be together, to be rich, and to live happily ever after. Blinded by his lust for Phyllis, Walter designs a foolproof plan. However, this is film noir at its best. In one plot twist after another, their plan unravels. Walter's boss and friend, Barton Keyes, is a brilliant claims investigator, whose intuition, which he calls his "little man," tells Keyes that Mr. Dietrichson's death was not an accident. Then, in a conversation with Lola, Phyllis' stepdaughter, Walter discovers Phyllis was a suspect in the death of her husband's first wife. He also learns that Phyllis is having an affair with Nino, her stepdaughter's boyfriend. Walter realizes that Phyllis never loved him; she only wanted to use him to kill her husband so Walter could take the blame and Phyllis could run off with the money and her young lover. Walter wants revenge; he decides to kill Phyllis and blame all the murders on Phyllis's lover, Nino. But when he arrives at Phyllis's home, once again things do not go as he plans. "Undermined by their own mounting distrust of each other, as well as by a shrewd and suspicious claims investigator," their elaborate scheme collapses and Walter and Phyllis shoot each other.[18] Suddenly, we are back at the start of the movie. After killing Phyllis, a critically injured Walter returns to his office and leaves a full confession on Keyes' Dictaphone. Walter explains that the only reason the brilliant Keyes could not crack the case was because Keyes trusted a friend and colleague too much to consider him as the criminal. Keyes appears at the office. Walter collapses while trying to leave, and the two friends have a smoke together while waiting for the ambulance and the police.

Gen X students love *Double Indemnity*. Class discussion after watching this film is always spirited and active, and it is the movie that students choose most frequently to discuss in their papers. Perhaps this should be predictable. As noted previously, they are educated and media savvy. They grew up in an age of multiplexes, VCRs, DVDs, and cable and satellite TV movie channels. They know movies. They recognize the classic Hollywood formulas, and they are aware of the genre conventions. These students are bored with predictable formula films, and they love and appreciate smart, complex films that provide something to think about, as well as something to discuss and argue about with their friends.

1. Double Indemnity Is an Intelligent Film

They see *Double Indemnity* as an intelligent movie right from the first scene. One Gen X viewer commented, " I really loved the way this movie started. It had a sense of death from the start. You can tell the character is hurt and hurt bad. He is confessing to what must have been his demise; the audience is drawn in already; they are hooked. They want to find out what happened to this crazed man and understand what he is confessing to."

Double Indemnity has many specific elements that appeal to and are appreciated by these smart and educated young Americans. Several intelligent aspects of this film are often noted by Gen Xers. For example, the Raymond Chandler dialogue is smart and playful; the narrative is complex with a non-linear narrative and multiple plot twists; symbols and metaphors are often used to support the dialogue; and the wonderful visual effects support the intent and content of the story.

DIALOGUE

For many of these students, the smart and playful Raymond Chandler dialogue is one of the appealing strengths of *Double Indemnity*. Adapted from a story by James M. Cain, *Double Indemnity* "represents a one-time-only collaboration between James M. Cain and Raymond Chandler, two of the leading writers of the hard-boiled school."[19] Although Chandler struggled with what he believed to be the "sensational elements," the "feverish erotic quality," [and the] "hothouse sultriness" of Cain's writing," these students thoroughly enjoy it.[20] Director Billy Wilder "had read two of Chandler's novels ... and was impressed with Chandler's lively narrative style and pungent, slangy dialogue,"[21] and these Gen X students agree.

Students often comment on the dialogue in this film. They love the hard-boiled language used by Walter as well as the comebacks of Phyllis. They enjoy (in their words) the "smart talk," "double talk," "put-downs," "comebacks," and "fast-talk." One scene in particular, that always appeals to students, is described by Frank Krutnik as the "sequence where a man and woman are engaged in playfully displaced sexual bargaining."[22] This scene occurs early in the film during the first time Walter and Phyllis meet. "Walter gets fresh with Phyllis after eyeing her provocatively draped in a beach towel. Phyllis responds in a playful, coy fashion that demonstrates that she is Walter's match when it comes to naughty innuendo." [23] "There's a speed limit in this state, Mr. Neff." "Suppose you get down off your motorcycle and give me a ticket," Walter replies. "Suppose I let you off with a warning this time," Phyllis answers with a smirk. [24] As one student noted, "I like hearing suave, smooth, smart-talkers who have the ability to twist words."

COMPLEX NARRATIVE

Double Indemnity features a convoluted narrative that students enjoy. It is a complex story that they have to follow carefully; it provides a mystery that they are trying to solve and unravel as they watch the film. Today's intelligent Gen X film-viewers often find simple and straightforward stories to be boring. The predictable formula film does not engage them or hold their attention. However, students love the complexity of the noir narrative that they encounter in *Double Indemnity*. They are typically impressed that this old film uses so many different techniques, and they are awed by how these tactics make the film so interesting. They especially note the effectiveness of the non-linear narrative, the plot twists, the use of symbolism and metaphors, and the visual elements that support the content of the film.

NON-LINEAR NARRATIVE

As noted earlier, *Double Indemnity* does not follow the typical genre film conventions and formula, and one example of this is the plot line of the story. Instead of a linear and predictable beginning, middle and end, this movie features a non-linear sequence. The story starts at the end, then returns to the beginning as the story is actually told in flashback. Then the movie returns to the beginning, which is really the end, to finish the story. Selby describes this non-linear narrative in *Double Indemnity* more simply. "The film actually begins when Neff arrives to dictate his confession. This dictation serves as the first-person narration that accompanies the flashbacks that make up the bulk of the film."[25]

The non-linear narrative style is not typically found in classic Hollywood movies, perhaps because it is disliked by many Americans who find it distracting and confusing. One student reported watching a noir film assignment with her parents. Whereas she enjoyed the film, her parents disliked the movie because they found it confusing; they could not follow the story that used a non-linear narrative. However, Gen X students enjoy the complexity that non-linear narrative adds to a story. In fact, one of their favorite neo-noir films, *Pulp Fiction,* also uses a non-linear narrative. They often associate this style with Quentin Tarantino and are surprised to discover that this non-linear style was used so long ago. They are also surprised to realize that learning the end of the movie at the start of the film does not take away from their enjoyment of the rest of the movie. They find the story so compelling that they still want to see the film. One student comment demonstrates a common reaction: "The beginning sucks you in. You have to watch the rest of the movie because you are trying to figure out what will happen next."

Another common element of the noir non-linear narrative is the use of flashbacks and first-person narration. This technique allows the protagonist to provide a voiceover to the flashback, thus injecting personal insight into the story. Andrew Dickos describes the benefit of the voiceover and flashback as follows: "Like the voiceover, the flashback gains privileged access to the perspective of each troubled character whose episode it presents."[26] The voiceover can also infuse a sense of truth to the story, almost as if the viewer is watching a documentary. Two student comments in particular help to illustrate what these students see as the benefits. "Flashbacks are a powerful tool in this film. They helped put the rest of the film into context." Another student commented, "flashbacks helped us develop him [Walter Neff] as a character and gave us insights into why he made some of the decisions he did."

PLOT TWISTS

"Every time I think I have this film figured out, there is a plot twist that puts me back to square one," notes one student. *Double Indemnity* is in fact, full of plot twists, which add a wonderful sense of complexity to this film. These plot twists challenge viewers who enjoy actively engaging movies, especially those people who like trying to figure out what will happen next. For students who enjoy this type of intellectual challenge, *Double Indemnity* presents an abundance of plot twists. For example, appearing to go against his nature, Walter decides to help Phyllis kill her husband. Even though the plan seems foolproof, it is not; Walter's boss Keyes is suspicious about the "accidental" death. Then, we discover that Phyllis does not love Walter; she is only using him to get rid of her husband so she can run off with another man. Next, Walter discovers he cannot trust Phyllis; in fact, he discovers that she was a suspect in the murder of her husband's first wife. Then, Walter decides to kill Phyllis and pin the murders on her young lover. But, before Walter can kill Phyllis, she shoots him. However, Phyllis can't finish the job because she might love Walter after all. Finally, Walter kills Phyllis and confesses to Keyes. It takes total and focused concentration to keep this story straight, and as noted earlier, Gen Xers love a puzzle; they enjoy "trying to figure out what will happen next."

SYMBOLISM AND METAPHORS

Classic Hollywood films typically tell their story in an easily accessible, straightforward fashion. This allows the viewer to sit back, relax, and be entertained by a simple story that guarantees a happy ending. These uncomplicated and undemanding movies are in direct contrast to film noir, where the viewer must be alert for the subtle clues and nuances imbedded in the film. One of the reasons that college students enjoy

The "love triangle" in *Double Indemnity*: Phyllis Dietrichson (Barbara Stanwyck), Walter Neff (Fred MacMurray) and Keyes (Edward G. Robinson).

Double Indemnity is because it is a complex text which provides an abundance of opportunities to search for these subtle cues. Thus, it provides them with material for endless discussions and debates. In a sense, locating and discussing these subtle elements seems to be an enjoyable form of intellectual recreation.

Typically, after watching the films in this course, students participate in class discussions and often write short reaction papers. One very popular topic in discussions and papers is identifying and analyzing the foreshadowing, symbols, metaphors, and recurring motifs in *Double Indemnity*.

Students often discuss examples of foreshadowing. Commonly cited examples include Walter ignoring the danger signals as he speeds through red lights in the opening scene of the film, just as he ignores danger signals throughout the film until it is too late. Another popular example occurs when Walter walks around Phyllis's living room while waiting for her to get dressed; the venetian blinds in the room cast what appear to be black and white stripes on Walter's suit, which makes it resemble striped prison garb. At the end of the movie, he does in fact go to jail.

In *Creatures of Darkness*, Gene D. Phillips discusses another popular example of foreshadowing.

> Walter's voice-over commentary provides a suggestively phallic metaphor for the danger and excitement of the enterprise. "I knew I had hold of a red-hot poker," Walter muses, "and the time to drop it was before it burned my hand off." Walter ignores his misgivings, however, and goes along with Phyllis's plot.[27]

There are a number of times in the film where characters use metaphors or words with double meanings, and the students enjoy discovering these moments. Comments such as, "the metaphors throughout the movie were very interesting and kept my attention," and "Walter used metaphors and would crack small jokes that were never acknowledged by the characters in the film." One example that a student particularly enjoyed occurred when Walter first meets Mrs. Dietrichson. She had been sunbathing and appears with no clothing, only a towel wrapped around her. Gazing up at her, an entranced Walter Neff explains that he wants to renew her insurance policy before it expires. He then adds with a smirk, "I'd hate to see you have an accident when you .. . [he pauses to signal the double meaning] are not fully covered."

Another student wrote an entire paper about the recurring motif of lighting your friends "smoke." Throughout the film, Neff always lights Key's cigar. At the end of the film, having confessed his betrayal to Keyes, a shot and bleeding Neff cannot light his own cigarette and Keyes lights it for him for the first time. This student used this motif as the starting point for an intriguing analysis about friendship and affection, and explores how Keyes finally lighting Neff's cigarette signals an important shift in their relationship.

VISUAL EFFECTS

One of the most noticeable characteristics that distinguishes film noir from most Hollywood films is the frequent use of visual effects. However, these visual cues go beyond style and appearance and are often used to support and illuminate the narrative. The intentional use of visual effects is widely recognized as a strength of *Double Indemnity* by both students and film noir scholars. James F. Maxfield writes, "*Double Indemnity* and *Murder, My Sweet* (both 1944) provided models for the visual style of the genre: expressionist lighting (dark shadows, sometimes with strongly contrasting highlighted areas), many night scenes, confined settings, tight close-ups,[and] high angle shots which diminish the stature of the characters."[28] In addition to the visual elements mentioned by Maxfield, students also note the interesting use of mirrors and reflections in *Double Indemnity*.

One student noted that the visual effects in *Double Indemnity* start immediately in the beginning of the movie and rush at the viewer throughout the film. He was especially dazzled by the first eight minutes of the film and described his experience in this way.

> Right after the opening credits the movie starts in darkness, with reflected lights, reflections, shadows, and angles assaulting the viewer. The movie opens with a car speeding through dark city streets, which are dimly lit with street lights and their reflections. Neff enters a dark and shadowy office building, and with sweat glistening on his face, begins to dictate a message to his boss. He then goes out into a bright, sunny, California day, which is immediately followed by his entry into a dark and shadowy house. He looks up to see a beautiful blonde wearing only a white towel, looking down at him from a second floor balcony in a way that communicates that this woman will dominate this man from this moment on. She leaves to dress while Neff wanders through the living room covered with black and white striped reflections from venetian blinds. Then a clothed Mrs. Dietrichson reappears and proceeds to gaze into a mirror while putting on her lipstick. At the same time, Walter Neff stares admiringly at her reflection in the mirror.

As this student noted, in the first eight minutes of the film the viewer has already experienced many of the film noir visual conventions, all of which communicate something about the content of the film, and all of which demand the viewer's attention.

Students love the visual effects in *Double Indemnity,* and the way these effects support and contribute to the narrative. Every semester that this course is offered, at least one student, and usually more, select the noir visual cues as the topic of their research papers. They are fascinated by German Expressionism, and by how much influence it has had on film noir. They enjoy discussing why angles are used in certain scenes: for example, Phyllis on a second floor balcony looming over Neff when they first meet, which immediately shows her sense of power. They speculate about how shadows and darkness can forewarn the viewer: At the end of the film, Walter and Phyllis meet in suffocating and claustrophobic darkness that surrounds the lovers with a sense of danger just before they shoot each other. And as briefly mentioned in the earlier student comment, at the start of the film, venetian blinds cast stripes on Walter that predict he will go to prison. Students find these visual cues to be so interesting that they often compile a collection of visual images on videotapes to accompany their research paper. As one student remarked, "we grew up on MTV, so we love seeing the creative use of visual images and visual effects." Another noted, "this movie was the first black and white film that I have ever seen. Because of the great contrast and use of negative and positive space, the angles of the camera, and the low key lighting, this film seemed more like a work of art."

2. *Double Indemnity* is Realistic

Gen Xers find *Double Indemnity* to be more realistic than the classic Hollywood films. One student noted, "life isn't always happy and there isn't always a happy ending. This contrasts greatly with most popular films." Another observed, "The story in *Double Indemnity* is dark and disturbing. However, it is these darker sides of life that depict and illustrate real life more truthfully and clearly. This film keeps the attention of the audience because they know this depiction is more realistic." Perhaps another student summarizes it best: "Murder, fraud, and adultery: all are vital parts of this story. It seems that this movie could be a film of today with all the crime that takes place."

In addition to perceiving *Double Indemnity* as a more realistic film because of its dark mood, less-than-happy ending, and lives affected by crime and morality struggles, students enjoy what they believe to be realistic characters in this film. One student asks, "who are the heroes in this film, if any exist at all?" In fact, there are no classic American heroes in this film. There are no unequivocal good guys or bad guys, and there are no superheroes. The characters in *Double Indemnity* seem like normal people: no one is perfect; everyone has their flaws. Another student observed, "these characters are far from the typical heroes and villains." Walter is often seen as a nice guy who gets deeply infatuated with a beautiful woman and makes a stupid decision. A third student remarked, "even though he is a murderer, there are times you can almost find yourself rooting for him."

Phyllis elicits a wider variety of responses. One student saw her as "scary and dangerous," whereas others viewed her as victimized by her husband. "Phyllis is devious and manipulative, but you find yourself feeling sorry for her when you meet her overbearing and cold husband." Another student commented, "there are times you find yourself admiring this woman because she is so smart and powerful. Besides, she never really murdered her husband; she simply had the idea." And, "it is possible to question if she really killed her husband's first wife, or if stepdaughter Lola is creating a story to undermine Phyllis, who she obviously hates."

The students also have some interesting reactions to the other characters in the film. The reactions to Keyes are a little more complex. Some students see Keyes as a good guy and admire his competence as a claims investigator. However, he also comes off as one of those one-dimensional people who is obsessed with his work, who has no life outside work, and who can be a pain to work with.

Even the minor characters have their flaws or moments when students disliked them. For example, the husband is cold and aloof. Nino is cheating on his girlfriend.

One student found innocent and naive Lola annoying because she is so susceptible to getting hurt. It is very interesting that the characters with whom audiences of the 40s connected so strongly, still connect so well with today's young audiences. One student summarizes this topic nicely when she says, "Moviegoers of today are searching for that same vision of reality, which is a dark side of society. It makes us feel better about our own lives when we can relate to the imperfect 'heroes' in the film." Students do not seem to like, nor can they relate to, the perfect people who populate classic Hollywood movies. Instead, because of their lives and experiences, these students connect with many of the characters in *Double Indemnity*. They seem to gravitate towards what one student described as a "hero who is the average depressed man with distorted morality."

3. *Double Indemnity* Examines Gender and Relationship Issues

Double Indemnity has been the focus of more student papers than any other film used in this course, and a favorite paper topic is gender and relationship issues. Students are fascinated by the way men and women are represented in this film: the way they interact with each other, the power struggles that result, and the way that relationship and gender issues are explored and illuminated.

Both male and female students are captivated by Phyllis. In fact, she generates more student interest than virtually any other female character in the films used in this film noir course. This is no small compliment given the fact that the course film list includes several stunning classic noir femme fatales including: Kitty in *Scarlet Street,* Cora in *The Postman Always Rings Twice,* Brigid in *The Maltese Falcon,* and Annie in *Gun Crazy,* to name a few. Students describe Phyllis as sexy, evil, dangerous, provocative, conniving, devious, smart, intelligent, manipulative, powerful, strong, seductive, controlling, self-centered, independent, and malicious. Some quotes from student papers further illustrate the degree to which students are fascinated by this character. One student wrote, "I enjoyed seeing a woman represented so strongly." Another student commented, "This is the kind of movie that you see and are so psyched that the woman has got a hold on the male. I even watched it a second time to get another feel for it." Another said, "I liked how Phyllis presented herself as the victim while in actuality she was the predator." One student liked how "Phyllis uses her sexuality along with the vulnerability of men to persuade them to do her will. She knows what she wants, and will stop at nothing to get it." Another student wrote, "this femme fatale had confidence, and beauty. People wanted to see her victimize men and still do." And lastly, "I loved the thought that although Phyllis was a horrible person, she is so powerful and smart." It is fascinating to see the degree to which this femme fatale connects with today's students.

Although most of the character oriented student papers focus on Phyllis, Walter also gets his share of attention from students who are captivated by this male protagonist who does not resemble the traditional male hero who is common in

The half-naked siren above, on the staircase, Phyllis Dietrichson (Barbara Stanwyck), who beckons to the "schlub" below, Walter Neff in *Double Indemnity*.

classic Hollywood films. The classic American male hero is a good guy who is tough, strong, smart, and in control; he is competent in his job, and he is in charge of male-female relationships.

However, this description does not necessarily fit the main protagonist Walter Neff. On the one hand, he is competent in his job and is even offered a promotion. Also, he does have his moments of being a nice guy, especially in the playful way he interacts with others. In fact, because he is likable, some viewers even root for him to succeed. He is also smart in some ways. In fact, he conceives a brilliant plan to murder Phyllis's husband. However, Neff has many other characteristics that interfere with classifying him as a hero. His ambiguous morality does not allow him to be identified as the classic good guy; he is after all, committing adultery with a married woman, and he does commit murder. Additionally, his judgment is definitely clouded when it comes to Phyllis. He is not strong or in charge of this relationship. Quite the contrary, he is weak, vulnerable, manipulated, seduced, controlled, cheated on, and dominated in his relationship with this femme fatale. He is totally susceptible to her charms and this is often seen by students as a sign of weakness.

Many of these characteristics classify Walter as an anti-hero, and yet it is these negative characteristics that seem to make his character intriguing to students. Students often recognize Walter's intelligence, and they react strongly to the fact that he uses his intelligence to commit a crime. One student observed, "Phyllis comes up with the idea of the murder, but Walter comes up with the plan." Another student noted, "Walter knows the insurance business well enough to cheat it."

Additionally, students are often intrigued by Walter's susceptibility to Phyllis, especially because he is intelligent, yet victimized, manipulated, and controlled by her. They wonder how such a smart man can be dominated by lust, and why "Walter does not recognize Phyllis's scheme until it is too late and he is in too deep." For most of these students, the personality traits that make Walter susceptible to Phyllis are typically viewed negatively in American society. Several student comments demonstrate their reaction to Walter's character. "Walter plays an intelligent yet extremely vulnerable man. He was merely a pawn in her little scandal." "The idea that a man could be manipulated by female sexuality, or even that a woman would dare to manipulate a man in this way must have been shocking at this time. However, it is much more common now." "Walter is a simple, innocent insurance man, who falls into the trap of a beautiful and tempting woman by the thought of having money *and* this gorgeous blonde as his own." "Walter cannot resist his overwhelming passion for Phyllis." "Walter takes it for granted that he has a dominant position in his relationship with Phyllis until it is almost too late. He is under the false assumption that he is controlling Phyllis, and also protecting her." One young male student made an especially strong connection to Walter's dilemma. "Movies such as *Double Indemnity* scare me. While some femme fatale movies, such as *The Hand That Rocks The Cradle*, disturb me, they do not frighten me. I can always remember that it is just a movie. *Double Indemnity*, however, is a movie about something that could easily happen to me if the right kind of woman bumps into me. Thus, seeing the plight of Walter touched a part of me that made me squirm and shortly thereafter cower."

4. A Dark Mood Permeates *Double Indemnity*

Film noir is widely recognized as a reflection of the dark side of American Society, and many of the descriptive terms used to describe these films reflect this dark nature. Interestingly, these dark themes are one of the qualities that make film noir so appealing to these students, and one of the reasons why film noir has such a resonance with Generation X. Film noir reflects the alienated, cynical, pessimistic, paranoid, anxious, entrapped, disillusioned, and hopeless state that many of these young Americans believe is true of their lives and their world today.

One student comment in particular, helps to clarify this student perspective. Film noir emphasizes " feelings of sadness, separation, isolation, cynicism, regret, pessimism, and paranoia. All of these emotions were present in the 40s and 50s, and they have now come back." In fact, all of these emotions are present in *Double Indemnity*.

Feeling trapped, stuck, seeing oneself as victim of fate, or living in a world that is outside one's control, is a recurring theme in the literature about Generation X, and as noted previously, is a recurring theme in many noir films. Often, these students recognize and identify with the feelings of being trapped experienced by the characters in *Double Indemnity*. Similar to Walter who is trapped in a boring job, or Phyllis who is trapped in a bad marriage, many Gen Xers feel trapped and are disillusioned about their opportunities or their ability to achieve the American Dream. In fact, these young post-cold war Americans are often surprised to see how many similarities they share with the disillusioned youth of post-World War II.

One example of how Gen Xers see themselves as trapped is demonstrated by what they see as their lack of future opportunities. For Generation X, one aspect of being trapped means being stuck in dead-end jobs, dead-end relationships, and what they see as the potential for dead-end lives. For example, Gen Xers define dead-end jobs, or "McJobs," as the "low-pay, low-prestige, low-dignity, low-benefit, no future job[s] in the service sector," that are most often available to them.[29]

Unfortunately, these concerns have some supporting evidence. In an *Atlantic Monthly* article, "A Politics for Generation X," Ted Halstead argues that this pessimism and cynicism might not be without some merit. "Xers may well be the first generation whose lifetime earnings will be less than their parents .... Falling wages and rising inequality have affected all young Americans, regardless of educational achievement. During the said-to-be economically strong years 1989–1995 earnings for recent college graduates fell by nearly 10 percent—representing the first time that a generation of graduates has earned less than the previous one."[30] Given this information, it should come as no surprise that students identify with the feelings of being trapped that run throughout *Double Indemnity*.

To varying degrees, all the characters in *Double Indemnity* are trapped. Walter is bored with his job. It doesn't present any challenge for him, yet the promotion he is offered seems to be a worse job, one where he is tied to a desk like his boss Keyes. Although Keyes does not seem bored with his job, his obsessive attention to it does not seem to provide him with much of a life outside work. Mr. Dietrichson seems bored with his life, and surly about the quality of his marriage. His daughter Lola is stuck in a loveless home and in a relationship with a man who is cheating on her. Phyllis is a bored housewife, in a bad marriage, with no escape except to find a way to murder her husband; this is the only way that she can be both rich *and* independent. All these people are trapped and bored, and the students recognize this fact and identify with it.

One student comments about how Walter is trapped: "Neff is in a way, the victim in this film because he is forced to make a choice to live his dreary insurance-selling life, or commit a murder for love and money: a choice-less choice. Either way, Neff will be choosing to lose something, whether it is his morals or the opportunity to have what every American man dreams of, sex and money."

Several students note that Phyllis is trapped. "Phyllis is stuck with an inferior husband and a stepdaughter who is her opposite." A second student adds, Phyllis "is in a troubled marriage which she doesn't want to be in. Her husband doesn't love her and her stepdaughter wants no relationship with her. Phyllis sees Walter as a way out, a chance to escape her misery." A third student comments directly to this point as well. "Phyllis is unhappy in her marriage and has every intention of ending it in a way that is most profitable to her, accidental death. This will provide her with freedom, both personal and financial."

Being bored with one's life seems to be an integral part of feeling trapped for these students. "Being trapped in a house all day and being married to a boring man was not what Phyllis was looking for. To her, love signifies danger, excitement, and freedom." It does not seem coincidental that a generation that feels bored and trapped would search for ways to generate excitement in their lives. Perhaps this is why some students recognized the excitement potential that was available to both Walter and Phyllis. One student commented, "many Americans long for a true love powerful enough to make you capable of murder."

Other students were intrigued by the possibility of escaping boredom by taking a risk and doing something dangerous and exciting. In fact, this interest in finding excitement in high risk behavior is not uncommon in the lives of Generation X. It does not seem coincidental that the recent rage on TV is high risk sports, also known as the "X Games." Accordingly, students enjoy seeing Walter participate in high risk activities such as adultery, fraud, and murder. One example of an activity that captures this sense of risk and excitement is planning, completing, and getting away with the perfect crime. As one student explained, "there is always the insider's temptation to cheat the system he knows. Walter wants to see if he can beat his own insurance company, to commit the perfect murder or perfect crime." The idea of "beating the system" seemed very exciting to these students. In his description of *Double Indemnity,* Spencer Selby seems to agree.

> Neff's motivation is directly linked to his relationship with Keyes in the important roulette wheel speech. Here Neff admits that it wasn't just desire and greed that prompted his decision to attempt the perfect murder. Like the man who runs the

roulette wheel, Neff has learned the mechanics of the system to a degree impossible for the average gambler. Since the wheel itself is right under his hand, Neff
feels that he has the power to beat the system, and the urge to do just that has
been building in him for a long time.... His attempt at the perfect crime is an act
of irreverent rebellion.[31]

It is interesting to note how many of these themes are also present in the 1999 Gen
X Noir movie, *Go,* a film that is very popular with Gen X students. The themes in *Go*
that also occur in *Double Indemnity* are: feeling trapped and underemployed; feeling
bored and taking dangerous risks for excitement; having the desire to get rich quick;
and taking one misstep and having your life spiral out of control. *Go* tells a story about
the dead-end lives of several college educated, intelligent, articulate, bored, young
"twenty-somethings" who are under-employed as grocery store checkout clerks. One
of the characters, a nice normal young woman—a Walter Neff type character actually—sees the opportunity to get some excitement and some fast money with a one
time sale of drugs, something she has obviously not done previously. Once she makes
this decision, her life spins wildly out of control with plot twist after plot twist making her situation worse and worse. The similar themes in both *Go* and *Double Indemnity* provide additional evidence for why these students thoroughly enjoy both films.

5. "Trust No One"

Another theme in *Double Indemnity* that has a powerful resonance with Gen Xers is
"trust no one." "Many Xers sense that the basic fabric of American Society is somehow fraying .... The result is a fundamental loss of trust: between citizens and elected
officials, between employees and employers, and ultimately between individuals and
their neighbors."[32] And similar to the post-World War II era, relationship and family
problems are a huge worry for many Americans today.

These young Americans have grown up in a dangerous world where they have
learned that they cannot trust public institutions. They have seen crime, corruption,
and moral lapses in the government, with political leaders, within the police forces, in
the corporate world, and even with religious leaders and institutions. Rall provides examples such as the high divorce rate, sex scandals in the churches, budget cuts in public education, corporate consolidation and more recently corporate scandals, voter
disillusionment because of cynicism about the government, and even a distrust of the
news media. [33] But perhaps where *Double Indemnity* is the most powerful is in the
statements it makes about the dangers of trusting those who are closest to you:
friends, co-workers, and family members.

In many ways, Barton Keyes is a friend and father figure to Walter Neff. Keyes obviously respects Neff, and in fact even offers him a promotion, which Walter declines.
Instead, motivated by lust, greed, a desire for some excitement, and the challenge of
beating the insurance system, Walter violates the trust that Keyes has placed in him

when he decides to help Phyllis defraud the All Pacific Life Insurance Company. Students point out that Keyes and his intuition were infallible until he trusted a friend and co-worker so much that he was unable to see Walter as a perpetrator. As Walter says during his confession into Keyes' Dictaphone, "I just wanted to set you right about something you couldn't see because it was right smack up against your nose." Keyes' "paternal rapport with Neff silences his inner suspicions and enables Neff to dupe the company."[34]

Another student describes how disturbing it is to discover the bad guy is your friend, neighbor, lover, or even someone who lives in your house with you. This comment was in reference to the fact that virtually every relationship in *Double Indemnity* is having a crisis in trust.

According to *Double Indemnity,* and many of today's students, you cannot even trust members of your own family. This family is in crisis. Mr. Dietrichson, the father and husband, dislikes and ignores his second wife, Phyllis. For her part, Phyllis killed her husband's first wife, presumably so she could marry a rich man and have a life of wealth and comfort. She certainly seems to have achieved this goal given the fact she lives in an expensive home and has the services of a maid. But this is obviously not enough. This wife cannot be trusted. She wants money and independence, and so she is planning to kill her husband, Mr. Dietrichson.

Additionally, Phyllis is the essence of the wicked stepmother. She has killed her stepdaughter's mother, she is planning to kill her stepdaughter's father, and she is having an affair with her stepdaughter's boyfriend.

This movie also strongly warns that you cannot trust your lover. Walter could not trust his lover Phyllis; she was having an affair with Nino, and she was planning to frame Walter for the murder of her husband and run away with Nino.

As a boyfriend, Nino cannot be trusted since he is cheating on his sweet and wholesome girlfriend Lola by having an affair with her stepmother. In response, students argue that this film is not about love; it is about greed, lust, and power. These people hide behind love to get what they want at any cost.

It should come as no surprise that Gen X can relate to this family. The news is full of stories about families in crisis: high divorce rates, divorced parents kidnapping children, child abuse, children killing their parents, and simply the stress of children coping with their parents' divorce, remarriage, and the adjustment to living in a stepfamily. Unfortunately, the trust issues raised in *Double Indemnity* are not uncommon. Many scholars argue that popular culture reflects the fears and values of a society, and that cultural rules are imbedded in popular culture texts, almost like cautionary tales. According to *Double Indemnity,* the moral to this story would have to be, trust no one. Unfortunately, this message is all too familiar to many Gen Xers.

In conclusion, at first it might come as a surprise to many that *Double Indemnity* is an incredibly popular movie with Generation X. Yet this 1944 film consistently gets positive reviews and generates a great deal of interest with today's college students. A deeper examination reveals that many of the values, issues, beliefs and fears that are explored in this 1944 film once again have resonance and importance to another generation of young people. Almost sixty years after its release, *Double Indemnity* connects with Gen Xers in a powerful and meaningful way. As one student so aptly concludes, "film noir presents an environment of menace, anxiety, uncertainty, realism, defeat, and entrapment. The main reason for its popularity today is our ability to connect to this side of life."[35]

NOTES

1. David Ansen, "The Neo-Noir '90s." *Newsweek*, October 27, 1997, p. 70.

2. John Housley, "Film noir, My Lovely." *Premiere*, March, 1992, p. 97.

3. Anonymous. *The Entertainment Weekly Guide to the Greatest Movies Ever Made*, New York: Warner Books, 1994, p. 15.

4. Ansen, p. 70

5. "Trust no one," is the slogan used by the TV program, *The X-Files*, a TV program that is very popular with Generation X. One of the two lead characters in the show, Fox Mulder, distrusts the government because he believes they are guilty of covering up evidence of para-normal activity. Many of the characters are paranoid and suspicious.

6. Douglas Coupland, *Generation X: Tales for an Accelerated Culture*, New York: St. Martin's Press, 1992.

7. Neil Howe and Bill Strauss, *13th Gen: Abort, Retry, Ignore, Fail?*, New York: Vintage Books, 1993, pp. 12–16.

8. Robert Owen, *Gen X TV: The Brady Bunch to Melrose Place*, Syracuse, New York: Syracuse University Press, 1997, p. 11.

9. Ted Rall, "Marketing Success: A Post-Mortem for Generation X." *Link*, August/September, 1997, p. 28.

10. Vann Wesson, *Generation X Field Guide and Lexicon*, San Diego, California: Orion Media, 1997, p. 7.

11. Owen, p. 5.

12. Susan Hopkins, "Generation Pulp." *Youth Studies* 14 (Spring, 1995), p. 1.

13. Rall, p. 31.

14. Idem

15. Ibid, p. 30.

16. Idem

17. Robert Ottoson, *A Reference Guide to the American Film noir: 1940–1958*, Metuchen, New Jersey: The Scarecrow Press, 1981, p. 1.

18. Foster Hirsch, *Film noir: The Dark Side of the Screen,* San Diego, California: Da Capo Press, 1981, p. 1.

19. Hirsch, p. 7.

20. Idem

21. Gene D. Phillips, *Creatures of Darkness: Raymond Chandler, Detective Fiction, and Film noir,* Lexington, Kentucky: University of Kentucky Press, 2000, p. 167.

22. Frank Krutnik, *In a Lonely Street: Film noir, Genre, Masculinity,* New York: Routledge, 1991, pp. 50–51.

23. Phillips, p. 174.

24. Idem

25. Spencer Selby, *Dark City: The Film noir,* Jefferson, North Carolina: McFarland, 1984, p. 15.

26. Andrew Dickos, *Street with No Name: A History of the Classic American Film noir,* Lexington, Kentucky: University of Kentucky Press, 2002, p. 179.

27. Phillips, p. 174.

28. James F. Maxfield, *The Fatal Woman: sources of Male Anxiety in American Film noir, 1941–1991,* Madison, New Jersey: Fairleigh Dickinson University Press, 1996, p. 26.

29. Wesson, p. 110.

30. Ted Halstead, "A Politics for Generation X." *The Atlantic Monthly,* August, 1999, p. 36.

31. Selby, pp. 15–16.

32. Halstead, p. 37.

33. Rall, p. 31.

34. Thomas Schatz, *Hollywood Genres: Formulas, Filmmaking, and the Studio System,* New York: Random House, 1981, p. 135.

35. A recent course syllabus for this film noir course is available at www.stlawu.edu/acsupport

Another modern-day "schlub" in the mold of Walter Neff: Ned Racine (William Hurt) lets his hormones and greed think for him and sinks deeper into the noir abyss in *Body Heat*.

Through the Past Darkly: Noir Remakes of the 1980s

Constantine Verevis

In *More Than Night*, James Naremore describes the category of film noir not as a set of narrative or stylistic features, but as a *discursive formation*: "film noir belongs to the history of ideas as much as to the history of cinema; ... it has less to do with a group of artifacts than with a discourse."[1] In the first instance, American film noir is a *critical genre*, "a belated reading of classic Hollywood that was popularized by cinéastes of the French New Wave, [and later] appropriated by reviewers, academics, and film-makers, and then recycled on television."[2] Naremore describes a first, "historical" age of film noir, enabled by the post-war arrival of Hollywood film into Paris, and a French predisposition to view the film noir as an "existential allegory of the white male condition."[3] In the late 1950s, French *auteur* filmmakers took film noir as a pretext for reinventing cinema as a mode of self-expression. In the United States, the expansion of film noir was assisted by factors such as the importation of the French *politique des auteurs*, the upsurge of repertory theatre short-seasons, the contribution of broadcast television to film literacy, and the expansion of film courses in American universities. Along with shifts in Hollywood production methods and commercial infrastructure, these factors led to a delayed new wave of American filmmakers whose early films were influenced by the French New Wave and were "somewhat noirish in tone."[4] By the late 1960s, the critical appraisal of noir had motivated something of a revival, but *film* noir did not become an *industrial genre* until revisionist and neo-expressionist productions (such as *Chinatown* and *Taxi Driver*, both 1974) generated a cycle of noir remakings. "At this point," Naremore concludes:

> [film] noir had fully entered the English language, and it formed a rich discursive category that the entertainment industry could expand and adapt ["remake"] in countless ways.[5]

Like the category of film noir, the concept of *film remaking* is never simply a quality of texts, but is the secondary result of broader discursive activity. Film remaking is both enabled and limited by a series of historically specific institutional factors, such as copyright law and canon formation, film reviewing and media literacy, which are essential to the existence and maintenance—to the discursivisation—of the film remake.[6] In the 1970s, the critical interest in film noir and the increasing development of a noir canon led to a number of direct remakes of classic noirs: *Murder, My Sweet* (1944) was remade as *Farewell, My Lovely* (1975), *They Live by Night* (1948) as *Thieves Like Us* (1974), and *The Big Sleep* (1946) was remade under the same title in 1978. The cycle continued into

307

the 1980s, with classic noirs like *Double Indemnity* (1944), *The Postman Always Rings Twice* (1946), *Out of the Past* (1947), *The Big Clock* (1948), and *D.O.A.* (1949) all providing material for remakes. More noir followed in the 1990s, with *Gun Crazy* (1950) remade as *Guncrazy* (1992), *Criss Cross* (1949) as *The Underneath* (1995), and *Kiss of Death* (1947) and *Night and the City* (1950) were remade with the same titles (1995/1992). This chapter does not seek to provide an exhaustive overview of these (and other) remakings,[7] but rather takes an interest in a cycle of noir remakes of the 1980s: namely, *Body Heat* (1981), *The Postman Always Rings Twice* (1981), *Against All Odds* (1984), *No Way Out* (1987), and *D.O.A.* (1988). In particular, this chapter looks at the role these remakes play in the commercial development of neo-noir, situated as they are between the revisionist (modern) noirs of the 1970s and the more formulaic (post-modern) neo-noirs of the 1990s.[8] Additionally, it is argued that these noir remakes depend not only on the repetition of existing textual structures but also upon audience knowledge of previous texts and an understanding of the broader generic structure of film noir.

Two noir remakes from the 1980s—*The Postman Always Rings Twice* (Bob Rafelson, 1981) and *Body Heat* (Lawrence Kasdan 1981)—provide an understanding of the critical discourses and industrial contexts attending neo-noir. Both appear at the beginning of the 1980s, but where *The Postman* looks back to the thematic and stylistic revisionism of 1970s noirs, *Body Heat* looks ahead to the more formulaic and commodified noir of the mid-1980s and beyond. Generally speaking, *The Postman* can be related to the revival and transformation of noir in films such as *Chinatown* (1974), Roman Polanski's revisionist private-eye movie; *The Long Goodbye* (1973), Robert Altman's adaptation of the 1954 Raymond Chandler novel; and *Thieves Like Us* (1974), Altman's period remake of the classic *They Live by Night* (1948). More particularly, *The Postman* is a *direct and acknowledged* remake of the 1946 MGM production *The Postman Always Rings Twice*, directed by Tay Garnett. Thomas Leitch describes *The Postman* as a "true remake" insofar as it establishes a relationship between itself, the earlier film it remakes and the "property"—James M. Cain's 1934 novel—upon which both films are based.[9] This triangular notion of remaking typically operates by "ascribing ... value to a classic earlier text [Cain's original literary property] and protecting that value by invoking a second earlier text [Garnett's 1946 adaptation] as betraying it."[10] Leitch argues that the rhetorical strategy of Rafelson's *Postman* depends on a distinction between "positive and negative textual markers":

> Richness, originality, and the imperial power of the classic on the one hand, and artifice, datedness, and repression of important material on the other. [...] In this way the [*Postman*] remake is able to valorize Cain's original text, toward which it adopts an attitude of hushed reverence, while ascribing any dated qualities in need of revision to [the earlier MGM] version.[11]

The original property, James M. Cain's *The Postman Always Rings Twice*, has been described as a "quintessentially American" novel.[12] Along with (then) contemporary authors, such as Dashiell Hammett, W. R. Burnett, Horace McCoy, Cornell Woolrich and Raymond Chandler, Cain belonged to a school of American writers of "tough guy" or "hard-boiled" mysteries and crime novels of the 1930s and 1940s.[13] Writing about Cain and his fellow "poets of tabloid murder," critic Edmund Wilson described Cain as a novelist intent upon making explicit all the things that had been excluded from classic Hollywood by the Catholic Legion of Decency: "sex, debauchery, unpunished crime, [and] sacrilege against the Church."[14] Between 1934 and 1976 Cain wrote some eighteen novels and although several of these were adapted to film, Cain's work is best remembered as the source for a cycle of 1940s film noirs: *Double Indemnity* (Billy Wilder, 1944), *Mildred Pierce* (Michael Curtiz, 1945) and *The Postman Always Rings Twice* (1946). Although the last to be adapted in this cycle, *The Postman* was Cain's first novel, an immediate best seller and an explicitly erotic work that was banned in some parts of the United States. In Europe, the novel quickly became the source of (at least) two continental versions: *Le Dernier Tournant* (*The Last Turning,* Pierre Chenal, 1939) and *Ossessione* (Luchino Visconti, 1942).[15] However, in Hollywood, the novel's explicitly erotic content saw a decade-long delay in its filming. When it finally appeared in 1946, the limitations imposed by the Production Code of the 1940s, together with the glossy production values that prevailed at MGM and the star presence of Lana Turner in the lead role of Cora, contributed to a "white washed" adaptation of the novel.[16] Richard Schickel provides a consensus view when he describes the MGM adaptation of *The Postman* as a "rather cold, sanitized (and miscast) version" and a film that "never did get the knack of noir."[17]

The 1946 version of *The Postman* effected a number of transformations on Cain's adulterous murder story, expunging not only the novel's scandalous depiction of aggressive sexuality but also its ethnicity (the Greek husband, Nick Papadakis, became Nick Smith; the Jewish lawyer Katz was renamed Keats). At the same time, the film remained in a number of ways surprisingly close to Cain's novel. It retained, for instance, *The Postman's* sense of foreboding by translating Frank's first-person delivery—"They threw me off the hay truck about noon"[18]—into a characteristically noir voice-over narration: "It was on a side road outside of Los Angeles. I was hitchhiking from San Francisco down to San Diego, I guess. A half hour earlier I thumbed a ride." In the novel, this mood of predetermination is further communicated through several doublings, and reinforced more generally by Cain's oft-quoted statement of a desire to *repeat* across a body of work some "[terrifying] wish that comes true."[19] These repetitions find perfect expression in the *rhyming effects* that characterize and contribute to the classical narrative style of the Hollywood studio film. At the global level (of action and event) the textual repetitions of Garnett's *Postman* include: two accidents with a lorry; two attempts (the latter successful) to kill Nick; two attempts to leave the café; and the two trials for murder. At the local level (of dialogue and motif) the doublings cover: the two notes in the cash register; the echoes at the lake; the name of the roadside diner ("Twin Oaks"); and (most eloquently) the lipstick roll that announces Cora's arrival in and departure from Frank's life. In a final repetition, Garnett (and screen writers Harry Ruskin and Niven Busch) made the decision to have Frank (John Garfield) spell out the metaphor of "the postman" (which only features in the title of Cain's novel) to the District Attorney Sackett in the death cell. Each of these repetitions communicates the mood of noirish foreboding and fatality conveyed by Cain's novel: "So I'm in the death house now, writing the last of this...."[20]

The place of Cain's *Postman* and Garnett's film version in the literary/film canon ensured that Rafelson's remake was discussed and evaluated in relation to both texts. The 1981 release of *The Postman* prompted a reprint of Cain's novel, and pre-publicity for the film focussed on its being a "corrective" to MGM's watered-down 1946 adaptation, a film described by one critic as "less noir than purplish melodrama."[21] Rafelson insisted that "they [MGM] never made the book … [T]he book was really a neglected minor classic."[22] Rafelson's claim to some greater fidelity centred in particular upon the 1981 *Postman*'s ability to depict the notorious sex scenes of Cain's novel:

> I took her in my arms and mashed my mouth up against hers. […] I bit her. I sunk
> my teeth into her lips so deep I could feel the blood spurt into my mouth. It was
> running down her neck when I carried her upstairs.[23]

In the first instance, Rafelson's version extended the strategy of censorship (Freudian and institutional) evident in the device of the lipstick, the fetish that stands (in the 1946 version) for the *problem* of Cora's dangerous sexuality. The *Postman* remake does this by developing (from the novel) the feline metaphor of sexuality that begins with descriptions of Cora as "cougar" and "hell cat,"[24] and persists throughout the story. Although present in a limited way in the 1946 version, this device is taken up in Rafelson's film through the narrative element of the domestic cat that thwarts the first murder attempt, the lawyer "Katz," the cat trainer Madge (Anjelica Huston), and (in another repetition) the "return" of the cat through the gift of the puma: "And the cat came back! It stepped on the fuse box and got killed, but here it [was] back."[25] More obviously, the pre-release publicity for Rafelson's version focussed on two scenes of "orgasmic … sex and violence"[26] omitted from the earlier film version: the violent coupling of Frank and Cora in the kitchen, and their mutual arousal while messing each other up at the scene of Nick's accident-murder.[27] These scenes were expected to bring to Rafelson's film an authenticity and *attitude* from the novel that oscillated between religious rapture—"I kissed her. Her eyes were shining up at me like two blue stars. It was like being in church," and sadistic contempt—"I was alone with her for a minute, and swung my fist up against her leg so hard it nearly knocked her over."[28] The promise that the *Postman* remake would deliver on those elements left out of the 1946 version was further reinforced by a report in *Variety* that Rafelson was going to shoot the film (on a closed set) as an X-certificate and then cut it to a R-rating for its theatrical showing.[29]

Upon *The Postman*'s release, David Thomson stated that the "restored" scenes were "among the least hindered views of sex the cinema [had] ever provided,"[30] but other critics complained that the "detached, meditative tone" of Rafelson's film was at odds with the "sleazy primitivism" of Cain's writing.[31] The perceived failure of Rafelson to bring to his adaptation the carnality and impulsiveness of Cain's novel appears to relate to a second (conflicting) claim to authenticity, namely the 1981 *Postman*'s careful reconstruction of the novel's setting in Depression era southern California. Rafelson said that he "thought it was owed to Cain for somebody to make it [*The Postman*] in the period he wrote it. I felt the story itself was *part* of the Depression."[32] Rafelson went to the trouble of having the Twin Oaks setting built from scratch, choosing for the

Above, Frank and Nora (Jack Nicholson and Jessica Lange) from the remake of *The Postman Always Rings Twice,* sharing wine as a prelude to violent passion. Below, the original *Postman* released by MGM in 1946: Nora (Lana Turner) helps the injured Frank (John Garfield) smoke a cigarette.

house a type of California architecture that was popular around 1915, specifically in order to avoid the Art Deco style featured in 1970s recreations of the thirties. In maintaining that he "didn't want everyone to be in awe of the period,"[33] Rafelson attempted to distance The Postman from the comfortable nostalgia of a recent cycle of neo-noirs such as Chinatown (1974), Thieves Like Us (1974), and Farewell, My Lovely (1975). These were films that seemed to satisfy the auteur predilections of their (nouvelle vague inspired) directors and meet the financial interests of corporate Hollywood, films that "both determined and reproduced the period's simultaneous impulses toward irony and nostalgia."[34] In an endeavour to avoid the self-knowing memorialization of the classic film noir, but at the same time meticulously recreate the story's period setting, Rafelson's earnest treatment of The Postman failed to capture its tough-guy manner. As Pauline Kael put it: "The words that would describe this movie [detached, meditative, studied] are at the opposite pole from how anyone would describe the book."[35]

Rafelson's "hushed reverence" toward Cain's story not only respects the latter's claim to being "the granddaddy of hot tabloid novels,"[36] but retrospectively (and somewhat unexpectedly) affirms the place of Garnett's version as a classic in the noir canon. More than this, Rafelson's Postman enters into the broader critical discourse of classic film noir (and its 1970s remakings). For instance, Thomson aligns it with the l'amour fou of Nicolas Ray's They Live By Night,[37] and Richard Combs suggests that Rafelson may have taken the opening of The Postman from Edgar G. Ulmer's Detour (1945), "the poor man's (or more downbeat, or simply more hysterical) Postman."[38] More importantly, the 1981 Postman can be related to Richard Martin's suggestion that "film noir in the hands of the post-classical Hollywood filmmakers became both an object of generic revisionism and a tool for [the] ... political investigation of American society."[39] Films such as Chinatown, The Long Goodbye, and Farewell, My Lovely developed their "ironic tone through [a] systematic contrast with the moral universe of 1940s private-eye films."[40] In Noël Carroll's account of Hollywood allusionism, this ironic reworking of genre was the legacy of American auteurism and the "unprecedented awareness" of film history that developed among filmmakers and audiences in the 1960s and 1970s.[41] In this context, The Postman becomes an extension of Rafelson's preoccupations as auteur of the New Hollywood. Best known for his work on low-budget BBS productions of the 1970s—in particular Five Easy Pieces (1970), The King of Marvin Gardens (1972) and Stay Hungry (1976)—Rafelson developed The Postman after being dismissed as director of the Fox production, Brubaker (1980). Given the opportunity to work again for a smaller production company (Lorimar) and with long time collaborator Jack Nicholson, Rafelson's version of The Postman is seen as an extension of the fatalism running through his earlier work.[42] Rafelson takes the rough-house style of Cain's novella, "retain[s] the plot but revise[s] the rhythm ... producing one of the formally most audacious of American mainstream movies [of the 1980s]."[43] In this auteurist interpretation, The Postman is read (alongside Rafelson's earlier allegories of America) as a mix of "carnality and capitalism":

> The precariousness of Frank and Cora's alliance becomes the heart of the film, and a shadowy metaphor for the pursuit of happiness and the American Dream, like the partnerships of love and profit in Marvin Gardens and Stay Hungry.[44]

The Postman's contemporaneous noir, Lawrence Kasdan's *Body Heat* (1981), deals with the same themes—sex and money—but reinvents the classic noir visual style for the 1980s. *Body Heat* is widely recognized as a remake of *Double Indemnity*, Billy Wilder's 1944 adaptation of James M. Cain's 1943 novel. Leitch categorizes *Body Heat*, alongside *The Postman*, as a "true remake"—a film that establishes a triangular relationship between itself, Wilder's film and Cain's novel—even though it does not credit the book as its source. *Body Heat* can be described as an *unacknowledged* remake, a film that repeats fundamental narrative units from the Cain novel (and Wilder adaptation) but alters the details of its title, setting, character names, and the like. In the absence of a screen credit acknowledging the original property, the remake becomes a theoretical construct, or function of the film's production and reception. Important here is Cain's reputation (and the early 1980s revival of interest in Cain's work[45]) but more significant is *Double Indemnity*'s privileged place in the noir canon. For instance, Naremore writes:

> Few would deny that *Double Indemnity* is a definitive film noir and one of the most influential movies in Hollywood history. [...] [It] was an unorthodox film, challenging nearly a decade of Production Code resistance to ... Cain's fiction.[46]

Frank Krutnik similarly declares that *Double Indemnity* was "historically significant in the development of the 1940s erotic crime thriller, establishing through its rendering of the Cain tale a model for the narrative ... structures of subsequent [film noirs]."[47] These accounts of *Double Indemnity*'s reputation and place in film history help explain why critics such as Leitch directly compare *Body Heat* to Wilder's adaptation, but fail to note that *Double Indemnity* had already been more directly remade as a lesser known movie for television, directed by Jack Smight in 1973.

Although Wilder's *Double Indemnity* is often taken as the "original" against which Kasdan's noir remake is evaluated, *Body Heat* can more broadly be seen as a remaking of Cain's *oeuvre* (or at least those works by which he is best remembered). Schickel goes so far as to argue that "*Double Indemnity* was created by [Cain] in full knowledge that he was doing his own homage to *[The] Postman*":

> Both tell essentially the same story: an all too compliant male is enthralled by a strong and scheming woman. With her motivating it and with him taking care of details, the adulterous couple execute a perfect murder of the woman's husband. Then, when they are virtually in the clear, fate (or irony) swipes them with its big blundering paw and they receive their just desserts—but for the wrong reasons.[48]

Such a connection enables one to recognize (in *Body Heat*) noir elements—such as the depiction of naked (and graphic) animal lust—that are common to both *The Postman* and *Double Indemnity* novels. However, at an even higher level of generality, it can be argued that *Body Heat* simultaneously refers to and remakes the noir genre to which its intertexts belong. David Chute understands this when he states that *Body Heat* refers to "just about every major film and novel in the hard-boiled and film noir genres."[49] Chute acknowledges that the "archetypal 'love kills' story line and the characters'

Detective Jake Gittes (Jack Nicholson) with the epitome of corruption, Noah Cross (John Huston), in the neo-noir trendsetter *Chinatown*.

doomed intensity" is borrowed from Cain, but he also finds in *Body Heat* elements of Chandler's novelette *Red Wind*, Howard Hawks' *The Big Sleep* (1946) and Robert Aldrich's *Kiss Me Deadly* (1955).[50] *Body Heat* director Lawrence Kasdan similarly cites various sources of inspiration: "*Double Indemnity* yes, *The Postman* not so much. Cain's writing was important... [but so too were] movies like *Out of the Past* and *Murder, My Sweet*. Also *The Killing* [1956]."[51]

While critical accounts of Rafelson's acknowledged remake of *The Postman* were often limited to a discussion of its (greater or lesser) fidelity to the spirit of Cain's novella, *Body Heat*'s disguised remaking of Cain and/or Wilder enabled it to be related to a broader category of noir fiction and film. While this led a critic like Kael to dismiss *Body Heat* as "a catalogue of noir clichés,"[52] others saw it as "a self-consciously knowing update of an archetypal film noir plot ... with every element cranked up to overdrive and overkill."[53] These opinions suggest that *Body Heat* (like *The Postman*) might be related to the revisionist and nostalgic tendencies of neo-noirs from the 1970s. Steve Jenkins, for instance, makes a connection between it and *Chinatown*, drawing out an analogous Oedipal pattern that sees the father figures of Edmund Walker (Richard Crenna) and Noah Cross (John Huston) as an "embodiment of material power and corruption."[54] Martin takes this further, locating the theme of patriarchal immorality in the socio-economic context of 1980s America, specifically in "the promotion of individualism, selfishness, and greed [that was] underpinned by Reaganomics."[55] In the case of a film like *Body Heat*, this "greed, both economic and sexual, ... results in an extended personal nightmare from which there is ... no escape [*no way out*]."[56] This is furthered through the character of Mattie (Kathleen

Turner) who, like her husband (Crenna), will do "whatever's necessary" to realize her (murderous) scheme. While *Body Heat* does not offer up the same damning critique of capitalism as Polanski's *Chinatown,* the figure of the politically corrupt and morally reprehensible patriarch launches itself forward into mid-1980s noirs such as *Against All Odds* and *No Way Out,* while the murderous (spider) woman is taken up in Rafelson's *Black Widow* (1987).

A further connection between *Chinatown* and *Body Heat* can be found in the suggestion that the latter's anachronistic dialogue and ambiguous costumes and setting make it (metonymically) a *nostalgia film.* Fredric Jameson states that "everything in [*Body Heat*] conspires to blur [its] immediate contemporary reference and to make it possible to receive this ... as nostalgia work—as a narrative set in some indefinable nostalgic past."[57] One could argue, though, that *Body Heat* does not recreate a (pseudo) period setting but rather *reinvents* the film noir, plundering a *critical* genre to promulgate a stylized, *industrial* cycle of neo-noir. In this respect the immediate precursor to *Body Heat* is not *Chinatown* or *The Postman,* but Martin Scorsese's *Taxi Driver* (1974). Naremore argues that "*Taxi Driver* is memorable not only for its [dense and mysterious] blacks but also for its neon, steam, and smoke."[58] Augmented by lurid color (and enabled by high-speed color negative film stock), the blacks of *Taxi Driver* become a "mannerism in all types of post-1970s noir."[59] A film like *Body Heat* extends this approach, employing desaturated visuals "to heighten the atmosphere of sex and violence, but also to evoke the monochromatic tradition of high-contrast, black-and-white thrillers."[60] *Body Heat* is a film that combines dark (and shadow) and heat (and color) to contribute to the commodification of a highly stylized late 1980s (and 1990s) noir look.

At the beginning of the 1980s, *Body Heat* re-presented film noir to an increasingly knowing and cine-literate audience, and set the agenda for later 1980s remakes of classic noirs. Chute described *Body Heat* as "one of the most accomplished American movies in years, and perhaps the most stunning debut movie ever."[61] Unlike *The Postman,* which arrived with exemplary credentials—Rafelson, Nicholson, David Mamet (writer), Sven Nykvist (cinematographer)—*Body Heat* was a first feature for its writer/director Kasdan, and a defining film for actors William Hurt, Kathleen Turner, and Mickey Rourke. More importantly, *Body Heat* anticipated the high-tech visual style and production design of the so-called "high concept" film of the 1980s.[62] At the level of composition, *Body Heat* adapted the visual style of classic noir to compose its high contrast and sometimes minimal color scheme. At the level of plot, it worked with a set of generic archetypes, enabling a more economical story line and schematic characterisations. In addition to this, *Body Heat* (rudimentarily) exhibited the importance that the high concept film was to place in such elements as pre-sold properties, genres, stars, and music: it was in the tradition of James M. Cain and film noir, it traded on William Hurt's star potential (earned in *Altered States* [1980]), and it introduced the character of Teddy Lewis (Mickey Rourke) through the lip-synching of the Bob Seger hit, "Feel Like a Number." Finally, *Body Heat's* frank sex scenes anticipated such neo-noirs as *Against All Odds* and *No Way Out,* and (the high concept films) *Sea of Love* (1989) and *Basic Instinct* (1992).

In the mid-1980s, *Body Heat* provided a kind of "rudimentary working proto-type"[63] for medium-to-high profile, noir remakings such as *Against All Odds* (Taylor Hackford, 1984) and *No Way Out* (Roger Donaldson, 1987). Like *Body Heat,* both films were *indirect* (or transformed) remakes in that they altered not only the title of their original properties but also characters, settings, and narrative units. *Against All Odds* took up the barest narrative outline from *Out of the Past*—one man is dispatched by another to Mexico to locate a beautiful woman who has gone missing—and rein-vented this as a romantic thriller for the 1980s. In a similar way, *No Way Out* retained (from *The Big Clock*) only a basic narrative framework—a man conducts a murder in-vestigation, *on himself*—but relocated the action from a bustling, 1940s New York media empire to a pre-glasnost, 1980s Washington Department of Defense. Both re-makes differ, however, from *Body Heat* in at least two respects. First, each of the films clearly *acknowledges* its noir sources: the credits of *Against All Odds* declare that it was "based on the film *Out of the Past* written by Daniel Mainwaring" (adapted from his 1946 novel *Build My Gallows High*);[64] and the titles of *No Way Out* announce that it is "Based on the novel *The Big Clock* by Kenneth Fearing" (filmed under the same title in 1948). Second, whereas *Body Heat* is a self-conscious re-creation of noir, *Against All Odds* and *No Way Out* are films that wear their knowledge of noir with a "light touch."[65] These are films that eschew any overtly noir mise-en-scène to embrace in-stead noir thematic elements and the generic conventions of the 1980s Hollywood thriller. While the noir originals provide a loose model (and ready point of reference), the absence of a noir style means that the identification of these films as noir remak-ings has as much to do with their critical reception as with any specific textual bor-rowings, narrative or visual.

Acknowledged copyright and a well-established noir canon saw *Against All Odds* and *No Way Out* consistently identified as *transformed* remakes of classic noirs. Headlined by *Variety* as a "sexy remake [that] just misses,"[66] *Against All Odds* struggled in the shadow of its precursor: "as subjects for remakes go, *Out of the Past* [is] a hard act to follow, since the original is such a paradigmatic [noir] work."[67] Foster Hirsch similarly describes *Against All Odds* as a "shamefully misbegotten remake," one that refuses the challenge of capturing the "pulp poetry" of Jeff Bailey's (Robert Mitchum's) voice-over or recreating the formidable presence of Kathie's (Jane Greer's) *femme fatale.*[68] Al-though not entirely misplaced, these kinds of comments fail to recognize the specific ways in which *Against All Odds*—like *Body Heat* before it—*transformed* classic noir via some of the commercial imperatives of 1980s Hollywood. In the first instance, *Against All Odds* traded on the popular success of Taylor Hackford's previous feature *An Offi-cer and a Gentleman* (1982) and on the profiles of its up-coming stars: Jeff Bridges, James Woods and Rachel Ward. Second, *Against All Odds* might well have translated the "hard sun and undulating shadows" and "erotic fever" of *Out of the Past*[69] into "'exotic' locations" and "dutifully sweat-drenched sex scenes,"[70] but this can be understood as a high concept promotion of a California-noir lifestyle. For instance, the image of Terry (Jeff Bridges) and Jessie (Rachel Ward) entwined on a tropical beach (reproduced for the *Against All Odds*' promotional poster, print advertising and soundtrack album) shaped the film's narrative *and* commercial identity. Finally, Phil Collins' song (and music

Evelyn Mulwray (Faye Dunaway) protects her sister/daughter in the explosive finale of *Chinatown*.

video) "Against All Odds (Take a Look at Me Now)" brought together the film's picturesque locations and star profiles in a cross-promotional strategy that most clearly
characterized the high concept film of the 1980s.

The re-makers of *The Big Clock* gave it a similar treatment, but (probably due to the
modest reputation of its original) *No Way Out*'s critical reception was more favourable
than that of *Against All Odds*. *Variety* headlined *No Way Out* as a "top notch remake with
[a] sure fire thriller formula,"[71] and Hirsch notes that in "reclaiming noir as a Reagan-
era star vehicle, [*No Way Out*] achieves a rare degree of independence while still satisfying genre requirements."[72] While *No Way Out* retains and revises some of the
details of the original—notably Louise Patterson's (Elsa Lanchester's) inspired abstract
painting of the suspected murderer, which is updated to an endlessly protracted computer rendering—the remake is constructed as a labyrinthine thriller for the 1980s. *No
Way Out* is primarily designed to showcase the talent of Kevin Costner, fresh off his
successful role as Elliot Ness in *The Untouchables* (1987), but also that of his co-actors,
Gene Hackman and Sean Young. While the fashion look of the film might now appear
as "anachronistic" as that of *Body Heat, No Way Out* is determinedly voguish in its costuming (especially Costner and Young's outfits), and also in the interiors of Young's
Georgetown apartment and the sounds of Maurice Jarre's electronic musical score. In
addition (and as in *Against All Odds* and *Body Heat* before it) the sex scenes are frank,
and Costner and Young's first sexual tryst takes place in the back of a limousine to the
(then) popular beat of Rod Stewart's "Da Ya Think I'm Sexy?" All of this suggests that,
for its contemporary audience, *No Way Out* appealed as much to the broad generic
conventions of the glossy Hollywood thriller as to any specific noir precursor.

Toward the end of the 1980s, *D.O.A.* (Rocky Morton and Annabel Jankel, 1988) extended the remaking strategies of earlier 1980s neo-noirs and anticipated the consolidation of noir as a commercial genre for the 1990s. Previously remade as *Color Me Dead* (Eddie Davis, 1969), the 1988 update of Rudolph Maté's *D.O.A.* (1949) might be described as a *non-remake*. Although Morton and Jankel's version retains the original title and gives Russell Rouse and Clarence Greene (the writers of the Maté film) a story writing credit, the *D.O.A.* remake transforms the original property beyond recognition. The basic narrative line becomes, in the remake, little more than a high concept story pitch for initializing the project and then marketing the product to the public: "Someone poisoned Dexter Cornell. He's got to find out why. He's got to find out now. In twenty-fours hours he'll be Dead On Arrival." In a similar way, the title "D.O.A." functions as a saleable generic marker of neo-noir and a readily identifiable (and transferable) logo for the promotion of the film. Following the trajectory signalled by *Body Heat*, *D.O.A.* announces itself as a high-tech noir, complete with a black-and-white prologue (brimming with shadows and titled compositions) in which Cornell (Dennis Quaid) staggers into a police station to report that a murder has been committed and that Cornell *himself* is the victim. The remake takes this basic set-up from the original and then spins it into a convoluted trail of bigamy and murder, infidelity and suicide. Consistently dismissed for being a "fantasia of classic noir motifs strained through an MTV filter,"[73] *D.O.A.* anticipates in its excessive reworking of its source a 1990s interest in the readily consumable "stylistic, iconographic, and narrative markers of classic film noir."[74] Despite its title, *D.O.A.* is less a direct remake of a noir classic than a generic noir remaking: "a sight-and-sound neo-noir spectacle."[75]

Morton and Jankel's MTV remaking of *D.O.A.* supports Martin's suggestion that the visual style of classic noir has been taken up and commodified not only by contemporary filmmakers, but also by television programmers and creators of music videos.[76] Following the early lead of *Body Heat*, noir remakes of the middle to late 1980s—*Against All Odds, No Way Out, D.O.A.*—chart the movement of film noir from its being primarily a *critical* genre to its emergence as an *industrial* genre and marketing category: "a major signifier of sleekly commodified artistic ambition".[77] Across these various 1980s reworkings, classic noirs are *transformed* through a number of "filters," such as "studio style, ideological fashion, political constraints, auteurist predilections, charismatic stars,... and evolving technology."[78] Moreover, as previously noted, the concept of noir is sustained across the decade through specific discursive formations, in particular a fully developed noir canon, and its contributing projects: the discussion and citation of noirs in popular and academic film criticism, the selective release and re-release of noirs to theatrical and video distribution windows, and (in circular fashion) the decision of neo-noir filmmakers to evoke earlier works and recreate cinema history. Beyond matters of narrative style and visual traits, beyond questions of originality and fidelity, an understanding of film noir and its 1980s remakings resides primarily in the determination of a discursive structure, in issues of cultural history and memory. As in classic noir, it's a question of how the past continues to inform—*has a firm hold of*—the present.

NOTES

1. James Naremore, *More Than Night: Film noir in Its Contexts*, Berkeley: U of California P, 1998, p. 11.

2. Naremore, p. 10.

3. Naremore, p. 26.

4. Naremore, pp. 32–33.

5. Naremore, p. 37.

6. See Constantine Verevis, "Re-Viewing Remakes," *Film Criticism*, 21.3 (1997), pp. 1–19.

7. For an account of noir remakes see Foster Hirsch, *Detours and Lost Highways: A Map of Neo-Noir*, New York: Limelight, 1999, pp. 23–65.

8. For accounts of neo-noir see: Alain Silver and Elizabeth Ward, editors, *Film noir: An Encyclopaedic Reference to the American Style*, Woodstock, NY: Overlook, 1992(3rd Edition), pp. 398–442; and Todd Erickson, "Kill Me Again: Movement becomes Genre," in Alain Silver and James Ursini, editors, *Film Noir Reader*, New York: Limelight, 1996, pp. 307–29.

9. Thomas M. Leitch, "Twice-Told Tales: The Rhetoric of the Remake," *Literature/Film Quarterly*, 18.3 (1990), p. 145.

10. Leitch, p. 147.

11. Leitch, pp. 145–46.

12. Dan Yakir, "The Postman's Words," *Film Comment*, 17.2 (March–April, 1981), p. 21.

13. Richard Schickel, *Double Indemnity*, London: BFI, 1992, p. 16.

14. Quoted in Schickel, p 20.

15. Dan Yakir, "'The Postman' Rings Six Times," *Film Comment*, 17.2 (March–April, 1981), pp. 18–20.

16. Robert G. Porfirio, "Whatever Happened to the Film noir?: *The Postman Always Rings Twice* (1946–1981)," *Literature/Film Quarterly*, 13.2 (1985): pp. 102–11, reprinted in Alain Silver and James Ursini, editors, *Film Noir Reader 2* (NY: Limelight, 1999), pp. 85–97.

17. Schickel, p. 24.

18. James M. Cain, *The Postman Always Rings Twice*, London: Pan, 1981 [1934], p. 7.

19. Cain, preface to *The Butterfly* (1947), quoted in Frank Krutnik, "Desire, Transgression and James M. Cain." *Screen*, 23.1 (May–June 1982), p. 32.

20. Cain, *The Postman*, p. 123.

21. Richard Combs, Rev. of *The Postman Always Rings Twice* [1981], *Monthly Film Bulletin*, 48.568 (May 1981), p. 96.

22. Quoted in David Thomson, "Raising Cain," *Film Comment*, 17.2 (March–April 1981), p. 28.

23. Cain, *The Postman*, p. 15.

24. Cain, pp. 16 & 19.

25. Cain, p. 113.

26. Tom Milne, Review of *The Postman Always Rings Twice* [1946], *Monthly Film Bulletin*, 48.568 (May 1981): 100.

27. Combs, p. 95.

28. Cain, pp. 21 & 16.

29. Review of *The Postman Always Rings Twice*, *Variety* (March 18, 1981), p. 133.

30. Thomson, pp. 27–28.

31. Pauline Kael, *Taking It All In*, London: Arena, 1987, pp. 179 & 182.

32. Qtd in Thomson, p. 28.

33. Qtd in Thomson, p. 28.

34. Robert B. Ray, *A Certain Tendency of the Hollywood Cinema, 1930–1980*, Princeton: Princeton University Press, 1985, p. 267.

35. Kael, p. 179.

36. Kael, p. 178.

37. Thomson, p. 25.

38. Richard Combs, Rev. of *Detour* [1945], *Monthly Film Bulletin*, 49.582 (July 1982), p. 146.

39. Richard Martin, *Mean Streets and Raging Bulls: The Legacy of* Film noir *in Contemporary American Cinema*, Lanham, Maryland: Scarecrow, 1997, p. 25.

40. Noël Carroll, "The Future of Allusion: Hollywood in the Seventies (and Beyond)," *October*, 20 (1982), p. 61.

41. Carroll, p. 54.

42. Thomson, p. 30.

43. Combs, Rev. of *The Postman*, p. 96.

44. Combs, p. 96.

45. See Krutnik, p. 31.

46. Naremore, p. 81.

47. Krutnik, p. 38.

48. Schickel, pp. 21–22.

49. David Chute, "Tropic of Kasdan," *Film Comment*, 17.5 (September/October 1981), p. 49.

50. Chute, p. 49.

51. Qtd in Chute, p. 54.

52. Kael, p. 255.

53. Steve Jenkins, Rev. of *Body Heat, Monthly Film Bulletin*, 49.576 (January 1982), p. 4.

54. Jenkins, p. 4.

55. Martin, p. 53.

56. Martin, p. 53.

57. Fredric Jameson, "Postmodernism and Consumer Society," in Hal Foster, editor, *Postmodern Culture*, London: Pluto, 1985, p. 117.

58. Naremore, p. 192.

59. Naremore, p. 192. See also Erickson, pp. 314–16.

60. Naremore, p. 192.

61. Chute, p. 49.

62. See Justin Wyatt, *High Concept: Movies and Marketing in Hollywood*, Austin: Texas University Press, 1994.

63. Martin, p. 29.

64. The novel was written under the pseudonym Geoffrey Holmes.

65. Hirsch, p. 33.

66. Review of *Against All Odds, Variety* (February 15, 1984), p. 24.

67. Tom Pulleine, Review of *Against All Odds, Monthly Film Bulletin*, 51.605 (June 1984), p. 171.

68. Hirsch, pp. 40–43.

69. Hirsch, p. 41.

70. Pulleine, p. 171.

71. Review of *No Way Out, Variety* (August 12, 1987), p. 12.

72. Hirsch, p. 33.

73. Hirsch, p. 54. See also Tom Milne, Rev. of *D.O.A.* [1988], *Monthly Film Bulletin*, 56.662 (March 1989), pp. 77–78; and Rev. of *D.O.A., Variety* (March 16, 1988), p. 14.

74. Martin, p. 118.

75. Hirsch, p. 55.

76. Martin, p. 29.

77. Naremore, p. 10.

78. Robert Stam, "Beyond Fidelity," in James Naremore, editor, *Film Adaptation*, London: Athlone, 2000, pp. 68–69.

Notes on Contributors

Stephen B. Armstrong is a doctoral student in the creative writing program at Florida State University. His work has appeared in several publications, including *Film Score Monthly,* the Tallahassee Democrat and American Writing.

Sheri Chinen Biesen is assistant professor of Radio, Television and Film at Rowan University. She received her Ph.D. at The University of Texas at Austin, MA at The University of Southern California School of Cinema-Television and has taught film at USC, University of California, University of Texas and in England. She has contributed to *Film and History, Literature/Film Quarterly, Popular Culture Review, Quarterly Review of Film and Video,* edited *The Velvet Light Trap* and is completing work on a book on *Film Noir and World War II.*

Beverley Carter has been studying film since 1997; when she discovered the wonder of *Film Noir.* She holds a BA (2002) in Film and Television Studies from Brunel University and has been a lecturer in film studies at Chichester College. The essay "Men in Film Noir and *D.O.A.*" is taken from her final year thesis entitled "The War of the Sexes: An analysis of gender roles and relationships in Film Noir."

Glenn Erickson is an Emmy-nominated film editor. He also writes articles on films, and reviews DVDs under the web alias DVD Savant. He is the co-author of *The Making of 1941* (1980), on the production of which he also served as Coordinator of miniatures and other effects. He has also written program articles for FILMEX and contributed to both *Film Noir Reader* and *Horror Film Reader.*

Michael E. Grost is a computer software analyst-designer. He has a Ph.D. in Mathematics from the University of Michigan. He has written extensively on popular culture and his pieces on film, which are focused primarily on a formal analysis of visual style, can be found on-line at *Classic Film and Television* (http://members.aol.com/MG4273/film.htm). He is also the author of a critical history of mystery fiction from 1830 to 1960, *A Guide to Classic Mystery and Detection* (http://members.aol.com/MG4273/classics.htm), and a detailed critical study of selected American comic books from 1935 to 1966, Classic Comic Books (http://members.aol.com/MG4273/comics.htm). He is also an abstract painter.

Kevin Jack Hagopian is a Lecturer in Media Studies at Penn State University, where he teaches courses in the history and theory of film, including a course in film noir. He is the former editor of the *Film Literature Index.* His writing on film has appeared in academic publications and the popular press, and he has frequently served as an expert on film and media for print and electronic media.

Daniel M. Hodges taught a course at the University of California at Berkeley, Extension, "From Center to Sidelines: The Transformation of Women in Alfred Hitchcock and Film Noir." He works as technical writer in the East Bay area of Northern California and is the president of a volunteer grassroots organization working for single-payer universal health care, Health Care for All-California.

Reynold Humphries is Professor of Film Studies at the University of Lille III, France. The author of *Fritz Lang: Genre and Representation in his American Films, The American Horror Film, An Introduction* and articles on such directors as Bunuel, Cronenberg, Losey, Mizoguchi, Peckinpah and Michael Powell. He is a contributor to the recent volumes of *Paradoxa* devoted to Horror and of *Postscript* to serial killers. He has also contributed to the on-line journal *Kinoeye* and to the collective volumes *Writing and Cinema* (edited by Jonathan Bignell, Longmans) and *Horror Zone* (edited by Ian Conrich and Julian Petley, forthcoming from Verso). His current project concerns the films written and directed by blacklist victims.

Gary Johnson is the publisher of *Images Film Journal* (www.imagesjournal.com). He contributed to *The Guide to United States Popular Culture* (Popular Press, October 2000).

Adrian Martin is film critic for *The Age* (Melbourne), author of *The Mad Max Movies* (Currency, 2003), *Once Upon a Time in America* (BFI, 1998) and *Phantasms* (Penguin, 1994). He is also Co-Editor of *Movie Mutations* (BFI, 2003) and the Internet film journal *Rouge* (www.rouge.com.au).

R. Barton Palmer is Calhoun Lemon Professor of Literature at Clemson University, where he teaches courses in literature and film. Among other books on film, Palmer is the author of *Hollywood's Dark Cinema: The American Film Noir* (Twayne)and the editor of *Perspectives on Film Noir* (G.K. Hall). Along with David Boyd, he has edited *After Hitchcock: Imitation/Influence/Intertextuality* (forthcoming from U of Texas Press). His Ethan and Joel Coen study will appear shortly in the University of Illinois Press's Contemporary Filmmakers series; and he has also edited two anthologies, *20th Century American Fiction on Screen and 19th Century American Fiction on Screen,* which are forthcoming from Cambridge University Press.

James A. Paris is a freelance writer, computer information specialist, and administrator for an accounting firm in West Los Angeles. He studied film at Dartmouth College and was in the film history program at UCLA. He has previously written on *film noir* in *Film Noir: An Encyclopedic Reference to the American Style.*

Robert Porfirio began his extensive work on film noir while in the Master's program at U.C.L.A. which culminated in his 1979 dissertation for Yale University "The

Dark Age of American Film: A Study of American Film Noir (1940–1960)." His articles include contributions to *Continuum, Dialog, Literature/Film Quarterly,* and *Sight and Sound.* He is co-editor of *Film Noir Reader 3* and *Film Noir: An Encyclopedic Reference to the American Style,* for which he wrote over sixty entries on individual films and also contributed to *The Noir Style.* He was formerly assistant professor of American Studies at California State University, Fullerton and is presently a real estate broker in Southern California and, when pressed, he occasionally lectures on film noir.

Nicolas Saada is a Paris-based screenwriter for film and television and a former critic for *Cahiers du Cinéma.* He worked as a program editor at the drama department of the Franco-German cultural channel ARTE between 1991 and 1998. For the past ten years, he has also hosted the radio program "Nova fait son Cinéma" dedicated to film soundtracks. He has written and co-written several films, including Pierre Salvadori's *Marchands de Sable* (1999) and Arnaud Desplechin's *Reading the Company of Men* (2002). He is currently working on several personal projects including a feature film. His original essay was written as a master's thesis for critic and professor Michel Ciment at Paris 7 University.

Ginny Schwartz teaches at St. Lawrence University, is a member of the Film Studies Advisory Board, and is the Coordinator of Academic Support. Her Ph.D. is in American Culture Studies, and her intellectual interests include American film, in particular film noir, and American youth culture. Her courses include Film Noir, Cold War History through Cold War Films, Popular Culture and History, and Identity and Popular Culture.

Alain Silver wrote, co-wrote and co-edited the books listed in the front. Shorter pieces have appeared in *Film Comment, Movie, Literature/Film Quarterly, Wide Angle, Photon,* the *DGA Magazine,* the *Los Angeles Times,* and the on-line magazines *Images, oneWorld,* and *Senses of Cinema.* He has co-written three feature films (*Kiss Daddy Goodbye, Time at the Top,* and *White Nights*) and produced numerous others as well as documentaries, music videos, and over sixty soundtrack albums for the Bay Cities and Citadel labels. His Ph.D. is from UCLA, and he is a member of the WGAw and DGA.

Eric Somer is in charge of store development and operations at Family Video Corporate Headquarters in Springfield, IL. He studied film at Central Michigan University, where he was a graduate assistant in the Department of Broadcast & Cinematic Arts, and principal film reviewer at Central Michigan Life, both in the mid 1990s. When time permits, he is currently at work on a study of the professional boxer in the film noir.

J. P. Telotte is a Professor in the School of Literature, Communication, and Culture at Georgia Tech, where he teaches courses in film history, film genres, and film and technology. Co-editor of the journal *Post Script,* Telotte has authored more than a hundred articles on film and literature, and such books as *Voices in the Dark: The Narrative Patterns of Film Noir, Replications: A Robotic History of Science Fiction Film, A Distant Technol-*

ogy: Science Fiction Film and the Machine Age, and The Science Fiction Film. His study of Disney television, Disneyland/The Wonderful World of Color, is forthcoming.

Grant Tracey, an Associate Professor of English at the University of Northern Iowa and Editor for the North American Review, has authored two books: A Filmography of American History (Greenwood Press, 2002), a reference resource guide for college and high school students, and Parallel Lines and the Hockey Universe (Pocol Press, 2003), a collection of short stories. He also plays drums in the cow-punk blues band, Atomic Hoss.

James Ursini is author and editor of the completed volumes listed in the front. He has also contributed articles to Mediascene, Femme Fatales, Cinema (U.S.), Photon, Cinefantastique, Midnight Marquee, and the DGA Magazine. He has produced Oral Histories and been a researcher for the American Film Institute and has also been associate producer and producer on feature films and documentaries for various school districts and public broadcasting. He has an MA in motion pictures from UCLA and had lectured on filmmaking there and at other colleges in the Los Angeles area where he continues to work as an educator and is writing noir novels.

Constantine Verevis teaches in the School of Literary, Visual and Performance Studies at Monash University, Melbourne. His articles have appeared in Australian Studies, Bright Lights Film Journal, Film Criticism, Framework, Hitchcock Annual, Media International Australia, Senses of Cinema, and other periodicals.

Tony Williams Tony Williams is the co-author of Italian Western: Opera of Violence (1975), co-editor of Vietnam War Films (1994) and Jack London's The Sea Wolf: A Screenplay by Robert Rossen (1998). He is the author of Jack London: The Movies (1992); Hearths of Darkness: The Family in the American Horror Film (1996); Larry Cohen: Radical Allegories of an American Filmmaker (1997); and the forthcoming Structures of Desire: British Cinema 1949–1955. His articles have appeared in Cinema Journal, CineAction, Wide Angle, Jump Cut, Asian Cinema, Creative Filmmaking, and the first Film Noir Reader. He is an Associate Professor and Area Head of Film Studies in the Department of English, Southern Illinois University at Carbondale.

Robin Wood whose numerous books on motion pictures include seminal English-language auteur studies of Alfred Hitchcock, Howard Hawks, Ingmar Bergman, and Arthur Penn and most recently Hollywood from Vietnam to Reagan, is now writing fiction. He is a former Professor of Film Studies at Queen's College and York University and remains a founding member of the collective which edits the film journal CineAction!